To Howard Clark and Devi Prasad

Gandhi the Organiser
How he shaped a nationwide rebellion:
India 1915-1922

© Bob Overy

First published 2019 by
Irene Publishing
Sparsnäs 1010
66891 Ed
Sweden

irene.publishing@gmail.com

www.irenepublishing.com

Layout: J. Johansen
Cover: Tom Howey
ISBN 978-91-88061-32-4 Softcover
ISBN 978-91-88061-38-6 E-book
ISBN 978-91-88061-39-3 Hardcover

ISBN 978-91-88061-32-4

90000

9 789188 061324

BOB OVERY

Gandhi
the
Organiser

How he shaped a
nationwide rebellion:
India 1915-1922

CONTENTS

Map of British India in 1915	7
List of Tables	8
Author's Preface	9
Introduction: What Gandhi Did	11

PART I

1. Champaran: Before and After	27
CASE STUDY 1: Champaran	29
2. Peasants and Workers Take Up Satyagraha	52
CASE STUDIES 2: Kheda and 3: Ahmedabad	61
3. Challenging the Raj	84
CASE STUDY 4: The Rowlatt Satyagraha	89

PART II

4. The Place of Constructive Programme	138
5. The Swadeshi Sabha	163

PART III

6. Muslim Outrage Against the Raj	181
CASE STUDY 5: The Khilafat and Noncooperation	182
7. Capturing the Congress: "Progressive Nonviolent Noncooperation" takes Shape	239
CASE STUDY 6: "The Punjab Satyagraha"	240
CASE STUDY 7(A): Noncooperation in Preparation	249
8. Boycotts Spread, Jails Fill and the Viceroy Offers Talks	288
CASE STUDY 7(B): Congress Takes up Noncooperation	288
9. Waiting for Mass Civil Disobedience	326
CASE STUDY 7(C): Noncooperation At Its Peak	326

PART IV

10. Gandhi's Method in the West	364
11. Constructive and Obstructive Methods	382
Acknowledgments	412
Glossary	415
Prominent Figures	417
Bibliography	422
Index	429

British India in 1915

This map of British India in 1915 was published in 1920. Gandhi returned to India in 1915. The province and city most associated with Gandhi are Gujarat and Ahmedabad, not shown on the map but located north of Bombay city and within the Bombay Presidency. At the time, the presidencies (Bombay, Bengal, Madras) and the provinces were under British control, while the princely states (shown as "Native States") were nominally independent.

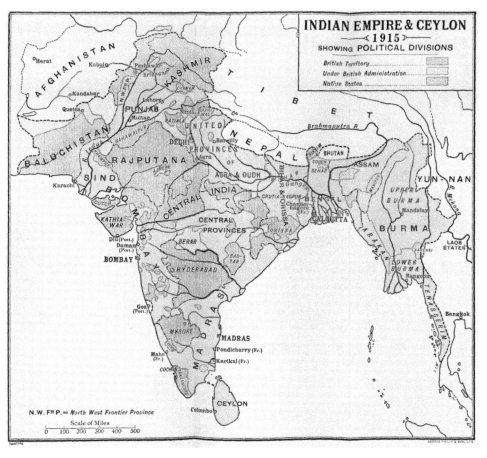

This map is in public domain and can be found:
www.en.wikipedia.org/wiki/File:IndianEmpireCeylon1915.jpg

List of Tables

Table	Title	Page
Table 0.1	Organisations in India founded or transformed by Gandhi 1915-1922	24
Table 4.1	Gandhi's Five Propositions on Combining Civil Disobedience with Constructive Programme in Nonviolent Struggle	141
Table 4.2	Gandhi's Propositions (Simplified) on the Relationship at Local and National Levels between Constructive Programme and Civil Disobedience	148
Table 6.1	Khilafat Satyagraha: Phases 1 and 2	197-198
Table 8.1	All-India Noncooperation: A Campaign in Three Stages	290-291
Table 10.1	Distinctions between Pragmatic and Principled Nonviolence	377
Table 11.1	The Essentials of Satyagraha in Action: Fundamental (and Additional) Rules	395-396
Table 11.2	The Two Sides of Satyagraha: The Balance between Civil Resistance and Constructive Programme during Noncooperation, 1919-1922	404
Table 11.3	Organising Satyagraha at a National Level: Rowlatt and Noncooperation 1919-1922	407-409

Author's Preface

I became interested in Gandhi in the early 1960s while taking part in demonstrations against Britain's nuclear weapons. Disillusioned with conventional politics and its failure to address the most important issue of the age, nuclear war, it made sense to me to challenge the state's legitimacy and to break some of its laws in public protests.

Substitute the imminent threat of nuclear war then with the unstoppable march of climate change today. My feelings then were probably not much different from many people's today, those who feel their lives and the lives of future generations will be cut short if they don't do something now to stop the madness.

The inspiration of Gandhi's campaigns in India and the eventual achievement of that country's independence had led some nuclear disarmers, within a few years of his death, to bring experiments with Gandhi's nonviolent methods of protest into British politics. They included not only marches and vigils, but also obstruction of traffic in city centres and incursions into nuclear bases. By the time I joined in, one campaigning objective, taken up enthusiastically by me, was "Fill the Jails".

I remember being arrested, found guilty of obstruction or breach of the peace, and fined, then refusing to pay and being jailed for a few days or the longest, two weeks, but I noticed after a year or so that the numbers following the same path were dwindling. That experience is one that has encouraged me to research and write this book.

Another has been the journey that the study of nonviolent direct action has taken in academia. In the years since I first became involved in thinking and writing about nonviolence, a field of study has opened up where nonviolence is seen as a substitute for violence, possibly to be adopted by military forces, increasingly to be taken up by civilian populations rising up in rebellion against authoritarian regimes.

The problem with much of this work is not the aim, which is often laudable, but the stance its practitioners have adopted. They insist on realism before idealism. In effect, the assumption is that nonviolent action can adapt to society as it is, rather then be part of a radical project to transform society. Nonviolence is rarely treated as a day-to-day tool to be used by all of us in our everyday undertakings. The result is nonviolent action substantially stripped of the experience and thinking of its greatest practitioner, Gandhi.

I decided to go back to Gandhi and see how his methods actually worked. This book is revised from a PhD I gained at the Bradford School of Peace Studies in the early 1980s.

At the time I didn't find a publisher and since then I have lived a most interesting life trying out my Gandhian ideas in a variety of contexts. Throughout that time various friends have suggested that I really ought to get the manuscript published because nothing like it was available.

Finally, when I retired a few years ago, I was persuaded that this really was the time to have another go. There was a huge amount to read, update and re-write. But at last it is done and I hope it proves challenging and useful.

Leeds, July 2019

INTRODUCTION

What Gandhi Did

Over many years, a wealth of material has been published magnifying Gandhi into a saint and politician of genius whose every utterance is worthy of reverent attention. Celebration of his immense personal achievement has tended to get in the way of understanding how he was able to do what he did, particularly in the years during and after the First World War when he came to political prominence in India.

With the publication decades ago now of Gandhi's *Collected Works*, the release of British official documents relating to the period, and also the systematic studies undertaken by historians of the part that many local areas played or failed to play in the Indian national struggle, it became possible to gain a much clearer picture of what Gandhi's role and influence actually was. Historians like Judith Brown broke new ground with her extensive, pioneering study of the Gandhian era in India, though with a detachment probably few Indians would want to adopt. (Brown 1972)

Other historians involved in South Asian studies, including Indian scholars, have brought to study of the period a variety of perspectives. These have not got in the way of the main task, which has been to dig beneath "nationalist mythology" and uncover what was actually going on during the Gandhi years. In my view, until recently, the best accounts of the Indian national struggle remained the broad studies written by authors who identify with the national movement and even with Gandhi himself. But more recent work, by scholars from east and west, has provided a wealth of new facts and speculative arguments which must be reflected in new studies of Gandhi and his methods.

The object of this book is not to develop the work of these historians, nor to duplicate or summarise them. Rather, drawing on some of their specific information and insights, it is to go back to Gandhi himself and to re-examine the basis on which he was able to present his method of nonviolent resistance to the Indian national movement and to win

11

widespread acceptance of it. The aim is to add to our understanding of Gandhian method by looking again in detail, in a series of seven case studies, at what Gandhi actually did in the years 1915 to 1922. During this seven-year period on returning to India from South Africa, he conducted the first of his three nationwide "experiments" with nonviolent rebellion.

There are numerous questions. For example, has the widespread development of nonviolent action theory recognised and reflected the new material on Gandhi's methods provided by historians? Are we sufficiently aware of how the theory and practice of nonviolent action evolved in those early years as Gandhi sought to organise political and social movements that would have a major impact on Indian society? How was Gandhi, without modern communications, able to shape and at times direct campaigns across a territory at that time containing not just modern day India, but Pakistan, Bangladesh and Myanmar as well?

Philosophy or Method?

Many non-biographical studies of Gandhi have tended to focus either on his philosophy or on his method of action. Interpreters of Gandhian nonviolence have tended to fall into two camps: those who embrace or describe the whole Gandhian philosophy of satyagraha and assume that Gandhian nonviolent action can best be understood from its roots in his religious and moral beliefs (Iyer 1973; Rothermund 1963; Dhawan 1957; Diwakar 1946); and those who wish to separate the practice of nonviolent action from its philosophical background and to look at it purely or principally as a technique in the political sphere for engaging in conflict. (Shridharani 1962, Sharp 1979, 1973, Bondurant 1965, Gregg 1960, Bose, N.K. 1947)[1] My own bias is unquestionably towards the first group – but in this book I will look not at Gandhi's philosophy, but at how he applied his philosophy. It was as a more effective organiser than any of his contemporaries that Gandhi was able to capture the leadership of the Indian National Congress in 1920.

---

1. More recent scholars, like Ackerman and Kruegler (1994), have tended to use Sharp as their starting point, rather than Gandhi.

What can be confusing is that Gandhi's term for nonviolent action, satyagraha, is commonly used with two overlapping meanings. *Satyagraha* (or truth-force) is Gandhi's philosophy of "right living"; but it also refers to a specific action or campaign carried out in accordance with this philosophy or with rules derived from it. Much of this book is comprised of the seven case studies of satyagrahas led by Gandhi. Analysis of these case studies will identify the philosophy in the way he organised these struggles, the decisions made and principles followed. It will also highlight the place of constructive work alongside conflict within the method of satyagraha.

Part of Gandhi's appeal was as an expert practitioner in a technique of conflict well suited to the conditions in which the Indian national movement found itself at the time of the first world war. But if he had been simply a "general" able to command civilian troops in nonviolent action, he would never have been called on to reveal his skills. The point about Gandhian nonviolent action in India is that a political context had to be created in which sections of the Indian political elite and large groups of the rural and urban "masses" were ready to take up nonviolent action and experiment with it under Gandhi's guidance.

Gandhi did not make a distinction between his ability to plan and organise political campaigns and his ability then to direct them in struggle. Although he frequently likened his leadership of civilians in nonviolent resistance to the generalship of an army, he did not differentiate clearly between the political and "military" spheres, nor between these and the conduct of social and economic life. For Gandhi, all of these were interlinked. This meant not only that his task as an organiser included work to create a political climate in which the Indian national movement would give him the opportunity to lead it in nonviolent struggle. But the very method, satyagraha, which he employed, expressed in itself his concern to reorganise social, economic and political life. Nonviolent action, as pursued by Gandhi, was not just a conflict technique. Simultaneously, it was a tool for transforming social, economic and political conditions. The two aspects, conflict and transformation, were combined. (Iyer 1973: 285, 306-307)

13

Thus a principal argument is that attempts to abstract from Gandhi's campaigns in India a technique of engaging in conflict called nonviolent action, and to leave aside the rest of his activity, have eliminated or made it hard to comprehend large areas of his practice. These need to be included if we want to understand how Gandhi was effective.

To put it more positively, Gandhi was an organiser of exceptional ability who had firm ideas on how to conduct political campaigns and build social movements. His success as an organiser of these campaigns was dependent on a certain set of principles and objectives which should not be sweepingly set aside. Certainly, his remarkable achievements in leading nonviolent campaigns were a springboard which encouraged those impressed to accept his leadership and to take up his larger social and political programmes. Social and religious values, his idea of how society should be ordered, were always uppermost in Gandhi's mind as he planned his civil resistance campaigns.

Constructive Programme

It was, for example, out of his opposition to a nonviolent tactic like economic boycott that Gandhi formulated his concept and plan of Noncooperation, first launched in 1920. For Gandhi, Noncooperation was positive – where economic boycott was negative – because those who supported the campaign withdrew their support not into bitterness, but into a movement to build alternative institutions. (Gandhi, M.K. 1965: vol 16: 480-482, 322-323) To him, the heart of the movement, the drive, was to build those alternative positive institutions, and after 1924 the promotion of the constructive programme became more important to him than the development of nonviolence as a conflict technique. The key factors here are order, discipline and self-reliance.

Gandhi is often described as a philosophical anarchist because he favoured fundamental decentralisation of society and wished political workers to abandon representative democracy at the centre and go to work in the villages. But he was in favour of a moral order of society where those who were morally the most advanced accepted responsibility and exercised authority. In order to achieve this new political and social order, where

14

the focus of political drive was not at the centres of power – as under the Raj – but in the villages and with the "masses", specific cultural changes were needed. The emphasis of his politics was on organising among the people to develop their capacity to solve their own problems, encouraging individuals and whole villages and districts to see themselves as models of social responsibility for others to emulate. In order to create a climate where this was possible, it was necessary to develop in the political workers and in the "masses" themselves a daily discipline, a notion of "good housekeeping", and a capacity to make sacrifices, which would sustain them personally and then fill out their lives and be assimilated by others. (Iyer 1973: 37-61, 113-148)

This effort to work a social revolution, which ultimately was more important than the political revolution and was based in individuals making changes in their own lives, became fundamental to the Gandhian movement in India. Whenever Gandhi was invited to lead the Indian National Congress into nonviolent conflict, he always placed great emphasis on the need to develop the social programme of nonviolence if nonviolent discipline in conflict was to be sustained. Thus the constructive programme – building a new social order directly by working among the people – was not only a long-term goal for Gandhi. Constructive work was also, in his view, an immediate requirement in preparing the movement for nonviolent struggle. In particular, it was an essential precondition for a mass nonviolent civil disobedience campaign where tens of thousands of people, in no way answerable to military discipline, might be expected to maintain nonviolent discipline under conditions of severe repression or provocation. (Gandhi, M.K. 1945)

In practical terms, there are broadly two ways of looking at the constructive programme. The first is as a moral imperative on individuals and groups who are concerned to live a way of life consistent with the values of nonviolence. They may be followers of Gandhi's philosophy. People who have adopted this approach, as a demonstration of their disinterested commitment to the good of the community, engage in socially useful tasks known as "constructive programme". "Has the movement undertaken positive, constructive steps with a view to providing services to its own members and to the public, and even in some cases to the opponent?"

15

asks Joan Bondurant, emphasising that constructive programme in this sense was an "earmark" of proper Gandhian satyagraha. (Bondurant 1965: 43)

A second use of the term, as with satyagraha itself, refers to a specific set of campaigns launched in India by Gandhi. The "constructive programme" comprised a specific list of initiatives devised by Gandhi to meet a number of important social questions. Each issue was taken up by his supporters as part of a nationwide campaign which had its own organisation; frequently there were targets for achievement which had to be achieved by a particular date. Over the years the number of these campaigns was gradually expanded. In the 1920s, the chief emphasis was on production of Indian-made cloths, on Hindu-Muslim unity and on abolition of untouchability, but prohibition of liquor selling and the uplift of women were soon added. By the 1940s, the programme consisted of 18 items. (Gandhi, M.K. 1945; Prasad R.1942; Kaushik, 1964)

Unfortunately, the ambition of this book, to reveal in detail how Gandhi made his decisions as an organiser, has made it impossible for me to pursue the history of his activities in India beyond 1922. Even so, analysis of just the seven years from 1915 to 1922 demonstrates that Gandhi was evolving the theory and practice of constructive programme, in both the above senses, as a specific response to setbacks and difficulties he experienced in pursuing his satyagraha campaigns at a national level. Gandhi's own conclusions in later years confirm that, in this intensive period of struggle, he developed a specific understanding and viewpoint, which was of the necessity to integrate a programme of social and economic transformation into his nonviolent civil resistance campaigns against the Raj.

After 1924, this part of Gandhi's strategy came to be known by the title of constructive programme. But it was not seriously propagated under this name until the 1930s and 1940s. As a result, my use of the term to cover projects that took place before 1924 is perhaps misleading in places. These campaigns – for example, the establishment of' national schools and arbitration courts, or the spinning wheel campaign – constitute strictly the origins of the constructive programme. But I have not attempted to describe in systematic fashion the origins of Gandhi's constructive programme in this early period. Some of the case-material does demonstrate the beginnings of this side of Gandhi's political work. For example, the formation of the Swadeshi Sabha of 1919; the evolution of Noncooperation out of the programme of the Sabha; and the emergence of the concept of "progressive nonviolent noncooperation" which became a crucial component of his strategy for confronting the British.

But my aim is to demonstrate, as an explanation of Gandhi's method as an organiser, that in this period he discovered the necessity to complement and consolidate "negative" campaigns of nonviolent protest with "positive" campaigns to improve social life. It is the balance between conflict and construction in Gandhi's method which interests me. I thus use the term "constructive programme" in a third sense, conceptually, combining the two practical meanings mentioned above. Constructive programme is a broad concept within Gandhian satyagraha theory which can be used to distinguish efforts to promote greater social harmony and higher standards of popular self-reliance within political campaigns against acts of central authority. A number of sources have followed Gandhi in presenting constructive programme in this way, as one branch of the satyagraha method. (Diwakar 1946: 47-48; Iyer 1973: 301; Dhawan 1957: 126-127, 190 ff)

I hope to demonstrate that this "constructive" concept was an integral part of the way Gandhi developed his method during the years up to 1922 – a concept which was applied and consolidated in a specific programme of campaigns in later years.

Planning his campaigns

I argue, first, that the now well-established division between interpreters of Gandhian nonviolence – over whether nonviolence should be viewed as a philosophy of life or as a conflict technique – can be bridged by looking at Gandhi as an organiser of social and political movements. From the point of view of the organiser, goals and ideals are interesting in so far as they can be realised and made practical in a concrete situation. The special genius of Gandhi as an organiser is his pragmatic spirit and inspiration which enabled him time and again to locate his high ideals in practical forms of action, accessible to large numbers of people and taken up by them. It is this process of visualising and shaping his ideals in practical proposals which deserves attention. The cleverness of Gandhi's choice of issues and of methods enabled his ideals to shine through again and again. Through examining his methods as an organiser, that is, his means, we shall discover in large measure what his goals, his ends, were – which is a good test of Gandhi's theory that ends and means are coincident! [2]

It is probably misleading though to see the process of organising as a linear one. Organising is above all a responsive art, requiring the organiser continually to adjust to constantly changing situations. Organising is the application of a strategy. Gandhi lived by his wits, calculating and pitching his initiatives, frequently improvising, in order to build and sustain broad social movements he could attempt to direct for social and political ends. Through the seven case studies of satyagraha struggles examined, we see him applying and evolving certain formulae, certain consistent patterns or rules for engaging in this process of organising. Elucidating these rules is a strong focus. I hope to show that Gandhian nonviolent action can better be seen in a broad perspective as a method of organising movements for social change than narrowly as a method of engaging in conflict.

The second main aim, already mentioned, is to show the balance between "constructive" and "obstructive" in Gandhi's method. How far did programmes of constructive work prove to be necessary and indeed indispensable to his method as an organiser – to his instrumental purpose of building and sustaining social movements? Could his extraordinary longevity as a leader, called upon by the national Congress to direct struggles on its behalf, be related to his simultaneous pursuit of short-term and long-term campaigns?

Two further broad themes also emerge. One is the observation that Gandhi's methods as an organiser necessarily adjusted as he moved from the local to the national scale. Scale is an important factor in the

---

2. I will argue that ends were important to Gandhi and that, rather than focusing simply on means, he sought to situate the end in the means.

organising of any social movement, because approaches and techniques for confronting an issue touching 80,000 people are inevitably different from those employed to reach tens of millions. As we shall see, there is a surprising consistency between Gandhi's methods at a local and national level, but there are also significant differences. One of the reasons for focusing on Gandhi's emergence as a leader in the province of Gujarat is to emphasise the crucial importance of localised support in his home region to his emergence as a national leader. This regional backing he was to rely on not only in achieving national leadership, but also in adapting his methods at the national scale.

Controlled Nonviolent Struggles

A further theme derives, practically, out of a comparison between Gandhi's approach to organising two all-India satyagrahas, the Rowlatt satyagraha of 1919 and Noncooperation of 1920 to 1922. It is expressed, theoretically, in an assessment of the balance between civil resistance and constructive programme in these two extraordinary adventures in nonviolent struggle. My conclusion is that Gandhi was drawn to place so much emphasis on the constructive side of satyagraha because of his difficulties when he relied too heavily on civil resistance. This suggests that the long, slow build-up of mobilisation through constructive action in Gandhi's method has been neglected in those theoretical accounts of nonviolent action which focus on the symbolic impact of confrontational civil disobedience.

It is tempting in the west to dismiss the relevance of Gandhi's experiments with satyagraha because of their background in the Indian context and in Hindu thought. The moralistic and religious basis of Gandhi's intervention in politics is foreign to many of us. It seems intellectually unsophisticated to base a political movement, as Gandhi did, on the principle of the unity of all that lives and the duty of those who are well-off and given high status to identify with the poorest of their fellows and to serve them. (Rothermund 1963: xii-xiv, 30-36) In other words, the idea of a single moral universe, where every action by anyone is linked on a cosmic scale to the welfare of everyone else, may seem preposterous or even irrelevant to the business of politics. (Iyer 1973: 38-61, 64-86)

Nonetheless, Gandhi's attempt to find another basis for political authority and social power – not based in control of the central institutions of representative democracy, not based in command of the military and the police – needs to be understood. It was because he had a view of political authority and of social responsibility different from most of his contemporaries that he made the political choices he did. (Iyer 1973: 53-57, 252-260; Sharp 1973: Part 1) With this view, he was able to initiate controlled nonviolent struggles and mass campaigns, which adopted and succeeded in maintaining to an astonishing degree, nonviolent discipline.

Flexibility and Pragmatism

At the same time, it is important not to present Gandhi simply as a moralist living strictly according to religious principles and refusing to bend them no matter what the circumstances or the emergency. This is a position which has been taken by some who look on Gandhi as a moralist or a spiritual guide and who have then taken over his personal principles and sought to apply them in their own lives and in the groups to which they belong. What is so remarkable about Gandhi is that, with his view that there was only one human nature and one shared system of values, he was willing all the time to make compromises with present reality. He was a pragmatist, happy to make any accommodation as long as, within the agreement, was some principle ensuring there would be moral progress. His view of progress was, like Plato's – the ideal was hidden somewhere, but we could dimly see its shadow and we should move towards that.

It was because of this flexibility, his determination to gear even his most idealistic campaigns to what was realistically achievable, that Gandhi was able to operate as a remarkably successful politician in pre-Independence India. If we want to understand how he was able to develop a mass following for nonviolence and how he was able to draw hundreds of thousands into nonviolent struggle, it is important to examine carefully how he planned and organised his campaigns. On what basis, for example, were the objectives for political struggles selected? Or what considerations persuaded him to seek alliances with other political figures who did not share his religiously-based political principles?

Seven Consecutive Case Studies

The greater part of the book is given over to a detailed examination of the principal satyagraha campaigns in which Gandhi engaged between 1915 and 1922. Seven case studies are contained in Part I (chapters 1-3) and Part III (6-9). Part II contains two chapters (4-5) discussing constructive programme, while Part IV (10-11) is devoted to analysis of the case studies and comparing the findings with the approach of some of the best known literature on nonviolent action in the West.

(There may be some readers who wish to avoid the more "academic" analysis sections. In which case you can follow the extraordinary story of Gandhi's activities during these years in Part I, in chapter 5 and in Part III.)

Chapter 1 contains the first case study. It presents a "classic satyagraha" in Champaran, usually seen as the first significant campaign in India to demonstrate his method of conflict. It was a local struggle and took place in 1917 when he was far away from his base in Gujarat. It is convenient to treat it first because it was so much an isolated campaign and relatively self-contained. The later struggles, particularly as Gandhi moved towards organising at a national level, are much harder to separate one from another and they sit within a developing narrative. Thus the second and third local case studies of the Ahmedabad and Kheda satyagrahas in Gujarat in 1918 took place simultaneously and within 30 miles of each other. They are discussed together in chapter 2. Their impact and partial success helped assure Gandhi's leadership of the nationalist movement in Gujarat and contributed directly to his next initiatives when he began to organise satyagraha on a national scale.

Champaran, because it is a self-contained case-study, gives me the opportunity to construct a framework for analysis of how satyagraha struggles were organised. An outline of the main events is followed by detailed consideration of different facets of the campaign. These include such topics as recruitment and preparation of co-workers, making an effective challenge in the particular local context, doing so in a nonviolent manner, engaging and involving the peasants whose cause he is championing and managing relationships with his opponents.

However, the later campaigns, particularly as they become national struggles with first the Rowlatt satyagraha and then Noncooperation, tend to merge into each other. They become complicated as they evolve and are shaped by the need to take part in and seek to influence the direction of nationalist politics both locally and at the centre. In some chapters, the historical material available and the issues raised have seemed to dictate a different structure. Therefore, I have not followed the Champaran framework rigidly.

The Champaran satyagraha lasted two months and fills an entire chapter. Noncooperation lasted two years, including the preparations for it, and occupies the largest part of four chapters. Gandhi designed and developed the Noncooperation campaign directly in response to mistakes made in the Rowlatt satyagraha and the tragic events which followed it, especially the riots in Bombay and Ahmedabad and the Punjab massacre (chapters 3 and 7). He was in frequent dialogue from the start with Muslim politicians on the Khilafat issue (chapter 6) and with Indian National Congress politicians as Congress was persuaded to become the vehicle for Noncooperation (chapters 7, 8 and 9).

Chapter 4 looks at the difference between local and national organising. It draws on the three preceding chapters and on Gandhi's own assessment to show that his methods in local satyagrahas should be distinguished from those devised for national or nation-wide satyagrahas. Looking back later in life Gandhi concluded that constructive programme is essential in national satyagrahas, but not in local ones.

Then chapter 5 explores an interesting historical question as Gandhi moved from local to national campaigns. Was he determined from the outset, if the opportunity arose, to put his approach to politics to the service of the nation as a whole? Or would he have been content to pursue local grievances only, if the turmoil in India at the end of the First World War had not thrust him to national prominence? The other section of chapter 5 describes one way in which Gandhi responded to the problems encountered in the Rowlatt satyagraha. It looks at the Swadeshi Sabha, a short-lived organisation he had set up in 1919 to develop constructive projects.

Part III is devoted to the all-India campaign to capture the Indian National Congress and, through it, to build an effective programme of noncooperation against the Raj for Independence. Most of the main published studies of Gandhi's life and methods have neglected the many complexities of Noncooperation; but for the student of nonviolent action, this satyagraha campaign proves to be a treasure trove. I argue that Noncooperation is made up of three satyagrahas – on the Khilafat and Punjab issues, and then finally for Swaraj. They eventually merge into one. Gandhi devised a key organising strategy, namely "progressive nonviolent noncooperation", as he wrestled with the difficulty of transplanting the simple concept of noncooperation into a workable plan.

In Part IV, the book concludes by drawing the various strands from the seven case studies together. It compares Gandhi's techniques as an organiser at a local and at a national level. It also presents a broader definition of the satyagraha method than is usually made in the west. In particular, it shows how Gandhi promoted both civil resistance and constructive programme, the two sides of satyagraha, by the same organising techniques.

The role of organisations

Within the eleven chapters, a lesser theme is also explored. Because Gandhi was such an original and extraordinary leader (and has acquired a reputation as a religiously-inspired, charismatic figure with timeless messages for humanity), many accounts tend to concentrate overwhelmingly on his personal role and neglect the mundane work of joining and building organisations to achieve his goals.

In Gujarat in 1917 his emergence as the principal Gujarati nationalist leader becomes clearer when he is invited to join the Gujarat Sabha as president after his success in Champaran; he immediately sets about transforming the organisation (chapter 2). Then he founded the Satyagraha Sabha 1919 to pursue his political agenda (chapter 3), in the process bypassing the Indian National Congress. The Sabha organised the Rowlatt satyagraha but shortly afterwards dissolved from failures of coordination. Then came the Swadeshi Sabha, which he founded following Rowlatt to pursue his social programme (chapter 5).

Table 0.1 provides a summary of the organisations he founded or transformed and a list of the chapters where they are described.

TABLE 0.1: Organisations in India Founded or Transformed by Gandhi 1915-1922

	Founded	Founded by Gandhi	Gandhi's leadership begins	Chapter
Gujarat Sabha	1885	-	May 1917	2
Satyagraha Sabha	-	February 1919	-	3
Swadeshi Sabha	-	June 1919	-	5
Central Khilafat Committee	July 1919	-	November 1919	6
All-India Home Rule League/ Swarajya Sabha	1916	-	April 1920	7
Indian National Congress	1885	-	September 1920	7, 8, 9
National Volunteer Corps	-	January 1922	Founded by Congress at his initiative	9

During 1919, with widespread uncertainty about how the nationalist movement would develop, he worked through the Central Khilafat Committee of Muslims (chapter 6), which planned and launched Noncooperation in August 1920, and also the all-India Home Rule League, re-named by him the Swarajya Sabha (chapter 7). They provided him with the support he needed to capture the Indian National Congress later that year.

In what was one of his greatest achievements, Gandhi then completely reorganised the Congress (chapters 7, 8 and 9) and transformed it into a campaigning organisation. Finally, seeking to strengthen the disparate set of volunteer organisations which were carrying out the Noncooperation programme across India, in early 1922 he set up the National Volunteer Corps, a campaigning wing of the Congress, still decentralised, but planned so as to improve coordination and discipline (chapter 9).

Gandhi the Organiser

Within this account of his early years back in India, there is no full attempt to place Gandhi relative to all the other forces and actors present at the time. There is no detailed presentation either of the changing and even chaotic economic, social and political conditions in India during and after the First World War. These created the possibility for a new type of political leader to emerge; without such a combination, Gandhi's career would have evolved quite differently. A fuller historical perspective on this period, however, can be gained from many other sources.

A more particular omission is discussion of the response Gandhi as an organiser evoked from the Indian people, both the educated and uneducated. At a general level, assessments of his impact have been made previously by social scientists and historians exploring the topic of charisma and also the religious themes from Hindu scripture Gandhi drew upon in making links with the peasantry. (Rudolph and Rudolph 1967: 155-249) In a discussion of Gandhi as an organiser, however, there could be a detailed examination of, for example, those groups in the Champaran peasantry who responded to his campaign appeal in 1917. Or how far Gandhi managed to reach and influence the behaviour of Muslim peasants during his championship of the Khilafat issue in 1920. That level of historical inquiry is beyond the scope of this book.

The emphasis will be on the rules developed by Gandhi for organising social and political movements: how, for example, he chose issues, how he made his judgements as to what was politically wise or expedient, and how he managed to balance his campaigns between maintaining the initiative for his side while sustaining respectful dialogue with his opponents (or failed to do so). We will see also how he achieved the position in Indian politics which enabled him to project his unconventional views to such a wide audience.

The focus, then, is on Gandhi the organiser – not exploring especially his philosophy and his principles, nor concentrating narrowly on his methods of engaging in conflict. With this special attention to Gandhi himself, it may seem that I have fallen back into the trap of isolating Gandhi as a remarkable figure from the context in which he operated. In some respects this is true. By picking out Gandhi as a particular character to study, I am judging that he had a special viewpoint and a role which make him interesting and even unique. It is not his personal qualities, though, remarkable as they were, which occupy me. It is the way he was able to take a set of unconventional and controversial political ideas – which his satyagraha creed and method always were – to the centre of political life in India.

PART I

CHAPTER 1

CHAMPARAN: BEFORE AND AFTER

It is common for commentators on Gandhi, allowing hindsight to colour their descriptions of his early years, to present him as a national political leader who emerged, as it were, complete, his destiny before him. Nonviolence, his message and method, took the people by storm; his charismatic presence drew all to him. The reality is different. Gandhi had to promote and "sell" his ideas to the nation. This was done through local campaigns, which brought him to national attention—but also just as significantly by his development of a reputation and organisation in the Gujarat province of the Bombay Presidency. Gandhi used success in Gujarat as a platform from which to launch initiatives at a national level. The importance of his regional base would provide a logical framework for a survey of his whole career.

It is also common for surveys of Gandhi's nonviolent campaigns to present his method as if there were no difference between his organising of campaigns at a local level in a limited geographical area and those struggles attempted on a vastly larger scale across the whole of India. It seems self-evident that mobilising on the vast scale of the Indian subcontinent posed immense problems for Gandhi, problems which were not so acute in struggles confined to a limited area.

These are broad themes which will be explored throughout this book: his promotion of satyagraha through local campaigns; the importance to Gandhi of his base in Gujarat; and the difficulties which he experienced in moving from organising at a local and regional level to a national level. We shall also hope to uncover some of the consistent patterns in his organising method.

Treading Carefully

When Gandhi arrived back in India at the age of 46 in 1915, he had spent twenty years in South Africa as a legal advocate and political organiser on behalf of the Indian community there. After 1907, when he realised that the British Crown could not be relied upon to protect the rights of Indians in South Africa, he had begun to experiment with methods of "passive resistance" which he called "satyagraha". His achievements there brought him to the attention of the nationalist movement at home in India and earned some approval from the government of India, the British Raj.

Back in India, Gandhi received a guarded welcome from the British and from the nationalist movement. To them he was an unknown quantity; while outside the circles of India's educated he was scarcely known. For his first years back, he was under a vow not to engage in political activity and he restricted himself primarily to building an ashram of his personal followers near Ahmedabad in Gujarat. Invited to address public meetings in different parts of the country on the position of Indians in South Africa he used his trips as an opportunity to learn about India. His appearance at receptions given in his honour in the clothes of a peasant caused some controversy, as did his insistence on some occasions on speaking in Gujarati or Hindi, rather than English. His main political achievement during his first eighteen months – an activity which did not break the terms of his vow to keep out of Indian politics - was to press successfully for the ending of the system of indentured labour under which Indians were sent to South Africa to work on terms close to slavery. (Brown 1972: 1-51; Tendulkar 1951)

Gandhi's position in the spectrum of Indian nationalist politics at this time was precarious and uncertain. He called himself a disciple of Gokhale, the great "Moderate" political leader who had died in 1915. G.K. Gokhale had been the principal leader of the Indian National Congress for nearly a decade and had visited South Africa to support Gandhi's struggles there. He was particularly identified with progressive causes such as the spread of education and the abolition of child marriage. The great split with the "Extremists" which had left Gokhale and the Moderates at the helm of Congress in 1907 was principally over the question of political methods. B.G. Tilak, the most prominent of the Extremist leaders, had openly advocated terrorism as a means of ejecting the British from India. Gandhi sided with Gokhale on this issue and with the Moderates' general approach of having the relationship between Britain and India change gradually on all sorts of issues through incremental reform. He also shared their active concern to promote social reform in Indian society, causes which traditionalists like Tilak often opposed.

Where Gandhi differed from the Moderates, however, was on two issues. First, their acceptance that the limits of political activity were set by the constitutional procedures established by the Raj, together with their unwillingness to risk popular campaigning. Second, he did not share their identification with British standards for economic development and cultural activity. Gandhi linked up with the Extremists as a populist and as a cultural nationalist who preferred the civilisation of India to that of the west.

What was he to do? The Extremists had returned to the Congress fold in 1916 and had seized the initiative from the Moderates in the economic and political turmoil gripping India at this time. Gandhi saw the popular movements they had founded to agitate for Home Rule making strong progress in the Bombay Presidency and elsewhere in these years; yet he hated the opportunism and stridency as he saw it of their agitations. The British of course were preoccupied by the First World War in Europe and the Home Rule rebellion in Ireland, both of which influenced political debate in India.

CASE STUDY 1: CHAMPARAN

Overview

When Gandhi arrived in the proximity of Champaran, a district of Bihar in northern India, in April 1917, none of the nationalist activists in that part of Bihar knew he was coming and none of them was campaigning politically on the issue on which he chose to make a stand. Within hours, however, of his hearing from a hurriedly grouped gathering of local lawyers about the conditions of the peasants forced to grow indigo in the district, he had decided to spend up to two years there. And within days he had organised this group of lawyers into a band of helpers who worked with him for the seven months that his work actually took.[3]

In Champaran about 200 European planters leased whole villages from Indian estate owners and sub-let to peasant cultivators. The *ryots* (peasants) were forced by the planters to grow indigo as a cash crop on a portion of their land. The indigo was then processed by the planters in their local factories into a vegetable dye for colouring blue clothing. Since payments to the ryots were on the basis of the number of acres sown with indigo, it was in the planters' interests to require the peasants to grow indigo on their best land giving the highest yield. This arrangement doubly penalised the ryots since they could get a higher price for other cash-crops such as rice, sugar-cane and maize. (Mishra 1963: 245-275). Various quasi-legal agreements had been struck with the tenants about the use of their land, of irrigation canals and of roads; these agreements were often secured by threats and physical intimidation; and if the tenants broke them they were frequently taken to court and fined.

Gandhi is unlikely to have had much awareness of the history of peasant activism in Champaran. In the 1860s, 1870s and in 1908-1909, outbreaks of rioting had been suppressed by the British authorities. These episodes – and other challenges within the law – had not achieved significant changes for the peasantry. Some of the larger peasant landholders were regularly in dispute with Indian land agents and British landlords, but on his arrival in 1917 there was no widespread agitation, particularly among the poorest peasants. (Pouchepadass 1999).

Gandhi had come to Bihar at the insistence of a particular peasant leader from Champaran who had met him at the annual session of the Indian

3. This account of the Champaran Satyagraha relies principally on Prasad R. (1949) and Tendulkar (1957). Also useful are two further accounts by Rajendra Prasad in Prasad R. (1955) and in Shukla (1949). Valuable documentation is contained in Gandhi (Gandhi, M.K, 1964; vol 13). Pouchepadass (1999: 188-289) provides a critical perspective. A useful overview is in Brown (Brown, 1972: 52-83).

National Congress held in Lucknow four months earlier. When he arrived, he informed the local British administration of his intention to go to Champaran - and quickly gathered that he was not welcome there. This assumption persuaded him to move into the district with all speed so that if he was arrested it would be in Champaran.

Within two days of arriving in Champaran, Gandhi was served with a notice externing him from the district, that is, instructing him to leave. Gandhi hurriedly organised his friends of less than a week into a team to carry on his inquiry into conditions in Champaran and offered himself in court. He made a defiant speech, a classic statement of civil disobedience, demanding the right to make the inquiry and insisting that he would not leave voluntarily. The magistrate had not expected this and did not know what to do because he did not want to jail Gandhi, so he postponed judgement. The local Champaran administration then was severely rebuked by the Bihar government for moving so precipitately; and Bihar was encouraged by direct attentions from the Viceroy himself, who was worried about Indian national opinion being roused against the British in India while British troops were fully stretched in the war in Europe. (Brown 1972: 70-72, 82-83) The case against Gandhi was dropped.

In the teeth of fierce political opposition from the planters and unease verging on hostility from the local administration – there were, of course, strong social ties between planters and local British officials – Gandhi then went ahead with his survey of peasant grievances. The survey involved his team recording up to 10,000 legal statements by the ryots. Pressure to get Gandhi out of Champaran before he had totally destroyed the planters' position and the authority of the local administration built up so much that the Bihar government began to think about externing him. They summoned him to the Bihar capital to the south in Ranchi where he met the Lieutenant Governor. But under pressure from the Government of India, the Lieutenant Governor completely changed his position. He decided to appoint a commission of inquiry into the conditions of the tenants in Champaran with Gandhi as one of its members.

Surprisingly, Gandhi was permitted to act as an advocate within the inquiry on the ryots' behalf while also serving as a member of the commission. He eventually managed to negotiate an agreement with the planters through the process of the inquiry, which met most of the tenants' main grievances. This agreement formed a part of the Commission's unanimous report, which was accepted by the Bihar government and enacted into legislation a year later. By any standards, it was an extraordinary achievement – though there were of course critics at the time and subsequently.

Gandhi then went back to his ashram in Gujarat, but immediately got involved in fighting a labour dispute on behalf of textile workers in the city of Ahmedabad and leading a civil disobedience campaign against high taxes in Kheda (Kaira), a rural area. Within a year he was also leading a markedly unsuccessful drive to recruit soldiers to fight on behalf of the British Empire in Europe from the very areas where he had been promoting nonviolent struggle – and simultaneously campaigning to get a leading Home Rule fighter and two Muslim leaders released from internment.

Here, we will examine the methods Gandhi adopted in Champaran. We will look at how as an outsider he was able so quickly to organise and build an effective campaign. We will also consider how he protected himself and his team by the manner in which he addressed his opponents and the various officials he encountered, including representatives of the Raj. In particular, we will see how he pitched his objectives throughout the campaign, in what Gandhians have called a classic satyagraha.

How Gandhi Organised Support

The First Days

When Gandhi arrived in Patna en route for Champaran, he was in the company of a peasant representative of the ryots from Champaran who had none of the connections with more educated people which Gandhi felt he needed if he was to establish himself in the area. Eventually, he remembered by chance to look up an old acquaintance from law school in London who was now a prominent member of the Muslim League; and this man gathered together a group of prominent Indian citizens to describe the situation in Champaran to Gandhi. Gandhi then decided immediately to go to Champaran and make an investigation. The Lucknow Congress had passed a resolution deploring the situation in Champaran, a resolution which Gandhi had been asked to move. He had declined on grounds of lack of knowledge and this gave him some authority to begin his inquiry.

Gandhi was given a contact in Muzaffarpur, the nearest large town to Champaran, and went to stay with him. This man brought together another group to discuss Champaran with Gandhi. Gandhi recognised directly from the situation of effective planter control of the local administration that this was a situation which could allow him to lead a nonviolent campaign to correct the injustice. But he was apparently conscious that he had no first hand knowledge of the situation and that if he was to engage in satyagraha against the administration he would need to be thoroughly identified with the cause of the peasants and have an indisputably established case. The power of satyagraha rested in the support of the peasants for what he was doing. If he was to find out exactly what was happening among the peasants and to build up support for a struggle on their behalf, he would need a group of full-time assistants.[4]

Gandhi straight away asked the group gathered with him in Muzaffarpur to help him, and a number of them agreed. The request was no small one because it meant abandoning for an indefinite period their families and established law practices and going to work in a subordinate capacity as clerks taking down statements. Gandhi also told the vakils (lawyers) that they should be prepared to go to jail. None of them agreed to this: but they did agree to work with him and to think about the question of jail - which must have seemed almost unthinkable to members of the legal profession, some of them quite prosperous, wondering what civil disobedience would mean for their legal careers. Gandhi offered no payment for their services. (Tendulkar 1957: 29)

Gandhi may have been successful in persuading a number of them to agree to go with him because he was a relatively senior man at 48 and

---

4. I am following here the conventional account in Gandhian commentary, which concentrates on Gandhi's role. More critical accounts such as Pouchepadass (1999) and Henningham (1976) focus on the role of peasant leaders who invited Gandhi to Champaran.

had a reputation as a national hero from his successful struggles in similar situations in South Africa. He had come to the area as a direct result of a decision of the Indian National Congress and displayed obvious sincerity and courage in being willing to go to jail on the Champaran issue when he was an outsider with no roots in the area. Moreover, changes in India were encouraging bold steps. The alignments of Indian political figures were shifting as the British showed themselves amenable to limited political reform. There may have been some jockeying for future position and an openness to experiment if it looked promising.

The next day Gandhi went to inform the Commissioner for the neighbouring district to Champaran of his intentions. He very quickly got the impression that he would not be allowed to enter Champaran. His reasons for rushing to the spot as quickly as possible are not recorded; but clearly the government's embarrassment in removing him from the area would be greater the closer he was to Champaran. His arrest there would pinpoint the peasant grievances nationally and help to focus local peasant opposition.

Gandhi had barely started his investigations from the town of Motihari in Champaran when he got an order from the local magistrate instructing him to leave the area. He immediately decided to disobey it and prepared instructions for his assistants of less than a week to follow in his absence.

From the start, Gandhi had fundamentally two objectives:

- To secure the legal abolition of the *tinkathia* system, where peasant tenants were obliged to grow indigo on the best portions of their land for their landlords, the planters and operators of the indigo factories; and

- To encourage in the peasants a spirit which would prevent the planters from re-establishing their grip on the area. (Tendulkar 1957: 29, 97; 1951: 200; Gandhi, M.K. 1964: vol 13: 35)

How he Organised His Assistants

As we have seen, Gandhi chose educated, professional men to be his assistants; he also made a point of choosing Biharis, that is, local men.

34

(He will have calculated that they knew the local dialects, had a better general knowledge of the area and its grievances, would perhaps be more acceptable to local peasants, would be better able to carry out the work if he was removed, and would be less vulnerable to attack as outside agitators.) The fact that the men were local, however, meant their reputation as legal advocates on behalf of the peasants and the involvement of some of them in Home Rule politics made them subject to criticism from the planters and the local administration. They were claimed to be biased men and well-known agitators. Gandhi's response to this charge was that his colleagues were, for the purposes of this inquiry, simply interpreters and clerks taking down statements, that they were entirely responsible to him and that if he felt that any of them were acting in an irresponsible way, he would instantly dismiss them. (Prasad, R. 1949: 133-134)

This assertion that he was master in his own camp seems to have been literally true. Gandhi set about organising his co-workers so that they became convinced (or pragmatic) followers of satyagraha and of his personal strategies and techniques. The first issue was to persuade them to come and work with him on a semi-permanent basis without money. A number of them decided to accept. Second, he wanted them to agree to take over the work from him in the event of his being jailed and to be prepared to go to jail themselves. On the morning when Gandhi himself walked to the courthouse in the conviction that he would go to jail rather than accept his externment from Champaran, his two key workers said they too were now ready to go to jail. Gandhi is reported to have said, "Now I know we shall succeed".

A third major achievement of Gandhi's brief but intensive association with these men was in the area of life-style. These were high-caste professional men who brought with them their servants and their cooks. This level of comfort was obviously distasteful to Gandhi who had thrown off the trappings of westernised, expensive living and who felt it his moral duty to engage in physical labour and to live like a peasant. He says that he "ridiculed" the men for their habits: arguing partly on a pragmatic basis that they needed to reduce their expenses. At any rate, all the servants were sent home and one cook only was kept who prepared vegetarian meals. One important aspect of this simplification of life-style, which extended to dress too, was that the gap between Gandhi's team and the peasants they were working with was reduced. Fourth, Gandhi quite simply worked harder than any of his associates (or opponents) and overwhelmed them with his energy and constant initiative. (Prasad R. 1955: 30-66; Prasad R. 1949: 111, 113, 118; Tendulkar 1957: 48)

Gandhi also refused to allow his assistants to identify their activity with the struggle for Home Rule, saying that if they were successful in their campaign in Champaran, it would do more for Home Rule than any amount of rhetorical agitation. (Prasad R. 1955: 27, 66; Shukla 1949: 274; Tendulkar 1957: 37)

Gandhi's Preparation for His Court Appearance

When Gandhi heard that he was to appear in court for disobeying an order to leave Champaran, he began a discussion with his assistants about what should be done - and was later gratified by the undertaking that some were willing to follow him to jail. He then prepared a list with the names of those who would take over in succession the direction of the campaign as others were arrested. He also wrote out a list of detailed instructions to his co-workers. (Gandhi M.K. 1964: vol 13: 369-370) It is clear that Gandhi immediately envisaged a structured and possibly prolonged campaign of civil disobedience in the event of his arrest (which he thought likely). He expected the principal leaders from the team he had assembled to follow him to jail, while offering no defence against the charge. Thereafter, a second tier of leaders from the peasantry should collect evidence from local centres. Peasants, where they considered that they were being treated unjustly, should simply refuse to grow indigo – and also be prepared to go to jail – rather than going to law. If necessary, a small All-India Committee should be consulted on the further direction of the campaign.

Gandhi then apparently spent the whole night writing letters to newspaper editors, explaining what was happening and asking them not to publish anything unless he was jailed. He also wrote to a number of leading Indian politicians including one who served on the Viceroy's legislative council: and addressed himself directly to the Viceroy, complaining that he was only interested in doing humanitarian service in Champaran. At the same time, he returned a medal that he had been awarded only a year previously by the Government of India for humanitarian work in South Africa.

Gandhi also prepared his statement for the court explaining why he was disobeying the order. (Gandhi M.K. 1964: vol 13: 374-375) The statement is in many ways a classic justification of civil disobedience. He expresses his sympathy for the magistrate: the local administration may have been poorly advised about his motive for coming to Champaran, which is to do a public service to the local area and to the Raj. His first instinct, he says, is to obey the law (and to leave the area) but, given his duty to study the situation in Champaran following a pressing invitation from the peasants, "the only safe and honourable course for a self-respecting man is… to submit without protest to the penalty of disobedience."

The statement illustrates a key feature of Gandhi's method at this time. He recognises and indeed endorses the authority of the state by accepting its penalty without complaint. At the same time, he proposes to challenge its authority by breaking this particular law (the order to leave the area). In so doing, he will place himself at the mercy of the magistrate; and simultaneously will challenge him (and a wider public) to consider the moral case which justifies his action. Gandhi plans to confront the state head on in the meekest way.

Gandhi's Relations with the Champaran Peasants

Gandhi was unknown to the ryots of Champaran, but by the time he was headed by train into the district word had got round that this man was coming to investigate – or solve – their grievances and numbers of people assembled at the stations to greet him and get a glimpse of him. When news of his court appearance came through more than a thousand peasants assembled at the court house and the magistrate had to rely on Gandhi to control the crowds.

A major part of Gandhi's considered approach to organising was that the peasant grievances would only disappear when they had the courage to stand up and insist that their situation must change. Gandhi's method of investigation at first was to go and visit a few villages and take depositions from peasants. (Hardiman 2003: 80-81) The presence of an Indian in the district conducting an inquiry of his own initiative was an encouragement to the peasants to believe that planter tyranny and the inactivity and bias of the local administration could be challenged and corrected. Each man who gave a statement about his position to Gandhi or his assistants (often in the presence of police officers) was confronting his own fear of the planters; and of course helping Gandhi build his case against the planters.[5] Eventually, 10,000 statements were taken by Gandhi's assistants.[6]

The people crowding round Gandhi's headquarters in Motihari or Bettiah and other more local centres to give their statements to Gandhi's assistants were mobilised by a second level of leaders, who came from the Champaran peasantry. These organisers were of a lower social status, wealthier peasants, shopkeepers, moneylenders, school-teachers and so on, who were able to work through existing village committees. Some historians have argued that the direction of the campaign lay in large measure with these men who had direct contact with the ryots on a daily basis. Their analysis is important in showing how Gandhi did not start completely from scratch and that he was able to utilise the energy and local knowledge of leading members of the peasantry who drove the

---

5. Strictly – according to the satyagraha method – Gandhi was not building a case against the planters, but compiling a case which (if well-established) would challenge them, or some of them, to change their behaviour and practices. His aim, in this sense, was to work with the planters to remedy the situation.

6. Both Prasad and Tendulkar report that 10,000 full-length statements were collected and, in addition, up to 15,000 shorter ones. One incentive for tenants to give statements was the belief that, if they did not come forward, they would be unable to benefit from any gains made by Gandhi's inquiry. (Prasad, R, 1955: 49) But Hardiman relates Gandhi's inquiry to the survey methods of Victorian reformers: "Gandhi understood [the need for investigations of problems on the ground] very well, and was a firm advocate of the careful and scrupulous social survey that was informed by a scientific spirit and open frame of mind. Following the principles of the great Victorian social investigators of Britain, he sought to identify problems through detailed fieldwork, involving the collection of testimonies and statistics." (Hardiman, 2003: 80)

campaign forward. At the same time, the occasion for this upsurge was Gandhi's survey and the taking of statements. (Pouchepadass 1999: 216, 220)

When a particularly bad situation was discovered in the landholding of one planter, Gandhi himself or some of his assistants would go directly to investigate and confront the planter with their information. This was to be done, if Gandhi's rules were followed, not in the spirit of exposure, so much as the desire of an investigator to hear the other side of the case. These direct approaches to the planters may have served to strengthen the reputation of the inquiry; in some instances they led to immediate and direct negotiations or proposals to resolve grievances.

The impact of Gandhi's arrival on the Champaran peasantry was immediate and unprecedented. Many of the ryots who came to the house where he was staying to give statements refused to leave till they had seen him. Gandhi's assistants arranged certain times of the day when Gandhi's darshan would be given, that is, peasants could get a glimpse of him. Rumours began that, for example, an avatar had come. One historian has collected and summarised concisely a number of these circulating rumours: Gandhi's power superseded that of all the local authorities; he was to abolish all the unwanted obligations imposed upon the peasants; and the administration of Champaran would be transferred to Indian hands, represented by Gandhi himself. His capacity to draw crowds wherever he went was a key factor in generating interest in the campaign. (Pouchepadass 1999: 216-221)

Privately, Gandhi expressed his concern with what he considered the ignorance and abject helplessness of the peasants. He extended his programme so far as to found schools in the area and to direct efforts for improving sanitation and personal hygiene. This emphasis on a constructive programme is an early example in India (though not a successful one) of how his method linked constructive work with resistance to injustice. Unfortunately, he was unable to find Biharis to take up these activities and had to recruit on an all-India scale. The school and other initiatives failed to take root and dissolved within a few months of his leaving the district. (Prasad R. 1949: 194-203)

With his triumph in the court room, his later successes in maintaining his inquiry in the teeth of planter opposition, and then securing a provincial government inquiry on which he himself was to serve, Gandhi's reputation with the peasants as some kind of miracle-worker became established. It is doubtful that direct training in the principles of satyagraha took place – though there were clearly intense discussions with his closest assistants. Gandhi seems to have assumed that his band of helpers, whatever their class and background, would follow his instructions to the letter; and that the poorest peasants would follow his leadership and that of his helpers and the peasant leaders without much or any knowledge of the satyagraha doctrine itself. It may be that the small number of reports of violence and other acts of militant resistance throughout the campaign (despite rioting having been a feature of the protests in previous decades) provides evidence of the influence of his personal charisma. The impact of Gandhi's presence in the area was to give the peasants unexpected hope that their situation would at last change for the better. (Pouchepadass 1999: 220-221; Sarkar 1983: 181)

Gandhi's Relations with the Press

Throughout his time in Champaran, Gandhi issued a series of background documents to the editors of newspapers. These were not for publication but were sent with the object of keeping them fully informed – so that they would not be tempted to publish ill-informed stories; and in the event of his being arrested, they would have accurate information on which to base any editorials they might write. Through this tactic, he was able to keep the press at bay at a time when he did not want anti-planter stories inflaming opinion.

How Gandhi Addressed His Opponents

The Planters

Before entering Champaran district, Gandhi went to see the secretary of the Bihar Planters Association (a group of Europeans) and told him what he was intending to do.

We may list some of the considerations of the satyagraha method which will have prompted Gandhi to seek this type of interview. By such an approach, which he maintained consistently throughout the inquiry, he confronted his opponents openly and personally. He forewarned his opponents and suggested honest intentions and invited trust. He implied a willingness to compromise and, by separating himself from the security of his supporters, indicated his own self-confidence and power, suggesting not only "I am my own master" but also, "You will find that I cannot be bought". Such an open, fearless approach stretches the credulity of the opponent, who knows that there are entrenched attitudes and does not readily understand this flexibility; and who may be tempted to talk to find out more.

This particular man seems to have been unsettled by Gandhi's courtesy, for he stated his personal willingness to assist Gandhi in his inquiry – though he added that he could not speak for his Association. (He later wrote to Gandhi, and told him not to go to Champaran, and got the whole planter network buzzing with the news.) (Prasad R. 1949: 101-102)

Gandhi's principal objectives, as we noted earlier, were to have the legal agreement whereby tenants were obliged to grow indigo abolished; to challenge a number of other unjust or legally doubtful obligations imposed on the tenants; and to develop in the peasant cultivators a spirit which would prevent the planters from re-imposing their tyranny. He had a further, more ambitious and idealistic aim – the very naivety of which shows the unusualness of his impact as an investigator and campaigner – which was to secure the willing agreement of the planters to his plans and to invite their support for his aims of social improvement in the area, such as schools and sanitation. (This approach could of course be misrepresented, and quite often was, as trickery and cynicism.)

Gandhi met with representatives of the planters on several occasions and with their full Association twice. When statements from peasants indicated a particular injustice or abuse, he would visit the planter concerned or write to him detailing the complaints and inviting his comments. In some instances, he offered immediate proposals for remedies. On one occasion, a planter denied that any of his tenants were unhappy with their arrangements and invited Gandhi to meet them in his company. In Gandhi's presence, large numbers of these tenants then complained against the planter to his face, and Gandhi immediately organised them to take action for a more just arrangement. (Prasad R. 1949: 143-147; Sharp 1960: 27-29)

These activities created apoplexy among the planter community in Champaran who used every type of pressure available to them to discredit Gandhi and have him expelled. The local and provincial administrations were saturated with complaints. European associations across India were activated to put pressure on the Viceroy; newspapers editorialised; biased press reports were published, as well as letters to the editor from planters. The main complaints were that the tenure system in Champaran had been in existence since "time immemorial" and so could not be challenged as unjust or illegal; that Gandhi had brought in Congress agitators; that Gandhi had established a parallel system of investigating grievances in Champaran which was undermining legitimate authority; and that the planters and their families were in fear of their lives from aroused peasants. Two small fires were started in indigo factories and blamed by the planters on Gandhi's inquiry. However, Gandhi denied that peasants were involved. (Prasad, R. 1949: 183-189)

When the Bihar Government appointed its own Commission to investigate peasant grievances, with Gandhi as a member, representatives of the planters on the Commission were in time persuaded to go along with major criticisms of the old system and recommendations to change it – these representatives were later disowned by other planters.

Gandhi and the Bihar Government were anxious to achieve a unanimous report from the Commission so as to make it possible for the Government to get through reforming legislation quickly. Gandhi therefore made quite major concessions to the planters' case, particularly on the question of compensation for the loss of revenues. In order to avoid costly litigation in the courts for the peasants, Gandhi was anxious that the report should detail agreed compensation terms for certain planters and agreed reimbursements to certain tenants of money already wrongly paid. After much fierce arguing with particular planters, terms were agreed, which were almost certainly generous to the planters. Gandhi was happy, once the principle of abolishing tinkathia was established, to concede on lesser issues. (Gandhi M.K.1964, 13: 435, 482, 490, 492, 500; Shukla 1949: 80; Tendulkar 1957: 95-98; Prasad R. 1995: 68-72)

Gandhi was severely criticised by some of the tenants for this compromise. (Shukla 1949: 273-274) It appears, however, that within ten years of his campaign (and with the market for indigo in decline), all the planters had left Champaran.

The Local Administration

Gandhi made it clear at one point that his strategy was first to persuade the planters; then if that failed, the local officials of the Raj; then if that failed, the Bihar Government; then the Government of India; and finally public opinion all over India. (Gandhi M.K.1964, 13: 572)

The local officials worked closely with the planters and in two days served Gandhi with notice to quit the area. When Gandhi appeared in court, refusing to obey the order but accepting any penalty the court might bestow, the magistrate did not know what to do. Gandhi had already won his respect (and undermined his authority) by helping to control the crowds around the courthouse. Sentencing was postponed and Gandhi released without any recognisance except his word to appear when called, because Gandhi refused to offer any money.

Later, on the orders of the Lieutenant-Governor of Bihar, the case was withdrawn. The Bihar authorities were furious because they felt that they did not have a strong enough case against someone of Gandhi's reputation, who had not actually done anything at that point except announce an inquiry. They instructed the local officers to offer their assistance to Gandhi's inquiry, and this was apparently done.

Gandhi met regularly with the local officials, informing them of what he was doing, sending them copies of some of the reports which others were sending to the Bihar government. These were uniformly negative, making the same arguments as the planters, that their authority was being undermined and serious trouble seemed likely.

When Gandhi received letters from these officials marked "confidential" he refused to accept them unless he was permitted to share the contents with his assistants. (When other "confidential" documents arrived from sources in the Indian civil service who supported Gandhi, he refused to use them because they had not been acquired openly.) (Shukla 1949: 273-274)

Gandhi's relations with the local authorities seem on the whole to have been courteous and even friendly.

The Bihar Government and the Government of India

After two months of Gandhi's inquiry, pressure from the planters and local officials grew so intense that the Bihar government summoned Gandhi to Patna to meet with one of its senior members. This man asked Gandhi to dismiss his assistants who were considered to be agitators and to end his inquiry; but Gandhi refused. The two then agreed that Gandhi should submit his preliminary conclusions to government in the form of a report. He would also slightly modify the conduct of his inquiry so that he, Gandhi, had most responsibility for the taking of the depositions.

Gandhi's report was produced in a single day. In this way he retained the initiative. He sent copies of it to the planters and to all the local officials, who were then given eight weeks to submit their comments to the government. This development further angered the planters and local officials who now felt their power being usurped, arguing that it appeared Gandhi's activities had the blessing of the government. They called for the Government to appoint its own Commission to replace Gandhi's inquiry.

When Gandhi was summoned to Ranchi, the capital of Bihar, to meet the Lieutenant-Governor, a month later, he and his co-workers thought it likely that he might not be allowed to return: the government obviously was not waiting to receive all the comments on Gandhi's report. They therefore made contingency plans for replacements to take over the inquiry if Gandhi was arrested. (Shukla 1949: 270; Tendulkar 1957: 73)

Apparently, the Governor had become alarmed with what was happening in Champaran, but at the same time he had received a letter from the Viceroy instructing him to establish a Commission with Gandhi as one of its members. The Viceroy had his "all-India reasons" for appeasing Gandhi while the First World War was in progress in Europe. Gandhi met with the Lieutenant-Governor for long sessions on three separate days. He insisted that, if he were to be a member of the Commission, he must retain the right to act as advocate on behalf of the peasants, that is, to present the evidence that his inquiry had gathered and also call witnesses. This was agreed. (Brown 1977: 69-72)

When the Commission was announced, the planters were delighted. When they heard a few days later that Gandhi was to be a member of it, they felt utterly betrayed. Gandhi then ended his inquiry, but retained his team in being to prepare evidence already gathered for the Commission and to provide an advisory service to tenants. (Shukla 1949: 170-171; Gandhi, M.K, 1964: vol 13: 478) The Commission met in Ranchi, Patna, Motihari and Bettiah, visiting many of the villages directly. Its report was argued over for more than two months but was finally unanimous. It supported in most particulars the preliminary report that Gandhi had prepared three months earlier. Planter reaction was predictably hostile; but the Bihar government piloted a bill closely based on this report through the legislative assembly and it became law within a year.

SUMMARY

1. Gandhi's aims were to abolish the "tinkathia" system whereby tenant cultivators were forced by their planter landlords to grow indigo; and to build up a spirit among the tenants which would mean that the old system of abuses against them could not be re-established. In this he succeeded.

2. This campaign, acting on a social grievance and organising the peasantry, moved Gandhi into an area of politics that had not been attempted by other contemporary Indian politicians.

3. Gandhi was able to assemble a strong team of local, educated men to work with him, who made considerable personal sacrifice to adopt his political methods and recognised his decisive authority.

4. Gandhi was able to reach the peasants with his campaign because:

- no Indian figure of his standing had tried to approach them before;

- he publicly out-manouevred the attempt by the local administration to expel him by his willingness to go to jail;

- his inquiry method was exceedingly thorough and conscientious; the survey he and his assistants conducted enabled thousands to make their contribution and take the risk individually and collectively of speaking out;

- he stood up fearlessly to the planters, visiting them personally when necessary;

- his life-style was simple and inexpensive and indicated a desire not to be vastly different from theirs; and

- rumours about his powers as a champion for the peasants – and the charismatic impact of his presence – appear to have had a calming effect. A hope grew among the peasants that changes would come without resort to rioting and clashes with the authorities.

5. Gandhi protected himself and was protected from government suppression by

- insisting on the neutral objective of his mission – an inquiry into conditions in Champaran;

- keeping public officials fully informed of everything he did, so he could not be accused of trickery;

- his willingness to go to jail – which might create serious all-India agitation at a time when Britain had few troops in India;

- the success of his mission in arousing peasant interest and support – which appeared to threaten disorder if action was taken against him;

- his outspoken and clearly genuine opposition to violence, thus neutralising charges that he was out to foment violence;

- his careful cultivation of all-India public opinion through press releases and personal letters;

- his deliberate dissociation of the campaign from Congress agitation for Home Rule;

- his links with higher levels of Government – and by uncertainty at Government level on how to deal with him;

- his insistence that he was taking personal responsibility for all aspects of the inquiry, thus forcing critics to debate with him; and by

- his energy and initiative, which meant that the other parties to the conflict were forced to react to him.

6. As a result of the survey, he was able to develop an excellent factual and legal case for reform in Champaran, which he was capable of arguing with all-comers.

7. He was friendly and courteous at all times in his dealings and obviously sincere.

8. His conduct in obeying all the rules of propriety indicated that he was not fundamentally against civil order (however threatening some of his actions seemed). If he was persevering with an inquiry which others wanted stopped, this was because they were party to an unjust system in Champaran, which – if they looked to their sense of truth and justice – they would have to admit must be changed.

9. He aimed to create social harmony between planter and cultivator in Champaran. In this he failed.

10. He aimed to develop his own idea of *swaraj* (Home Rule) in Champaran through constructive work in education, sanitation and hygiene. In this he failed.

11. He showed a willingness to negotiate and to compromise on what he saw as inessentials, which demonstrated his complete personal authority and also invited criticism from some tenants later.

CONCLUSION

Champaran is in some respects an isolated example of Gandhi's political activities in India – not least because of its great distance from his base in Gujarat in west India. Apart from the one act of civil disobedience by Gandhi himself when he refused to leave the district after being ordered to do so, there was no direct confrontation with the British authorities, nor with the planters. Nor was there a protest campaign as such of public meetings and processions.

On the other hand, as the planters and local administrators were quick to point out, Gandhi's initial act of civil disobedience, followed by the manner in which his inquiry was conducted and the response it drew from the peasantry, did constitute in practice a continuous demonstration which involved effectively a succession of public meetings across the whole district. It could be seen for what it certainly was felt to be by the planters, a carefully pitched strategy of confrontation, where Gandhi never quite lost his stance of outside impartial investigator and so was able to protect himself from charges of simply stirring up an agitation. Nationalist opinion also saw Champaran as a confrontation in which Gandhi won a "victory" by his novel technique of satyagraha.

Champaran has often been presented by Gandhians as a "classic" satyagraha because of the "purity" of its execution. A highly antagonistic confrontation between irreconcilable groups was turned creatively by Gandhi's intervention into an exercise where the provincial government of Bihar was forced – by defiant and respectful pressure – to address itself to a popular grievance and to respond to it positively. Moreover, as a result of the satyagraha, relations between the planters and their tenants were changed to the extent that the Champaran peasants were less afraid to stand up for themselves. We can see here Gandhi's argument that, in Champaran, he and his co-workers were doing the work of preparing

India for Home Rule, even though he refused to allow it to be linked to other Home Rule agitation.

It is interesting to speculate on why Gandhi chose Champaran in remote Bihar for the first major demonstration of his new method of satyagraha. As we shall see in the next chapter, early in 1917 he had begun to take an active part in the politics of Gujarat. It may be that he was now seeking to engage in an exemplary struggle and that Bihar seemed "riper" than areas nearer home.

There were undoubtedly many other parts of India where peasants suffered grievously under cruel landlords. What was distinctive about Champaran was a similarity between the situation there and that of indentured labourers in South Africa whose cause Gandhi had consistently championed. Moreover, these peasants were growing cash crops; their horizons had been stretched through buying and selling in the market-place. The landlords were Europeans, mostly British. The symbolic value of a struggle against exploitative British landlords in India, at a time when India was being asked to support Britain by sending troops and money to assist the war in Europe, will not have escaped Gandhi.

It is relevant to note, too – though Gandhi is unlikely to have known this at the outset – that the cultivation of indigo in this part of Bihar had gone into rapid decline at the turn of the century. From 96,000 acres under cultivation with indigo in Bihar and Orissa in 1899-1900, the figure had declined to 8,000 acres in 1914-1915. Production of a cheap synthetic dye in Germany had destroyed the market for natural indigo. War with Germany brought a renewed demand for the natural product, and the area under production increased to 22,000 acres in 1916-1917 and 26,000 in 1917-1918. It was during this period that Gandhi was in the district. After the war, demand collapsed again and, following attempts to switch from indigo to other cash crops, most of the European planters left the district. (Mishra 1963: 249)

In practice, the Champaran satyagraha had a number of all-India implications. It was seen as a victory for the nationalist cause; it showed the potential for drawing new social groups from a "backward" area,

Bihar, into politics; it showed a new method of engaging in struggle, satyagraha, whose potential was unknown; and it introduced a new nationalist leader to prominence. What it also did was to reveal Gandhi's highly individual approach to the British Raj.

For several years afterwards, Gandhi used to face arguments that it was disloyal and opportunist of him to organise such campaigns against the Raj while a bitter war was being fought in Europe. He replied that his struggles were in fact of benefit to the Raj because they brought about a closer identity between the rulers and the ruled, and helped to clear up blots on the record of the Raj in India that would otherwise justify disloyalty.

In a similar fashion, he used to argue that civil disobedience could be used only by those who respected the law. In fact, to break the law in a civil manner – the emphasis was important – when it offended one's conscience, constituted the highest form of respect for law and for the government. This was so, he argued, because one was willing to offer oneself in a spirit of civic sacrifice to one's belief that the law should be changed or was being used wrongly. Nonviolent, and especially violent, lawbreaking not carried out in this spirit, he considered to be "criminal disobedience", which he strongly deplored.[7]

Only later, when Gandhi came to believe that the British must leave India altogether, did he come to present civil disobedience as a means of challenging the very authority of the Raj in India – though he still retained this stress on the civil character of civil disobedience. As his views on the value of the British connection changed, so he began to

---

7. Later, in 1922, Gandhi used exactly the same formulation of "criminal disobedience" to describe the rioters of Chauri Chaura, whose violent actions caused him to call off Noncooperation. Some of the rioters went willingly to jail as Gandhi wished them to do – but unfortunately the national movement distanced itself at the time and for many years afterwards from those jailed (some for long periods) and from those executed. It viewed them, as did the Raj, as criminals, rather than peasant satyagrahis whose protest had got out of hand. (See Amin, 1995)

place more emphasis on constructing a political instrument which could replace the British as rulers of India and a social programme which would unify and prepare the nation for independence.

But in Champaran, Gandhi challenged authority as someone who in his own unique fashion was a loyalist, and this accounted in part for the care with which he was treated by the Raj. It helped also to define the gap between himself and the Home Rule agitators among the nationalist movement at the time, especially the Home Rule Leagues which were much more anti-British in temper.

When he returned to Gujarat from Champaran and organised another peasant agitation, this time against the Raj's own land revenue system, Gandhi still remained "loyal". Before long he went so far as to start active recruiting on behalf of regiments serving with the Indian Army. But in Gujarat, Gandhi came much more strongly into contact with a few experienced political activists who had been brought into nationalist politics by the activities of the Home Rule Leagues. He discovered here that his companions in struggle were not so "pure" as in Bihar and he was less satisfied with the exemplary quality of his satyagraha campaigns. In Gujarat, and more especially nearby Bombay City, Gandhi encountered the emerging mainstream of nationalist agitation in India. In coming to terms with it, he lost some of his isolation in politics and Gujarat became a power-base for him as an all-India nationalist leader.

CHAPTER 2

PEASANTS AND WORKERS TAKE UP SATYAGRAHA

Prior to 1919 nationalist leaders did not seriously attempt to develop personal followings and political organisation much outside their own home provinces. India is after all a vast country with distinct religious, language and caste groups and wide regional differences. Politics at the centre was a matter of forging alliances with leaders of other regions.

Annie Besant, a British woman already in her sixties when she entered Indian politics as a Theosophist after 1910, was perhaps the first to try to organise on an all-India scale. Her All-India Home Rule League, formed in 1916, drew on the network of Theosophists established across India: it gathered strong support in Madras in the south and in Bombay city and Gujarat in the west, and to some extent elsewhere. The leader of the other Home Rule League, Bal Gangadhar Tilak, tended to confine his intensive organising to his home province of Maharashtra also in the west and in the Bombay Presidency. Tilak's organisation, known as the Indian Home Rule League, was founded in part as a means of preventing Mrs Besant from gaining too strong a following in Maharashtra. (Owen 1968: 159-195)

Sumit Sarkar comments that Gandhi's experience in South Africa had made him at this time already "potentially much more of an all-India figure... than any other politician". His work in South Africa had been with Indians from various religious, caste and regional backgrounds and with upper-class merchants and lawyers as well as mineworkers. He was also "something of an international celebrity". (Sarkar 1983: 178)

Gandhi's first three years back in India, from 1915, coincided with the emergence of the Home Rule movement as a force in Indian politics.

He saw at first hand in his home province of Gujarat and elsewhere the potential for nationwide organising in the response the movement drew from previously unorganised regions. The Home Rule agitation demonstrated that the older "moderate" politicians who had played a careful game of diplomatic pressure in the central councils of the Raj could be outflanked in the foremost meeting-place of Indian nationalists, the Indian National Congress. For in 1917, the Home Rule Leagues captured Congress and Mrs Besant was elected Congress President for the following year.

During 1918, for a variety of reasons, Mrs Besant lost control of the movement; but the possibilities opened up by the agitational politics of the Home Rule Leagues were obvious. It was clear, too, that if mass politics could be consolidated and brought under control by Indian nationalist politicians, then Congress would be transformed, and would have to be, into a quite different sort of political body.

The purpose of the next two chapters is to do two things. First, to show how important was the organising work which he undertook in his home state of Gujarat to Gandhi's triumph at the two sessions of the Indian National Congress held in 1920. Even after establishing himself as the foremost all-India leader, Gandhi still relied on the support he knew he could command in Gujarat. And, secondly, to examine in detail three of Gandhi's early satyagraha struggles: the Ahmedabad and Kheda satyagrahas of 1918, both local campaigns, followed by the first national campaign, the Rowlatt satyagraha of 1919. (Yajnik 1933: 2)

This emphasis on his Gujarat origins may seem to belie the argument that Gandhi was the first all-India politician to develop mass support outside his home region. But it was primarily through the work he conducted in Gujarat that Gandhi was able to bring himself and his methods to the attention of a wider Indian public. His work in Gujarat was crucial and remained until the 1930s central to his success as an all-India leader: it is chiefly in Gujarat that Gandhi personally engaged in satyagraha struggles; and in Gujarat Gandhi found a base of support in the peasantry and to some extent in the industrial working class who together acted as exponents of his satyagraha method for the rest of the nation. Some prominent Gujarati business owners also supported him at different times.

Gandhi builds a following in Gujarat

When Gandhi returned to India in 1915, he looked to Gujarat as his home base because this was the province of his birth. In a typically symbolic gesture, Gandhi met the reception committee assembled to greet him as he got off the boat at Bombay in the clothes of a Gujarati peasant. Later in 1915, he founded his Ashram just outside Ahmedabad, the leading city of Gujarat. The ashram was a living and working community of his most devoted companions and followers, some of whom had returned with him from South Africa.

Much of the thinking behind Gandhi's choice of Gujarat had to do with language. He was a native speaking Gujarati and had developed the conviction that in making bonds between the educated classes in India and the common people, as he was determined to do, it was essential to use the common speech. But there was another calculation too, Gandhi was a member of the *bania* caste, a trading not a warrior or a scholarly caste, and he reckoned that he was likely to win financial support from the bania merchants of Ahmedabad and Bombay. Also, Ahmedabad was a traditional centre for handloom weaving and Gandhi thought that he would be well-placed there to revive the craft of hand-spinning. (Gandhi M.K. 1982: 357)

As a Gujarati of national prominence (established by news reports of his satyagraha campaigns in South Africa in the years 1906 to 1914), Gandhi was guest-of-honour at numerous public events held on his return throughout India, and especially in his home province and in the Bombay Presidency. There were several opportunities open to him immediately to assume a position of leadership in Gujarat politics.

But Gandhi, to the perplexity of some of the young Gujarat Home Rulers who were looking to him to give a lead, did not take advantage of them.

(Yajnik 1933: 4-6)[8] He appears to have passed over these opportunities for two reasons. First, because his view of politics was very different from most of the young nationalists who in 1915 and 1916 were coming under the influence of Annie Besant's propaganda for Home Rule. Gandhi felt it necessary to delay because he did not want to act until he had a group of capable co-workers who would follow his lead. (Yajnik 1933: 14) Second, it is reasonably clear that Gandhi did not think of himself as a Gujarati leader in the usual political mould; he saw himself as a potential all-India leader whose mission was to lead a national movement according to the principles of satyagraha he had developed in South Africa. Indulal Yajnik, one of the young Home Rulers who was looking to Gandhi to direct agitation in the province – and was continually disappointed – got a glimpse he says of the "fire within" in 1915 when Gandhi told him flatly that he was destined to secure a large following in "due course". What worried Gandhi was whether he would be able to retain that following when they discovered how determined he was to maintain "strict adhesion to my principles – which they may fail to understand". (Yajnik 1933: 9)

Gandhi, it appears, needed time to develop his knowledge of the whole of India, not just Gujarat, and equally he needed to establish contact with individuals and groups across India to whom he was unknown. It is also true that Gandhi had made a vow at the request of a senior Indian politician, Gopal Krishna Gokhale, who had befriended Gandhi and supported him in South Africa, that he would refrain from political involvement for his first year back in India. (Tendulkar 1951: 157) Within six weeks of Gandhi's return, Gokhale died and Gandhi, characteristically, took a further vow not to put on footwear for a year. (Tendulkar 1951: 160) Gokhale's memory was celebrated all over India and it is certain that Gandhi in his bare feet remained conscious of his friend's injunction.

The Gujarat Sabha

While Gokhale was still alive, Gandhi was honoured by a reception organised by the Gujarat Sabha. The Sabha, founded in 1885, the same

---

8. Yajnik, although a critic of Gandhi, provides a most persuasive account of his first years back in Gujarat, and I have followed it extensively. (See also, Owen 1968: 169-170)

year as the Indian National Congress, was the principal nationalist organisation in Ahmedabad, though the reception was held in Bombay city, which is 300 miles away. Gandhi was introduced by the leading Muslim Home Ruler in Bombay at that time, M. A. Jinnah, who was also a Gujarati. Jinnah, of course, was to become Gandhi's implacable opponent twenty years later when he was leading the separatist struggle to partition India; and the relationship between them was always cool. Jinnah and others made their welcoming speeches in English. Gandhi delivered an unambiguous rebuke to his hosts by replying in Gujarati, urging that the English language be discarded in national and political work, and that the provincial language, or Hindi, be substituted for it "in order to appeal to the masses". (Yajnik 1933: 5; Tendulkar 1951:158)

One of the main issues that Gandhi promoted during his first years of touring very widely throughout India was the spread of Hindi. In 1916 he presided over the All-Indian Common Script and Common Language Conference held in Lucknow simultaneously with the annual Congress session (Dalal 1971:11) and, in 1918, he was elected President of the Indore session of the Hindi Sahitya Sammelin "in recognition of his services to Hindi". Rajendra Prasad reports that while he was active in Champaran, Gandhi was also beginning to organise the propagation of Hindi in Tamil-speaking southern India. (Prasad, R. 1955: 77-80; Dalal 1971: 18) It was through this language work that Gandhi made contacts with like-minded individuals in many parts of India, some of whom would visit him at his Ahmedabad ashram to learn more about his methods.

At home in Gujarat, Gandhi held aloof from the Home Rule agitation during 1916 – though in his ashram his followers were reading and discussing Thoreau's classic text On the Duty of Civil Disobedience, which Gandhi had translated into Gujarati. (Yajnik 1933:14) Gandhi did accept invitations to preside over a number of meetings of the Gujarat Sabha, which has been described at the time as "moribund" (Yajnik 1933: 30) and "quiescent" (Gillion 1971:131) but he did not get heavily involved and restricted himself to non-political topics. In June, in Poona, he spoke against Home Rule agitation which would embarrass the British Government while it was engaged in "a life and death struggle" during the war in Europe, but he added that once the war was over he was quite prepared to start any movement he thought necessary to secure the people's rights to Home Rule. (Yajnik 1933: 30)

By December 1916, however, when the Congress session was held in Lucknow, it may be that Gandhi was forced to recognise that the Home Rule movement had captured "a rising tide of political awakening" and that whatever his personal opinions about launching agitation, he now had to make up his mind on whether to move into the political arena or not. Indulal Yajnik comments:

"I believe that he rightly read the signs of the times at the Lucknow session and it was practically about this time that he decided to lead the political tide that was then rising in the country in his own characteristic manner." (Yajnik 1933: 17-18)

At a meeting in rural Gujarat at Godhra in February 1917 – held to commemorate the second anniversary of Gokhale's death – Gandhi spoke of "a tide of great political enthusiasm now running all over the country, nearly as big and wide as the Ganges in flood", which was "running to waste for want of people's control".

He also proposed at a second meeting a resolution which was adopted, that the Government be given a specific time limit to end the indentured labour system – by May 31 , 1917. Under this system, Indian labourers were induced to go to South Africa and other British colonies to work virtually as slaves. It was a particular cause of Gandhi's to have the system abolished for he had seen its results in South Africa. Gandhi explained his resolution in these terms:

"If Government does not take necessary measures within the appointed time, you must be prepared to suffer, to go to prison or even to die in order to redress the grievous wrong."

Other bodies under Gandhi's influence adopted similar resolutions. In April, the Government announced that it had stopped the shipping of indentured labour to South Africa – and Gandhi was seen to have won his first victory in India. (Yajnik 1933: 18-19; Tendulkar 1951: 198-199)

In April 1917, Gandhi became involved in Champaran, nearly a thousand miles away from Ahmedabad. When his successful defiance of the order externing him from the district won him praise all over India, the repercussions back in Gujarat were immediate. Gandhi was invited to accept the Presidency of the Gujarat Sabha in June 1917, which he did. (Watson 1969: 72) Having delayed accepting leadership for two years, he was now in a position to impose his own authority and programme on the organisation.

His first action as President of the Sabha was to arrange a huge petition addressed to the Secretary of State for India in London, Edwin Montagu. The petition voiced support for the scheme of constitutional reform jointly agreed by the Indian National Congress and the Muslim League at their annual sessions at Lucknow. Signatures were collected all over rural Gujarat. (Yajnik 1933: 30) It has been suggested that, like Tilak with his Indian Home Rule League in Maharashtra, one of Gandhi's motives was to counter the successes Annie Besant's League was having in Gujarat. (Hardiman 1977: 57) At the time, Gandhi is said not to have been much impressed with the Congress-League Scheme itself, but he favoured the petition because "this seemed a splendid opportunity to reach out into the villages and give the educated a chance to come into contact with the illiterate." (Brown 1972: 92-93) Over a million signatures are reported to have been collected, including some thousand from the Kheda district, where he was shortly to become involved in a local struggle against land taxes. (Kaushik 1964: 31; Hardiman 1975: 108)

Dissatisfaction with Besant's Home Rule League

In June 1917, Annie Besant was served with a Government order restricting her to the area of Madras in the south where she lived. The All-India Home Rule League got a tremendous boost and new branches were opened in many parts of India, especially Gujarat. (Brown 1972: 92; Owen 1968: 176) Gandhi was again approached to lead the Home Rule League in Bombay Presidency, but declined. However, he did offer advice to the militant young Home Rulers, which impressed them. In Madras, the police had forcibly removed Home Rule flags from some houses. Besant was proposing to take legal action against the police.

Gandhi thought the proposal ridiculous:

> "The matter could be settled in an incredibly simple manner. All you have to do is to make thousands of small Home Rule Flags and hoist them in thousands of houses in Madras. Surely Government will not send its police officers to remove all these flags, and thus you will win a decided moral victory against the Government".

The Bombay "youngsters" also asked him what should be done about the restriction order itself. Gandhi apparently drew up a pledge offering satyagraha, which he said was to be "signed solemnly and sincerely by all those who were really determined to take direct action in the matter". If a sufficient number of signatures could be collected, he proposed that the satyagrahis should march the 1,000 miles from Bombay to Madras and there offer civil disobedience under Besant's leadership. Over 1,000 signatures were collected, but Besant rejected the proposal. (Yajnik 1933: 25-27) She was by this time worried about the dangers of civil disobedience and as a result quickly lost the support of many of her followers. Yajnik says that at this time he and other Home Rulers "were trying to make our own synthesis between the political demand of Mrs Besant and the political method which was so dear to the heart of Mr Gandhi". (Yajnik 1933: 27)

Gandhi, however, wanted the Home Rulers to adopt his "political demand" too. In November 1917, he was invited to preside over two important conferences held in Gujarat, the second Gujarat Educational Conference at Broach and the first Gujarat Political Conference at Godhra. Both Conferences were conducted in Gujarati at Gandhi's insistence, to enable the non-English educated to participate. At the Broach conference, Gandhi piloted through a programme dealing with mass education, women's education and the adoption of the vernacular. At the Godhra political conference, attended by over 9,000 people, a detailed programme to deal with local political, economic and social grievances was agreed. But the customary loyalty resolution to the King was not put to the gathering. Gandhi took the view that "their loyalty could be presumed, until they declared as rebels". (Hardiman 1975: 117)

At the Godhra conference, too, Gandhi was able to announce to the public session that he had received that day a "communication" from the Government indicating that a particular local grievance, the Viramgam customs cordon, would be ended. Viramgam is a small town about 40 miles from Ahmedabad where railway passengers were subject to the humiliation of a customs search. In 1915 Gandhi had threatened to lead civil disobedience on the matter and had been in correspondence with the Bombay Governor and the Viceroy. (Tendulkar 1951: 159-160) The subjects committee for the Godhra conference had already agreed to put before the full session a resolution demanding the removal of the cordon. Gandhi had informed the Government that he would be forced "to 'begin public agitation on the subject at this political conference if he did not receive a satisfactory reply by then." When the Bombay government responded by removing the cordon, Yajnik comments that, in the eyes of the young Home Rulers, Gandhi had now won three victories against the Government: over indentured labour, the indigo workers in Champaran, and now Viramgam. (Yajnik 1933: 27-29; Gandhi, R 2007: 180)

After these two conferences, Yajnik asserts that Gandhi had "succeeded in placing himself at the head of the forces of political discontent in our province". (Yajnik 1933: 30) Gandhi himself in a letter to a friend in South Africa a few months later said that his activities In Gujarat were "multifarious" and consisted "in carrying out the programme set out in the Godhra and Broach addresses" - that is, the presidential speeches he had made at these sessions. (Desai 1968: 33) At the Broach and Godhra conferences Gandhi had made contact with a woman who scoured rural Gujarat and neighbouring Baroda for him till she discovered some disused spinning wheels. These he then used as a basis for his experiments with spinning at the ashram. (Tendulkar 1951: 174-175)

Gujarat at the end of 1917 was proving to be the base for his activities Gandhi had been seeking. Over the three years he had discovered a number of co-workers who were now ready to follow his direction in their political and social work, to experiment in their own lives with satyagraha.

CASE STUDY 2: KHEDA
CASE STUDY 3: AHMEDABAD

An Overview

It was directly as a result of the Godhra conference that Gandhi became involved in his first peasant agitation in Gujarat, the Kheda satyagraha in 1918. Peasant agriculturalists and local political leaders who had attended the conference contacted Gandhi about their problems with the land revenue tax charged on their crops by the Bombay government. Efforts to raise these grievances through Indian representatives of the Bombay Provincial Assembly had achieved nothing. Gandhi began his investigation in rural Kheda in his capacity as president of the Gujarat Sabha, and members of the Sabha worked alongside supporters of the Home Rule League who were already involved, though in practice these memberships overlapped. (Yajnik 1933: 35-36; Hardiman 1977: 57; Gandhi 1968: 75-76; Brown 1972: 94-95)[9]

At the same time, Gandhi also became involved in a second satyagraha, again through the Gujarat Sabha. The Sabha had been recruiting mill-owners in the city of Ahmedabad to its membership during 1917. Early in 1918, Gandhi was invited by representatives of the mill owners and millworkers to arbitrate in a dispute about the wage rates for weavers in the city's factories. When the arbitration broke down, Gandhi felt himself obliged to act on behalf of the workers. (Brown 1972: 113, 115-116)

In most accounts, the Kheda (or Kaira) satyagraha is discussed separately from the Ahmedabad satyagraha. This can be misleading, however, because the two struggles, both personally directed by Gandhi, went on simultaneously. It is also helpful to an understanding of how he organised these campaigns to compare his methods in each directly.

---

9. Brown tends to favour police reports, which accused Gandhi of acting as an "outside" agitator in Kheda, rather than responding to a local grievance. Hardiman (1967: 47) has, however, criticised her account in general and demonstrated the genuine nature of peasant unrest.

To discuss the circumstances of the rural struggle, which began first and continued longer, the Kheda District of Gujarat is often referred to by its anglicised name, Kaira. Only thirty miles south-east of Ahmedabad, Kheda, with a population of 700,000 had been by Indian standards a prosperous agricultural district. Peasant farmers, the *Patidars*, had acquired land-ownership rights under the British in the 19th Century and had experienced a "golden-age" - until a disastrous drought at the turn of the century had brought on famine, the death of cattle, consequent loss of soil fertility due to lack of manure, a lowering of the water table, and other calamities. Many of the peasants had been unable to recover from this disaster because of the high land revenue charges imposed by the Raj. Beside the Patidars, the other main caste group in Kheda consisted of landless labourers, the *Baraiyas*, many employed on Patidar holdings. In 1917, severe flooding during the monsoon had damaged the crops, and the Patidar farmers – who also suffered severely from an outbreak of plague which hit Ahmedabad – were agitating for remission of revenue. (Hardiman 1977: 47-59)

Ahmedabad was the scene of Gandhi's labour satyagraha. The second city in the Bombay Presidency after Bombay city itself, Ahmedabad in 1918 had a population of nearly 300,000. Based on the cotton industry, the city experienced a boom during the war years as supplies of imported cloth dried up and India became dependant on home-produced cotton goods. Several mill owners became millionaires and wages increased too – putting further pressure incidentally on the Patidar farmers in nearby Kheda who had to increase wages for their labourers. Late in 1917, plague broke out in Ahmedabad causing the booming cotton mills to pay a special "plague" bonus to their workers to encourage them to stay in the city. This increased their wages by up to 75%, which helped the workers to meet the increase in prices brought on by wartime shortages. But early in 1919 demand for cloth dropped at the same time as the plague epidemic eased. The employers then withdrew the "plague" bonus leaving the workers to cope as best they could with continuing shortages of consumer products and price inflation. As a result, 10,000 weavers out of the 70,000 workers employed in the mills in Ahmedabad went on strike. (Brown 1972: 114-116; Gillion 1971: 129-132). Quite apart from the particular grievance that led to this strike, the millworkers in

Ahmedabad suffered from appalling poverty. A Government report on housing conditions in India (published more than ten years later) spoke of the "terrible squalor" in the areas occupied by the working classes in Ahmedabad. (Brailsford 1931: 59-60; Yajnik 1933: 30)

In taking up satyagraha in India, Gandhi was faced with two particular difficulties. First, as we have seen, there was the need to train a band of reliable lieutenants who would organise actively on his behalf. Second, there was the problem of securing mass support for nonviolent action according to his theories, support strong enough to sustain nonviolent discipline through fierce struggle and in circumstances of great sacrifice. Gandhi's conception in both struggles, Kheda and Ahmedabad, was not simply pragmatic, to win the victory; he also wanted the struggle to be exemplary in the sense (1) that it demonstrated the effectiveness of his method and (2) that the participants were strengthened in their self-image as people who would stand up for their rights and their dignity, whatever the cost to themselves.

The Team of Helpers

In Gujarat, Gandhi had acquired the team of helpers which he needed, but having been blooded in the Home Rule agitations, which were not controlled by Gandhi, several of them were more independently-minded than the recruits he had made in Bihar. Gandhi was less satisfied with them. (Desai 1968: 52, 72) Mahadev Desai, who had been recruited by Gandhi in 1917 to act as his secretary, reports in his diary on a revealing conversation at the time. He was talking with one of Gandhi's chief co-workers about their leader's method of attracting new followers:

> "In loving admiration for Bapuji (an affectionate name for Gandhi), I gave him the epithet 'The Slave Hunter' in my talks with Pandyaji. He (Gandhi) goes on, I explained, catching some one or other, and yokes him to the national work, a passion of his life, which he pursues day and night." (Desai 1968: 34)

Initially, in Ahmedabad, a team of volunteers carried out the organising work among the 10,000 striking mill-hands. As the struggle moved quickly to confrontation when the employers began a lockout, Gandhi himself assumed direct command of the strikers and, with the help of his most trusted associates, like Shankerlal Banker and Anasuya Sarabhai, addressed nightly meetings of the mill-hands.

Gandhi decided that their advice to the strikers would be superficial and would fail "without intimate knowledge of the outer and inner life of the workers". They therefore paid daily visits to the workers in their homes, gathering information about their conditions – discussing the strike with them, finding temporary work for those who wanted it, dealing with health problems, and so on. Mahadev Desai, in his pamphlet on the Ahmedabad struggle, emphasises that, as a result, the advisers could "feel the pulse" of the entire labour community, and Gandhi "knew exactly what steps to take at the critical moments in the struggle".

In addition to the nightly meetings with the strikers, which were switched to the mornings when the employers ended their lockout, Gandhi and his advisers prepared daily leaflets for distribution among them, discussing the conduct of the workers during the strike, the behaviour of the employers, and so on. Mahadev Desai stresses the results that these speeches and leaflets had on "the inner life of the people" – and notes that, as in Champaran, to avoid polarisation, these speeches were deliberately not supplied to the press. (Desai 1951: 4-10; Desai 1968: 48)

In rural Kheda, thirty miles from Ahmedabad, a first group of workers associated with the Gujarat Sabha carried out an assessment of the value of the crops in a few villages, led by two representatives on the Bombay Legislative Council who were also Ahmedabad lawyers. When the government questioned their findings, Gandhi himself led a much fuller investigation "with the assistance of over 20 capable, experienced and impartial men of influence and status". Gandhi personally visited over 30 villages, engaging in "a searching cross-examination of the villagers". By these methods, 400 villages out of the 600 in the district were investigated. Indulal Yajnik, who was one of Gandhi's volunteers in Kheda, describes what happened:

> "Some of us had already gone round a few villages in the course of the Home Rule agitation. But Mr Gandhi for the first time put us to the test of covering every one of the 600 big and small

villages of the district - some having a population of nearly 10,000 and others consisting only of a few homesteads. He ruled us with the iron rod of discipline. The inquiry had to be finished within ten days. The workers therefore were divided into ten or twelve groups, and each group had to cover four or five villages a day. And yet we were all forbidden the use of carts or any other vehicles…" (Yajnik 1933: 36)

Gandhi also suggested that one particular village be assessed as a test case by the responsible local official, with himself present. But this suggestion was rejected by the government, as was Gandhi's report of his team's investigation and his proposal for an independent committee of inquiry. (Desai 1968: 326-328) The Gujarat Sabha then decided on satyagraha, in this case, civil disobedience, which was commenced on March 22, 1918, with the taking of an oath by villagers refusing to pay the revenue. By the end of April over 2,000 villagers had taken the pledge not to pay. Organisation of the struggle was conducted through regular public meetings, Gandhi himself engaging in several speaking tours through the area and, after initial reluctance to publicise the dispute, by statements in the press. (Desai 1968: 63; Brown 1972: 101) Volunteers went on foot through the villages eating only simple foods. Gandhi himself commented later:

"It was the Kheda campaign that compelled the public workers to establish contact with the actual life of the peasants. They learnt to identify themselves with the latter. They found their proper sphere of work, their capacity for sacrifice increased." (Gandhi M.K. 1982: 396)

To give a brief timetable of the two satyagraha struggles: Gandhi first became involved in arbitration between mill owners and workers in Ahmedabad in February 1918, two months after the Kheda agitation had started. Events moved to a head much more quickly in Ahmedabad, though. The mill-hands' strike began on February 22 and lasted 25 days until March 18. Only four days after the Ahmedabad satyagraha was over, Gandhi launched civil disobedience in Kheda, which continued there for nearly three months.

The Satyagraha Pledges

At the beginning of the Ahmedabad strike, which went on significantly longer than Gandhi's side had expected, the workers were invited to take a pledge, which they apparently did unanimously. This pledge was repeated at the nightly meetings. It committed the workers, first, to remain on strike until their demand, which was a moderate one, had been met and, second, to conduct themselves with dignity and restraint throughout the dispute. This oath took the form of a religious vow and Gandhi consistently stressed its seriousness. On the fifth day he discussed in his speech people's hopes that the strike would soon be over:

> "I repeat that even though we may hope that our struggle will soon end early, we must remain firm if that hope is not realised, and not resume work even if we have to die." (Desai 1951: 10-13)

Later, when after three weeks the strike began to weaken, Gandhi realised that their commitment to maintain the vow had tested the workers beyond their capacity. He then took his decision to fast:

> "I cannot tolerate for a minute that you break your pledge. I shall not take any food nor use a car till you get 35 per cent increase or all of you die in the fight for it."

In his eyes, the effect on the millworkers was "electric". Gandhi claimed that the workers experienced a moment of sublime religious awareness as he announced his decision and they regained the confidence that they could keep their vow. (Desai 1951: 24-29; Desai 1968: 67-68)[10]

---

10. See Gandhi's prayer speech in the ashram, March 17 1918 (Desai, *Day-to-Day with Gandhi*, pp 67-68):

"For the last twenty days. I have been moving among ten thousand millworkers. In my presence they took a solemn oath with Ishwara or Khuda [both names for God]... as their witness. And they took it with great fervour... [T]hese labourers are believers in their God.

"They had supposed that God was sure to rush to their rescue as they had strictly kept the vow for full 20 days, but when God did not help them even then, and chose to put them to a severer test, their faith in him weakened.

Gandhi's action, though spontaneous, was the product of a highly self-conscious project he had set himself. As he told the mill-hands later that day:

"I was not unmindful of what I had realised during my widespread travels in India that hundreds of persons take an oath and break it at the very next moment. I also knew that the best among us have just a feeble and irresolute faith in God. I felt that it was a golden opportunity for me, that my faith was being tested." (Desai 1951: 25)

Two days later at a prayer meeting at his ashram, Gandhi was even more explicit:

"... I saw in the fast a good opportunity to give out to the world one sublime principle of action ... From the mine of our ancient culture and civilisation, a gem has come into my possession, i.e. I have learnt a principle of life which, if thoroughly assimilated, can enable even the very few of us who are here to rule the world..."

Gandhi then went on to compare the "gem" he had to offer India with

---

They felt: 'Trusting the word of this one man, we suffered so long and gained nothing. Instead of listening to his advice to remain peaceful, had we indulged in violence we would have got within quite a few days, not merely the 35% increment we demanded but even more.' That was their changed outlook after 20 days.

"It was impossible for me to put up with this mentality. It appeared to me as the victory of Satan, if a vow, taken in my presence, could be so easily broken and if the people's faith in God faded away, life would become intolerable to me if I remained a passive witness ... I realised I must make the millworkers understand the seriousness of a vow and show them how far I would go to honour it... I had to save those ten thousand persons from a moral fall and I took the only possible step for it."

"My fast had an electric effect... Thousands of men were present there and streams of tears flowed through their eyes. A wave of conversion - an awareness of the Soul - swept them... Their spirits rose high and they regained the confidence that they could keep the vow. The sight convinced me... that Indians are still their true selves, capable of realising the Self within and knowing its power."

the contributions being made by Tilak, the leading nationalist figure of the time, and by Madan Mohan Malaviya, the most prominent orthodox Hindu in politics. He continued

"... deep down in me, the feeling persists that (Tilak) has not imbibed the true spirit of Mother India, viz. her age-old pursuit after soul force. And that is why the country still welters in its present plight... Were Tilak's object in his sufferings spiritual and not political, our condition today would have been far better, because astounding benefits might have come out from them. It is this central point - the spiritual background behind my suffering through the fast - that I want him to understand...."

Gandhi then claimed that Malaviya too...

"... does not quite understand, I am sorry to say, what India really stands for... To both these great men I must show the true spirit that has been animating India since ages past... It appeared to me as the victory of Satan, if a vow, taken in my presence, could be broken so easily and if the people's faith in God faded away... My fast had an electric effect, beyond my wildest hope ... a wave of conversion - an awareness of the Soul - swept them... The sight convinced me beyond doubt that the light of dharma in India is not yet extinct, that Indians are still their true selves, capable of realising the Self within and knowing this power. If Tilak Maharaj and Malaviyaji open themselves to this, the true spirit of India, we can achieve miracles."

He concluded:

"And if ten thousand labourers went back upon their solemn resolve, the country would head straight for disaster. It would become impossible to raise again the question of the amelioration of labour conditions. Everywhere the disgraceful precedent of Ahmedabad would be cited and they would say, 'Ten thousand labourers suffered for 20 long days - and with such a leader as Gandhi - and yet they failed' ..."

Thus Gandhi quite self-consciously presented himself at Ahmedabad as giving a lead to the Indian nation and a lesson to its senior nationalist leaders. (Desai 1968: 64-68; Tidrick 2013: 122-125) At the time, he was 48, and only three years back in India. Malaviya was 57; Tilak, 62. Annie Besant was 71.

Gandhi entered the Kheda Satyagraha with the same conception and the same suggested means of binding the Kheda peasants together, a religious vow not to pay their revenue unless certain conditions were met. (Desai 1968: 345)[11] By April 21, 2,337 signatures to the pledge had been gathered. Gandhi was again thoroughly aware of the national implications of this action. He wrote to an acquaintance in April 1918:

> "You have only to come and see with what perfect good humour the fight is being carried on, how the people are steeling their hearts for any kind of loss, and how elderly men and women too are taking part in the demonstration. You, at least, ought to see that this self-inflicted suffering must exalt "the nation", whereas the same suffering unwillingly undergone hitherto has only degraded the nation." (Desai 1968: 76)[12]

___

11. This reference contains the full text of the March 22 pledge.

12. In her useful and original case study of the Vykom temple roads satyagraha – which took place 7 years later in 1924 (and 900 miles away from Gujarat in the south of India) – Mary King is extremely critical of Gandhi's advocacy of "self-suffering". She presents it as a method of converting the opponent, which she says rarely succeeds. She argues that "conversion" as a mechanism of nonviolent action has been over-emphasised in the literature. (King 2014: 266-270)
To my mind, the acceptance and advocacy of "self-suffering" should rightly be questioned. But King (with her focus on conversion of the opponent within a limited time period) does not address two other aspects: those who undergo it have taken a strong stand on a matter of principle from which they will not be budged. And it takes courage, determination and self-discipline to sustain it. Gandhi recognised that soldiers under orders are prepared to show immense courage and endure terrible suffering. He wanted his nonviolent troops to be just as brave. To me, it is important not to exclude these two priorities from presentation of his nonviolent method: (1) sticking to a principle even at cost to one's self and (2) disciplining oneself to endure possibly severe mental stress and physical hurt.
Also, while the self-suffering may not directly persuade the opponent, it can have

As he wrote to the Kheda satyagrahis two weeks later:

> "Lest we weaken in our resolve, we have bound ourselves down with a solemn vow. No nation ever rises without taking resolves and a vow is nothing more than an inflexible resolve. The man who cannot be resolute is like a rudderless boat tossed hither and thither in an ocean till it meets its doom". (Desai 1968: 336)

When, however, despite all Gandhi's exhortations and those of his co-workers, the resolve of the Kheda satyagrahis did weaken, he adopted a quite different method of restoring their determination than he had taken in Ahmedabad. This time he escalated the struggle from non-cooperation to nonviolent intervention. Five volunteers went out to reclaim a crop of onions confiscated by the government in lieu of revenue payment. These civil disobedients when arrested and jailed became local heroes, and peasant morale was boosted. (Brown 1972: 101)

Refusal of Outside Support

In both places Gandhi also adopted a novel, many would say perverse, method of sustaining the morale of the strikers, and of demonstrating their integrity and determination to their opponents and to the country at large. In Ahmedabad, he refused to allow a strike fund to be started for the workers. At their daily meetings he told the striking workers that it was beneath them to ask for financial aid – "the world will ridicule you by saying that you fought on the strength of others' money." (Desai 1968: 20) Gandhi tried to stiffen the workers' resolve in this regard by finding alternative employment for them, including hand spinning among the women. (Desai 1968: 162) In an exultant letter to a Bombay businessman, he commented:

> "That 10,000 workmen are observing a strike quite peacefully without a rupee being spent after them, is by no means a small achievement and yet it is a fact. People have realised the truth of the principle 'Self-help is the best help'. The strikers have been

---

a large impact on third parties and public opinion generally and lead ultimately to a positive resolution, as it did with the Vykom satyagraha.

given these two keynotes for success: 'On you, not on others, depends your success' and 'No victory without voluntary self-suffering'." (Desai 1968: 59)

In Kheda he took exactly the same attitude. He thought that collecting thousands of rupees to pay the peasants' assessment could easily be done and might make an effective agitation, but it would make no impression on the Government; whereas, "it will be a serious headache for the Government to impound and sell the peasants' cattle. The object behind the idea of offering satyagraha is to make the people fearless and free, and not to maintain our own reputation anyhow." (Desai 1968: 18) Gandhi claimed later that he had accepted only two or three thousand rupees as travelling expenses for his workers in Kheda, but had returned 25,000 rupees to their donors and declined many other offers.

> "If I accepted contributions, the spirit of the fight would be vitiated, immorality would creep in, and the people instead of rising higher would sink lower. Refusal to take any amount from outside has saved me from all those dire consequences and enabled me to keep the battle on a high moral plain. The whole of India understands and backs the struggle..." (Desai 1968: 127)

It was in this way that Gandhi advanced his principle of self-suffering, a method designed simultaneously to ennoble the sufferer and convert the opponent (but see footnote 12 above). He also developed his principle that Indians to be free must not be afraid to rely on their own efforts and not look for support from outside. Mahadev Desai notes Gandhi's pleasure after one public meeting in April with the English Commissioner in Kheda, Mr Pratt. Pratt tried to make the peasants back down but failed to over-awe them. (Desai 1968: 93)

Pitching the Demands Low

Yet the sacrifices demanded of the mill hands and peasants were very great. Here were unsophisticated people being directed by a man many of them viewed as a saint – and so they could not easily speak out against him – to risk starvation and death or the loss of property and their rights of ownership to hereditary farms. Gandhi has frequently been criticised because the extreme methods he advocated produced so little by way of direct result. (Yajnik 1933: 22-24, 31, 33-34, 37, 39)

In Ahmedabad, for example, the mill-hands, as we noted, had suffered a cut in wages at a time when prices were rising rapidly. Higher wages had been paid to those who were prepared to carry on working during a period of plague in the city. When this epidemic ended, the management withdrew the "plague bonus". The workers demanded a 50% increase in their basic wage to meet the higher cost of living; the employers offered 20% and Gandhi was called in as an arbitrator. When arbitration broke down, the employers staged a lock-out and Gandhi felt obliged to side with the workers. He then recommended the workers to concentrate on the demands of the weaving section, and waive the question of the spinning workers for the time being (Desai 1968: 48); advised them to reduce their demand to a minimum increase of 35% and also to maintain the demand for arbitration. Thus when, after Gandhi's fast was begun, a settlement was quickly reached, the major direct result was the appointment of a new arbitrator. This decision the workers agreed to accept even if the award was less than 35%. In the event, the arbitrator found that several companies were already paying 35% and 50% increases – there was a breakdown in employer solidarity – and his verdict went in favour of the strikers. (Desai 1951: 48) But even after their victory in the strike, the workers were still receiving less in wages than they had been during the plague bonus period.

In Kheda, Gandhi's demands were equally moderate. Many of those calling for relief in the district were reasonably prosperous. Their contention, as drafted by Gandhi, was that even though they might be able to afford to pay the revenue assessed on their crops, the assessment itself had been calculated unfairly and should be re-examined by an independent inquiry. If, on this re-examination, the crops were found to have been valued too highly, the richer peasants would still be willing to pay their full assessment, on condition that the obligations of the poorer peasants were cancelled. Gandhi was quite explicit that the reason why those able to pay were withholding payment was to protect those unable to afford the revenue from being isolated and forced into panic selling, or into debt.

After nearly three months of tax refusal and six months agitation in all, the government had granted no independent inquiry; but Gandhi advised most of the satyagrahis to pay the assessment when eventually it became clear that the government would not proceed against those unable to pay. He himself called this an unsatisfactory solution because the government showed no conciliatory spirit whatsoever and the satyagrahis were left without a clear-cut sense of victory. (Desai 1968: 345-348)

Gandhi's Aims and What was Achieved

Thus what Gandhi aimed for in both these desperately fierce struggles, as in Champaran, was simply arbitration or an independent inquiry. In the nine "Steps in a Satyagraha Campaign" that are listed by Joan Bondurant in her analysis of Gandhian satyagraha, negotiation and arbitration are itemised as the first stage in an escalating series of actions leading up to "usurping the functions of government" or "parallel government" (Bondurant 1969: 40-41).[13] But as Bondurant herself makes clear in her discussion of the Ahmedabad satyagraha, arbitration was generally not only the first step, but also the last, in these Gandhian satyagrahas. (Bondurant 1969: 72-73: Yajnik 1933: 46)[14] In fact, Gandhi stated on several occasions that he was fighting the Ahmedabad satyagraha for the principle of arbitration between management and labour (Desai 1968: 47; Desai 1951: 34, 67, 68); and the Kheda satyagraha for the principle that the government should call an independent inquiry in those cases where its decisions were frankly and sincerely called into question by the citizens most affected. (Desai 1968: 328, 331-333, 343; Brown 1972: 97-98)

---

13. Bondurant's scheme is adapted from Shridharani 1962 (first edition 1939): 15-57.

14. Yajnik's observation was: "And even when he could not secure immediate redress from the authorities, and was compelled to resort to direct action, he as invariably hoped and anxiously waited for the resumption of negotiations with the Government, negotiations which would eventually lead to a truce or a settlement."

While neither of these would seem on the face of it to be radical demands they were extremely important in the Indian context at the time. By insisting on the principle of arbitration in the Ahmedabad dispute, Gandhi was able to construct the basis of peaceful industrial relations in that city which were maintained for several decades; moreover, both mill-owners and mill-hands were drawn into support for Gandhi's later campaigns, the links between the Bombay Presidency factory owners and the peasantry being a significant factor in Gandhi's later achievements. (Brown 1972: 119-121; Bondurant 1969: 70-71, 73; Gillion 1971: 143-144) In Kheda, what Gandhi had orchestrated was a major challenge to the presumption of the Raj that it could undertake the assessment and collection of revenue from the peasantry without being subject to democratic control. No tax campaigns, as they were called, continued in this part of Gujarat for almost the next twenty years, until finally in the 1935 government reforms, Indians were granted some political control over the gathering of revenue. (Hardiman 1977: 58-59; 70-72)

Nevertheless, as Bondurant points out, making a principle out of arbitration – that is, the sound judgment and good faith of an independent third party – was a risky business. (Bondurant 1969: 73) And the powerful long-term forces which these struggles set in motion could not have been predicted – though Gandhi might have argued that an alliance between workers and employers in Ahmedabad and sustained militancy in rural Gujarat were implicit ends to be gained from the means he adopted in these struggles. What Gandhi was doing by pitching his demands so low was seeking to establish an unassailable case, so that in the event of arbitration or an independent inquiry the findings could not but be in favour of his side. Thus the extreme test to which the satyagrahis were put in Ahmedabad and Kheda was likely to end in victory and without them having to pay the ultimate penalty. Moreover, his opponents, the mill-owners and the revenue officials of Bombay Presidency, because of the basic unreasonableness of their position and the obvious reasonableness of the satyagrahis they were fighting, would find it relatively easy to reach a conciliatory position.

Gandhi, in a sense, was trying to eat his cake and have it. He wanted the mill-hands and the peasants to be immeasurably strengthened by staking their lives, their property, their honour and their religious conviction on a fierce struggle against entrenched power, which they would win. And, on the other hand, he wanted relations between the competing parties at the end of the struggle to be immeasurably improved. In Gandhi's conception, however, there was no contradiction. By setting his demands so low, he ensured that there was no "victory" in the conventional sense for his side or the other. By insisting that the mill-owners and the revenue officials of the Raj learn to respect the Ahmedabad workers and the Kheda peasants he was, in his own eyes, establishing the only true basis for partnership between capital and labour in industry and the British Raj and the Indian people in public affairs. (Desai 1931: 14-16, 44-50; Desai 1968: 331-338) This was the "victory" Gandhi wanted. In Ahmedabad, he was in many ways successful; in Kheda, he discovered just how intransigent the British Raj was to be, but the Kheda peasants played the part that he wanted.

Kheda and Ahmedabad: A Comparison

How Gandhi Organised Support for his Activities

If we examine these two satyagraha struggles by the same criteria which we used in analysing the Champaran satyagraha, we can see Gandhi organising in the following way.

First, he brought his team of workers together and gave them instructions – in both instances setting them tests which would be educational for them and would demonstrate their sincerity to the labourers and the peasants with whom they were working. In Ahmedabad they were to go daily into the workers' homes and render them services much as a social worker would do. When Gandhi himself came under criticism from workers who were starving for continuing to eat and to ride in one of the mill-owners' cars while they suffered, he then took his vow that he would share their conditions until the dispute was ended and began his fast. In Kheda, Gandhi had his volunteers walking as much as 20 miles a day in the scorching sun, eating only peasant food. (Yajnik 1933: 36) Later some of them repossessed a confiscated field of onions on behalf of the peasants. What Gandhi was doing, of course, was training workers who would identify with the common people and he was trying to make that identification as deep and as practical as possible; a psychological experience for the volunteer and a visible or symbolic action to those observing the volunteer. (Rothermund 1963: 17-36)

Second, in Ahmedabad, he organised the mill-hands by calling regular meetings and processions through the town. Leaflets were circulated daily discussing the progress of the struggle. It has been suggested that the men's foremen constituted an intermediate leadership, who looked directly to Anasuya Sarabhai, Shankerlal Banker and Gandhi himself as their figureheads. Gandhi was clearly worried from the start about the mill-hands' likely behaviour during the strike. He tried to maintain discipline by getting the workers to take a vow, which was repeated daily at the meetings; "Keep the Pledge" was a slogan chanted on the processions. A large proportion of the vow was concerned with the strikers' conduct during the struggle.

The morale of the strikers began to suffer when Gandhi strongly criticised some of the leading activists who were intimidating fellow-strikers who wanted to return to work. In order to restore morale, Gandhi then announced his fast. He also organised the payment of work-parties, drawn from the strikers, to help in the construction of his ashram, which was then being moved from one part of Ahmedabad at Kochrab to the riverbank at Sabarmati.

A year later, in 1919, Gandhi was invited to lead Bombay millworkers in a major strike. He seriously considered getting involved, but eventually withdrew on the grounds that the majority of the Bombay millworkers were from Maharashtra and he thought that, as a Gujarati leader, he would have great difficulty in controlling them. (Gillion 1971: 133)

In Kheda, the peasant farmers were also disciplined by a vow. Meetings were held throughout the district. At first, the police were distraining only "movable" property from the farmers who refused to pay their revenue. A system was devised where the local volunteers would warn a village by runners when the officials were coming. They would then lock their houses so the officials couldn't get in and allow their cattle to wander off their property so they couldn't be identified. (Masselos 1971:

171-172) Later, as the struggle intensified, police were given warrants to break into the houses, to remove standing crops and to forfeit land from those refusing revenue and sell it at auction. Gandhi escalated the conflict in return by sending in the volunteers to remove the confiscated crop. They became heroes when they were jailed for a month. (Yajnik 1933: 38-39; Gandhi 1982: 394-395) Gandhi also made defiant speeches in which he denied absolutely that the Government would be bold enough to sell the farmers' hereditary lands. (Desai 1968: 338)

In both Ahmedabad and Kheda, Gandhi vastly increased the sacrificial element in the struggle by denying to the labourers and the farmers a strike fund. In Ahmedabad, to avoid polarisation, he kept the struggle out of the press, but once he announced his fast, telegrams poured in from all over India pressing the mill-owners to settle. In Kheda, he restricted publicity prior to the declaration of "satyagraha", but once the revenue refusal was launched, he invited the support of public opinion across India while still refusing donations.

How Gandhi Approached his Opponents

Gandhi's leadership of satyagraha in Ahmedabad was complicated by the fact that his opponents, the mill-owners, included as their principal representative a young man, Ambalal Sarabhai, who though only 25 was a personal friend and benefactor of the ashram. Throughout the strike they continued to meet socially and maintained cordial relations. Also, Gandhi's principal co-worker was Anasuya Sarabhai, Ambalal's 23-year old sister, and it was through his friendship with both that he first became involved in the dispute. When his arbitration broke down, Gandhi and Anasuya sided with the workers. Erik Erikson, in his book on the Ahmedabad strike suggests that this conflict with Ambalal Sarabhai set off an intense personal crisis in Gandhi resulting, six months later, in a severe illness which brought him close to death. (Erikson 1969)

As we have seen, Gandhi's objectives in Ahmedabad were pitched extremely low. His chief goal – as in all his struggles – was to develop the character of the mill-hands by helping them discover depths of courage and self-sacrifice of which they did not know themselves capable. If by

77

intense suffering they could win a victory, then their self-respect and the respect in which they were held by their employers would immeasurably improve. The Ahmedabad satyagraha was, in this regard, an exercise in industrial relations for Gandhi – not based on anti-employer polarisation and the build up of independent worker power to compel a settlement. If Gandhi had sought this he would have launched a strike fund so as to prolong the strike and compel the employers to submit.

Gandhi's concept – similar to his conception of caste in which, with specific strong reservations, he was a firm believer at this time – was of the mutual rights and obligations of employers and employees, both of which deserved recognition. He therefore favoured the principle of arbitration, rather than what we today know as "collective bargaining", as a way of balancing the scale. But he also believed that the workers were much weaker than the employers and deserved his support, not least because of the appalling conditions in which they were living.

Ambalal Sarabhai, the mill-owner, was like Gandhi a religious man and appears to have convinced Gandhi that he was sincere in his principal argument. (Gandhi 1982: 388-390) This was that the employers were unwilling to give way, not because the workers' claim was unjust, but because if they did power would swing to the workers, whose demands in future would become unreasonable. (Desai 1951: 14) To complicate matters, some of the employers, including Sarabhai, bound themselves by a religious vow not to pay more than a 20% increase. This, of course, was directly counter to the workers' vow not to accept less than 35%. When Gandhi undertook his fast in order to sustain the workers in their vow, the employers capitulated quickly, with some bitterness. Gandhi confessed to feeling guilty, partly because his fast had put undue pressure on them, but also because it was his act that had "won" the strike, rather than the sufferings of the workers.

Eventually, the fresh arbitrator appointed as a result of the settlement found in favour of the mill-hands. But the remarkable result was the development of a unique system of industrial relations in Ahmedabad.

Under the leadership of Anasuya Sarabhai and Shankerlal Banker, the Textile Labour Association of Ahmedabad was formed as a means of protecting and educating its members. By the 1930s, it was running 23 schools for 1,600 children; a hospital with 30 beds, and two dispensaries; restaurants; a grain shop; a savings bank; a credit union; a cinema; a library; choirs; and five gymnasiums. With over 50,000 members it exercised a strong influence at municipal elections and had imposed on the Town Council a relatively ambitious housing programme. In addition it had won for its officers the right of access to the mills to investigate complaints, and where disputes remained unresolved, Gandhi stepped in as mediator.

After 1923, there was no general stoppage of all the mills in the city. (Brailsford 1931: 86-90) By 1940, the Textile Labour Association had established as its goal co-ownership of the mills "on a footing of equality with the so-called owners". (Desai 1951: v-vi) Indulal Yajnik commented that "Mr Gandhi and his lieutenants have succeeded in turning Ahmedabad labour into their own special preserve." (Yajnik 1933: 34; Sarkar 1983:186)

In Kheda, Gandhi's principal opponents were officials of the British Raj, though he also encountered some opposition from local nationalist representatives at the Bombay provincial council who disapproved of civil disobedience. (Yajnik 1933: 35-36) The British commissioner for the Northern District, Mr Pratt, was the responsible official for both Ahmedabad and Kheda and he had gone on record in Ahmedabad, at the public celebrations to mark the end of the strike, in advising labourers to continue to follow Mr Gandhi. However, in Kheda, he was defending the British system of revenue collection and his attitude was quite different. Revenue assessment was frequently arbitrary and unfair, but the British could not afford to have the system undermined by agitation. As Hardiman says, "The British were always afraid that if they yielded an inch, peasants throughout India would refuse their revenue." (Hardiman 1977: 71) Democratic control of the revenue collection system by the Indian electorate was not secured until 1935.

In Kheda, Gandhi maintained regular contact with Mr Pratt. Again, his demands were pitched extremely low but, as with the Ahmedabad mill-owners, Pratt clearly felt he could not afford to concede. Gandhi used all his skills as an advocate to argue that the British must base their rule on consent rather than fear, but to no avail. Pratt had the support of both the Bombay Government and the Government of India in refusing to budge. (Brown 1977: 96-103) In the end, Gandhi discovered that the British were not exacting sanctions against those strikers least able to pay. He decided that this was a concession and that it met his original objectives as set out in the vow taken at the beginning of the struggle. The British, however, made no public statement of the concession and no negotiation had taken place. So Gandhi felt extremely disappointed with this "victory".

Nevertheless, refusal of revenue became a consistent tactic as a weapon against the Raj adopted by peasants in this part of Gujarat over the next 15 years up to 1934. They clearly saw it as an effective weapon. And Hardiman points out that while assessment was increased in many areas surrounding Kheda in subsequent years, in Kheda itself the rate remained the same until a new increase was made in 1924 and this contributed directly to the pivotal Bardoli revenue refusal in 1928. Kheda peasants remained strong supporters of the Gandhian campaigns subsequently, including especially the 1930-31 movement. (Hardiman 1977: 58-59, 70-72)

Interestingly, one of the Bombay councillors who spoke openly against Gandhi while the Kheda struggle was continuing, later wrote to him as follows:

"I must admit that I considerably under-rated the power of combination of the Khaira agriculturalists under the leadership of a gentleman of your high magnetic influence. The result valued in money may not be big, but to my knowledge there was hardly any district in which the icon of authority was venerated and respected as much as in Kaira (Kheda), and you have done the greater service to the country by smashing the icon within its own temple and exposing all its internal deformities. One can do nothing better than let the people perceive where is the real source of authority. I believe that the Government and the people will not easily forget the lessons you have taught." (Desai 1968: 229-230)

Also, in 1920, Gandhi received a letter from Mr Pratt, the British Commissioner, who had then returned on leave to England. Pratt admitted that "there have been hard thoughts and hard words against you which were not justified", and added that in future "I wish to grasp the hand of fellowship and cooperation". Pratt had been impressed by the pro-government stance Gandhi took at the 1918 Amritsar Congress. (Desai 1968: 54-55)

Indulal Yajnik, who parted company with Gandhi in 1920, reviewed the Ahmedabad and Kheda campaigns some years later, having been on the edge of the first and a participant in the second. By the time of writing he was a convert to Marxism and he concluded that in Ahmedabad, Gandhi had virtually starved the workers into submission to the employers, but that they were "so thoroughly hypnotised" by Gandhi's fast they thought they had won a "victory". (Yajnik 1933: 33) Also, in Kheda, the campaign "achieved practically nothing".

Yajnik adds a comment about Kheda which has remained a standard criticism of Gandhi's methods from many other political radicals: "The end of the struggle ... showed Mr Gandhi after leading a revolutionary struggle up to a certain stage could console himself and others with the achievement of success when none had really been obtained..." Yajnik found himself forced to admit, nonetheless, that the Kheda struggle "at least served to awaken a new spirit among the peasants, not only of the district and the Province, but of the whole of India". (Yajnik 1933: 39)

Even if he had achieved nothing for the peasants, at least Gandhi had awoken the peasantry across the whole of India – though this is an exaggeration. We see, though, how Gandhi's methods had more to do with changing consciousness than with winning specific material concessions from opponents. This made him vulnerable to criticisms from conventional political standpoints of left, centre and right, examining objectively what he had "won" for his side – in these and other struggles. It is a criticism which cannot be ignored and which may be decisive in the end. But Gandhi had other and larger objectives than the specific grievance at hand, as we have seen. In this respect his battles in Ahmedabad and Kheda had many of the results he wanted. Erik Erikson doubts at one point "whether this wily little man ever was drawn into a decision which he did not choose for long- (very long) range reasons". (Erikson 1969: 45)

SUMMARY

1. Gandhi kept aloof from the activities of the Home Rule Leagues and the Gujarat Sabha on his return from South Africa, but after his success in Champaran he felt able to accept an invitation to take charge of the Gujarat Sabha.

2. Immediately, he placed his stamp on the organisation by directing its members into political and social work projects among the peasantry.

3. Over three years, he had recruited a team of co-workers who worked under his direction during the refusal of land revenue by peasants in rural Kheda and a strike against reduction in their wages by mill-hands in Ahmedabad.

4. Features of both campaigns were:

- the taking of religious vows by peasants and workers to maintain their struggle until their minimum demands were met;

- the pitching of low demands so as not go beyond the strength of the satyagrahis;

- a demand for third-party arbitration or a public inquiry as a way of resolving the conflict;

- the refusal of outside support for the struggle as a demonstration of self-reliance;

- Gandhi's sense that the struggles must set an example in integrity and fortitude to the whole nation; and

- a weakening of morale which led Gandhi to improvise an escalation of the conflict (through the fast and through removal of the onion crop).

5. Gandhi's fast was designed to identify himself with the weakening mill-hands who were starving. It had an electrifying impact on all parties to the conflict and across India. The employers quickly capitulated and claimed that Gandhi had used unfair pressure.

6. The intransigence of the Raj in a struggle affecting its land revenue system prevented any public inquiry in Kheda – but Gandhi found that there had been a concession and it secured the position of the poorest peasants, so he called off the campaign.

CHAPTER 3

CHALLENGING THE RAJ

Gandhi's promotion of satyagraha in Ahmedabad and Kheda in 1918 transformed politics in Gujarat. "By mid-May", says Judith Brown, "when the Ahmedabad satyagraha drove home the implication of the Kaira campaign, Gandhi was the most powerful leader in the region's public life." (Brown 1972: 120-21) As a result he began to receive invitations from nationalist leaders prominent in other provinces and from the Government of India itself to play a part in some of the great decisions facing the nation at the end of the First World War.

From this point, Gandhi began to operate increasingly as an all-India political figure and his activities, even when confined to Gujarat, had direct implications and repercussions outside the province. The period between 1918 and 1920, during which Gandhi launched the Rowlatt Satyagraha as a first attempt to organise on a national scale, was a time when he began to rely on Gujarat as a base which would take up his activities while he mobilised new support for his efforts elsewhere. This is especially clear in the build-up to Noncooperation in 1920. After 1920, as a principal figure in the National Congress, Gandhi sought to become a politician whose programme and appeal touched all parts of the subcontinent. Nonetheless, he was always able to look to Gujarat for that exemplary first step, the leading role, which would encourage the rest of the nation.

Thus Gujarat first helped Gandhi to prominence and then remained loyal to him when he became a pre-eminent national figure. By focusing on his activities in Gujarat we can see the importance to him as a national leader of his regional base. We can also begin to explore the relationship between local and national action. On the one hand, there is a dynamic relationship illustrated here – Gandhi's activities in Gujarat propelling him to national prominence. On the other, there are strategic questions for the organiser – how to deal with the different demands imposed by a local campaign in a defined area as against those of a national campaign over a vast subcontinent.

Recruiting in Rural Gujarat for the Indian Army

Throughout the Champaran and Kheda struggles, Gandhi had been protesting his loyalty to the Raj, while simultaneously he organised civil disobedience against it. In the spring of 1918, only six months before the Armistice, the Secretary of State for India in London began to put pressure on the Viceroy in Delhi to raise more money and troops for the war. (Rumbold 1979: 28-30, 118-119) Gandhi was among a number of national leaders whom the Viceroy, Lord Chelmsford, invited to a war conference in Delhi in April 1918. (Brown 1972:145-148; Gandhi M.K. 1982: 399-405; Yajnik 1933: 51-56) Gandhi attended but only very reluctantly when he discovered that Tilak and other major nationalist figures had been excluded. He made it clear publicly that he opposed more funds being raised in India for the war ("India has already donated to the Imperial Exchequer beyond her capacity"). Nevertheless even more decisively he supported the British call for men throughout India to enlist. (Desai 1968: 112-116) He also created a mild sensation at the war conference by speaking only in Hindi.

Few Home Rulers actively supported recruiting for the Indian Army because they had no love for the British Raj – but they did not speak out openly against it for fear of charges of sedition. Their principal argument was that support by them as nationalist leaders for recruiting must be conditional on the British promising to bring forward major constitutional reforms towards Home Rule. Gandhi utterly rejected this argument, which he saw as immoral. Until the Indian nation was ready to throw off British rule in its entirety, which he did not think it was – and neither, he believed, did the Home Rulers – it should support Britain in its hour of danger unconditionally. If it did this wholeheartedly, he added, he believed the British would be much more willing to grant the

Indian nation Home Rule. (Desai 1968: 118-119; 128; 169; 185-186; 191-192)[15]

As a follow-up to the Delhi war conference, all provincial governors were asked to call regional war conferences. In Bombay in June, Tilak and the other nationalist leaders were invited along with Gandhi to the conference for the Bombay Presidency. When Tilak was stopped by the Governor of Bombay, Lord Willingdon, from presenting his argument – that nationalist India would be willing to cooperate in recruiting if specific reform proposals were announced, but not otherwise – the Maharashtrian political leader walked out with his supporters. Gandhi, as a protest at the insult to Tilak, declined to second a resolution moved in support of recruitment and remained silently in his seat. He then, however, threw himself wholeheartedly into recruitment.

From Gandhi's own accounts and others, the work became an obsession with him. Inevitably, the district where he chose to concentrate his recruiting effort was the Kheda district of Gujarat where he had just organised a partially successful six months' campaign involving mass peasant participation. Most of Gandhi's co-workers took up the campaign with him, despite some having doubts about how Gandhi could square recruiting work with his faith in ahimsa, or nonviolence. The Kheda peasants, however, fresh from their perilous confrontation with the British revenue system, were not impressed by the campaign and Gandhi gained few recruits and little cooperation from the Kheda district. Gandhi, nevertheless, spent seven weeks of intensive work in the district, moving from village to village with his team of workers, until in August he fell seriously ill. (Gandhi, R. 2007: 200-201)

---

15. P.H.M. Van Den Dungem argues that after his experiences in South Africa between 1906 and 1909, Gandhi was not strictly a loyalist; when he was engaged in recruiting in 1918 Gandhi was following the satyagraha principle of "helping the opponent in a time of trouble in order to secure a sympathetic response." This is surely correct; but Van Den Dungem does not explore Gandhi's belief that India in 1918 was not yet ready for Home Rule, nor his assertion at this time that the "disarmed Indian nation had been 'emasculated'." (Van Den Dungem 1971: 43-63)

Gandhi, as we have seen, was opposed to raising money for the war. He also argued strongly that one of the greatest crimes of the British in India had been to weaken the ability of the nation to fight by depriving the citizen of the right to bear arms. Nonviolence, according to Gandhi, was rooted in the voluntary renunciation of weapons, rather than in an imposed and compulsory disarmament, which was humiliating. Enlisting in the army, he argued, would give Indians training in the use of weapons and encourage the development of a fighting spirit, which he felt was essential for the attainment of independence or Swaraj. (Desai 1968: 156-157; 166-167; 172-178; 186-187; 217) This surprising argument was the one said to have appealed most to Gandhi's young Home Rule co-workers in Gujarat.[16] (Yajnik 1933: 51)

Part of Gandhi's appeal in Kheda was his religious asceticism. Gandhi followed very much in the bhakti tradition of Hinduism which was strong in Kheda. In the early 19th century an ascetic bhakti saint called Swaminarayan had won many converts in the area stressing good works and the doctrine of ahimsa, or nonviolence, in contrast to the emphasis of an earlier bhakti sect in the area associated with Vallabhacharya. The British had actively encouraged the Swaminarayan sect because of its emphasis on quiescence before authority. Gandhi's religious programme and ashram life were very similar to the Swaminarayan doctrine and someone like Vallabhbhai Patel, a native of Kheda district, who had been brought up in a strict Swaminarayan household and had then rejected the doctrine, initially scorned Gandhi because he thought he was promulgating the same message. When, however, Vallabhbhai saw after Champaran that Gandhi was an activist, he became an active supporter. (Hardiman 1967: 59-60)

In 1918, during his recruiting work, Gandhi came up directly against the influence of these two sects in Kheda. He wrote to his son in July 1918:

---

16. Privately, Gandhi told his secretary, Mahadev Desai: "My mind refuses to be loyal to the British Empire and I have to make a strenuous effort to stem the tide of rebellion... But a feeling deep down in me persists that India's good lies in [the] British connection, and so I force myself to love them." (Gandhi, R. 2007: 199)

"What has cut me to the quick is the perception that the teachings of Swaminarayan and Vallabhacharya have made us completely unmanly... The love taught by Swaminarayan and Vallabhacharya is effeminate sentimentality. True love cannot grow out of it. They have not even an inkling of the true spirit of Ahimsa... Their influence has spread most widely in Gujarat..."

In another letter written at the time, Gandhi explained this further:

"I find great difficulties in recruiting, but do you know that not one man has yet objected because he would not kill? They object because they fear to die. The unnatural fear of death is ruining the nation." (Desai 1968: 203)

In his discussion of the influence of Swaminarayan and Vallabhacharya, he went on to announce "the great change in my thinking". This had nothing to do with abandoning his faith in the superiority of Indian culture over "western civilisation", but he now distinguished between the letter of nonviolence and the spirit of nonviolence. He had decided that the spirit of nonviolence (*ahimsa*) could be contained in a violent act (*himsa*), as for example in killing a rabid dog. In the same way, he speculated, children should be trained in fighting techniques so that they would be "physically strong enough to practise true ahimsa, or nonviolence". (Desai 1968: 197-200) He wondered whether children in the ashram could be trained to hit back when attacked "without their becoming aggressive and insolent". (Desai 1968: 206-207)

Much of this thinking stayed with Gandhi when his fruitless recruiting work was over. As we have seen, his first question to prospective satyagrahis had often been, "Are you prepared to die?" After his 1918 recruiting experience he began to place more emphasis on "manliness" and physical courage and to see even more strongly in martial qualities the potential for ahimsa or nonviolence. But, ironically, it was during this time that Gandhi's own physical health collapsed. While in Kheda, Gandhi had come to realise that the diet he developed in South Africa, of fruit and nuts, was beyond the means of most Indian peasants. He therefore was in the process of transferring to the local peasant diet based on vegetables, including beans and grains. This harsher regime appears to have caused him great problems, for in August 1918 he fell seriously ill with dysentery and believed he was going to die. (Yajnik 1933: 56) He was confined to bed for three months. During this time, the Armistice was signed ending the war. Gandhi's recruiting team turned its efforts to work on famine relief in several parts of Gujarat.

CASE STUDY 4:
THE ROWLATT SATYAGRAHA

Gandhi Takes Up His First All-India Issue

If Gandhi's recruiting efforts in Kheda were unsuccessful, they do not appear to have damaged his standing in Gujarat. Relations with the Raj were profoundly uncertain as the First World War drew to an end and nationalist politicians had no clear-cut position on the recruitment question. A second issue was preoccupying Indian nationalism at this time. While he was still recruiting in Gujarat and, later, when confined to his sickbed, Gandhi began to receive attentions from leading nationalists anxious to know where he stood in a fresh controversy. Proposals for constitutional reform had been introduced by the Raj as a direct response to changes in political conditions stemming from the war. Opinion was divided on whether to welcome or reject these proposals. As part of a gradual process of preparing India for a form of self-government, the Raj intended to enlarge the franchise and increase representation at the central level and, in particular, at provincial and local levels. Control on key issues would remain with the Viceroy.

One group of Indian politicians, the Moderates, who had been until 1917 in control of the Indian National Congress, favoured collaboration with the Raj. The other group, the "Extremists", were the Home Rulers, led by Tilak and Besant who, as we have seen, had gathered an active following in the country and had captured Congress in December 1917. Pressed by the Moderates to support the reforms and by the Extremists to oppose them, Gandhi refused to become involved and developed his own position critical of both sides.[17] Broadly, Gandhi supported the Moderates in their arguments in favour of reforms, but felt that they were not prepared to press with enough determination – that is, go to the length of civil disobedience – to ensure that the limited modifications they did wish to see were actually carried out.

Early in 1919, a third issue became an equally important focus of nationalist opinion. During the war, the Raj had faced a terrorist movement in Bengal. As the war ended, the Government of India was nervous about developments in Turkey and the possible impact of the Russian revolution. It felt that, in addition to a political gesture towards Indian nationalism such as the proposed constitutional reforms, some extension of emergency powers that were about to lapse under the Defence of India Act, was needed in peacetime to protect the state against further terrorist outbreaks throughout India, not just Bengal. Thus the Rowlatt Bills were drawn up to fit this purpose. The Bills provoked uproar throughout India, including the unprecedented, unanimous opposition of all Indian representatives on the Viceroy's Council. They included provision for retrospective application for offences committed before they were passed, and for detention without trial. They also abridged normal court procedures and restricted rights of appeal. (Brown 1972: 161; Nanda 1989: 177) Gandhi, in choosing the Rowlatt Bills as the first issue on which to organise an all-India satyagraha, selected an issue which united all nationalist opinion in outrage, as opposition to the constitutional reforms did not.

The Rowlatt Bills offered an opportunity to lead a united campaign rather then one divided. It would be focused on a limited issue, the reservation by the Raj to itself of emergency powers after the war had ended, rather than on a general issue like the progress of Indian nationalism towards

---

17. Gandhi was out of sympathy with the narrow political concerns of the Indian elite. "Without our penetration into the villages, our Home Rule schemes are of little value. With the people really at our back we should make our march to our goal irresistibly. We must give the fruits of our western learning to our millions; whereas we, circulating ideas among ourselves, describe like the blindfolded ox (round the well) the same circle and mistake it for motion forward." (Quoted in Nanda 1989: 167)

some form of self-government. In Gandhi's eyes, limited issues offered a greater chance of success. A focus on the Rowlatt Bills also gave him the chance to define a campaign which he could lead himself and accordingly develop his method of satyagraha, rather than share leadership with others whose methods and aims were different. But he now had to find a way to organise for the first time on an all-India scale.

Formation of the Satyagraha Sabha

Gandhi had not yet played a leading role in any of the annual sessions of the Indian National Congress. Nor had the Congress yet established itself as an organisation capable of launching mass political agitation, despite efforts by Besant and Tilak in that direction since 1914. (Owen 1968: 164-184) Gandhi was not in control of any other national body capable of organising satyagraha. He was by this time more complimentary of the work of Annie Besant's League, but still resisted pressure from his Gujarati colleagues to join the organisation ("one scabbard cannot hold two swords"). (Yajnik, 1933: 27) Thus when the group of young Bombay and Ahmedabad Home Rulers, several of whom had worked with him in Ahmedabad and Kheda, approached him in February 1919 with the request that he lead a nationwide satyagraha struggle against the Rowlatt Bills, they jointly agreed to form a new organisation, the Satyagraha Sabha, to conduct the agitation.

The 24-member executive of the Satyagraha Sabha, established at a meeting in Gandhi's ashram on February 24, 1919, was composed almost entirely of members of the two Home Rule Leagues, drawn from Bombay city and Ahmedabad, with Gandhi as President. Unsurprisingly, Gandhi's collaborators from his local campaigns were prominent among them, including Vallabbhai Patel (who became secretary), Indulal Yajnik and Jamnadas Dwarkadas from the Kheda satyagraha and Anasuyaben Sarabha and Shankerlal Banker from the Ahmedabad mill strike. Other prominent members from Bombay included the poet, Sarojini Naidu, Umar Sobhani, a Muslim mill owner, and the editor of the Bombay Chronicle, B.G. Horniman. The Sabha envisaged semi-autonomous branches being established in other parts of India, and this did happen in a few cases; for example, Gandhi secured the involvement of Rajendra Prasad and J.B. Kripalani in Bihar, who had worked with him in Champaran, and a new collaborator from Madras, Chakravarti Rajagopalachari. But Gujarat and Bombay city remained the driving force. (Owen 1971: 65, 68-74, 77-82, 90; Nanda 1989: 178; Gandhi, R. 2007: 206-207)

Within a month, on 18 March 1919, the first of the Rowlatt Bills was passed into law by the Government of India. Nationalist opinion had been ignored. The government's action precipitated a quick response.

The newly-formed Satyagraha Sabha, despite allowing themselves only two weeks to plan a major event of protest – the April 6 Rowlatt *hartal* – succeeded in promoting simultaneous demonstrations in many parts of India, several of them extremely well supported. The hartal was an attempted closing-down of all commercial businesses, accompanied by prayers, fasting, public meetings and processions. One widely noted feature was its almost entirely peaceful character throughout the country. Subsequently, of course, serious violence did break out in a number of places, causing Gandhi to suspend and finally abandon the Sabha's programme of civil disobedience. But extraordinarily, these later destructive and in some respects insurrectionary events prompted Gandhi to do no more than hesitate in promoting his method of satyagraha and his claims as a national leader.

The Rowlatt Hartal

Gujarat and Bombay city played a key part in the Rowlatt events. As part of its organising activities, the Satyagraha Sabha had circulated a pledge to be signed by those willing to offer civil disobedience at its direction. By mid-March 1919, across the whole of India, 982 signatures had been collected – of these, over 80% were from Gujarat and Bombay. By April 7, the day after the hartal, it is reported that 1,645 signatures had been collected in Bombay. (Owen 1971: p 81, 81n) Much of the promotion for the April 6 hartal was done through contacts and membership lists across India to which the Bombay and Ahmedabad members of Annie Besant's League had access.

Gandhi spent April 6 in Bombay. At the beach, he was with more than a hundred Home Rulers and satyagrahis who assembled early in the morning and bathed in the customary purification ceremony for holy days. They were joined by a crowd variously estimated at 5,000 by the police and 150,000 by the nationalists. It listened to a speech by Gandhi read by a prominent Bombay Home Ruler and to a Muslim religious leader. The crowd then went in silent procession to a Hindu temple bearing a banner saying "mourn for justice" in Gujarati and English; and then on to another meeting in a mosque, which Gandhi and Sarojini Naidu had the rare experience as Hindus of being permitted to address. Muslim support for the Rowlatt agitation had been won by their recognition that the Rowlatt Act might be used against their own leaders. (Masselos 1971:174-181)

It has been estimated that 80 percent of shops closed in Bombay on April 6. Gandhi had requested workers to attend for work unless given permission not to do so by their employers. Eleven mills out of 82 in Bombay closed during the day. Most of the support for the hartal came from Gujaratis, though there was a noticeable participation too from the Maharashtrian community. One commentator notes cautiously, "Larger numbers were involved in the hartal than had perhaps ever previously participated in any Bombay political demonstration". Even so support did not go much beyond the educated classes already mobilised – "the working class and masses" had not yet moved in Bombay in a decisive way to support Gandhi. (Masselos 1971: 179-181)

In Ahmedabad, Indulal Yajnik was one of those who addressed a crowd estimated by him at "almost a hundred thousand" and elsewhere at well over 80,000. (Yajnik 1933: 66; Gillion 1971:135) Meetings were held in Viramgam and other towns in Gujarat. On the evening of April 6, when the day's fast was broken, workers from the Satyagraha Sabha committed civil disobedience in Bombay and Ahmedabad by selling several banned books and an unauthorised newspaper. Since these were available only in the Gujarati language, this action was largely confined to the Bombay Presidency; but the Bombay government quickly chose not to prosecute. The following day, as a means of preparing individuals for satyagraha struggle on a national scale, the Sabha invited people to take two new pledges drawn up by Gandhi. One, the Swadeshi Pledge, committed the signatory to wearing only clothing manufactured in India; the other was a pledge to observe Hindu-Muslim unity. Neither pledge drew much support in Bombay. (Yajnik 1933: 63-64, 67)

Delhi, then Bombay and Ahmedabad

Through a failure of communication, Delhi, 900 miles from Bombay, had observed the Rowlatt hartal a week early on March 30. Police shootings led to serious rioting, and Gandhi was pressed strongly to come to Delhi and help. (Ferrell 1971: 23) In the Punjab (before the worse events which followed), supporters of the Rowlatt hartal were also confronted by an obdurate provincial government and appealed to Gandhi for assistance.

Thus Gandhi left Bombay for Delhi by train on April 8, intending to visit both places. However, as he neared Delhi on April 9, he was served with a government order restricting him to Bombay Presidency, which he refused to obey. He was then returned under police escort to Bombay city, which he did not reach until two days later. When the news of Gandhi's arrest reached Ahmedabad and Bombay on April 10, the result was angry demonstrations, which took the form of hartal in Bombay but quickly developed into severe rioting in Ahmedabad. Gandhi arrived in Bombay on the afternoon of April 11 and was able to help bring the crowds under control. In Ahmedabad, fifty-one government and several municipal buildings were burnt down and a European police sergeant murdered. Twenty-eight people were killed and 132 wounded as the police and military restored order under martial law.

In Viramgam, near Ahmedabad, six rioters were shot and, in retaliation, an Indian official burnt alive. In Kheda district, two houses were burnt down, telegraph wires cut, and a train carrying troop reinforcements to Ahmedabad was derailed, though without injury to the 200 British soldiers on board. (Gillion 1971:136-138, 142)

Gandhi had hoped to go to Delhi and the Punjab to restore calm. In Delhi, following news of his arrest, more demonstrators were shot by police. In the Punjab, martial law was declared and a regime of repression imposed which became notorious internationally as a symbol of British imperial domination in India. The "Punjab Wrongs" of April 1919 were later taken up by the nationalist movement as a main grievance behind the Noncooperation struggle of 1920-22.

Impact of the violence

Gandhi was horrified by these events. Under the terms of his banning order, which restricted him to the Bombay Presidency, he returned to Ahmedabad from Bombay on April 13 and immediately put his energies alongside the British authorities in restoring calm. Gandhi's view, characteristically, was that his supporters should not have been angered by his arrest and they should not have reacted violently to the further arrest of demonstrators or to the fatal shootings. He spoke of his shock that in a community in which he was well known and had gone some way to explaining his principles of satyagraha, the people should have so little understanding of these principles and should riot in his name.

He announced that just as he intended to maintain his satyagraha against the Rowlatt Act, as he had vowed to do, he now thought it was his duty to exercise satyagraha against his own supporters. What pained him most was having to forego his pledge to commit civil disobedience, since he had intended to return to Delhi in contravention of his restriction order. But he would also undertake a further penance – Gandhi was still very weak after his illness – of a three-day fast. (Desai 1968: 27-29; Tendulkar 1951: 253-255)

At subsequent meetings, Gandhi went on to make a distinction between civil disobedience conducted in a spirit of lawlessness and civil disobedience undertaken as a branch of satyagraha. He thought that to continue civil disobedience against the Rowlatt Act in the prevailing atmosphere of lawlessness would harm the satyagraha movement. In order to encourage the respect of the government and to reduce the enmity between Europeans and Indians, he thought that satyagrahis should now support the government wholeheartedly in seeking to restore law and order.

Gandhi organised a fund for the families of the victims in Ahmedabad. Nationalist opinion in the city appears broadly to have accepted that the police and military acted "properly" in the imposition of their authority – though it did object to the maintenance of martial law and also to the subsequent trials and sentences of people arrested and to the levying of a punitive tax on the city for the reconstruction of the property destroyed. (Gillion 1971:138-141) Yajnik recounts that when he and other satyagraha workers went round in fulfilment of Gandhi's campaign to promote the principles of satyagraha, he found people cowed and terrorised by the heavy military and police action. (Yajnik 1933: 79-80) In the long run, K.L. Gillion, a scholar who has written a history of Ahmedabad, concludes:

> "The events of April 1919 marked the transfer of moral authority in Ahmedabad from the British... The government's formal authority was restored without difficulty, but the Congress... soon turned the city into a moral and financial base for the freedom movement... Gandhi always regretted the violence that had taken place and it showed him the dangers inherent in mass political action. But it was the violence of April 1919 that broke the spell of the Raj." (Gillion 1971:143-144)

Standing up to the Raj on an issue which united Indian opinion appears to have had a striking effect on popular confidence and morale. Gandhi of course wanted the protests to be nonviolent, not least because he felt that would make it easier for the Raj to listen and respond flexibly. His role in these events confirmed his position as a leader who was prepared to take action, even when he made mistakes and unrest led to riot and bloodshed.

If the violence of April 10 and 11 was cathartic for Ahmedabad, the news of the terrible events in the Punjab as it gradually became known across the subcontinent, had the same effect for the Indian nation as a whole. Government press censorship ensured that the news spread slowly. But the violence of the masses shocked the educated classes in Ahmedabad, who were also alienated by the Rowlatt Act itself, by the arrest of Gandhi and by the punitive reaction of the government in the city. Instead of causing disillusionment with Gandhi, therefore, the events of 1919 strengthened their alliance with him. Despite the immediate damage to the satyagraha movement caused by the outbreak of violence, Gillion notes that these events paved the way for Gandhi's constructive political work – the development of the Ahmedabad Textile Workers Association, the support of the mill-owners for Congress, and the struggle for control of the Ahmedabad municipal authority waged under the leadership of Vallabhbhai Patel. Gandhi, he implies, offered an alternative path to the educated classes from that of violence.

Organising Against the Rowlatt Bills: The Satyagraha Sabha

We have focused so far on the support the agitation against the Rowlatt Bills achieved in Gujarat and nearby Bombay city, the headquarters for Gandhi's first nationwide satyagraha. But the Rowlatt Satyagraha also got a response from many other parts of the Indian subcontinent, and this posed problems of co-ordination for the Sabha in Bombay.

These matters are the subject of a paper by Hugh Owen "Organising for the Rowlatt Satyagraha of 1919". (Owen 1971) According to Owen, the Rowlatt Satyagraha:

"posed new problems of organisation; of communication of ideas; of mobilization of a wide array of social groups; and last, but not the least, of exercise of control and restraint over the social groups thus mobilized under conditions of excitement, provocation, or repression. " (Owen 1971: 64)

It was, of course, through the Home Rule Leagues that Gandhi was able to draw on pre-existing networks of support across India. Owen notes that branches of the Leagues were activated in different parts of India in the run-up to the April hartal; but in two regions where the Home Rule Leagues had been weak, in Bengal and in the Punjab, communications were more difficult. Gandhi himself went on a speaking tour north to Delhi, Allahabad and Lucknow in the United Provinces and south to Madras city, Tamilnad and Andhra, as well as making special efforts in Bombay city itself. Owen comments,

"This tour of Gandhi's amounted, in a sense, to a substitute for organisation: by personal contact he communicated his ideas to people scattered over much of India, mobilized lieutenants and a broader following, and strove to co-ordinate, to control and to restrain them. Having hitherto directed campaigns in more-or-less limited areas, Gandhi was trying to direct this all-India campaign in the same personal manner. Indeed he was nervous about the conduct of the campaign in Bengal, and disowned responsibility for the violence in the Punjab since he had been unable to visit either province personally. But India was clearly too vast for effective face-to-face leadership on a countrywide scale by Gandhi himself; more elaborate organisation and preparation were obviously needed." (Owen 1971: 88)

Branches of the Satyagraha Sabha were established in Bombay, Ahmedabad, Delhi, Allahabad, Madras, and Karachi. In Delhi and Lucknow, Gandhi secured the support for the Rowlatt Satyagraha of the leaders of a section of Muslim opinion, the Pan-Islamists, who were already agitating about the Khilafat question. But in the province of Madras, Annie Besant was able to exercise strong pressure against members of her All-India Home Rule League supporting the hartal call, and major support was confined to Madras City and to parts of Andhra where Gandhi had visited.

Within this loose framework, there was even among the branches of the Satyagraha Sabha disagreement about how far they should follow Gandhi's ideas and philosophy, a lack of clarity about decision-making and poor co-ordination. Gandhi commented in his *Autobiography*, written in the late 1920s, about early signs of disunity in the Bombay branch of the Sabha:

"I soon found that there was not likely to be a chance of agreement between myself and the intelligentsia composing this Sabha. My insistence on the use of Gujarati in the Sabha, as also some of my other methods of work that would appear to be peculiar, caused them no small worry and embarrassment ... (From) the very beginning it seemed clear to me that the Sabha was not likely to live long. I could see that already my emphasis on truth and Ahimsa had begun to be disliked by some of its members..." (Gandhi M.K. 1982: 411)

Owen comments that, "while Gandhi had a clearer conception of the organisational needs of agitational politics than any of his predecessors or rivals for power in the Indian movement, he remained fundamentally anarchist in temperament". (Owen 1971: 91)

Thus early in March Gandhi informed the Allahabad Sabha that they could either recognise the Bombay committee as a central committee, co-ordinating activities across the whole of India, or they could form their own independent committee if they wished. By mid-March he had decided that the Bombay committee would have its jurisdiction limited to the Bombay Presidency; and later in the month he confirmed that each province should have its own independent autonomous organisation. Yet at the same time, he assumed that the Sabhas would follow his lead as President on the strategy and even the tactics of the campaign, refusing to allow provincial Sabhas to adapt the wording of the Pledge for use in their own areas, or to permit one province to extend the grounds for civil disobedience to the refusal of land revenue tax. When he personally conceived of the idea of an all-India hartal, Gandhi announced this to the press before consulting the Sabhas. Later, when violence broke out, he sent instructions to the Sabhas without discovering what were the local conditions. (Owen 1971: 78-79)

This imperious quality of Gandhi's leadership, he justified by his claim, which was true, that he had superior experience and understanding of satyagraha. The formation of the Satyagraha Sabha itself was at his suggestion because, as he admitted, "all hope of the existing institutions adopting a novel weapon like Satyagraha seemed to me to be in vain. " (Gandhi 1982: 411)

The Congress itself at this time was not geared to political agitation and even if it had been, Gandhi would not have been in a position to direct the campaign. But Gandhi went ahead with the Rowlatt Satyagraha without any reference to the working committees of the national Congress or the Bombay Provincial Congress. As Owen suggests, the campaign seems in many respects to have been a personal tour de force. In areas where Gandhi was known, he was able to exert direct personal influence. In provinces like the Punjab, Bengal or the Central Provinces, where his reputation was slight, whether the Rowlatt agitation was taken up or not depended on the particular local conditions. In Punjab, the end of wartime restrictions contributed to a massive upsurge of political activity in the province, which took up the Rowlatt agitation without any individuals signing the Satyagraha Pledge or forming a branch of the Sabha. In Calcutta, in Bengal, the radical wing of Congress opinion supported the hartal, but without enthusiasm for the religious aspects of satyagraha. In the Central Provinces, there was little response at all.

Despite all these organisational weaknesses, one feature of the Rowlatt satyagraha and of the Sabha itself is that it brought together from the local satyagrahas in Champaran, Ahmedabad and Kheda and from Gandhi's speaking tours across India, many of the leaders who were to play a major part in his later campaigns for independence. Others, like Jawarhalal Nehru, were impressed that a leader had emerged with a novel method of action who could mobilise astonishingly wide support. Gandhi was assembling a group of national co-workers who were coming to appreciate and understand satyagraha and, whether they fully agreed with him or not, mostly stayed with him.[18] (Gandhi R. 2007: 206-208)

Civil Disobedience, the pledge and the hartal

Gandhi had conceived of the Rowlatt Satyagraha much like his earlier campaigns in Gujarat. The basis of the Satyagraha was a pledge to be signed by people willing to disobey the Rowlatt Bills if they became law, or some other laws to be declared by a committee of the Satyagraha Sabha.[19] Only those who had signed the pledge were entitled to commit

---

18. In the North West Frontier Province, 25 miles from the Khyber Pass, Abdul Ghaffar Khan, then 28, organised a rally in support of the Rowlatt hartal. Ghaffar Khan was of course a Muslim and became known later as "the Frontier Gandhi". (Gandhi R. 2007: 207)

19. The text of the Satyagraha Pledge, February 24, 1919 reads: "Being conscientiously of opinion that the Bills known as the Indian Criminal Law (Amendment) Bill No. 1 of 1919 and the Criminal Law (Emergency Powers) Bill No. 2 of 1919 are unjust, subversive of the principle of liberty and justice, and destructive of the elementary rights of individuals on which the safety of the community as a whole and the state itself is based, we solemnly affirm that, in the event of these Bills becoming law and until they are withdrawn, we shall refuse civilly to obey these laws and such other laws as a Committee to be

civil disobedience; and only signatories to the pledge could be members of a branch of the Sabha. It was when support for civil disobedience across India, registered by the number of pledges signed, seemed to be confined to little over a thousand that Gandhi literally dreamed the idea of an all-India hartal – a day of purification and prayer when all businesses would be closed across India. Hartal had traditionally been applied as a form of protest in India, with all the markets in a town or province closed in protest against the activities of a ruler. But this was the first time it had been proposed on an all-India scale. (Yajnik 1933: 64-65; Masselos 1971: 181)

Thus a two-tier level of commitment was created in the Rowlatt agitations – firstly, those who had signed the Satyagraha pledge who were ready to engage in civil disobedience and, secondly, those who took part in the hartal, which was not an act of civil disobedience at all. Gandhi tried to link the two by defining the hartal as a day of preparation for civil disobedience. (Gandhi 1964-66: vol 15: 145) He also introduced a lesser (or third) pledge for those who were willing to commit themselves to "the truth part" of the Satyagraha Pledge, but not to the civil disobedience. (Gandhi M.K.1964-66: vol 16: 415-416; Gandhi M.K. 1951: 145)

We see here Gandhi developing a flexible basis for satyagraha activities which could engage potentially large numbers of people, while at the same time reserving civil disobedience for those who were sworn and disciplined satyagrahis.

In the areas where a Sabha had been formed, the members of the Sabha became – without much consultation or planning – the organisers of an extensive programme of purificatory bathing, fasting, religious services, processions and public meetings which constituted the April 6 hartal. Yajnik claims:

> "The 6th April was observed as a day of national penance and mourning - of fast and prayer - millions of people following

---

hereafter appointed may think fit and we further affirm that in this struggle we will faithfully follow truth and refrain from violence to life, person or property." (Gandhi 1965: vol 15: 101-102)

the custom of centuries went in the morning bare-foot to tanks or rivers, or to the seas, to purify themselves by bathing in the holy waters. And after finishing the bath, the crowds formed themselves into monster processions..." (Yajnik 1933: 66)

The terms of the pledge, which was an individual vow to disobey laws selected at some future date by a committee, caused some problems for the Sabha. Some critics argued that they were willing to disobey only the Rowlatt Act itself, and they objected to the extension of civil disobedience to other laws; another criticism came from those who felt that they could not be bound by the unspecified dictates of a committee. (Brown 1972: 168-169)

Gandhi put a great deal of thought into these questions, distinguishing between "good" or "moral" laws which should never be disobeyed, and laws without moral content, which could. (Desai 1968: vol 1) It was impractical to organise a mass campaign against the Rowlatt Act itself because it was an emergency measure, held in reserve by the government – and in fact was never used. He actively considered both the Salt Act and the land revenue system as targets for civil disobedience but, in the event, restricted his choice to the Press Laws governing journalists and publishers, a system of censorship he had been complaining about for some time. (Gandhi M.K. 1964-1966: vol 15: 147-148)

The idea was that the pledged satyagrahis would circulate selected illegal texts banned by the government and print newspapers without an official permit. The committee of the Sabha designated in the Pledge did not issue its "Statement on Laws for Civil Disobedience" until April 7, the day after the Rowlatt hartal. Gandhi had imagined the sale and circulation of dissenting literature. He envisaged both books and newspapers being sold openly and, as they were confiscated and the publishers and sellers arrested, copies being made by hand and reading clubs started. Ultimately, satyagrahis should remember "that we have in India the tradition of imparting instruction by oral teaching". In selecting the Press Laws and making their choice of prohibited literature to be circulated, the Sabha were to be guided by the following considerations:

" (1) To cause as little disturbance as possible among the governors and the governed;

" (2) Until satyagrahis have become seasoned, disciplined and capable of handling delicately organised movements, to select such laws only as can be disobeyed individually;

" (3) To select as a first step, laws that have evoked popular disapproval and that, from the satyagraha standpoint, are the most open to attack;

" (4) To select laws whose civil breach would constitute an education for people, showing them a clear way out of the difficulties that lie in the path of honest men desiring to do public work:

" (5) Regarding prohibited literature, to select such books and pamphlets as are not inconsistent with satyagraha and which are, therefore, of a clean type and which do not, either directly or indirectly, approve of or encourage violence. " (Gandhi M.K. 1965: vol 15: 192-194)

Thus a tactical decision was taken to engage only in individual rather than mass civil disobedience. (Dhawan 1957: 242-243) As he stated more clearly in his speech on the Bombay sands on the morning of the April 6 hartal:

"When we have acquired habits of discipline, self-control and qualities of leadership and obedience, we shall be better able to offer collective civil disobedience, but until we have developed these qualities, I have advised that we should select for disobedience only such laws as can be disobeyed by individuals." (Gandhi M.K. 1965: vol 15: 186-187)

Moreover, distinguishing as ever his activities from those of the Home Rule Leagues under Tilak and Besant, Gandhi declared in the first issue of his hand-produced paper *Satyagrahi*, published in Bombay on April 7, that the business of the paper itself was to secure the withdrawal of the Rowlatt legislation by means of civil disobedience.

"This publication... is... committing civil disobedience in the very act of publishing... " (Gandhi M.K. 1965: vol 15: 190-191)

Though this particular campaign did not develop as planned, we see here the subtlety of Gandhi's method. Preaching civil disobedience, the production and distribution of these papers would constitute an act of civil disobedience. His hand-written newspaper could be copied – and others were to be independently edited and produced "in every satyagraha centre" – and circulated indefinitely among literate sympathisers and read and then passed on by word of mouth among the illiterate ("It need not occupy more than one side of half a foolscap") until "at last the process of multiplication is made to cover, if necessary, the whole of the masses of India".

In practice, though, this civil disobedience campaign did not get off the ground. The violence in different parts of India, following Gandhi's arrest on his way to Delhi, caused him to suspend the programme after a few days. But in any case the prohibited books – which were mainly works written or translated by Gandhi himself – and the newspaper *Satyagrahi*, were available only in the Gujarati language and so not suitable for all-India distribution. Also, the government of the Bombay Presidency decided not to prosecute either the sale of the prohibited books or the unregistered newspaper. The prohibited books, they judged, such as Gandhi's political testament, *Hind Swaraj*, had been published in South Africa in 1909; and the new edition published in Ahmedabad in 1919 had not been prohibited! Similarly, a hand-written unregistered newspaper was deemed not to contravene the law since this applied only to printed newspapers. (Watson 1969)

Thus, Gandhi's campaign of civil disobedience against the Rowlatt Act, such as it was, caused even less "disturbance among the governors" than he had intended. If, on the other hand, the campaign had not been suspended so quickly, it is clear that Gandhi would have widened the programme of civil disobedience to the point when arrests would have been made.

Returning to the second objection against the Rowlatt Pledge, that signatories could not agree to be bound by the unspecified dictates of a committee, Gandhi made two responses. Firstly, he said that permitting the satyagrahi to commit civil disobedience only against the laws chosen by the committee was a useful restraint against indiscriminate and uncoordinated lawbreaking. But, secondly, if individual satyagrahis did not agree with the choice of law to be broken made by the committee, then they had the right to refrain from civil disobedience: this was clear in the pledge by the satyagrahi's commitment to "follow truth". As he wrote to C.F. Andrews, who was one of the critics:

"... as a check upon individual extravagance, (the signatory) surrenders his judgement to that of experts as to the selection of breakable laws and the order in which they are to be broken. That surely is not a matter of conscience. If the committee, which is bound by the same Pledge that binds the individual satyagrahi, commits an error and selects laws whose breach will be inconsistent with satyagraha, naturally the individual signatory who conscientiously thinks so refrains from breaking such a law. In all satyagraha organisations, this final liberty is understood." (Gandhi M.K. 1965: vol 15: 169-170)

In this passage, we see again Gandhi's clear conception of his role within the Satyagraha Sabha, as an expert in satyagraha. In his view, he had a right and a duty to direct and control the behaviour of those he was leading into civil disobedience and other forms of nonviolent activity. Having voluntarily surrendered their judgement to his, or more exactly to a committee, the individual satyagrahis, nonetheless, retained a prior and overriding commitment to the dictates of their own consciences. They could choose not to follow him if they wished.

Religious basis of Rowlatt Pledge and Hartal

This overriding emphasis on individual conscience draws us into another aspect of the Rowlatt satyagraha. During the Ahmedabad labour strike, as we have seen, Gandhi spelled out his conception of his personal mission which was to draw upon the spiritual resources of the Indian nation and turn them into a political weapon. The Rowlatt satyagraha was Gandhi's first attempt to apply this novel approach to politics on an all-India scale and he was quite explicit on many occasions that this was what he was doing. On March 14, 1919, in a speech in Bombay, Gandhi said:

"We may expect to be told ... that the government will not yield to any threat of passive resistance. Satyagraha is not a threat, it is a fact; and even such a mighty government as the Government of India will have to yield if we are true to our Pledge. For the Pledge is not a small thing. It means a change of heart. It is an attempt to introduce the religious spirit into politics. We may no longer believe in the doctrine of tit for tat; we may not meet hatred by hatred, violence by violence, evil by evil; but we have to make a continuous and persistent effort to return good for evil." (Gandhi M.K 1965: vol 15: 135-136)

By this, Gandhi meant that the Rowlatt Pledge constituted a change of heart for the Indian nationalists who had signed it. Through the Rowlatt satyagraha, and through the Pledge in particular, Gandhi was organising directly to counter and supersede the agitational methods of the Home Rule Leagues – "tit for tat" – with which he so disagreed. He said much the same thing at a public meeting in Madras, six days later: the movement "constitutes an attempt to revolutionise politics and to restore moral force to its original station." (Gandhi M.K. 1965: vol 15: 141-143)

Gandhi was asking nationalist political radicals to pledge themselves to a quite different kind of politics from what most of them were used to. Of course, his nonviolent method because of its appeal to the masses did prove itself capable of building power close to the conventional sort for those who joined the movement. This helps to explain why a great many nationalist political figures later worked with Gandhi – some of whom were greatly influenced by him – even though they never fully accepted that they were "revolutionising" politics by introducing into it the religious spirit. But this was what Gandhi intended and what he thought he was doing.

At a public meeting in Tamilnad on March 28, 1919, Gandhi showed again how much closer he felt himself to be to the spirit of the people than were the conventional politicians:

" [The temples of south India] demonstrate to me as nothing else does that we are a people deeply religious and that the people of India will be best appealed to by religion... Many of us think that in the political life, we need not bring out the religious element at all. Some even go so far as to say that politics should have nothing to do with religion... We have seen that all our meetings, all our resolutions and all the speeches of our councillors in the Imperial Legislative Council have proved to be of practically no avail. There are two ways and only two ways open to us [to remove the Rowlatt legislation]. One is the modern or the Western method of violence upon the wrongdoers. I hold that India will reject that proposition... The other method is the method known to us of old. And that is, of not giving obedience to the wrongful things of the rulers but to suffer the consequences. The way of suffering is satyagraha." (Gandhi M.K. 1965: vol 15: 159-162)

Gandhi held that the ancient civilisation in India was superior to that of the West. He saw himself as trying by the method of satyagraha to mobilise the residual confidence of the masses in their own heritage and to use it as a weapon against their Western rulers and a guide to their future development as a nation.

In the Rowlatt Satyagraha, Gandhi used two principal methods to promote this fundamental strategy. The first was the Pledge. We have noted in our discussion of the Ahmedabad and Kheda pledges, Gandhi's identification of the vow with religious faith, his belief that in the keeping of a sacred vow was the presence of God. He laid down strict and detailed instructions to Sabha volunteers on the procedure for ensuring that signatories fully understood the nature of their vow – "a single intelligent recruit to satyagraha is worth a hundred signatories who have not realised their responsibilities." (Gandhi M.K. 1965: 118-120) In his speech on March 28, he added in typical fashion:

"The taking of the Pledge is a sacred act undertaken in the name of the Almighty. Whilst therefore I invite every man and woman to sign the Pledge, I beseech them also to consider it deeply and a number of times before signing it... The satyagrahi when he signs the Pledge changes his very nature... Before he signs the Pledge he might get irritated against those who differ from him but not so afterwards." (Gandhi M.K 1965: vol 15: 159-162)

Moreover, on the day of the Rowlatt hartal, April 6, Gandhi introduced two further pledges, which were to be taken up and promoted by the Sabhas in addition to their civil disobedience against the Press Laws. The first was the *Swadeshi* vow – pledging the signatory to wear only Indian hand-made clothing – and the second the vow of Hindu-Muslim unity. (Gandhi M.K 1965: vol 15: 183-184, 188-189) "A vow", Gandhi said, in a leaflet published on April 8 while he was on the way to Delhi, "is a purely religious act which cannot be taken in a fit of passion. It can only be taken with a mind purified and composed and with God as witness." (Gandhi M.K 1965: vol 15: 201-203) But in partial contradiction of this, he stated in two messages to the press sent on the same day:

"This is the right time for (the foundation of swadeshi) as I have found that when a purifying movement like satyagraha is going on allied activities have an easy chance of success." (Gandhi M.K 1965: vol 15: 198)

and

"When the religious sense is awakened the people's thoughts undergo a revolution in a single moment... The spirit of sacrifice pervades the Indian atmosphere at the present moment. If we fail to preach swadeshi at this supreme moment, we shall have to wring our hands in despair." (Gandhi M.K 1965: vol 15: 200)

And again in another leaflet prepared on April 8, Gandhi proposed the vow of Hindu-Muslim unity:

"I hope that on this auspicious occasion – and surely the occasion must be auspicious when a wave of satyagraha is sweeping over the whole country – we could all take this vow of unity. " (Gandhi M.K 1965: vol 15: 203)

Gandhi was attempting to seize the opportunity, which the hartal and the launching of civil disobedience gave him, to consolidate a wider programme of activity and to do this by means of further pledges.

However, in addition to the use of pledges, Gandhi adopted a second method during the Rowlatt Satyagraha to promote his idea of a "purified" politics. This was the all-India hartal itself. The hartal was not, of course, an act of civil disobedience because it did not involve challenging any laws. But, for Gandhi, because he saw the Rowlatt civil disobedience as the moment when a religious spirit was entering politics, the hartal constituted both a means of preparation of members of the Sabha for civil disobedience and a way of preparing the masses to understand the nature of civil disobedience – and in the long run to take it up themselves. The civil disobedience against the Press Laws, it will be remembered, was to be undertaken by individual members of the Sabha only, whereas the hartal was intended as a mass activity.

The core of the hartal on April 6, as Gandhi conceived it, was a 24-hour fast. He gave this pride of place, rather than the suspension of business and the holding of processions. (Gandhi M.K 1965: vol 15: 145-146) He saw the fast as "an expression of grief, an act of self-denial, a process of purification". (Gandhi M.K 1965: vol 15: 149) As he said in a speech in south India on March 25:

"My first suggestion is that ... we shall all observe a 24 hours fast. It is a fitting preliminary for satyagrahis before they commence civil disobedience of the laws. For all others, it will be an expression of their deep grief over the wrong committed by the Government. I have regarded this movement as a purely religious movement and fast is an ancient institution amongst us... It is a measure of self-discipline, it will be an expression of anguish of the soul ... I have also suggested that on that Sunday all work should be suspended, all markets and all business places should be closed. Apart from the spiritual value of these two acts they will form an education of first-class value for the masses." (Gandhi M.K 1965: vol 15: 154-155)

Two weeks later the idea of the hartal had developed and was described in the directions issued to demonstrators on April 6 as "a day of humiliation and prayer and also of mourning by reason of the Delhi tragedies". (Gandhi M.K 1965: vol 15: 177-178) Demonstrations began with a purificatory bath; the processions were to be carried out in complete silence; no pressure of any kind was to be put on those who ignored the hartal. In a number of centres, religious services constituted part of the programme and breakthroughs occurred with joint Muslim-Hindu services.

It is hard to understand some of these ideas from a secular standpoint. An expression of mourning for the 14 people who had been shot by the Raj in Delhi a week before the Rowlatt hartal, is an action readily understood.

So too is the idea that grief and even anguish should be expressed at the damage done to the nation's pride by the imposition of the Rowlatt Act against the wishes of Indian political opinion. This helps explain a "day of humiliation". But beyond this Gandhi wanted to signify by this religious demonstration on a political issue the arrival of a new method, which was to be a major break with the methods of political agitation pursued previously. The hartal signified this new direction not only as a public manifestation visible to outsiders, but also as a statement to themselves by the individuals who took part in it – hence the fasting and notions of penance and purification – that they themselves would in future act differently. They should throw off those practices which prevented their community and the nation as a whole from rising to its proper stature and in this way compel respect from the British. They should find within their own religious culture a means for doing this.

By implication, Gandhi in particular was upbraiding the Indian people for their own condition at the same time as he showed them a way to change it. The hartal was intended to promote for the individual quiet reflection, penance, purification and discipline for the struggle ahead.

Use of Religion as a Means of Organising

In the editorial introduction to his *Essays on Gandhian Politics: the Rowlatt Satyagraha of 1919* (Kumar 1971), the author suggests that Gandhi "intuitively realised that India could be united only through means which affected the emotions instead of touching the purse-strings of the common people." Kumar is struck by the absence of class-rhetoric in Gandhi's appeals to the Indian people in support of the Rowlatt campaign. Gandhi assumed, says Kumar, that Indian loyalties were to their community and their religion rather than their class or profession. There was an influential argument among the apologists for British rule in India that the divisions between different castes, religions, language groups, classes and communities made progress to democratic government in the sub-continent unrealistic. Gandhi, says Kumar, had no illusions about the nature of political society in his country, but was seeking to unite it because of his belief that "religion provided the fundamental basis for political action in India." Kumar continues:

"A community embraced a number of castes with comparable hierarchical status and related cultural values. Gandhi realised and herein lay the great reason for his success, that only a 'romantic' issue could persuade different communities and religious groups to participate in agitation against the British government, because only a romantic issue could give them the freedom to voice their grievances on a common platform without surrendering their distinct identities. Gandhi's romanticism rested upon his attempt to relate political aspirations to moral instead of material objectives; to the flowering of the character and personality of his countrymen rather than to the achievement of economic and social goals. By drawing different castes, communities and religious groups into the penumbra of romantic politics, Gandhi sought to transform social groups which were loosely held together into a cohesive, articulate and creative political society. The support which the Rowlatt Satyagraha won in different parts of the country and the wide range of classes and communities which participated in the movement, are measures of Gandhi's success in transforming the peoples of India into such a society." (Kumar 1972: 15-16)

To make his point, Kumar tends to overemphasise Gandhi's lack of interest in economic and social goals: rather Gandhi looked at these goals within the context of a religiously-based ideal of society. In some respects, Kumar's argument mirrors the well-established observation that nationalism, as a "romantic" ideal, can triumph over class politics. Kumar also points out that Gandhi's religiously-based political appeal could draw together Indians of different religions and castes because he recognised each one as a "distinct community" of equal status and dignity. Mutual aid between these groups was the basis for action against the Raj. Equally, as we will examine shortly, the constructive programme was necessary to correct abuses within Indian society which were a blot on its reputation and a barrier to unity.[20]

---

20. Nanda (1957: 185-192) strongly objects to the depiction of Gandhi as pursuing a "romantic" issue. Nanda locates his success in a number of economic and political events which enabled the Rowlatt satyagraha to have an impact and adds that Gandhi's unique personality and charisma began to play a major part in the response he gained from a newly-emerging popular movement.

Kumar, in common with other critics, however, goes on to point out that while Gandhi's romanticism "was conspicuously successful in mobilising new classes and communities", it was inadequate to exercise control over these groups once they had been drawn into political agitation. In particular, he makes the common charge that Gandhi's "religious idiom ... widened the gulf between the two major communities of the sub-continent" and probably contributed to Partition in 1947. It is a fundamental criticism of Gandhi's political method, which I have not seen satisfactorily answered.

Gandhi's "Himalayan miscalculation"

Gandhi stated that he made a "Himalayan miscalculation" during the Rowlatt Satyagraha when he decided "to launch upon civil disobedience prematurely". (Gandhi M.K 1982: 422) This famous phrase has been reproduced many times to illustrate Gandhi's sense of shock when his elaborately conceived assault upon the nation's political life through the new weapon of satyagraha, collapsed in the rioting in Ahmedabad, Bombay and rural Gujarat and the repression in Delhi and the Punjab. Gandhi suggests in his *Autobiography* that he first used the expression at Nadiad in the Kheda district of Gujarat when he went there a few days after the Ahmedabad riots on April 24, 1919, (Dalal 1971: 23) and "saw the actual state of things there". (Gandhi M.K 1940: 346) But other records make it seem clear that he made the remark almost three months after the riots, on July 6, 1919, when he visited Nadiad again, and was inviting the citizens to support him in a resumption of civil disobedience against the Rowlatt Act. (Gandhi M.K. 1965: vol 15: 434-439)

According to Gandhi in his Nadiad speech in July 1919, his error lay "in trying to let civil disobedience take the people by storm". While in his Autobiography, he gives a fuller explanation:

> "... willing and spontaneous obedience [of the law] is required of a Satyagrahi. A Satyagrahi obeys the laws of society intelligently and of his own free will because he considers it to be his sacred duty to do so. It is only when a person has thus obeyed the laws of society scrupulously that he is in a position to judge as to which particular rules are good and just and which unjust

and iniquitous. Only then does the right accrue to him of civil disobedience of certain laws in well-defined circumstances. My error lay in my failure to observe this necessary limitation. I had called on the people to launch upon civil disobedience before they had thus qualified themselves for it and this mistake seemed to me of Himalayan magnitude." (Gandhi M.K 1982: 423)

Gandhi is here making the same distinction between passive resistance and satyagraha that he made throughout his career in politics.

Immediately after the April rioting, he made the point in a slightly less abstruse way, talking about the difference between civil disobedience carried out in a spirit of lawlessness and civil disobedience as a branch of satyagraha. This again was the distinction which he used when he wrote the Report of the Congress Inquiry into events in the Punjab. (Gandhi M.K. 1965: vol 15: 229-231, 244-245; Brown 1972: 239) He made the same criticism of the agitational methods of the Home Rule Leagues, that they carried out legitimate radical activity in the wrong spirit, thus undermining and invalidating their actions. Gandhi obviously reached the conclusion after the Rowlatt rioting that he had overestimated the extent to which satyagraha had superseded the old methods of nationalist agitation. In his *Autobiography* he goes on:

"As soon as I entered the Kheda district, all the old recollections of the Kheda struggle came back to me, and I wondered how I could have failed to perceive what was so obvious. I realised that before a people could be fit for offering civil disobedience, they should thoroughly understand its deeper implications. That being so, before restarting civil disobedience on a mass scale, it would be necessary to create a band of well-tried, pure-hearted volunteers who thoroughly understood the strict conditions of Satyagraha. They could explain these to the people, and by sleepless vigilance keep them on the right path." (Gandhi M.K 1982: 423)

This was indeed Gandhi's principal conclusion from the breakdown of the Rowlatt Satyagraha and he continued for the rest of his life to try to build that core of convinced supporters of satyagraha. But Gandhi's own assessment of his "error of Himalayan magnitude" in the Rowlatt

Satyagraha seems to be highly suspect. Despite what he says, the Rowlatt Satyagraha was not based on civil disobedience "on a mass scale". The civil disobedience actions proposed by Gandhi during the Rowlatt Satyagraha were specifically restricted to breaking the Press Laws and to a type of action – publishing and selling a newspaper or book – which was to be carried out only by individuals and they must have taken what amounted to a religious vow. Gandhi, in his speech on the morning of the April 6 hartal, had explicitly excluded "collective civil disobedience" from his programme of action – "until we have acquired habits of discipline, self-control, qualities of leadership and obedience." (Gandhi M.K. 1965: vol 15: 186-187) Certainly, the Rowlatt hartal itself was a mass action, but it was not in any sense civil disobedience, and Gandhi always claimed subsequently that the hartal itself had been a complete success.

As we have seen, no-one was arrested for civil disobedience against the Press Laws. Gandhi had taken enormous pains in devising his plan of civil disobedience to guard against the breakdown into lawlessness, which nevertheless happened. He had inserted into the Satyagraha Pledge a condition that only those laws could be broken which had been selected by a committee of the Sabha, which included himself. This, he admitted, was specifically designed to check "individual extravagance". During the March 1919 build-up to the April 6 hartal, a procession of satyagrahis in Sindh had been prohibited. Gandhi was delighted that the protesters obeyed this police order, even though the procession was "innocent", "because they are bound by the Pledge not to commit disobedience, except where authorised by the committee." (Gandhi M.K. 1965: vol 15: 169-170) When he was called upon to make an assessment of the March 30 hartal in Delhi, when 14 people were killed, the principal criticism of the participants which Gandhi made was that a crowd had assembled at the railway station demanding the release of some men who had been arrested. As he wrote on April 3:

> "... the conduct was premature, because the committee contemplated in the Pledge had not decided upon the disobedience of order that might be issued by Magistrates under the Riot Act... The essence of the Pledge is to invite imprisonment and until the committee decides upon the breach of the Riot Act, it is the duty of satyagrahis to obey, without making the slightest ado, the

magisterial order to disperse etc. and thus to demonstrate their law-abiding nature." (Gandhi M.K. 1965: vol 15: 174-176)

Three days later, on April 5, when Gandhi wrote his "Directions to Demonstrators" taking part in the April 6 hartal, one paragraph stated:

"It is the duty of the demonstrators to obey and carry out all police instructions as it is as yet no part of the movement to offer civil dis-obedience against police orders that may be given in connection with demonstrations, processions organised by Satyagraha Associations". (Gandhi M.K. 1965: vol 15: 177-178)

It is ironic that the one clear breach of these instructions by a member of the Sabha was that by Gandhi himself, when he refused on the train to Delhi on April 9 to obey an order issued by the police, restricting him to the Bombay Presidency. Gandhi commented in a statement released the same day, "I had no hesitation in saying to the officer who served the order on me that I was bound in virtue of my Pledge to disregard it, which I have done... It was galling for me to remain free whilst the Rowlatt legislation disfigured the Statute book." (Gandhi M.K. 1965: vol 15: 207-209)

While this assertion that he was bound by his Pledge to refuse to obey the order was repeated by him subsequently, and I have not seen it challenged by any commentator, Gandhi was bound by his Pledge, as we have seen, not to disobey any police instruction or orders until authorised to do so by the Satyagraha committee. This "Himalayan miscalculation" appears to have been a headstrong action, an impulsive breaking of his own carefully constructed rules for the conduct of the Rowlatt Satyagraha.

If their leader, who was of course the author of the instructions coming from the committee of the Satyagraha Sabha, felt free to extend the grounds for civil disobedience suddenly and unilaterally on April 9, no wonder this sowed confusion in the minds of his immediate supporters, and gave the impression to a wider public that now was the moment for general disobedience to take place. It is questionable whether Gandhi actually intended to launch mass civil disobedience by refusing the order to turn back. As Gandhi had clearly stated, the people were in no measure ready for general disobedience according to the rules of satyagraha.

This was why he had restricted civil disobedience to individuals and to breaking the press laws. But the careful distinction he had made between the pledged satyagrahis who were to engage in civil disobedience and the mass of non-pledged supporters who were to support quiet and disciplined protests, like the hartal, swiftly broke down. It seems, then, that Gandhi's miscalculation was not, as he said, that he "launched civil disobedience prematurely", but that he implied by offering himself for arrest on April 9 and breaking the careful restriction of the grounds for civil disobedience which he himself had devised, that the time for general or mass disobedience had arrived.

In 1941 Gandhi published a pamphlet, which in one part attempted a classification of the functions of civil disobedience. The second function, he said, had been demonstrated at Champaran in 1917 when he disobeyed an order externing him from this district of Bihar.

> "It (civil disobedience) can be offered without regard to effect, though aimed at a particular wrong or evil, by way of self-immolation in order to rouse local consciousness or conscience. Such was the case in Champaran when I offered Civil Disobedience without any regard to the effect and well knowing that even the people might remain apathetic. " (Gandhi MK, 1945: 35-36)

It seems Gandhi attempted to repeat the tactic two years later in 1919 on a national scale, with disastrous results. He appears to have taken on the hero's part in a moment of impetuosity, which caused him to throw over all his earlier careful calculations.

Gandhi also said that his "Himalayan miscalculation" lay "in trying to let civil disobedience take the people by storm". (Gandhi M.K. 1965: vol 15: 436) This reflects in a general way what happened. He had been talking in his Swadeshi and Hindu-Muslim Unity leaflets, both published on April 8, the day before his arrest, about people's thoughts undergoing "a revolution in a single moment" when their religious sense is awakened; and also about "a wave of satyagraha ... sweeping over the whole country". He may have been deceived by his own rhetoric into believing that satyagraha had taken root more deeply than it had.

In addition, in planning the April 6 hartal he had prescribed three forms of action. The first was the 24-hour fast; the second was the closing of businesses and the third was to hold public meetings and processions all over India.

> "The third suggestion is to hold in every hamlet of India public meetings, protesting-against the Rowlatt legislation and asking the Secretary of State for India to repeal that legislation. "
> (Gandhi M.K. 1965: vol 15: 161-162)

A number of these meetings and processions did take place on the day of the Rowlatt hartal, mainly in the urban areas of India. After Gandhi's arrest, the closing of businesses and staging of marches and protest meetings continued, leading in some places to the breakdown of nonviolent discipline, which so appalled him. Possibly these traditional political activities would not have led to violence if he had obeyed the order restricting him to Bombay; but having decided in so precipitous a manner to go ahead with individual civil disobedience himself, a programme of public street demonstrations was disastrous.

Gandhi quickly decided not repeat his mistake. When a British member of the Satyagraha Sabha executive, B.G. Horniman, was deported a month later, he successfully forbade street demonstrations. Later, in July, when he was planning to resume individual civil disobedience against the Rowlatt Act by offering himself as the first to be imprisoned, he again explicitly forbade public demonstrations to be staged in protest. (Gandhi M.K. 1965: vol 15: 207-209) Subsequently, Gandhi tried to keep civil disobedience separate from a programme of street demonstrations.

Thus Gandhi's "Himalayan miscalculation" on April 9, 1919, was not that he misjudged the mood of the Indian people and launched mass or individual civil disobedience prematurely. The elaborate restrictions he had placed on the conduct of a civil disobedience campaign by confining it to laws which could be broken only by individuals at the direction of a committee, showed that he was well aware of the dangers. What seems to have happened is that a miscalculation on his part by offering spontaneous personal civil disobedience against a police restriction order, breached his own carefully prepared plan of action. It helped precipitate rioting in a number of centres by people aroused and prepared by the mass demonstrations staged during the Rowlatt hartal on April 6.

What these events also showed is the difficulty he was having in organising satyagraha on a national scale.

The second phase of the Rowlatt Satyagraha

When he suspended individual civil disobedience just over a week later on April 18, Gandhi insisted that the Rowlatt Satyagraha would be continued. Mass participation in the campaign ended as the protests set off by Gandhi's arrest gradually petered out. But the Satyagraha Sabha went on to carry out a revised programme of activities during April, May and June. This was the second phase of the satyagraha. It consisted of attempts to calm the situation in areas where order had broken down; to put greater efforts into teaching the principles of satyagraha on a wide scale; and to demonstrate that the satyagraha movement was a responsible movement which should not be identified with the outbreaks of violence. At the same time, Gandhi's objective was to prepare simultaneously for a renewal of civil disobedience against the Rowlatt Act, and to engage in correspondence and discussions on all these matters with the Raj as part of the ongoing satyagraha.

Gandhi's self-confidence and even temerity in believing that he could pursue such diverse objectives is extraordinary. One effect was to confuse British officialdom who welcomed his support in restoring public order but were astounded by his effrontery in promising to take up civil disobedience again.

On June 18, 1919, Gandhi announced that individual civil disobedience would be resumed in July, and he proceeded with preparations – including, for example, his speech at Nadiad in Kheda district where he spoke about his "Himalayan miscalculation". However, within a few weeks, he felt able to claim that his correspondence and occasional meetings with the Governor of the Bombay Presidency and with the Viceroy had borne some fruit. Accordingly, he suspended his proposals for the renewal of civil disobedience again on July 21. (Brown 1972: 175-185)

The main events of this second phase began on April 14 immediately following the riots in Ahmedabad, when Gandhi insisted that the duty of satyagrahis was to help the authorities restore order. (Gandhi M.K.: vol 15: 219, 245) Over subsequent days, he deliberately resisted the temptation to criticise the military for their excesses during the period of martial law in the city. He felt he had a higher duty to support the authorities at such a moment. (Gandhi M.K. 1965: vol 15: 226, 228) He also placed a strong emphasis on the Swadeshi and Hindu-Muslim Unity constructive campaigns he had launched on April 3 and issued a series of leaflets explaining the principles of satyagraha. These leaflets were used as a basis for their campaigning by Sabha volunteers.[21] (Gandhi M.K. 1965: vol 15: 239, 384, 437) Their activities were mainly confined to the Bombay presidency.

The Delhi Branch of the Sabha

In Delhi, the Satyagraha Sabha branch had staged its Rowlatt hartal a week early on March 30. Confrontation with the authorities on that day led to a number of fatal shootings, but the local Satyagraha Sabha under the leadership of Swami Shradhanand managed to contain the explosion of anti-British feeling which followed and staged a second peaceful hartal on April 6. (Ferrell 1971: 189-235) They appealed, however, to Gandhi himself to come to Delhi to assist them in disciplining the crowds and in educating them in the principles of satyagraha. On April 3, Gandhi released a letter to the press commenting on the coming all-India hartal in the light of what had just happened in Delhi. "The Delhi tragedy", he said, "imposes an added responsibility upon satyagrahis of steeling their hearts and going on with their struggle..." Broadly, he accepted Shradhanand's published account that the authorities had over-reacted, but he criticised the Sabha for not dispersing the crowds after it was ordered by the authorities. He also, publicly congratulated Shradhanand and "the people of Delhi" "for exemplary patience" and for the sacrifice of "such innocent blood as Delhi gave". (Gandhi M.K. 1965: vol 15: 172)

---

21. A photograph of the sixteenth satyagraha leaflet issued in Bombay from April 16 onwards appears in Tendulkar's biography (Tendulkar 1960: vol 1: 257). Eleven of these satyagraha leaflets discussed the Horniman deportation.

Privately, he wrote to moderate Indian leaders like Srinivasi Sastri and Pandit Malaviya arguing that the methods used by the Delhi police and the consequent sacrifices, demanded that they speak out more strongly against the Rowlatt Act. (Gandhi M.K. 1965: vol 15: 173, 174)

It was while he was on his way to Delhi on April 9 in answer to Shradhanand's request, that the authorities prevented him from entering the city. In Delhi, this set off a further hartal and series of demonstrations which lasted for over a week until April 18 – even though Gandhi himself was released from police custody as he returned to Bombay on April 10. Two more riots occurred in Delhi and, in all, over the three-week period of unrest from March 30, nineteen people died. (Ferrell 1971)

Before he knew what had happened in Delhi, or in Ahmedabad or the Punjab, Gandhi was faced with the riot in Bombay. On April 11, on his return to the city, he issued a "Warning to Satyagrahis and Sympathisers" published as the third Satyagraha leaflet. In it, he criticised Bombay supporters of the satyagraha demonstrations for obstructing trams, stone-throwing and demanding the release of arrested people. He went on to say that "satyagrahis", meaning members of the Sabha who had taken the Satyagraha Pledge, were responsible for the conduct of sympathisers who joined the demonstrations. If it proved impossible to prevent "the slightest violence from our side", then it might be necessary to abandon the satyagraha in its existing form or greatly restrict it. (Gandhi M.K. 1965: vol 15: 211-212)

On April 12, before he returned to Ahmedabad and saw the destruction there, he issued the following "Instructions Regarding Satyagraha":

"In order that satyagraha may have full play and a chance of permeating the masses, in my humble opinion, the following instructions should be STRICTLY obeyed. Some of the items may require change later. The rest are inviolable principles of satyagraha.

"No processions.

No organised demonstrations.

No hartals on any account whatsoever without previous instructions of the committee.

All police orders to be implicitly obeyed.

No violence.

No stone-throwing.

No obstruction of tram-cars or traffic.

No pressure to be exercised against anyone.

"AT PUBLIC MEETINGS

No clapping of hands

No demonstrations of approval or disapproval.

No cries of 'Shame!'

No cheers.

Perfect stillness.

Perfect obedience to instructions of volunteers or management.

MOHANDAS K. GANDHI"

These strictures of course should not be taken out of the context of the complete breakdown of discipline following the Rowlatt hartal, which Gandhi by April 12 was becoming aware of. They illustrate how he saw a direct link between conventional political partisanship and antagonism in public meetings and demonstrations, and the descent into lawlessness. This was the antithesis of satyagraha.

When the Delhi branch of the Sabha, in the midst of the second upheaval provoked by Gandhi's arrest, read Gandhi's "Warning to Satyagrahis and Sympathisers" of April 11, they wrote to him through Shradhanand asking for clarification. Were members of the Sabha really responsible for all actions taken by people who joined their demonstrations, including (i) those who were non-satyagrahis who were provoked by police violence into retaliation and (ii) those who joined the demonstrations and actively opposed the leadership of the Sabha members? If any violence whatsoever stemming from either of these groups caused injury to others, had Gandhi really meant to say that the satyagrahis themselves were responsible for that "sinful injury"? (Gandhi M.K. 1965: vol 15: 502-503) Gandhi replied uncompromisingly on April 17 stating, "I... hold that we are just as responsible for the action of non-satyagrahis when they act with us as we are for our own". (Gandhi M.K. 1965: vol 15: 238-240)

The following day on April 18, Gandhi announced the "temporary suspension" of the programme of individual civil disobedience against the Press Laws and of his own plans to challenge his restriction order. However, the Delhi branch of the Sabha had disbanded the day before and burned its membership list. Faced with what Ferrell calls, "the complete loss of control, the violence and the actions of the government..." a general feeling had grown in the city that things had gone too far and "They began to doubt the validity of mass agitation because such agitations invariably led to violence." (Ferrell 1971: 232) Swami Shradhanand wrote to Gandhi withdrawing from the Satyagraha Sabha on May 3. (Brown, 1972: 184n)

Lahore and then Amritsar

Furthermore in the Punjab, according to one commentator, its principal city, Lahore was "ripe for revolution" in 1919 (Kumar 1971: 275):

> "All that was required in April 1919 to launch a popular movement against the British government was an issue which would provide a channel of expression for the discontents which affected various classes and communities in Lahore. By initiating a satyagraha against the Rowlatt Act, Gandhi provided such an issue, and he thereby set afoot a movement whose intensity surprised the local administration no less than it surprised the local leaders of Lahore. " (Kumar 1971: 297)

For four days, from April 11 to 14, control of the city passed out of the hands of the British and into those of a People's Committee. Martial law was declared and order restored by troops, with the city being placed under the direction of a military administrator. More than thirty people were killed by police and army units firing into crowds.

It is Amritsar, however, 30 miles from Lahore, which is most associated with the Punjab atrocities by the British in April 1919, which fuelled the later nationalist movement. The forcible removal of Gandhi from the train, coupled with the arrest and deportation of two local leaders, set off severe rioting in Amritsar, which led to the murder of several Europeans.

In retaliation, troops were sent in to teach the citizens of Amritsar a lesson. On April 12, a proclamation was issued prohibiting all gatherings in the city, but this was read in English and probably not widely understood. On the following day, a meeting of about 10,000 people assembled in the Jallianwala Bagh, a large open air meeting place, was fired on by troops without warning. Under the command of an Englishman, General Dyer, fifty soldiers fired into the crowd for 10 minutes at a range of 100 yards. (Payne 1969: 337-339) The official figure of deaths is 379, but that is disputed. As a nationalist history records:

"When Dyer withdrew after all his ammunition was exhausted, he left about 1,000 dead and several thousand wounded." (Chandra, Tripathi and De 1972: 130)

The troops turned round and marched off without giving any thought to the wounded: Dyer is said to have commented that it was not his job to care for them. (Hardiman 2018: 188-191)

Martial law was declared in the Punjab on April 15 and continued for nearly two months until June 11. During this lengthy period, a regime of deliberate humiliation was imposed on Amritsar and other parts of the Punjab. The most notorious abuse of power was the "crawling order" – Indians who passed the spot in Amritsar where a European woman had been severely beaten, were forced to crawl on their bellies. If they refused, they were publicly whipped. Other abuses included public floggings, numerous summary trials, dubious convictions and punitive sentences under martial law; cruel punishments like the skipping order; the commandeering of Indian-owned vehicles and other property, and providing them to Europeans for their use; compelling thousands of students to walk 16 miles a day for roll-calls; the arrest and detention of 500 students and professors; forcing school children aged between 5 and 7 to attend parades and salute the flag; and rigid press censorship. (Tendulkar 1960: vol 1: 257-259)

The "Punjab events" of 1919 occurred at the periphery of the Gandhian movement, where Gandhi's personal influence had been least felt. There was no branch of the Satyagraha Sabha in the Punjab and Gandhi had never visited the province. The pretext for the Governor of the Punjab suppressing local political leaders was the taking up in Amritsar, Lahore and elsewhere on April 6 of the national Rowlatt hartal, but it was later claimed by Gandhi that his satyagraha movement had nothing to do with the explosion of feeling which took place in the province. This view has been broadly accepted by historians subsequently.

The causes of the "Punjab events" were grievances specific to the province. If the Amritsar massacre had taken place in Bombay or Ahmedabad, where Gandhi's ideas were much more widely known; moreover, if the victims of this calculated butchery had been pledged satyagrahis, fully committed to the campaign of nonviolence which Gandhi was promoting, then the consequences for the development of the Gandhian programme would have been far-reaching. As it was, political conditions in the Indian sub-continent were diverse, British governors of the Indian provinces were allowed considerable autonomy and few were as inflexibly disciplinarian as the Governor of the Punjab, Sir Michael O'Dwyer. Moreover, as a result of the press censorship, it was some weeks before Indian nationalists outside the Punjab were able to grasp what had happened in Amritsar on April 13 and what was still going on under martial law.

As reports of what was happening in the Punjab began to seep out, these seemed to confirm in many nationalist minds the argument Gandhi had made to justify the Rowlatt Satyagraha; namely, that the reform programme which the Government was introducing to increase Indian representation at municipal, provincial and national levels was meaningless while the Raj retained such fundamentally contemptuous attitudes to expressions of popular Indian opinion and continued to exercise arbitrary power against the Indian people when they defied its dictates.

Broadening the terms of the Pledge

At the end of May – after the Satyagraha Sabha in Bombay had staged a peaceful hartal in protest against the deportation of its English vice-chairman, B.G. Horniman[22] – Gandhi called a meeting of Sabha representatives from across India to discuss extending the grounds for civil disobedience to "The Punjab Matter". Their objectives should be to press the government to stage, firstly, an impartial inquiry into the Punjab disturbance and the administration of martial law and, secondly, to empower an independent tribunal to review and revise the sentences handed out under martial law. (Gandhi M.K. 1965: vol 15: 332-333) In the middle of June, he informed the Viceroy and the Secretary of State for India in London, E.S. Montagu, that he would be resuming individual civil disobedience in July in order to secure (i) the withdrawal of the Rowlatt Act, (ii) the appointment of an inquiry into the Punjab events and (iii) the release of the editor of a Lahore-based nationalist paper, Babu Kalinath Roy, who had been jailed for two years' "rigorous imprisonment" for his writings on the Rowlatt events. (Gandhi M.K. 1965: vol 15: 377-378, 387)

In drafting the Rowlatt Satyagraha pledge, Gandhi had given the Sabha committee authority to extend the range of laws against which civil disobedience would be offered. But he had not allowed for increasing the number of issues, which would justify civil disobedience. Gandhi readily admitted that, in bringing in the question of the Punjab, he was going beyond the original objectives of the Sabha. He was able nonetheless to win support for this expansion from the May 28 Sabha meeting. (Gandhi M.K. 1965: vol 15: 332-333)

Gandhi's aim in launching the Rowlatt Satyagraha had been to challenge the Raj for retaining to itself its arbitrary wartime powers in peacetime and for its contempt for Indian opinion. It was therefore consistent for him to extend the campaign to questioning the use by the Raj of arbitrary power in the Punjab. Moreover, as Judith Brown points out, by taking up the Punjab question Gandhi was able to move on to familiar ground:

> "On the Punjab issue Gandhi repeated the tactics he had employed in Champaran and Kaira. Simultaneously with his criticisms on specific cases he campaigned for a government enquiry..." (Brown 1972: 233)

22. Horniman as editor of the Bombay Chronicle had defied press censorship by publishing accounts of British repression in the Punjab.

But even though the Punjab issue – as a "real" grievance – came to assume more importance to Gandhi and to the national movement than the Rowlatt question (which was "abstract", given that the powers given to the government by the Act were never used), Gandhi did not easily drop the Rowlatt campaign. Rather than suspend the campaign indefinitely, his plans for a renewal of individual civil disobedience were detailed elaborately in a new set of "Instructions to Satyagrahis" issued to secretaries of the Sabha on June 30. He had already secured for himself, in the Bombay Presidency, "the power to select the exact moment of starting civil disobedience and the satyagrahis who should take part in it and to decide upon the manner of offering civil disobedience". (Gandhi M.K. 1965: vol 15: 364-365)

His new plans envisaged that he alone would launch the action by breaking the restriction order confining him to the Presidency. Because entering the Punjab would have seemed too "theatrical" and might have threatened renewed violence, he would break the order by entering Madras Province to the south. (Gandhi M.K. 1965: vol 15: 430, 424-425; and vol 16: 3-4) As with the Horniman hartal in May, there were to be no demonstrations at all when he was arrested. No further acts of civil disobedience by other individuals would be undertaken for at least a month, and then only if "full peace" had been observed over that period. This programme was to be confined to the Bombay Presidency.

However, he did write to the Madras branch of the Sabha suggesting that they should adopt a similar strategy. In Bombay, Gandhi selected five "independent self-sustained centres, each seeking cooperation with... advice from the rest, with none being under the orders of any". He named the leaders who from these centres were to operate a "constructive programme" to discipline and prepare individuals for civil disobedience. Moreover, his effort to control tightly the form of the action is evident again. No more than two at a time were to offer civil disobedience from any one centre, nor should civil disobedience be commenced simultaneously at all the centres. (Gandhi M.K. 1965: vol 15: 412-416)

How Gandhi Addressed his Opponents

In Champaran and Kheda, Gandhi had demonstrated that a key part of his method was to engage openly and respectfully with his opponents. When local officialdom tried to obstruct him he stood up to them fearlessly; and he was also able to rely on his reputation with the Raj and its more senior officials for some protection or even intervention in support of his cause. When he launched the Rowlatt campaign challenging the Raj itself, he took the same approach – only this time he was engaged not only with the Viceroy and provincial and local officials, but also with the Secretary of State for India in London. He wanted the Raj to appreciate his sincerity and hear his argument.

A new liberal Secretary of State, Edwin Montagu, had visited India in 1917 to assess what reforms might be introduced in recognition of its contribution to the war effort in Europe. At that time, Montagu met various national leaders, including Gandhi. (Gandhi, R. 2007:192; Nanda 1989: 165) From July 1918, when the reform proposals were published, Gandhi was in occasional correspondence with Montagu and with the Viceroy, Lord Chelmsford, as well as the Viceroy's secretary, J.L. Maffey. He also secured meetings with the Viceroy himself and the Governor of Bombay, George Lloyd.

Chelmsford appeared to accept that Gandhi, despite his readiness to pursue civil disobedience, was a useful ally. He had supported the war effort and seemed genuinely opposed to violence. On 5 March 1919, Gandhi was in Delhi to inform the Viceroy about the formation of the Satyagraha Sabha and its proposal to pursue civil disobedience. However, the Raj took advice from many quarters and Chelmsford remained persuaded that some additional emergency powers were needed. A few weeks later, on 22 March, it became known that the Viceroy had signed one of the Rowlatt Bills into law. (Brown 1972: 168, 174, 178-180; Gandhi, R. 2007: 207)

This rebuff was of course the signal for Gandhi to plan for the April 6 hartal and the start of individual civil disobedience. His removal from the train on his way back to Delhi then set off the rioting in Gujarat, the Punjab and elsewhere.

Immediately on his return to Bombay, Gandhi was released and found himself confronted by a stone-throwing crowd being charged by mounted police. He went straight to complain to the Bombay police commissioner, Griffith, about the police conduct. In response, Griffith told him what had happened in Ahmedabad and that he held Gandhi responsible. Gandhi replied that if he had been allowed to go to the Punjab there would have been peace there and in Gujarat. But he added that he would consider suspending the campaign.

In Ahmedabad, he went straight to see the commissioner, Pratt, who was well known to him from the Kheda satyagraha. Pratt was "in a state of rage". Gandhi expressed regret for the violence and said that martial law was not necessary. Extraordinarily, when Gandhi offered to co-operate with Pratt to calm the violence, Pratt agreed to suspend martial law. This episode is a straightforward example of power being passed from the Raj to an Indian leader, or at least shared. Gandhi was allowed to address a public meeting the following day, where he spoke of his shame at the actions of his followers and said he would undertake a three-day fast. (Gandhi, R. 2007: 209-210)

Gandhi's focus for the next two months, particularly in Gujarat, was on promoting his satyagraha method, including constructive projects like the Swadeshi cloth campaign and Hindu-Muslim unity. On April 30, he wrote confidently to the Governor of Bombay inviting him to sign the Swadeshi pledge and a week later to the Viceroy's Secretary with the same request. (Dalal 1971: 23) He also cabled the Viceroy to protest about the floggings in the Punjab, and promised to resume individual civil disobedience when the time was right. By his work in helping the authorities bring the situation in Bombay under control, as well as in Ahmedabad, and by the restraint with which the hartal against Horniman's deportation was carried out, Gandhi imagined that he was getting through to the government the difference between satyagraha and conventional political agitation. Also, typically, respecting the Raj's estimate that it was under pressure, he waited until June 18 when martial law had been withdrawn in the Punjab, before announcing the renewal of civil disobedience. (Brown 1972: 177-178; Tendulkar, 1960: vol 1: 258)

Time after time in his speeches and interviews he distinguished between civil disobedience and criminal disobedience. Civil disobedience was a branch of satyagraha, and satyagraha was the ancient law of India which the Indian people were rediscovering. On many occasions, Gandhi argued that satyagraha provided the only possible restraining force which was preventing Indians from exploding in violence. He appears to have convinced himself that the uprisings following the Rowlatt hartal were inevitable, and that satyagraha and civil disobedience itself had had a slight restraining influence. Gandhi engaged in regular correspondence in this vein with the Viceroy, his Private Secretary and with the Secretary of State for India in London. (Gandhi M.K. 1965: vol 15: 218-220, 274-275, 334-335, 367-368, 377-378, 387, 397-398)

On July 12, he met with the governor of Bombay, George Lloyd, to discuss his upcoming campaign of civil disobedience. He had already gained the impression from the British officials that the Rowlatt Act was to be withdrawn and appears to have received information about a Punjab Inquiry and a resolution to the Roy case too. Gandhi made it clear to the governor that if the Viceroy publicly asked him to call off the renewed campaign of civil disobedience, he would do so. This offer appears to have been unconditional. (Gandhi M.K. 1965: vol 15: 425; Brown 1972: 178)

His intentions in giving the Viceroy this apparently easy let-out are not recorded – but it seems likely that he was hoping to establish further his integrity as a satyagrahi, one who would not embarrass the authorities at a time of instability in the subcontinent. Thus when the Viceroy did send Gandhi a letter giving him a grave warning of the consequences to public security if he went ahead, Gandhi on July 21 duly announced publicly that he was suspending civil disobedience again. He added to his statement news of two successes: the sentence of the jailed Lahore editor, Kalinath Roy, had been reduced from 2 years to 3 months; and he had received an assurance that a Committee of Inquiry into the Punjab events would be appointed. (Gandhi M.K. 1965: vol 15: 468-471)

The Rowlatt Act was never withdrawn, however, and Gandhi was to look a little foolish for this climb-down. His principal objectives at this time seem to have been both to restore his credit with the Raj after the trauma of April and, equally, to oblige the Viceroy to recognise the continuing strength of Indian feeling against both the Rowlatt Act and the handling of the Punjab events. He was also attempting to instil a sounder grasp of the principles of satyagraha among his supporters. It was a difficult balancing act, particularly when the dangers of losing control of a renewed civil disobedience programme – his trump card – were so great.

A remarkable tribute to his skill as a tactician and to the uncertainty his new political method of satyagraha had sown in the minds of the British rulers, was that he, the spark for a widespread rebellion against the Raj in April, had been permitted to go free when he threatened to launch the movement again in July. Gandhi was undoubtedly seen by the British as a "special case", not bound by the rules normally governing the treatment of political agitators – internment, deportation, jail or hanging. At one level, this was because, as the Rowlatt hartal had demonstrated, he already commanded widespread popular enthusiasm at all levels of Indian society and it would be risky to move against him. But, at another level, he pitched his objectives so close to the middle ground of nationalist opinion and he argued so consistently, and demonstrated by his actions, that his radical method of civil disobedience should display the highest principles of citizenship and be conducted with the utmost respect for authority – that it was less easy to isolate him and portray him as a wholly irresponsible extremist or rebel.

Moreover, the Raj's senior officials were divided on how to deal with him, and he appears to have won a sympathetic response from the India Office in London. In September, Montagu, the Secretary of State, privately cabled Chelmsford that "he had never heard of a case where the appearance of Gandhi has not had a tranquillising effect" and that Gandhi to his knowledge was a man "who always kept his word". (Brown, 1972: 180; Gandhi, R. 2007: 211)

The Collapse of the Satyagraha Sabha

The second suspension of civil disobedience in July, however, caused ructions inside the Satyagraha Sabha. Judith Brown reports:

"After Gandhi's second suspension of civil disobedience satyagrahi critics became more vehement, and at a Bombay meeting of about 200 of them on 26 July he was mercilessly cross-examined on his decision. One anonymous correspondent ... called Gandhi 'disappointing as a leader', and said, 'I fall at your feet to resume the vow. Or else leave your leadership'." (Brown 1972: 182)

Hundreds of resignations had been received from different parts of India and the Sabha was disintegrating. Yet Gandhi, as late as July, had written to a member of the Madras branch, suggesting that they establish the Sabha as a permanent organisation with a broad programme of objectives:

"I see that we will have to extend the scope of satyagraha activity to all spheres of life and to all other questions. I am seriously thinking of altering the constitution of the Sabha and make [sic] it a permanent body." (Gandhi M.K. 1965: vol 15: 429-430)

At the end of July, this was no longer possible. The Satyagraha Sabha had served a useful purpose in co-ordinating the April hartal and sustaining a much-reduced programme for several months afterwards. It had also enabled Gandhi to get his ideas across for the first-time on a national scale; and helped him incidentally to acquire control in Bombay and Gujarat of two newspapers. It had established for him, too, links with most of the national leaders in other parts of the country, a number of whom were later to become his followers or his allies. But with the virtual demise of the Sabha itself in July 1919, Gandhi was left again, in Judith Brown's phrase, "isolated at the centre of institutional politics".

Gandhi's Refusal to Give Up

Even so, Gandhi still did not abandon his campaign against the Rowlatt Act. Having suspended civil disobedience for a second time and effectively lost the Satyagraha Sabha, he tried to shift the burden of leading opposition to the Act on to the moderate politicians who had pressed him to call off radical action. (Gandhi M.K. 1965: vol 16: 6, 16) In turn, they accused him of not having fully exploited constitutional methods of protest.

In response, Gandhi supported a Home Rule League petition against the Act in October. (Gandhi M.K. 1965: vol 16: 236) He also organised his own petition through *Navajivan* in November 1919. (Gandhi M.K. 1965: vol 16: 274, 544-545) But he refused to accept that it was enough that the Act was being held in reserve and unused. He insisted that through the power of satyagraha it would be withdrawn before its three-year period was completed.

Gandhi was reluctant to ask the Viceroy to remove the restriction order confining him to the Bombay Presidency because he was planning to break this order if the time came to renew civil disobedience. (Gandhi M.K. 1965: vol 16: 3-4) When in September 1919 he felt obliged to ask permission to go to the Punjab to investigate conditions there himself, and within three weeks the Raj granted his request, he was quite explicit that he was sacrificing his means of civil disobedience:

> "...So long as the Rowlatt Act remains on the statute book the release order can be no joy for me. In the internment order I had a ready-made weapon for offering civil resistance."

He went on:

> "I hear people saying that satyagraha is as dead as Queen Anne and that Mr Montagu will never repeal the Rowlatt Act, although he is quite sure that the Act will never be enforced. Those who make the first statement do not know what satyagraha is and how it works. Those who make the second do not know the power of satyagraha. He who runs may see that satyagraha is slowly but surely pervading the land. So far as Mr Montagu's supposed declaration is concerned, the strongest man of South Africa had to yield to that matchless force... General Smuts... said that, although the Transvaal Asiatic Act would not be enforced, he would never formally repeal it, but in 1914 he revealed his strength by repealing that Act... I have not the slightest doubt that Mr Montagu and the Viceroy will yield to the same ancient force and repeal the Rowlatt Act long before the expiry of its time limit. But whether they do or not the lives of the satyagrahis are dedicated to securing among other things the repeal of that Act." (Gandhi M.K. 1965: vol 16: 239-241, 293)

Again we see Gandhi's ultimately religious concept of satyagraha, a force acting on society in mysterious ways.

In the world's terms, October 15 1919, when at Gandhi's request the Viceroy lifted the restriction order confining him to the Bombay Presidency, should probably be seen as the final conclusion of the Rowlatt Satyagraha. However, in April 1920 Gandhi launched National Week from April 6 to April 13, which was to commemorate annually thereafter the Rowlatt hartal and the Amritsar massacres, and to signify the moment when a new phase of the nationalist struggle under his leadership was launched. He also contemplated renewing civil disobedience against the Act. (Dalal 1971: 30n; Tendulkar 1960: vol 1: 302)

For the rest of his life, he fasted for 24 hours on April 6 and April 13. (Dalal 1971: 204) From Gandhi's perspective, a satyagrahi never gives up, particularly when he or she has taken a vow, and is never disheartened. By 1922, when the Act's three-year term lapsed, the Rowlatt Satyagraha effectively in his eyes was merged into other more immediate struggles.

Conclusion

As a mass movement the Rowlatt struggle lasted for less than two months in March and April 1919. (Bondurant 1958: 73) Even in that short time, it showed Gandhi's immense creativity and confidence in striking out on his own through the Satyagraha Sabha. He declared that he would lead an unprecedented civil disobedience campaign despite strong disagreement from fellow nationalists; identified the Rowlatt Bills as the issue on which to do this and proposed suitable "civil" actions with which to challenge them; planned carefully how to prevent civil disobedience leading to unrest; and re-invented the hartal in a form that reflected his satyagraha philosophy. Events did not go as he had hoped, but he succeeded throughout in keeping in touch with the officials of the Raj.

Despite the damage unleashed by his "Himalayan" blunder, the Rowlatt campaign demonstrated that Gandhi could trigger an upsurge of feeling across much of India. Perhaps just as important, it showed in the suspension of civil disobedience and the ending of public demonstrations that he had the determination to bring the movement under control when it did not develop as he had intended. Particularly in the Bombay Presidency, especially Gujarat, he had the ability to do this. Thus Gandhi also demonstrated a certain authority to the other political leaders in India and suggested his unique capacity to assume leadership of a popular movement as part of the national struggle.

Brown, noting the multitude of grievances which moved different groups across India to support the Rowlatt hartal, comments:

> "The Rowlatt satyagraha showed Gandhi as an all-India leader of immense potential. His personality, his ideology, his novel approach to politics, and his technique of satyagraha enabled his campaign to become the focus for multifarious local grievances and gave him access to the power they generated." (Brown 1972: 187)

Owen's conclusion, as we saw earlier, is that Gandhi recognised through the Rowlatt Satyagraha the impossibility of coordinating renewed countrywide agitation by personal face-to-face leadership, and became committed to more elaborate organisation and preparation. (Owen 1971) Gandhi himself concluded that he would have to train a team of committed co-workers closely identified with himself and his philosophy. It also seems probable that with a secondary leadership of reliable co-workers, he saw himself as better able to centralise a future struggle under his personal direction.

SUMMARY

1. When called upon to launch a national campaign against the Rowlatt Bills, Gandhi formed his own organisation, the Satyagraha Sabha, because "all hope of the existing organisations adopting a novel weapon like Satyagraha seemed to me to be in vain."

2. The principal means which Gandhi used to bind the members of the Sabha together and to discipline them for the struggle, was a religious vow. He saw this as a direct opportunity for those taking the satyagraha pledge to commit themselves to a new form of political life. He later

broadened the scope of the Rowlatt pledges to allow people unwilling to engage in civil disobedience to be involved too.

3. Because he was determined to launch a disciplined campaign of civil disobedience against the Rowlatt Bills, Gandhi refused to contemplate "collective" civil disobedience; but restricted the action to "individual" civil disobedience by signatories to the pledge.

4. Against criticism that signatories could not bind their consciences to act at the decision of the Sabha committee, Gandhi argued that the vow contained a conscience clause, that is, the commitment to "truth". The clause allowed them to opt out if they wished, without breaking their word. This reliance on the Sabha committee, however, helped to establish the practice of Gandhi's followers effectively surrendering their judgement to him, because of his "superior wisdom".

5. Against criticism that it was legitimate to commit civil disobedience only against the Act in question, the Rowlatt Act, Gandhi argued that civil disobedience could be extended reasonably to "bad" laws such as the Press Acts, the Salt Laws or certain Land Revenue laws; but not to "good" laws of benefit to society.

6. When only a few hundred people had signed the satyagraha pledge Gandhi added a second category of action to the Rowlatt Satyagraha. This was the nationwide hartal, a genuinely mass action involving (as he envisaged it) a day of religious observance, fasting, closing down of businesses, processions and meetings.

7. Effectively, organisation of the hartal across the country was handed at short notice to members of the Sabha and other nationalist leaders who were not necessarily versed in organising mass nonviolent street demonstrations.

8. There was no branch of the Satyagraha Sabha in the Punjab, nor were there any signatories to the pledge. The Rowlatt hartal was nonetheless supported in Lahore and Amritsar. Gandhi disclaimed responsibility when ongoing popular agitation led to martial law and brutal repression..

9. His arrest triggered uprisings in several parts of India and Gandhi suspended the programme of "individual" civil disobedience. Satyagraha volunteers, supporting the authorities in restoring law and order, were instructed by Gandhi to demonstrate the distinction between civil and criminal disobedience. Efforts to promote Swadeshi and Hindu-Muslim unity and to explain satyagraha principles were extended.

10. Gandhi's "success" in calling off the civil disobedience and calming crowds in Bombay and Ahmedabad demonstrated his determination to lead a satyagraha campaign according to his own methods and strategy, or not at all. It also showed his residual control of the movement in the Bombay Presidency.

11. Gandhi did not immediately abandon his programme for individual civil disobedience but reformulated it, proposing to begin again by challenging the order confining him to Bombay. Other individuals were selected by him to carry on the campaign after his arrest. Gandhi also secured the agreement of the Sabha to extend the grounds for civil disobedience to a government inquiry in the Punjab. When such an inquiry was announced, he responded to the Viceroy's request and called off civil disobedience again, causing the Satyagraha Sabha to collapse in dissension.

12. Pressure to call another hartal in response to the Bombay Government's expulsion of the British journalist Horniman was cautiously accepted by Gandhi. This time no processions or meetings were conducted and the action was confined to Bombay city. It passed off peacefully.

13. Operating on a national scale with the hartal and with subsequent demonstrations in a number of provinces and cities, Gandhi was inevitably less able to maintain the face-to-face dialogue with opponents he had achieved with the planters and British officials in Champaran; or with the mill-owners in Ahmedabad. With events escalating out of control quickly and his communication with the senior officials of the Raj more remote, it was difficult for him to grasp quickly what was happening when things went wrong. However, his confidence in his Rowlatt aims, thanks to careful preparation, and his determination not to compromise them or to abandon his underlying doctrine of satyagraha, enabled him

to respond quickly to events and to act decisively in co-operation with initially hostile local officials, so as to calm unrest in Bombay and Gujarat. His contacts with Montagu in London and Chelmsford in Delhi survived the breakdown of order in various cities and towns across India. Gandhi's negotiating skills appear to have been rewarded when an inquiry into the Punjab events was instituted; but he was shocked that Montagu never withdrew the Rowlatt Act.

14. Gandhi's approach to the opponent, therefore, was mainly expressed indirectly through the conduct of the satyagraha campaign itself. His emphasis on civil disobedience as a responsible method of dissent for citizens denied any other means of redress, did not persuade the Hunter Commission later when they investigated the Rowlatt events as part of their inquiry into the Punjab massacre. But the Commissioners were impressed by Gandhi's sincere effort to restore order after the rioting had stalled his satyagraha movement.

15. Even though it was critical of civil disobedience and public demonstrations, Gandhi had too much support among Indian political "moderates" on the Rowlatt and other issues for the government to move strongly against him.

16. Paradoxically, Gandhi's determination to challenge the British Raj without relying on Congress and then to call off satyagraha when events got out of hand, consolidated his position as a national leader of great originality and with an important contribution to make.

PART II

CHAPTER 4

THE PLACE OF CONSTRUCTIVE PROGRAMME

With the collapse of the Rowlatt Satyagraha in the violence which followed his arrest on the train to Delhi, Gandhi was faced with the problem which remained with him for the rest of his life – how to organise nonviolence successfully on a mass scale.

His immediate reaction was to direct his co-workers into a campaign to promote hand spinning. This seeming diversion provoked much bemusement at the time, a state of incomprehension, which persisted in varying degrees through all the years that followed as Gandhi acted to consolidate his programmes of constructive work. In 1941, Gandhi was told by some of his co-workers that they felt "the want of something from my pen showing the connection between the constructive programme and civil disobedience. " (Gandhi, M.K. 1945: 36)

In response he wrote his pamphlet called *Constructive Programme: Its Meaning And Place*, which was thoroughly revised in 1945. This pamphlet is basically a presentation of the different campaigns constituting the constructive programme in the early forties. By that time, the programme had developed far beyond the early swadeshi efforts we have noted; it included a list of eighteen items. These ranged from the long established campaigns to promote Hindu-Muslim unity, the removal of untouchability and production of khadi, to newer organising initiatives around education for village children and adults, together with campaigns to improve village sanitation and health education and projects to set up new village industries. The pamphlet also includes a summarised analysis of the relationship between civil disobedience and constructive programme, making specific reference to two of the satyagrahas we have

138

already discussed in the case studies, Champaran and Kheda. This brief analysis throws light on Gandhi's organising methods as he moved to a national scale.

Under the heading, "Place of Civil Disobedience", Gandhi writes as follows:

"I have said in these pages that Civil Disobedience is not absolutely necessary to win freedom through purely non-violent effort, if the co-operation of the whole nation is secured in the constructive programme. But such good luck rarely favours nations or individuals. Therefore, it is necessary to know the place of Civil Disobedience in a nation-wide non-violent effort.

"It has three definite functions:

1. It can be effectively offered for the redress of a local wrong.

2. It can be offered without regard to effect, though aimed at a particular wrong or evil, by way of self-immolation in order to rouse local consciousness or conscience. Such was the case in Champaran when I offered Civil Disobedience without any regard to the effect and well knowing that even the people might remain apathetic. That it proved otherwise may be taken, according to taste, as God's grace or a stroke of good luck.

3. In the place of full response to constructive effort, it can be offered as it was in 1941. Though it was a contribution to and part of the battle for freedom, it was purposely centred round a particular issue, i.e. free speech. Civil disobedience can never be directed for a general cause such as for Independence. The issue must be definite and capable of being clearly understood and within the power of the opponent to yield. This method properly applied must lead to the final goal.

"I have not examined here the full scope and possibilities of Civil Disobedience. I have touched enough of it to enable the reader to understand the connection between constructive programme and Civil Disobedience. In the first two cases, no elaborate constructive programme was or could be necessary. But when Civil Disobedience is itself devised to the attainment of

Independence, previous preparation is necessary, and it has to be backed by the visible and conscious effort of those who are engaged in the battle. Civil disobedience is thus a stimulation to the fighters and a challenge to the opponent.

"It should be clear to the reader that Civil Disobedience in terms of Independence without the cooperation of the millions by way of constructive effort is mere bravado and worse than useless. " (italics added) (Gandhi, M.K. 1945: 35-36)

We should note two broad distinctions which Gandhi makes here – concerning the scale of the campaign, whether local or national, and the choice or scope of the issue, whether particular or general. Dhawan quotes Gandhi making the same distinctions in more summarised form more than ten years earlier, writing in *Young India* in 1930:

"Constructive programme is not essential for civil disobedience for specific relief, as in the case of Bardoli. A tangible common grievance restricted to a particular locality is enough. But for such an indefinable thing as Swaraj people must have previous training in doing things of All-India interest. " (Dhawan 1957: 193)

Gandhi's Five Propositions

In the long extract quoted from Gandhi's pamphlet, he lists only three categories in placing civil disobedience in the context of "a nationwide non-violent effort". I think, however, that the passage can be systematised into five related propositions:

1. Civil disobedience can be offered effectively in a local struggle without constructive programme.

2. Civil disobedience can be offered at a local level without constructive programme in the form of sacrificial action – "self-immolation" by which Gandhi does not mean burning, but perhaps "burning one's bridges", denying oneself the possibility of retreat – which takes no thought of the consequences and therefore may or may not be effective.

3. Where constructive programme has not been taken up at a satisfactory level across the nation, civil disobedience can be offered effectively at a national level only on a subsidiary issue – as "a contribution to" the larger struggle – but not on the main issue itself.

4. When civil disobedience is offered on the main issue – in this case, national independence – then a full programme of constructive work must have been taken up by the people.

5. In theory, if the nation as a whole has taken up constructive programme to the fullest level possible, then Independence could be won without the use of civil disobedience at all.

These five propositions can be expressed as in Table 4.1:

Table 4.1: Gandhi's Five Propositions on Combining Civil Disobedience with Constructive Programme in Nonviolent Struggle

Proposition	Constructive Programme	Civil Disobedience
1.	Not essential	Effective on its own at a local level
2.	Not essential	"Self-immolation" may or not be effective on its own at local level
3.	Partially taken up at national level	Effective at a national level on a subsidiary issue
4.	Almost fully taken up at national level	Effective at a national level on the main issue
5.	Effective on its own if fully taken up at national level	Not essential

If we look at these propositions in turn, it will be possible to suggest some of the thinking about the practicalities of organising nonviolence which Gandhi developed over the years.

1. Local Civil Disobedience, with Constructive Programme Not Essential

Examples where civil disobedience was "effectively offered for the redress of a local wrong" are easy to identify. The Kheda struggle mentioned above, and two other local campaigns, Borsad in 1923 and Bardoli in 1928 (both led by Gandhi's Gujarati colleague, Vallabhbhai Patel) are among the most obvious. All of these were conducted in rural Gujarat. Common to them was the leading role taken by "public workers" associated with Gandhi who devoted themselves full-time to organising peasant farmers in resistance to a strongly felt local grievance, the imposition of an unreasonably high local government tax. The basis of the organising was a solemn pledge taken by the peasants not to pay this tax whatever the consequences; and the object of the organising was to maintain peasant morale so that they could sustain their commitment to the pledge until government concessions were made. The specific aims of these campaigns were moderate and the moderation of the satyagrahis was underlined by their willingness to respect the findings of an independent inquiry, the demand for which became one of the principal issues in the campaigns.

According to Gandhi, in these campaigns, "no elaborate constructive programme was or could be necessary". However, Joan Bondurant, in her analysis of the Bardoli satyagraha, indicates that constructive programme, by which she means spinning, the wearing of *khadi* cloth and the conduct of social work activities, did play a part in the organisation for civil disobedience. There is no doubt that *khadi* propaganda was important in maintaining morale. (Bondurant 1965: 55; Gandhi, M.K. 1951: 218-219) Nonetheless, Gandhi suggests that an "elaborate" programme was not strictly necessary because of the "tangible common grievance".

All of these actions are civil disobedience actions involving the refusal to comply with the legally-sanctioned demands of the provincial government revenue department. Another civil disobedience action of this type would be the Vaikom temple satyagraha of 1924 to 1925, when satyagrahis attempting to secure untouchables the specific right to use a road passing a Hindu temple were first arrested and later blocked by a police barricade. Bondurant again points out that constructive programme, that is, the maintenance in good order of their camp, hand-spinning and the building of a school, constituted an important discipline for the satyagrahis. But the satyagrahis were a relatively small group; the campaign did not rely much on mass action. (Bondurant 1965: 47-48, 51; Shridharani 1962: 93-95) In her otherwise highly critical account of the Vaikom satyagraha, Mary King, too, specifically identifies constructive programme as a feature of this action and recognises its importance to Gandhi's method. (King 2015: 245-246, 296)

Another similar campaign was the Ahmedabad labour strike of 1918, though this was not a civil disobedience action since it did not involve the breaking of a law. The Ahmedabad satyagraha, according to Gandhi's concept, was a local campaign of civil resistance to a specific injustice. Constructive programme – visiting the mill-hands in their homes, providing paid spinning work for some of the women and paid construction work for some of the men –was a factor in Ahmedabad. But the decisive leadership role played by Gandhi in the daily meetings and then his assumption that it was his duty to fast, indicates what is common to all these local satyagrahas: direction of the campaign by an absolutely determined and resourceful leadership, sincerely committed to nonviolence as a tactic, but experimenting as well with some aspects of nonviolence as a way of life, and commanding widespread local and some national support.

2. Local Civil Disobedience as Self-Immolation, with Constructive Programme Not Essential.

Gandhi himself quotes Champaran as an example of this type of civil disobedience – "aimed at a particular wrong", "without regard to effect" "by way of self-immolation in order to rouse local consciousness" - referring to his action in 1917 in refusing to obey the order externing him from this district of Bihar. There are no other examples of which I am aware which exactly match the Champaran case and it is surprising perhaps that Gandhi should isolate it in this way.

The Ahmedabad Fast, on the other hand, during the 1918 labour struggle, was a spontaneous action, "aimed at a particular wrong or evil" (the refusal to pay workers a just wage) "by way of self-immolation" (the fast) "in order to rouse local consciousness or conscience" (help the

143

workers stick to their pledge). Gandhi could not really calculate the effect it would have and took the action as a matter of conscience. But it was not civil disobedience.

At a national level, though, there is a striking example of Gandhi's trying to repeat the Champaran tactic. In 1919, on the train to Delhi following the Rowlatt hartal, Gandhi refused to obey the order confining him to the Bombay Presidency. This was "self-immolation" "in order to rouse consciousness or conscience" "without any regard to the effect" and without prior preparation of the people by way of constructive programme. It failed disastrously. Major rioting was set off in Ahmedabad and parts of Gujarat and the Punjab. We can see why, after this disastrous experiment at a national level, Gandhi specified twenty years later, that this type of civil disobedience should be confined to a "local" level. All Gandhi's later attempts at aggressive civil disobedience of this type were very carefully prepared in advance, as for example, the Salt Satyagraha in 1930 and Individual Civil Disobedience in 1941.

However, Gandhi did attempt a number of other acts of "self-immolation" on national issues. These, though, constituted acts of civil resistance to what he saw as injustice or disastrously wrong political steps, rather than civil disobedience to law. Such would be his public fasts – the Communal Award Fast of 1932 when he fasted in protest against the government decision to introduce a separate electorate for untouchables; or the Hindu-Muslim Unity Fasts of 1947 in which he attempted with startling success to bring the rioting between Hindus and Muslims under control at the time of partition between India and Pakistan. Gandhi could not know what the results of these acts would be, they were moral gestures "aimed at a particular wrong" and designed "to rouse consciousness or conscience" – but they were not aggressive acts against constituted authority. In fact, interestingly, these fasts were related directly to two of the principal and most longstanding campaigns in the constructive programme – the campaign against untouchability and for Hindu-Muslim Unity. When these central facets of the constructive programme (as designed and outlined by him constantly over ten or more years) came under threat, then Gandhi's whole concept of how India must prepare itself for swaraj was threatened, and he resorted to "self-immolation". But

THE PLACE OF CONSTRUCTIVE PROGRAMME

it should be emphasised that this was not civil disobedience and there was some preparation.

3. Civil Disobedience on a National Scale on a Subsidiary Issue, with Partial Constructive Programme.

Gandhi indicates that a third function of civil disobedience is at the national level; the first two functions he confines to the local level. At the national level it can be used effectively on a "particular issue" as a substitute "for full response to constructive effort". He gives as an example the Individual Civil Disobedience Campaign of 1941, when chosen satyagrahis went out individually to commit civil disobedience by speaking against India's involvement in the Second World War. These were the same tactics Gandhi had chosen in 1919 for the Satyagraha Sabha to use against the Rowlatt Act, though the campaign was never launched.

In fact, virtually all Gandhi's nationally organised civil disobedience campaigns were of this type. The Rowlatt Satyagraha of 1919 was addressed to a "particular issue" rather than Home Rule. Noncooperation, from 1920 to 1922, though not in its early stages a civil disobedience movement, became that when the government declared the Congress volunteer organisation illegal – the "particular issues" chosen were the Khilafat question and the Punjab inquiry, though at one point Gandhi suspended both these objectives in order to fight simply for the rights of freedom of association and free speech. Again, the Civil Disobedience Movement from 1930 to 1933 was focused on a whole set of economic and political grievances, most famously the Salt Tax, which were far short of the "general cause" of independence. As far as Gandhi was concerned in planning the strategic objectives of these campaigns:

> "the issue must be definite and capable of being clearly understood and within the power of the opponent to yield. This method properly applied must lead to the final goal."

4. Civil Disobedience on a National Scale on the Main Issue with Full Constructive Programme.

Gandhi never seriously attempted civil disobedience for the "general cause" of Independence. He was never able to secure "the co-operation of the millions by way of constructive effort" to the requisite level.

When he launched the Quit India Movement in 1942, this was civil disobedience on the main issue of Independence. But Gandhi was well aware that from his own perspective the adoption of constructive programme had not gone deep enough in the nation to develop the level of discipline necessary. He therefore launched civil disobedience with the expectation that it would break down into violence – because he felt he had no alternative – and this is what happened.

Similarly, one of the principal slogans of the Noncooperation campaign (1920-1922) was "Swaraj in One Year"; and Civil Disobedience from 1930 to 1933 was fought with the objective of achieving Independence. Nonetheless, when Gandhi was drawn into negotiations with the Raj, these were not his demands. He considered that the constructive programme had not been taken up to an adequate level to make these fundamental goals achievable; and preferred to focus on "particular" issues which "must lead on to the final goal".

5. Constructive Programme on a National Scale without Civil Disobedience

The assertion that "if the co-operation of the whole nation is secured in the constructive programme", then swaraj would be achieved automatically and "Civil Disobedience is not absolutely necessary", was advanced consistently by Gandhi from 1920 onwards. It is an almost mystical view, which he adapted to most of the items in the constructive programme. That is, if the nation could achieve perfection in Hindu-Muslim Unity, or in hand-spinning, or in the abolition of untouchability, and so on, then it would achieve such moral strength and practical vigour that the British would be compelled to recognise the stature of the people and would introduce Home Rule, quite possibly without the necessity for a struggle. This was the basis of Gandhi's promise in 1921 of "Swaraj in one Year", if the nation fully adopted his constructive programme. (Tendulkar 1951b: 19-21, 63, 73-74, 239-240)

In practice, this level of commitment to the constructive programme was never approached during Gandhi's life-time or since, though in the 1930s, as it became clear that the time was approaching when the British would grant independence, he made a major effort to institutionalise the constructive programme with a series of all-India boards to direct the work and a great deal of discussion within and outside Congress. It would have been consistent for Gandhi to argue that the shift in British opinion in favour of granting Independence during the 1930s was, at least in part, a product of the consolidation of the constructive programme across the nation – but I have not seen a statement by him or his followers arguing this.

After Independence, however, Vinoba Bhave adopted the same viewpoint. Civil disobedience was not necessary to the achievement of "nonviolent revolution" in India. As the successor to Gandhi leading the Gandhian workers after 1949, Vinoba used this perspective as his strategic concept in planning the Bhoodan and later the Gramdan movement for land revolution. (Ostergaard and Currell 1971: 265-271)

Civil Disobedience at Local and National Scales

We have explored these five propositions in some detail to see what Gandhi saw as the relationship between civil disobedience and constructive programme. To go further, however, it is useful to simplify them down to two[23] as shown in Table 4.2 below.

As an all-India leader Gandhi had the utmost difficulty in persuading his fellow Congressmen to accept that, if they wanted him to organise civil disobedience, they must also adopt his ideas on constructive programme.

23. In her classic interpretation of the method of satyagraha, Bondurant neglects this distinction which is important to an understanding of how Gandhi organised his campaigns of civil disobedience. She tends on the contrary to emphasise the importance of constructive programme at the local rather than the national level. (Bondurant: 1965: 36-104)

It will be useful therefore to examine more closely why Gandhi reached this conclusion.

Table 4.2: Gandhi's Propositions (Simplified) on the Relationship at Local and National Levels between Constructive Programme and Civil Disobedience

Proposition	Civil disobedience	Constructive programme
1.	At a local level	Not essential beforehand
2.	At a national level	Essential beforehand

Why Gandhi Thought Constructive Programme Essential at National Level

Returning again to the long passage from his pamphlet on Constructive Programme, we found Gandhi making two key distinctions. The first is the question of scale, whether civil disobedience is conducted at a local or a national level. The second concerns the choice of issue, whether it is a main or a subsidiary issue; or in Gandhi's terminology, whether it is a "general" or a "particular" issue.

In general we would expect that the larger the scale of the campaign, the more difficult it was:

i) for the leader to maintain personal supervision of the campaign

ii) to establish an organisation of co-workers knowledgeable in satyagraha principles and techniques

iii) to maintain the morale and discipline of the organisation under the stress of conflict

iv) to avoid the campaign being undermined by a particular group or locality breaking ranks and showing indiscipline.

As a corollary of the above, however, the smaller the scale of the campaign the easier it was:

i) for the leader to maintain personal supervision

ii) for the leader to train and supervise a team of co-workers,

iii) to maintain discipline and morale,

iv) to deal with local breakdowns or indiscipline.

On the face of it, all these points are confirmed by our discussion of local satyagrahas in Bihar and Gujarat. These campaigns were distinguished first by the highly visible and directive leadership roles assumed by Gandhi himself and, later, by his chief lieutenant Vallabhbhai Patel. Second, Gandhi delayed for two years his activities in Gujarat, enabling him in time to draw people from the Home Rule Leagues and elsewhere who would accept his authority and follow his satyagraha principles. Third, the fast in Ahmedabad is the best example of Gandhi using his personal position to maintain discipline and morale. Fourth, in Kheda, it was possible for Gandhi to go personally to parts of this district where peasants were wavering in their resolution.

On the other hand, as soon as the context shifted to the national scale with the Rowlatt satyagraha, Gandhi encountered all sorts of difficulties. First he was unable to maintain personal supervision in Delhi and the Punjab of the activities of the Satyagraha Sabha and people outside the Sabha. Second, one explanation he gave for the outbreak of violence following his arrest on the train to Delhi, was that his co-workers had not sufficiently grasped the principles of satyagraha. Third, under the stress of his arrest, the popular movement erupted in violence at various places causing Gandhi to draw back from civil disobedience and the Sabha eventually to collapse. Fourth, Gandhi's trip to Delhi was prompted by the difficulties the Sabha was having in controlling the crowds there; his arrest en route led to the loss of control in a number of centres across India.

If we turn to the second distinction which Gandhi emphasised in the passage quoted – the selection of the issue around which to centre a campaign – a similar analysis can be made. The broader, or more general, the issue under which the campaign was fought:

i) the more difficult to reach a settlement

ii) the more people's expectations would be aroused unrealistically

iii) the more groups operating from different political perspectives could offer a different analysis and campaigning programme and so divert the movement.

It will be remembered that one of Gandhi's criticisms of the Home Rule Leagues was that their demand could not be realised in the short term, therefore they were rousing peoples' expectations unrealistically and contributing to a generally negative spirit in the people.

The corollary of this perspective, again, is that the more limited, or more particular, the issue:

i) the greater likelihood of reaching a settlement,

ii) the more realistic are the people's expectations of success,

iii) the less easy is it for other groups to take over or undermine the campaign.

Our discussion in earlier chapters illustrates the first two of these points at least. Gandhi's reputation in India prior to 1920 was achieved on the basis of his tackling particular grievances and winning, or winning concessions. For example, his successes with the abolition of indentured labour, the Viramgam customs cordon, the Champaran indigo question, the Ahmedabad labour strike and the Kheda no-tax campaign gave him the reputation as a leader who could take on the British or local vested interests and win. The fact that these were mass campaigns, or potentially so, and that he was able to remain on speaking terms with his opponents, had important effects on national morale.

In his presentation and analysis of Gandhi's early years, Indulal Yajnik places great emphasis on what he calls Gandhi's "particularist ideology" in politics, which he compares unfavourably with Tilak's concentration on the "central demand", the "fundamental issue of transfer of political power from Government to the people":

"Mr Gandhi would busy himself chopping off innumerable heads of the hydra-headed monster of foreign oppression that sucked the life-blood of India, while Mr Tilak concentrated his attention and energy on the sovereign method of destroying the monster itself"." (Yajnik 1933: 55)

Yajnik, however, admits Gandhi's "initial" success with this method:

"While Mr Tilak dominated like a giant the whole scene with his single slogan of 'Home Rule' and 'Self-government' as a panacea for all evils, humble workers sought comfort and solace in the advice of Mr Gandhi, who had been trained by his past experiences to act as a suitable mediator for the redress of special wrongs between the people and the Government. As Mr Gandhi went on settling one question after another ... he commanded increasing faith and following among the people. "

Yajnik goes on to add that Gandhi, by securing redress for grievances, "really helped the Government partially to reinstate itself in the affections and confidence of the people". He continues: "modern militant fighters would have no hesitation in defining all such activities – however militant they might appear at a certain stage – as distinctly counter-revolutionary in as much as they would end... by securing only a few crumbs from the rich table of Government. " Yajnik calls Gandhi "essentially a reformer" who had been habituated by his experiences in South Africa "to study and grapple with the various symptoms of a disease rather than to work for the eradication of the disease itself. " Really, he says, Gandhi retained the method of the political Moderates in India, "of tackling separate grievances – local, provincial and national" – and stresses Gandhi's ability throughout his political career to retain his links with the political moderates who collaborated with the British Raj. (Yajnik 1933: 45-50)

Gandhi, however, would probably have rejected this analysis as superficial. He would have accepted some of the criticisms of his "particularist" method as tributes to its success. But ultimately there are two aspects of Gandhi's approach with which Yajnik's criticisms here do not deal. First, as Gandhi was quick to argue the Indian nation really had little choice but to follow his nonviolent programme for achieving independence because it had been disarmed and could not win by Tilak's methods. Second, Gandhi was not "essentially a reformer". He would deny that the "central demand", "the monster itself", "the disease itself", was as Tilak presented it. As we have seen, Gandhi's view of the central issue went beyond and deeper than what he saw as the superficial question of the transfer of power into Indian hands. In this he is a political leader of great originality.

Another writer who has noted both Gandhi's concentration on particular issues and his sensitivity to the question of scale, is Indira Rothermund in her book significantly titled *The Philosophy of Restraint, Mahatma Gandhi's Strategy and Indian Politics*, she argues that Gandhi evolved a method of "strategic" and "stylized" answers to political problems. The aim of this method was to restrain the use of power by both sides in the national dispute; his political approach involved the "restraint of power". He experienced two particular problems in developing this method. One was the problem of mass participation, how to discipline participants - this is the problem of scale. The other was the problem of the definition of the issue, or the scope of the action - what we have called the choice of the issue. Rothermund does not make the distinction between local and national campaigns as we have. In considering the scale of participation she discusses only national campaigns. Her classification indicating Gandhi's response to the problems of scale and choice of issues is as follows. He might organise a national campaign involving: (i) mass participation; or (ii) participation by a selected local area or group; or (iii) individual action by the leader only. Similarly, in dealing with the problem of the scope of the action, he might organise a national campaign around (i) a general issue -- for example, independence; or (ii) a specific issue – for example, No-tax campaigns; or (iii) a definite point -- the Communal Award of 1932 which was to set up a separate electorate for untouchables .

This analysis is extremely helpful, but Rothermund goes on to argue that the problems which Gandhi experienced in organising mass civil disobedience led him over a period of 25 years to evolve his method progressively to the point where he could control mass campaigns by inviting the nation to identify with action undertaken by himself alone. Thus the importance in Gandhi's political method, she suggests, of the symbolic action, where only the individual leader participated, focusing his action on a definite point, or specific issue, which the watching nation could clearly understand:

> "…millions would refrain from action so that one man could act under complete control of the action: because of this, the action of this one man assumed million-fold importance. The action was symbolic because millions watched and listened, and these millions watched and listened because they knew that the action

would be a symbol. Gandhi arrived at this method because he had recognised that it was impossible to train large numbers of participants for disciplined satyagraha." (Rothermund 1963: 64-74)

This argument is elegant and describes well the conception behind Gandhi's political fasts and explains their impact; so, too, it gives a helpful perspective on the drama of a symbolic action like the Salt March in 1930. But Rothermund is surely overstating her case when she says that Gandhi progressively abandoned organising around general issues and also when she says that he gave up the possibility of organising mass action.

Gandhi's own view, stated in December 1945 when he wrote the introduction to the *Constructive Programme* pamphlet, was as follows:

"Civil disobedience, mass or individual, is an aid to constructive effort and is a full substitute for armed revolt. Training is necessary as well for civil disobedience as for armed revolt. Only the ways are different. Action in either case takes place only when occasion demands. Training for military revolt means learning the use of arms ending perhaps in the atomic bomb. For Civil Disobedience it means the Constructive Programme.

"Therefore, workers will never be on the look-out for civil resistance. They will hold themselves in readiness, if the constructive effort is sought to be defeated." (Gandhi, M.K. 1945: 4)

Thus Rothermund's analysis is one to which we will return when we examine in more detail Gandhi's organising efforts on a national scale. But for the present we remain with the points already established. It was easier for Gandhi to organise and maintain nonviolent discipline at a local level than at a national level. Because of the difficulty of maintaining discipline for civil disobedience on a national scale, he devised programmes of constructive work to prepare, supplement, or act as a substitute for it. While the constructive programme was in its infancy, he directed campaigns on particular rather than general issues.

The Connection Between Constructive Programme and Civil Disobedience

But how did Gandhi imagine that a programme of constructive work would "train" a people for civil disobedience? In what way does constructive programme prepare people for campaigns of civil resistance? How can it act as a support for those engaging in civil disobedience, or even as a substitute for it? How did the great movements to challenge the British help forward the campaigns of constructive work?

To answer these questions we must return to the two practical ways of looking at constructive programme.[24] First, it can be seen as a moral imperative on individuals who wish to live a way of life which expresses the values of nonviolence. By examining constructive programme in this sense, as a discipline for the individual or committed group, we can suggest the impact it may have on the behaviour of individuals who take it up. Second, the term also describes a set of specific campaigns organised in India to change society. By looking at constructive programme in this second way, we can suggest its function and effect as a means of mobilising the Indian nation for struggle.

Looking at its effect on the individual, Gandhi made great claims for constructive programme in his pamphlet. Independence was to be not the nominal transfer of power to an Indian government but "the independence of every unit, be it the humblest of the nation". Communal unity was to be achieved not by an accord between Hindu and Muslim politicians, but by "an unbreakable heart unity" among the people. Power does not come down to a people when they achieve parliamentary self-government, but resides in them already if they will recognise this and find a means of exercising it. (Gandhi, M.K. 1945: 9-11) Thus "swadeshi mentality" meant "a determination to find all the necessaries of life in India and that too through the labour and intellect of the villagers." Such a reversal -- throwing off the exploitation of "half a dozen" cities in India and Britain –

"vitally touches the life of every single Indian, makes him feel

_____
24.. As outlined in the Introduction.

154

aglow with the possession of a power that has lain hidden within himself, and makes him proud of his identity with every drop of the ocean of Indian humanity." (Gandhi, M.K. 1945: 14-15)

Gandhi hated the modern city. It was ugly and godless. But his preference for a society of villages did not rule out technological improvements, including labour-saving devices. They should be appropriate to the needs of the majority of people and must provide dignity for manual occupations and support a more equitable division of labour. (Hardiman 2003: 77-80)

Gandhi made further claims. Basic education, the educational programme promoted by him in the late thirties to develop standards and skills related to Indian village life, was "meant to transform village children into model villagers". Adult education was not to be satisfied with combating illiteracy but "true political education of the adult by word of mouth":

> "They do not know that the foreigner's presence is due to their own weaknesses and their ignorance of the power they possess to rid themselves of the foreign rule." (Gandhi, M.K 1945: 19-21)

It was essential to work in provincial languages in order to give the masses the opportunity to make their solid contribution to the construction of swaraj. Because of the neglect of the great languages "the mass mind" remained "imprisoned".

> "The languages of India have suffered impoverishment. We flounder when we make the vain attempt to express abstruse thought in the mother tongue. There are no equivalents for scientific terms. The result has been disastrous. The masses remain cut off from the modern mind. " (Gandhi, M.K. 1945: 24)

Tribal peoples must be brought into the political nation through constructive programme. "Unless every unit has a living consciousness of being one with every other", India could not make good its claim to be one nation. So too should lepers – "For what the leper is in India, that we are, if we will but look about, for the modern civilised world. " (Gandhi, M.K. 1945: 30-31)

These are some of the broad moral arguments used by Gandhi in the 1940s when seeking to inspire his readers to take up the mature constructive programme and engage in what today might be called consciousness-raising. Constructive programme is presented as a method by which individuals and groups can achieve personal self-confidence and self-reliance as well as a national self-consciousness through serving each other. These characteristics provide a basis for national unity and the exercise of political power, and hence a realistic background and complement to the campaigns of civil disobedience.

Assessments of Constructive Programme

In 1941, the American Gandhian Richard Gregg published a pamphlet which attempted to demonstrate systematically for a Western reader the value of physical labour as a discipline for nonviolence. (Gregg 1941) Manual work was to constitute one first essential part of a "fourfold discipline" of body, emotion, mind and spirit, which would prepare people both for nonviolent resistance and for "a better civilisation, a nonviolent world". (Gregg 1941: 32)

Gregg argued from military authorities that the key to success in war, beyond questions of weaponry and firepower, was organisation, discipline and morale. Just as military training relied considerably on physical drills and discipline, so training for nonviolence could be obtained through manual work. Gregg explores a list of qualities engendered by military training – the habit of obedience; self-respect, self-reliance and self-control; tenacity of will; sense of unity with others; endurance of common hardship; sense of order and co-operation; protection of community; energy; and courage. He then argues that each of these can be achieved through the discipline of manual work and lists further qualities necessary for "pacific resistance" which can also be developed – equanimity and poise; patience and humility; love of truth; faith in human nature; satisfactions; and relief from moral strain. (Gregg 1941: 1-6, 9-27) In one intriguing passage he addresses the difficulty that "war provides a wide channel and allows people to vent all the energy of their accumulated resentments... [which] explains in part why many men get such satisfaction from war". His response is predictable enough, but entirely relevant to our discussion:

> "It is that huge reservoir of unconscious, suppressed energy of resentments of long ago which is so unmanageable and takes us off our guard. A wise discipline will find ways to train off that energy into creative channels. By so doing it will enable its followers to develop more poise and equanimity. The nature of this manual work and of its organisation is similar to that of much of the causes of the original frustrations, namely social, economic and natural. Also the deep evolutionary connection between mind and hand, and between emotion and physical action, makes sublimation by means of manual activities peculiarly effective and complete. " (Gregg 1941: 20-21)

Gregg does not make the simple error of arguing that manual workers are by nature nonviolent. But he insists that they do display many of the qualities necessary for disciplined nonviolent action. These can be drawn out and cultivated if linked to a self-conscious nonviolent movement. (Gregg 1941: 6-9) In the concluding section of the pamphlet, he searches for a manual activity which, first, produces something beneficial to the community, especially to the poor and unemployed, and second, which the poor themselves can take up as a form of "self-respecting" self-help. He thinks that if "one kind of work could be found which exemplifies the discipline with special power and which could be universally practised, it would be especially valuable. " It should also be "elemental", concerned with either food, shelter or clothing.

Unsurprisingly, perhaps, Gregg reaches the conclusion that this "universal physical disciplinary activity for nonviolence" should be the making of yarn and cloth by hand. (Gregg 1941: 28-36) In summarising, we may have made his argument sound trite, but it is a coherent thesis. Gandhi approved of the pamphlet and had it printed in India with a foreword by himself. We may therefore assume that Gregg was expressing some of the linkages between constructive work and civil resistance which Gandhi himself envisaged.

Constructive programme was, however, also a specific set of campaigns launched to have a direct impact on Indian culture and society, especially the character of its villages and the activities carried on there. In our discussion of the Swadeshi Sabha in Chapter 5 and also of Noncooperation we will find that Gandhi saw in the swadeshi cloth campaign a means of developing organisation at village and district level which would help to draw people into the national movement. He maintained that such organisation in itself would make good the Congress claim to be an effective and representative national political movement. It would also give it a network to be employed in building up support for civil resistance campaigns. It is this factor of developing, testing and demonstrating effective organisation which is emphatically claimed by J. B. Kripalani, one of Gandhi's co-workers, in his defence of constructive programme, *Politics of Charkha*, published in 1946. (Kripalani 1946) "The capacity to organise", he states flatly, "is the one quality the nation sadly lacks and which it must cultivate if it is to assert its dignity and achieve its independence". Comparing centralised organisation "imposed from above" with "small decentralised cottage industry organisation... of a voluntary and democratic character", Kripalani saw individuals mobilised by the decentralised approach better educated for "united, co-operative, disciplined and self-regulated activity." Examining, on the one hand, the spinning and weaving centres established across India, as well as the procedures for supplying tools to the workers; and, on the other, the arrangements for marketing the finished cloth, Kripalani claimed that "*Charkha* (the spinning wheel) can organise the country-side". In terms of organisation, he said, it involved a tremendous voluntary and co-operative effort towards the mitigation of poverty and unemployment across the nation. Moreover,

> "The organisers of village and cottage industry are a body of disciplined volunteers from whose ranks, if need be, satyagrahis can always be recruited. As a matter of fact, constructive workers constitute a standing army of Satyagrahis." (Kripalani 1946: 16-25)

Gandhi saw in decentralisation of the swadeshi cloth movement its greatest strength:

> "... centralised khadi can be defeated by government but no power can defeat individual manufacture and use of khadi." (Gandhi, M.K. 1945: 4, 15-17)

Developing effective decentralised organisation capable of resisting central government – in this case, the Raj – is another expression of the relationship between constructive programme and civil resistance. Such resistance as a popular civilian activity requires organisation on a wide scale in order to sustain the movement.

A further factor is the effort to offer all citizens, however poor, a means of playing their part in the national struggle. This we saw was one of the factors guiding Gregg in his search for a universal, manual activity suitable for developing nonviolent discipline. But an important consideration which Gregg does not mention is that citizens who are not engaged in civil resistance can still make their contribution by engaging in constructive programme, by for example wearing swadeshi clothing or undertaking some other aspect. The national struggle was reinforced by the effort to reclaim a key area of essential production, in this case clothing. As a result, the cloth campaign came to be identified by both sides with the national movement, and producers, sellers and wearers of swadeshi cloth all became liable to sanctions from the Raj.

Gandhi saw too in the spinning campaign a link between the educated classes and the masses of India:

> "Consider the levelling effect of the bond of common labour between the rich and the poor."

One of his perpetual themes was of the "divorce between labour and intelligence" in India. The reluctance of the educated classes to employ their talents on behalf of their fellow Indians had resulted in "stagnation". Discussing village sanitation, another item in the later constructive programme, he writes, "Divorce between intelligence and labour has resulted in criminal negligence of the villages". (Gandhi, M.K. 1945: 17-19) Constructive programme was designed to express in practical terms a unity across class and caste which would prepare the nation for struggle and for independence.

There are links in the other direction, too. Campaigns of civil resistance provided Gandhi with the opportunity to launch new constructive campaigns to help sustain the struggle. As we shall see when discussing Noncooperation, boycotts of Government schools were launched quite deliberately before national schools had been established. The schools boycott provided constructive workers with a pressing incentive to establish their own "national" alternative. So too lawyers and litigants were pressed to boycott the law courts before arbitration courts had been set up; and the failure of the movement to establish widely these constructive alternatives greatly limited the impact of that particular boycott. Boycott of the legislatures took politicians who previously had been oriented towards the Raj's elite forums, out into rural areas where they worked for the first time to build up the Congress organisation. Boycott of foreign cloth automatically gave strong support to the swadeshi campaign as an effort to substitute for imported goods through home production. Inevitably, the success or failure of these constructive campaigns helped to determine whether the boycotts could be sustained or not.

Change with the Times

In an interesting analysis of constructive programme, Jayantanuja Bandyopadhyaya explores the complementary relationship between constructive programme and civil disobedience, as we have done. He then distinguishes between the specific projects Gandhi developed in India to address Indian conditions and a set of general or universal proposals for constructive programme which he identifies as a key part of Gandhi's method.

In discerning those elements to be applied universally, he reduces the number of projects from eighteen to four. The "essential features of the Gandhian constructive programme", he says, are: (1) the political institutions of village self-rule (like village councils); (2) hand-woven cloth and other village industries as the economic base; (3) basic education as the intellectual and moral base; and (4) non-political peasant and labour associations as the organisational base. He notes that village councils are not actually listed in the programme in Gandhi's pamphlet but argues, convincingly in my view, that this is an oversight and not a deliberate omission. (Bandyopadhyaya 1969: 203-213)

The four universal elements of the constructive programme are not to be pursued exclusively, however – but complemented by other projects relevant to the political and social context at the time.

However, returning to the constructive programme in its Indian context, Bandyopadhyaya considers that it has not evolved as it should have done. He points out that Gandhi's motto throughout his political life was "One Step At A Time". As a result, he says, when India assumed self-government (and the situation was no longer one of opposition to a colonial government), Gandhi was prepared to accept transitional arrangements short of his ideal and geared to the readiness of the nation, including for example state ownership in preference to private ownership. (Bandyopadhyaya 1969: 216-217) Bandyopadhyaya criticises the Gandhian movement after Gandhi's death for not updating constructive programme pragmatically (One Step At A Time) to take account of the changed conditions, including the cooperation of the state:

> "If instead of wasting valuable national resources on a highly unproductive and inefficient programme of spinning throughout the country, and depending in the process on heavy governmental subsidies and protection, these organisations had engaged themselves in organising modern small and medium scale industries on a cooperative basis, including handloom and power-loom cooperatives, cooperative consumers', marketing and housing societies, adult education schools etc and identified themselves with the community development programme launched by the government... they would probably have been truer to the ideals of Gandhi and rendered greater service to the country at the same time". (Bandyopadhyaya 1969: 377-386)

Hardiman makes much the same point about khadi production:

> "Much of its problem has probably stemmed from the fact that khadi-spinning and weaving were fetishised... What this brings out is that alternative economic systems cannot be dreamed up and applied in dogmatic ways." (Hardiman 2003: 79-80)

Constructive programme (as a specific programme in a given context and as a universal method) must be expected to change with the times.[25]

---

25. Bandyopadhyaya also argues that constructive programme with civil disobedience is a revolutionary method only in predominantly agrarian societies. (Bandyopadhyaya 1969: 213-214)

Here, though, we are focused on Gandhi's method as it was developed and carried out during his times, alongside civil disobedience.

Conclusion

To sum up, what the constructive programme did was to provide, on the one hand, a basic moral or patriotic training and orientation, together with some practical discipline, for individuals who might join campaigns of civil disobedience. On the other, it also provided part of the infrastructure of support for these national campaigns, and a training in establishing all-India organisations, particularly in the rural areas. It vastly improved the moral case for civil disobedience too, since those involved as leaders and organisers were devoting their lives in a spirit of service to a programme of social and spiritual improvement for the nation. Since what Gandhi was looking for was a basis on which to invite mass participation in civil disobedience across India, the constructive programme, made up as it was of a number of simultaneous all-India campaigns involving mass participation on a daily basis, provided the means of preparation he was seeking. (Sarkar 1983: 229-231)

Mass commitment to constructive work was, Gandhi felt, essential before campaigns of mass civil disobedience could be launched at a national level. But at a local level, where there was a "tangible common grievance" and where the direct influence of a leader and co-workers thoroughly immersed in the principles of satyagraha could be used to exercise direct control over the direction of the struggle, mass civil disobedience could be undertaken without constructive programme being essential.

CHAPTER 5

THE SWADESHI SABHA

Ambition and Circumstances

Gandhi's local campaigns in Gujarat in 1918 had served as a sign to the political nation that a highly original leader was emerging not identified with either of the main nationalist camps, the Moderates or the Extremists. His launching of the Rowlatt Satyagraha in 1919 had demonstrated that from the organisational centre of Bombay City and a core of support in Gujarat, he could inspire an all-India campaign capable of drawing support from many parts of India.

Prior to 1920, all Gandhi's initiatives were conducted outside the framework of the Indian National Congress and in splendid isolation from the established leaders of the national movement. Judith Brown, in her pioneering study *Gandhi's Rise to Power, Indian Politics 1915-1922* (Brown 1972), explains Gandhi's move into the centre of Indian politics during 1920. Gandhi's isolation from the main political factions enabled him to establish an independent political position and, when the time came, to deal directly with other national leaders.

Gandhi was successful in mobilising social classes and geographic regions which had previously been politically dormant, and in bringing them into the arena of Congress politics. He was able to forge a (temporary) political alliance between Muslims and Hindus on a key political issue, the Khilafat question, bringing Muslims for the first time in significant numbers into Congress politics, with himself as the indispensable bridging leader, the "lynch-pin", holding the alliance together. He had a method of political agitation to offer – civil resistance, or satyagraha – which went beyond the limitations of parliamentary collaboration adopted by previous nationalist leaders, but stopped short of violent insurrection, which was felt to be unrealistic by most contemporaries.

These points are extremely helpful to an understanding of how Gandhi, a leader of regional importance early in 1919, was able to take over the direction of the national struggle just 18 months later. We may also add another observation. Gandhi had a practical political programme to offer, which demanded personal sacrifice and dedicated service to the nation, a scheme which met the mood of a nationalist movement unable to proceed directly to its long-term goal of Home Rule.

There is a point of interpretation in Judith Brown's analysis, however, which seems to misrepresent Gandhi's behaviour during this period. Thus, when she says that the First World War "transformed" Gandhi into an all-India political leader and was a "watershed in his career", she adds:

> "...If India had not felt the repercussions of the European conflict it is possible that Gandhi would have remained a public worker in the small world of the district and the market town, only occasionally participating in the activities of the political nation...

> "...This was the situation in which Gandhi felt forced into public action, but he was no politician in the ordinary sense of the word. He seems to have had no clear plan for a career or ambition for power, but to have visualised himself as a religious devotee and a public worker, whose duty it was to forward his ideal of Swaraj in his ashram and through the constructive work of his assistants in Champaran; while the 'wrongs' he had discovered were local ones, felt more sharply because of the effects of the war, the incentive to work on a larger scale, and so come face to face with the politicians and the raj in the political arena, only came when 'wrongs' occurred which were not confined to a particular locality and yet appeared to be within his compass or when opportunity offered to spread his vision of true Swaraj before a wider audience." (Brown 1972: 123)

It is true that there was a particular combination of circumstances at the end of the First World War which made India ripe for the type of struggle which Gandhi launched, and it follows that if these circumstances had not occurred then Gandhi might never have achieved national prominence. It is also true that Gandhi's ambitions were not those of a conventional politician. He strongly deprecated the views of people like Tilak and Besant that politics had its own rules and could not be governed by the dictates of religion. He did indeed devote his life to social service of individuals and local groups and would almost certainly have been "content" to have remained at this level, if his understanding of the national question and the nature of political power had not told him that many of the smaller or more local issues could only finally be resolved in the context of tackling larger ones. And, as we have seen, it was his political method to select particular issues to organise around, what Brown calls "wrongs to be righted".

But our account so far has not shown such a discontinuity between Gandhi's local and national campaigns, nor that Gandhi had not thought of moving into the national political arena before 1919. It is also questionable whether his selection of particular wrongs as the focus for his campaigns was piecemeal and not informed by a deeper political ideology, long-term objectives and a sophisticated sense of strategy and tactics. It seems more accurate to see Gandhi in the years between 1915 and 1919 as a mature figure, biding his time (as he said on many occasions) before he made his move into the national arena, content to wait precisely because his ambitions were different from those of other political leaders and therefore the ground had to be thoroughly prepared in advance.

For example, Gandhi did not, with the Rowlatt Satyagraha, move directly from the "market town" and the "tiny worlds of particular districts" to a national campaign. Through his local campaigns he had established himself, as Brown herself states, as the leading political figure in Gujarat; he was a regional or provincial leader of national importance. Moreover, the Rowlatt issue was not much different from the concerns which prompted his first act of civil disobedience in Champaran and the campaign in Kheda. Gandhi believed that the Raj should accord to its Indian citizens the respect owed to a nation of equal status.

The Rowlatt Bills did, as Brown suggests, affect directly only the nation's political elite, whereas Champaran and the other campaigns took up the struggles of peasants and workers, but Gandhi's objection in principle to the Bills was the same as when he refused to obey his externment order from Champaran: the emergency powers of the Raj were being used in his eyes to suppress legitimate national activity. There seems to be no reason why Gandhi should have viewed an insult to the nation's political leaders, as he considered the Rowlatt Bills to be, as essentially different from the failure of British officials in Bihar and Gujarat to protect the peasantry from the unjust behaviour of indigo factory owners and local revenue officers.

We have seen too that at the time of the Ahmedabad strike in 1918, Gandhi was directly comparing himself with Tilak and Malaviya, suggesting that his spiritual approach to politics was more appropriate to the Indian nation than theirs. Moreover, the local struggles were not directed, as Brown suggests, at "'wrongs' confined to a particular locality", nor at issues that were without "all-India implications". Especially in the case of Kheda, the campaign addressed itself to a grievance against the revenue officials which was felt widely in different parts of India. Even in Champaran and Ahmedabad, the particular struggles signified Gandhi's identification with peasants and workers across India and his ability to suggest a dramatic new weapon of struggle; thus they had an impact way beyond the particular locality.

Later, when Gandhi was organising national struggles, he would, on several occasions, select a local area within which to conduct a struggle on a national issue because he understood the importance of symbolic local struggles in focusing the attention of the nation and raising consciousness and morale. Again, Gandhi had formulated his views on the national question in India in his pamphlet, *Hind Swaraj*, published in 1909. These were very different from those of other Indian political figures. It does not go against the evidence to suggest that from 1909 onwards and when he returned to India in 1915, Gandhi was holding himself in readiness for a possible all-India role in politics.

We have also noted, third, that Gandhi's distinctive political method, formulated in South Africa and maintained by him subsequently, was distinguished by what Yajnik called a "particularist" approach to politics. His selection of issues, or wrongs to be righted, was not as haphazard as

Brown (and Yajnik) imply. Gandhi believed from experience that tackling particular issues successfully would demonstrate the effectiveness of his methods, commend himself and those associated with him to the nation as leaders to be taken seriously, and build popular confidence that the problems of British India could be tackled and changed. At the same time, he was critical of organising on remote issues like Home Rule, which called forth fiery speeches and antagonistic feelings against the British, but produced no direct political results or immediate benefits.

Thus, moving from a particular local issue to a particular national issue marked no change in Gandhi's analysis, method or ambition. In 1919, a particular affront to nationalist opinion occurred with the publication of the Rowlatt Bills. Gandhi, by this time, felt he was ready to take the initiative on the issue as he would probably not have been able to do earlier.

The general point that Gandhi was not a religiously-minded humanitarian worker, who rather fortuitously got swept up into national politics as a result of the First World War, is important because his career prior to 1920 should be seen as a period when he was experimenting with methods of inserting himself into Indian political life. Brown is right that Gandhi did not concern himself with the day-to-day politics of the nationalist leaders who were wondering, in 1918, how to formulate proposals for a reformed Indian constitution and, in 1919, how they should react to the British response made in the Montagu-Chelmsford reforms. Gandhi was not interested in these matters not because national politics did not interest him, but because he believed that little could be achieved until the basic relationship between the Indian people and the British rulers had been changed. Such a transformation demanded in his eyes the organisation of a popular movement different in its character and objectives from the popular agitations started by the Home Rule Leagues.

Gandhi was also aware that, since his political principles were markedly different from the other nationalist leaders, he would not be able to make headway amongst them until he had established his credentials and authority by his achievements, by the "results" he was able to secure in his local campaigns and then his first all-India campaigns. It is true that Gandhi was undecided about which organisations to work through during this period; hence his hesitation about joining the Gujarat Sabha, his refusal to join, but close collaboration with, the All-India Home Rule League of Annie Besant, and his bold step in bypassing the Indian National Congress when he formed the Satyagraha Sabha and launched the Rowlatt Satyagraha. But these hesitations do not show a reluctance to enter nationalist politics; rather they indicate an understandable uncertainty over tactics and an underlying determination to define for himself an independent position and base of support before he made his entry.

The Swadeshi Sabha

What is swadeshi?

The Swadeshi Sabha was begun in 1919 with Gandhi's characteristic energy and determination, but it was not a great success. There is no mention of the Swadeshi Sabha in Gandhi's autobiography, nor in the biographies by Tendulkar or Rajmohan Gandhi, and little has been published about it. Even so, it provides a useful example of Gandhi's early attempts at organising constructive programme on a national scale.

Swadeshi was not a new concept. (Sarkar 1983: 111-125) At the time of the partition of Bengal in 1905 a major movement for the boycott of British goods and the promotion of Indian manufactures had been launched by nationalists in Bengal and was supported elsewhere in India. According to one commentary, the Bengal campaign had two aspects.

"On the one hand, British wares were burnt at public places and shops selling them were picketed; on the other, a vigorous drive was made for the production and sale of Swadeshi goods. The confectioners vowed against using foreign sugar, washermen against washing foreign clothes, priests against performing puja with foreign materials. Women of the Deccan and Bengal gave up foreign bangles and glass utensils. Students refused to use foreign paper. Even doctors and pleaders refused to patronise dealers in British manufactures." (Chandra, Tripathi and De 1972: 89)

Fourteen years later Gandhi acknowledged his debt to the earlier movement, but decided that it was totally impractical to substitute across the board Indian goods for British goods as the Bengal movement had tried. People who took a vow not to use British goods of any sort would find this vow impossible to keep and the movement would break down. Therefore, he proposed to be selective in promoting swadeshi, or home manufacturing. As he said to a meeting in Bombay in June 1919:

"When swadeshi was introduced in Bengal, the people there were not ready for it, nor the traders. The leaders then embarked upon the task of spreading swadeshi far and wide among the people, and gave it up, for in the attempt to take too big a step, they lost everything... If we think of using everything swadeshi, all at once, the result will be that we shall succeed in using none. I am placing before the people a programme which they can assimilate and carry out." (Gandhi M.K. 1965: vol. 15: 376)

He repeated the same thought to a Swadeshi Sabha meeting in Ahmedabad later in the same month:

"The fault, then, which I have noticed in the earlier movement is this, that it was organised on too large a scale. It is plain enough that we cannot have everything swadeshi all at once." (Gandhi M.K. 1965: vol. 15: 405)

Gandhi, typically, was reluctant to advocate "too big a step". Too often political and social movements overreached themselves and collapsed because they went beyond the capacity for sacrifice of their supporters. He wanted a swadeshi campaign which the people could "assimilate and carry out". Gandhi felt that the place to start was with cloth for a number of practical reasons.

After food, clothing was a primary necessity of life; (Gandhi M.K. 1965: vol 15: 324) the largest proportion of Indian income spent on foreign goods was used to buy imported cloth and, historically, India had had a flourishing textile industry. (Gandhi M.K. 1965: vol 15: 305-306, 329) In addition, Gandhi wanted to tap the unutilised energy of women and he felt that this could be done if they took up spinning in their own homes. (Gandhi M.K. 1965: vol 15: 439-445, 485-486) Moreover, spinning and weaving in the villages would bring in extra income for rural families during the months when there was no work on the land. (Gandhi M.K. 1965: vol 15: 437-438) To launch such a programme on a large scale was an extraordinarily ambitious conception, which naturally demanded a concentration of effort. When later the proposal was made to extend the swadeshi campaign to sugar, Gandhi agreed in principle with encouraging Indian manufacture of sugar but declined to make this an objective of the campaign, which was still confined to cloth. (Gandhi M.K. 1965: vol 15: 199; vol. 16: 125, 184)

Opposition to boycott, Particularly of British goods

Gandhi's swadeshi campaign, however, was distinguished from the earlier Bengal movement in another significant way – and this presumably had a lot to do with the slow growth of the movement. He was strongly opposed to the boycott of British goods. (Gandhi M.K. 1965: vol 15: 197, 401) He thought that such a boycott was impractical; also, it was a negative concept and it might encourage dependence on other foreign goods which would be imported as substitutes.

Eighteen months later, in the national Congress programme of Noncooperation, he was forced to modify his opposition to boycott; but in 1919, through the Swadeshi Sabha, Gandhi placed his emphasis on swadeshi alone. He felt that boycott would generate antagonistic feelings towards the British and could only be considered effective if it drew overwhelming support so as to materially affect or "punish" British cloth producers. It was preferable to promote swadeshi without boycott, because this was a positive programme to develop Indian skills and resources. It could be said to be effective even if only one individual adopted it. Boycott in Gandhi's view was a short-term movement, solely geared to a political objective; whereas swadeshi was a lifelong principle for building a new social order. (Gandhi M.K. 1965: vol. 15: 480-482)

With this conception, Gandhi tried to construct a campaign geared realistically to the practical capacities of the Indian people and to their needs. He sought at the same time decisively to modify the swadeshi idea. He transformed it into a religious rather than a political principle, or rather a religious principle which would underlie and help to shape political activity. (Gandhi M.K. 1965: vol. 15: 439-445; vol. 16: 60) This principle of swadeshi – which was expressed primarily in the campaign to promote hand-spinning, but later in many other forms – was to become a guiding concept behind all his constructive work in India. In a report on a speech Gandhi made in Poona in July 1919 the religious standpoint is stressed:

> "He had defined swadeshi as restricting oneself to the use and service of one's immediate surroundings to the exclusion of the more remote... He felt that the first and elementary duty of man was to use and serve his neighbours and that if he went farther for his needs and services, it argued on his part more regard for self than for others." (Gandhi M.K. 1965: vol 15: 454)

In rural Gujarat in August, he was more specific, as another report shows:

> "To him the religious aspect was all sufficient. That elementary religion which was common to mankind taught him to be kind and attentive to their neighbours. An individual's service to his country and humanity consisted in serving his neighbours. If that was true, it was their religious duty to support their farmers, their artisans, such as weavers, carpenters, etc. And so long as the Godhra farmers and weavers could supply the wants of the Godhra citizens, the latter had no right to go outside Godhra and support even (say) the Bombay farmers and weavers. He could not starve his neighbour and claim to serve his distant cousin in the North Pole. This was the basic principle of all religions and they would find that it was also of true and humane economics." (Gandhi M.K. 1965: vol 16: 30)

Thus Gandhi devised a specific campaign to promote his religious ideal of swadeshi. He later called swadeshi "an eternal principle whose neglect has brought untold grief to mankind." (Gandhi M.K. 1965: vol 16: 480)

Swadeshi and Rowlatt

The basis of the swadeshi campaign was inevitably a religious vow. Gandhi launched the new movement on the day of the Rowlatt hartal, April 6, inviting his listeners on the beach at Bombay to take the vow three days later – during a religious festival. In two leaflets distributed on April 8, Gandhi gave the text of the vow:

> "With God as my witness, I solemnly declare that from today I shall confine myself for my personal requirements to the use of cloth, manufactured in India from Indian cotton, silk and wool; and I shall altogether abstain from using foreign cloth, and I shall destroy all foreign cloth in my possession."

He thought that while the "purifying movement" of satyagraha was going on, that is, the work of the Satyagraha Sabha in organising the April hartal and civil disobedience, this was a supreme and "revolutionary" moment, during which "allied activities have an easy chance of success". (Gandhi M.K. 1965: vol 15: 98, 200) Moreover, when the riots following the hartal forced him to suspend civil disobedience, swadeshi propaganda became a useful substitute for action against the Rowlatt Act – "in order to keep the people fully engaged". (Gandhi M.K. 1965: vol 15: 384, 437, 471)

Yet in principle and practice Gandhi was determined to keep the swadeshi campaign separate from the Rowlatt Satyagraha. (Gandhi M.K. 1965: vol. 15: 306, 327-328) At the same time as he was confronting, or planning to confront, the Raj with civil disobedience, he wrote to the Viceroy and to the Governor of Bombay with his extraordinary request that they sign the swadeshi pledge. (Gandhi M.K. 1965: vol 15: 262, 263, 275; vol 16: 60-62, 220) Swadeshi, he explained, was not a political movement – though it was "fraught with political consequences" – and could be supported by people not in sympathy with his political work. In this way, Gandhi tried to signify his bona fides as a satyagrahi, one who was working for the good of Indian society at the same time as he challenged the Raj on a contentious political issue. Unsurprisingly, British officials did not adopt the swadeshi pledge, but he did receive guarded support from some of them in promoting swadeshi. (Gandhi M.K. 1965: vol. 16: 62, 28-31) Similarly, Indian and Anglo-Indian leaders who opposed him in his civil disobedience programme publicly supported his swadeshi work. (Gandhi M.K. 1965: vol. 15: 385-386, 503-504)

Launching the Sabha

However, despite his initial promotion of the swadeshi vow through the two leaflets published at the time of the April 6 hartal, Gandhi delayed launching the Swadeshi Sabha for two months until mid-June. In the intervening period he appears to have been brought face-to-face with a great deal of resistance to his proposal. As he stated in a new leaflet on the swadeshi vow published in May, the idea had "now been fully thrashed out" and a number of clarifications and practical alterations made.

First, he stressed the point that the swadeshi vow was not related to the Rowlatt agitation, but would continue long after the repeal of that Act. Second, he had to emphasise the importance of "commercial honesty". In the previous swadeshi campaign during the time of the Bengal partition, mill-owners and shopkeepers had taken advantage of the campaign to charge inflated prices for Indian goods of inferior quality, and this had not been forgotten. (Gandhi M.K. 1982: 444-446) Third, he had to ask people not to buy large quantities of swadeshi cloth because Indian suppliers could not meet the demand. This understanding forced him later to emphasise in his campaign the production of swadeshi cloth as much as its consumption.

Finally, there were problems in obtaining Indian yarn from which to weave the cloth. He was thus obliged to introduce two new vows, a "pure swadeshi vow" which was similar to that proposed in April, and a "mixed swadeshi vow" which committed the signatory to wearing Indian cloth irrespective of where the yarn came from. Both vows, however, could be restricted to a limited number of years, rather than committing the signatory for a lifetime, as in April; and neither mentioned the destruction of foreign cloth. Also, Gandhi had relaxed somewhat his idealistic requirement that the yarn and cloth be hand-spun and hand-woven in order to constitute pure swadeshi. (Gandhi M.K. 1965: vol 15: 305-308)

When the Swadeshi Sabha was finally launched with the publication of a fourth leaflet on the swadeshi vow on June 18, Gandhi admitted:

"We advisedly deferred issuing this leaflet so long for the reason that we thought it necessary to make some provision for the

173

supply of cloth to intending signatories before giving the vow wider publicity." (Gandhi M.K. 1965: vol 15: 372)

Shops selling "pure swadeshi" were opened in Bombay and Ahmedabad and branches of the Swadeshi Sabha started in both these cities. Over the next few months, Gandhi opened a number of other swadeshi stores in Gujarat. (Dalal 1971: 24-27) On July 1, the Central Swadeshi branch was founded in Bombay to co-ordinate branches of the Sabha throughout the Bombay Presidency, with Gandhi inevitably as President. The managing committee of the Sabha was to consist of 30 members; branches were to have a minimum of ten members. In addition to the "pure" and "mixed" vows, there was now a third vow, permitting those who were already in possession of foreign clothing to retain this, but committing them in future to buy only cloth manufactured in India. (Gandhi M.K. 1965: vol 15: 421-424) Gandhi confessed later to be embarrassed by this compromise.

These swadeshi stores were committed to selling at a profit of no more than 5.5% to 7.5%. (Gandhi M.K. 1965: vol 15: 372, 484) Gandhi, on learning that only 25% of the demand for cloth in India could be met from Indian mills, had shifted a great deal of his attention to the production of swadeshi cloth. He concluded that it was impossible to expand mill-production quickly enough to meet the demand and that therefore the only realistic approach coincided with his religious standpoint, that home production of yarn and cloth was the best way to produce the required amounts of swadeshi cloth in a short period. (Gandhi M.K. 1965 vol 15: 329, 372-374)

Members of the Sabarmati Ashram in Ahmedabad had been weaving for some years; Gandhi now instructed them to concentrate on hand spinning. Gandhi quite self-consciously saw the ashram setting an example to people interested in the campaign. (Gandhi M.K. 1965: vol 15: 276-277, 321, 339-340, 346-347) Experiments in spinning and weaving at the ashram were complemented by a contest launched through Navajivan to invent a more efficient spinning wheel. (Gandhi M.K. 1965: vol 16: 217-218, 348) One of Gandhi's followers was despatched to research handloom weaving in all parts of India. (Gandhi M.K. 1965: vol 15: 369-370)

In his many speeches to women's meetings in Gujarat, Gandhi urged the women to take up spinning and their husbands weaving. Frequently, he pointed out the example of Gangabehn, the woman he had met at the Broach conference in 1917, who had succeeded in establishing a network of over 100 spinners and weavers in a rural part of the princely state of Baroda, which adjoined Gujarat. He also persuaded high-class Indian ladies in Bombay to take up regular spinning lessons as an example to other Indian women. (Gandhi M.K. 1965: vol 16: 79-81, 161-162; Gandhi M.K. 1940: 362)

Gradually, a network was established where the Sabha branches supplied cotton to the spinners and cloth to the swadeshi stores. (Gandhi M.K. 1965: vol 16: 132) Much of this was of poor quality – and Gandhi began to argue for the superior aesthetic pleasure of wearing homespun, however coarse, to being clothed in fine machine-made or foreign garments! By September he was able to claim:

> "As a result of the present movement, about 2,000 wheels are working and 200 weavers have begun to weave afresh." (Gandhi M.K. 1965: vol 16: 126)

Swadeshi and Congress

This project of course was a significant beginning for the Khadi campaign, producing and wearing hand-spun cloth, which was to become an integral part of the constructive programme launched in later years. But it did not provide the revolutionary impact which Gandhi had anticipated in April. Moreover, sales of Swadeshi cloth and signatories to the three vows did not spread as he had hoped. In July he admitted:

> "The vow of the third category is so simple that I even felt ashamed when including it, for there can be no vow which does not entail some suffering. I cannot understand why people have not taken such a simple vow in large numbers. There should be none in Bombay who has not taken one or other of the three vows. " (Gandhi M.K. 1965: vol 15: 431)

Opening a new swadeshi store in Bombay in September he complained:

"If the swadeshi movement were flourishing in India as we want
it to flourish, we would have swaraj this very day. But, friends,
it is not. "

He said he had received letters telling him that if he were to open a
swadeshi store where they lived, then the people would take up swadeshi
cloth; but this hadn't happened where he had done so. The explanation
that it was the poor quality of the Indian-made cloth that was the
problem did not mollify him – "No cloth anywhere in the world can
stand comparison with what I am wearing. Surely the Bhagavad Gita
doesn't say that we should dress ourselves in delicate Japanese fabrics."
But he seems to have accepted at this point that a gradual adoption of the
swadeshi campaign was the best he could hope for and then only if "the
young people" took it up. (Gandhi M.K. 1965: vol 16: 112-113)

One major restriction on Gandhi's promotion of the Swadeshi Sabha
was that (following the Rowlatt Satyagraha) he was still confined at
this time to the Bombay Presidency. When finally in November he was
permitted to go to the Punjab, he found there a much healthier tradition
of hand spinning and weaving than in Gujarat. (Gandhi M.K. 1965:
vol 15: 285, 286-287, 331) He continued to speak on the subject of
swadeshi, especially to women's groups, and to open Swadeshi stores in
different parts of India, but perhaps because of the effort he was putting
into the Punjab Inquiry and simultaneously into building up the Khilafat
movement, he seems not to have put a major organisational drive into
promoting the Swadeshi Sabha outside the Bombay Presidency. His
promotion of swadeshi was personal and piecemeal until eventually it
became absorbed into the concept and programme of Noncooperation.

Indulal Yajnik devotes a chapter to the Swadeshi Sabha in his account
of Gandhi's activities at this time. He shows how the Gujarat workers
were directed to take up spinning following the collapse of the Rowlatt
civil disobedience campaign and how many of them abandoned this
difficult craft, and neglected the Swadeshi Sabha itself, when they got
swept up into the Khilafat agitation and work for the Amritsar session of
the Congress in December 1919. (Yajnik 1933: 81-84)

Gandhi was clearly casting around for direction at this time (Gordon 1970: 1-2, 10-11) but his underlying and long-term faith in the swadeshi campaign is demonstrated by a remarkable article he published in Young India just before the Amritsar Congress, under the heading "Swaraj in Swadeshi". This was the Congress session where the political leaders had to decide whether to accept or reject the Montagu-Chelmsford Reforms. Gandhi comments:

"The much-talked of Reforms Bill will become the law of the land within a few days and in due course the new legislature will take the place of the old... I have refrained from expressing an opinion on the report of the Joint Committee for I do not feel sufficiently interested in it. It is not possible to be enthused over a thing which when analysed means little for the people... I would simply urge that we should take the fullest advantage of it...

"But the real reform that India needs is swadeshi in its true sense. The immediate problem before us is not how to run the government of the country but how to feed and clothe ourselves ... The Reform Scheme, no matter how liberal it is, will not help to solve the problem in the immediate future. But swadeshi can solve it now...

"I know that means a revolution in our mental outlook. And it is because it is a revolution that I claim that the way to swaraj lies through swadeshi. A nation that can save sixty crores of rupees per year and distribute that large sum amongst its spinners and weavers in their own homes will have acquired powers of organisation and industry that must enable it to do everything else necessary for its organic growth.

"The dreamy reformer whispers 'Wait until I get responsible government and I will protect India's industry without our women having to spin and our weavers having to weave.' This has been actually said by thinking men... (But) India cannot wait for a protective tariff and protection will not reduce the cost of clothing. Secondly, mere protection will not benefit the starving millions. They can only be helped by being enabled to supplement their earnings by having a spinning industry restored to them. So whether we have a protective tariff or not, we shall still have to revive the hand-spinning industry and stimulate hand weaving."

Gandhi went on to say that, if he had his way, he would make spinning or weaving compulsory for all Indians and he would start in the schools and colleges because they presented "ready-made organised units". Starting new factories would not deal with the problem in time and would not succeed in distributing the extra wealth to the peasantry, but would concentrate money and labour and thus make matters worse. (Gandhi M.K. 1965: vol 16: 335-337)

The Amritsar Congress was the session where Gandhi made his mark as a member of this body for the first time. In the "Swaraj in Swadeshi" article he presented himself to congressmen as a mature political figure with a range of practical concerns, which went far beyond the narrow preoccupation with political representation, which had been the prime focus of Congress up to then. He professed himself not much interested in the political reforms because they missed the point, which was the poverty of the people, which he felt they should tackle by their own direct efforts. The Swadeshi Sabha was Gandhi's first effort to practice what he preached through a constructive programme launched on a wide scale.

Though it remained formally in being for some years, the Sabha did not have the impact Gandhi had hoped. What it did was to bring many of his political co-workers much closer to the philosophy and way of life he was promoting in his ashram. It also provided a pool of skilled workers and technical experience for the later Khadi movement. What it did too was announce to the Indian National Congress a fresh way of building a popular movement for national independence. Many of Gandhi's political co-workers, now committed to the swadeshi programme, were with him when he made his bid to capture the organisation of Congress less than a year later. And they constituted his loyal supporters when he tried to introduce swadeshi as a main plank in the programme of the Congress in subsequent years.

Summary

1. Gandhi joined or initiated a number of organisations in the years after his return to India. Each time – initially at a local level in Gujarat and thereafter at a national level – he saw them as a means for organising campaigns according to his particular set of principles.

2. Gandhi launched the swadeshi campaign on April 6, 1919, the same day as the Rowlatt hartal, thus indicating the broad satyagraha movement he was hoping to initiate. Later he chose to differentiate the swadeshi campaign from the political movement against the Rowlatt Act, which was co-ordinated by the Satyagraha Sabha. The Swadeshi Sabha itself was not founded until June.

3. The basis of the swadeshi campaign was again a religious vow, which committed the signatory to wearing only Indian cloth manufactured from Indian yarns, and to destroy all foreign cloth in his or her possession. Later, the vow was modified and variations introduced to meet various practical objections.

4. The practical nature of Gandhi's organising method is well illustrated in this, one of the more idealistic of his campaigns:

(i) Swadeshi had established itself in Bengal more than ten years earlier in an effort to find substitutes for all British goods during a boycott campaign. Gandhi viewed this as hopelessly impractical. He therefore isolated cloth as the sole item to concentrate on in a new swadeshi campaign, which he felt could actually be implemented on a vast scale. This "limited" objective was reinforced by an "extreme" method, taking a sacred vow.

(ii) In the earlier Bengal campaign, swadeshi stores had apparently exploited the shortage of Indian cloth to make large profits. Gandhi proposed 5.5% to 7.5% as a maximum profit for stores; he also shifted attention from the consumption of swadeshi cloth to its production, which he thought could be met most effectively by cottage industries.

(iii) Gandhi seems to have believed that individuals spinning and weaving in their own homes could meet the demand for cloth more quickly than could an expansion of factory production. He also argued that the distribution of income gained from increasing production of cloth would be more equal if the emphasis was on cottage industries.

(iv) Consolidating his earlier work in the Ahmedabad ashram to develop skills in weaving, ashram workers and other supporters were now instructed to improve their techniques of spinning. Also classes were started with educated women to try by example to take the craft of spinning to the villages.

(v) Once permitted to enter the Punjab, Gandhi discovered there a flourishing tradition of spinning and weaving and he proceeded over the next few months to open new swadeshi stores in several parts of the country.

5. The Swadeshi Sabha did not have the impact for which Gandhi had hoped and the more politically-oriented workers were pulled back into other activities as Gandhi took up the Khilafat and Punjab issues.

6. Gandhi persisted in a romantic view that the British in India might support his swadeshi campaign. He wrote to the Governor of Bombay and to the Viceroy requesting their support, without result. His public meetings to promote swadeshi were occasionally patronised by British officials, though.

7. The swadeshi campaign met with support from a number of Indian political and cultural figures, as for example some associated with the Servants of India Society, who would not have supported Gandhi's civil disobedience movement. The swadeshi campaign was one of the factors which enabled Gandhi to maintain the high personal regard of some prominent "moderate" leaders.

PART III

CHAPTER 6

MUSLIM OUTRAGE AGAINST THE RAJ

Most accounts of Gandhi's activities in 1919, if they refer to the Swadeshi Sabha at all, treat it as a short-lived experiment he took up in some desperation and dropped quickly when he got involved in the Khilafat campaign.[26]

The Swadeshi Sabha did not have the sweeping effectiveness Gandhi had expected. Pledging oneself to wear only clothing made in India, or devoting hours of one's time to learning the arts of spinning and weaving, were not commitments that could be made easily. Moreover, Gandhi tended to be caught up in more immediate political causes. He does appear to have neglected the Swadeshi Sabha itself after his initial enthusiasm.

But the principles of swadeshi were to play an important part in the programme of Noncooperation he developed between 1919 and 1922: first, as a strategy for the Khilafat movement in confrontation with the Raj, and then, in more extended form, for the national movement itself under the leadership of Congress. The concept of a positive movement to develop self-reliance among the people was a principle he refined and extended throughout the rest of his career.

Always this work provoked hesitation and scepticism among some of his supporters. They followed him on the one hand as a national

---

26. Yajnik, for example, dismisses the Swadeshi Sabha in this way. (Yajnik 1943: 84; also Gordon, 1970)

leader of outstanding insight and energy, but they were reluctant, on the other, to go "the whole hog" and adopt all the requirements of his social programme. There was a tension too between his insistence that the constructive work was non-political "national work" or "public service", and his simultaneous assertion that only through the medium of this constructive programme could a genuinely unified and successful nationalist movement be built.

The failure of the Swadeshi Sabha to take root in 1919; Gandhi's shift on to more short-term "political" issues like the Khilafat and Punjab questions; and his development and promotion of the swadeshi programme within these new campaigns – these illustrate the difficulty he found in promoting his religiously-based social programme. In the late summer of 1919, Gandhi might have persisted in the narrow task of assembling in the swadeshi campaign a company of true believers; but his drive to put his ideas across to the Indian nation as a whole led him into alliance with nationalists and radicals of other persuasions whom he then tried again to lead in his direction.

CASE STUDY 5: THE KHILAFAT AND NONCOOPERATION

The Khilafat campaign was one of the strangest alliances Gandhi forged.[27] In London as a law student in the 1890s and in South Africa before returning to India, Gandhi had formed firm attachments with Indian Muslims. On the basis of the unity that had been achieved in the satyagraha struggles in South Africa, Gandhi believed that a similar alliance between Muslim and Hindu was possible in India itself.

Hindu-Muslim unity was a precept of his in 1916 at the same time as the national leaderships of the Congress and Muslim League were effecting

---

27. This account of the Khilafat movement relies mainly on Judith Brown (Brown 1972: 151-157, 190-229, 250-304); B.R. Nanda (Nanda 1989: 198-251); Sumit Sarkar (Sarkar 1983: 195-199); and Rajmohan Gandhi (Gandhi, R. 2007: 219, 223-229, 231-234).

a political alliance for the first time to press for constitutional changes from the Raj. (Nanda 1989: 198-200) Where the approach between the established national leaderships and Gandhi on the question of unity was different, however, was that Gandhi looked to a unity among the people based on reconciliation and mutual respect at a local and village level, whereas the approach of the established politicians was for the two separately organised "monolithic" communities to come together through political bargaining and accommodation between their separate leaderships. (Rothermund 1963: 6-75, 98-115)

The Congress and League politicians moved in 1916 towards a negotiated compact through which they could jointly press their claims on the British. Gandhi, typically, was more radical, though he did support the Congress-League Pact. He sought a lasting solution organised from the bottom-up through a change in the religious and social customs of the ordinary Hindu and Muslim people. He thought that the way to achieve this was through emphasising rather than playing down or neglecting religious identities. He sought to mobilise the best elements in the religious traditions and among the respective religious leaderships, promoting tolerance, integrity and respect for diversity.

On his return to India in 1915, Gandhi pursued his populist strategy for communal unity by seeking links with the pan-Islamic movement among Indian Muslims. Pan-Islamic leaders were questioning the conservative, pro-British line adopted by the Muslim League, based on cooperation with the British Raj in order to secure the position of the Muslim minority in an India dominated by Hindus. The pan-Islamists felt that this approach had failed to protect the interests of Indian Muslims, who were being left behind by the emergence of popular Indian nationalism. They were also critical of a secular drift in League policy. They favoured the re-assertion of a Muslim unity across national frontiers, focused on the religious leadership of the Sultan of Turkey, the Khalifah, with his command of the Holy Places in the Middle East.

When the First World War saw India, as part of the British Empire, automatically pulled into a war against the Ottoman Empire which had aligned with Germany, this posed a conflict of loyalties for the Indian pan-Islamists. Many of the Indian troops fighting on behalf of the Empire were Muslim. Islamic countries in the Middle East were undergoing major upheavals as the rival imperial powers undermined more than 400 years of stable Turkish rule, encouraging nationalist movements in the course of the war to upset the old order. Indian Muslims looked on powerless as European armies and European-sponsored nationalist movements overthrew the Turkish Empire, dislodged the Khalifah, and occupied the Holy Places. Then the spoils of war were divided up in the peace treaties following the Allied victory.

For the pan-Islamists and their supporters in India, a fundamental tenet of their religion was under threat. Muslim control of the Holy Places through the religious institution of the Khilafat was about to be abolished, despite British political leaders making public wartime promises that Muslim sensitivities in the Middle East would be respected. The Ali brothers, Mohammad and Shaukat, were Delhi journalists who publicly stated the dilemma the war placed them in. For their pains, they were put under house arrest – and Gandhi pursued their case and their friendship, along with that of other pan-Islamic leaders like Abdul Bari. (Nanda 1989: 201-209)

Established nationalist Hindu leaders were more circumspect in taking up the Khilafat cause, but Gandhi as a radical, religiously-motivated figure, critical of the political calculations of the established politicians, had no such qualms. His position was that Indian Hindus were obliged to support their Muslim brothers when fundamental tenets of their religious faith were under threat. Moreover, the British government had pledged itself on several occasions to protect the interest of the Indian Muslims in the Middle East and must be held to those pledges. (Gandhi M.K. 1965: vol 17: 412-413, 435, 456-460; Nanda 1989: 203-205) His support for the campaign of the Ali brothers against their detention first gained him the confidence of the pan-Islamist leadership. Then the Rowlatt Satyagraha indicated that a popular alliance might be achieved between the pan-Islamist Muslims and nationalist supporters of Gandhi. As the Rowlatt Satyagraha came to an end, Gandhi continued to support the pan-Islamist claims on the Khilafat. As a result, when the Khilafat movement itself was put to the test towards the end of 1919, Gandhi's commitment to the cause was tested too.

The issue was the peace terms imposed on Turkey at the end of the war. Supporters of the Khilafat movement realised that they needed Hindu support if they were to mount a serious challenge to the British government. They also needed an effective method of struggle falling short of violent rebellion. Therefore they looked to Gandhi to cement an alliance and to advise them on their campaign. Crucial to this alliance was the new method of struggle Gandhi was developing. B.R. Nanda comments that, throughout 1919, for Gandhi:

> ""How to conduct a struggle against injustice without hatred and violence was a problem which taxed his intellectual and moral resources to the utmost. With one satyagraha struggle [Rowlatt and its aftermath] still on his hands, he was not in a hurry to launch another on the Khilafat issue. He had, however, commended satyagraha to Muslim leaders as an alternative to violence." (Nanda 1989: 209)

By the summer of 1920, Gandhi felt that "the moment of moments" had arrived. He called upon Hindus to do all in their power to support the Muslims. Such an opportunity of uniting the two communities, he said, "would not arise in a hundred years". (Hamid 1967: 144; Gandhi M.K. 1965: vol 18: 203; Gandhi R. 2007: 224)

Preparations For Taking Up the Khilafat Issue

We look in this chapter at the preparations for noncooperation by the Khilafat movement, including the success it achieved when its proposals were taken up by the Indian National Congress in December 1920.

Following the breakdown of the Rowlatt Satyagraha, it appears that Gandhi quickly learned the key lesson. Thorough preparation for a national level satyagraha struggle had become an essential prerequisite. The Khilafat campaign, organised by the Central Khilafat Committee, drawing on Gandhi's advice and under his leadership, was effectively a second national satyagraha for him within a year. In its design, it could be called "the Khilafat Satyagraha" and I will analyse it from this perspective.

With the Khilafat campaign there was an extended period of preparation as approval was sought from the leaders of the Muslim community and various tests made of the capacity and readiness of the Muslim population to engage in a mass nonviolent struggle. These preparations were accompanied by a drive to win over the institutions of Indian nationalism and to prepare the Hindu population too. Effectively the programme was built up in phases. It continually evolved as it was debated at national conferences and reformulated through political resolutions.

Gandhi himself was engaged also in work on behalf of the Congress on the Punjab issue. On this issue, in December 1920, what can be seen as a third national satyagraha under Gandhi's leadership was taken up by the Congress. We will consider Gandhi's approach to "the Punjab Satyagraha" in Chapter 7. Finally, in Chapters 7, 8 and 9, we assess the programme of Noncooperation followed by Congress from 1921 to 1922, as it challenged the Raj on both the Khilafat and Punjab issues and added its demand for Swaraj.

In 1919, as the reality of an impending struggle between the Raj and its Muslim subjects became clearer, Gandhi concentrated on two things. First, was the need to assure himself, and have the agreement of Muslim religious leaders, that satyagraha, the nonviolent method of struggle, was consistent with Islamic teaching. Gandhi never sought to deny that a violent struggle was consistent with the Islamic religion; his problem was to achieve consent among Muslim divines that nonviolence was not specifically excluded by the Koran as a means of struggle for Muslims, and that a programme of nonviolent action could be taken up by the Muslim community of India in a life and death struggle, with the authority of the Koran behind it. (Gandhi M.K 1982: 446-447)

Discussions with the Ali brothers, with Abdul Bari and other Muslim religious leaders, eventually convinced Gandhi that he was on the right lines. Thus in a speech on the Khilafat issue to a meeting of Muslims in Bombay in May 1919, only a month after the Rowlatt hartal (and before he had given up the idea of renewing civil disobedience on this issue), Gandhi commented on the need for Muslims to be able to enforce their demands on the Raj:

> "When people have become enraged against governments for a deliberate failure to carry out their wishes, they have resorted to

violence and I know that many consider that violence is the only remedy open to them when ordinary agitation has failed. This is an age-long remedy. I consider it to be barbarous and I have endeavoured to place before the people and the Government another remedy which does away with violence in any shape or form and is infinitely more successful than the latter. I feel we are not justified in resorting to violence for asserting our rights. It is nobler by far to die than to kill. Had it not been for my talks with Barisahib (Abdul Bari) I would have hesitated to talk to you on a subject which is deeply religious. But he assured me that there was a warrant enough for satyagraha in the Holy Koran. He agreed with the interpretation of the Koran to the effect that, whilst violence under certain well-defined circumstances is permissible, self-restraint is dearer to God than violence, and that is the law of love. That is satyagraha – violence is a concession to human weakness, satyagraha is an obligation." (Gandhi M.K. 1965: vol 15: 295-299)

In February 1920, Gandhi stated in Navajivan his side of the "agreement" he had reached with the Ali brothers and with the Muslim divine, Hasrat Mohani: "When you offer satyagraha, invite me to join you; at other times, I am not with you." He went on to describe the response he had received from the three Khilafat leaders:

"The Brothers do not put unqualified faith in satyagraha. Hasrat Mohani Saheb, however, whispered to me in passing, 'I cannot say whether satyagraha can always be practical but for this purpose and in these times, I too believe that there is no other weapon like it. I shall certainly therefore propagate it'." (Gandhi M.K. 1965: vol 16: 516-517)

The second fundamental requirement for which Gandhi pressed in 1919, as the likelihood for the Khilafat movement of conflict with the Raj came nearer, was that the movement should define carefully what its objectives were, and then commit itself to them seriously and devise a method for enforcing them. His correspondence and speeches in the summer of 1919 are full of suggestions to the Khilafatists that they should state their claims straightforwardly and plan a realistic campaign which would bring significant pressure on the Raj. Addressing a meeting predominantly of

Muslims in Bombay in September, Gandhi upbraided his audience in his familiar style when preparing a community for nonviolent struggle:

> "...I confess I do not fear the ministerial neglect of duty so much as I fear yours – the leaders on the platform and this vast audience. If you and I do not do our duty today, we shall rightly deserve the curses of the millions of Mohammedans who are hoping that somehow things will come out right... The British rulers... take no time to find out whether we are serious or at play. I want therefore to ask you to ask yourselves whether you are serious about this very serious matter... A sincere and true man is ready to sacrifice himself for a cause. Are you ready to sacrifice yourself for a cause? Are you ready to sacrifice your ease, comfort, commerce and even your life? Then you are satyagrahis and you will win." (Gandhi M.K. 1965: vol 16: 151-152)

Earlier in May, Gandhi had invited Bombay Khilafatists themselves to experiment with satyagraha by joining the hartal organised so cautiously to protest against Horniman's deportation. (Gandhi M.K. 1965: vol 15: 298) This was a test in Gandhian terms of their capacity to maintain nonviolent discipline.

By October 1919, when a Khilafat Conference in Lucknow had called for a "Khilafat Day" of 24 hours of fasting and prayer, Gandhi took up the proposal and used it as another test. He urged non-Muslims to make it a "national fast and national prayer", accompanied by suspension of business. (Gandhi M.K. 1965: vol 16: 206-208) As with the earlier Horniman hartal, Gandhi's proposal for the Khilafat Day was significantly restricted when compared with the Rowlatt hartal; again there were to be "no processions, no meetings". Gandhi felt sure enough of his authority with the Khilafat leaders to write almost peremptorily to Abdul Bari advising him to issue "public instructions" to Muslims asking them to observe his proposed limitations on the form of the action. (Gandhi M.K. 1965: vol 16: 229-230) In the event, the first Khilafat Day passed off peacefully on October 17, and the call for prayer, fasting and suspension of business was observed in many parts of India. Nanda calls it "a great success" and says that a notable feature "was the widespread participation of Hindus". (Nanda 1989: 210; Brown 1972: 197-201)

Thus by October, Gandhi had won recognition from the major Khilafat leaders in Bombay and northern India as a trustworthy ally and his general approach, advocating satyagraha and a deadly serious campaign to challenge the British, was being heeded. When in November, a two-day conference of Khilafat leaders was held in Delhi to discuss the outlines of a strategy for the Khilafat movement, Gandhi was the only non-Muslim invited to attend the first day's proceedings, which were private. He was also honoured by the invitation to preside as chairman over the second day's session, which was held in public. (Gandhi M.K. 1965: vol 16: 306n, 307n, 309-310)

The Second All-India Khilafat Conference, Delhi, November 1919

This all-India Khilafat Conference in Delhi on November 23 and 24 was of decisive importance for the Khilafat movement and for Gandhi's future as a nationalist leader. Despite considerable differences of viewpoint, Gandhi was able to impose his personality on the gathering and to carry the decision on several important points.

Invitations had been sent to Hindu leaders to attend the public session of the conference; their cooperation had been sought by the proposal that the conference would discuss ways of preventing cow-slaughter in the Muslim communities, a practice causing great offence to Hindu religious feelings. Gandhi had gone on record as opposing any attempt to win Hindu support for the Khilafat cause by making a bargain on cow-slaughter. (Gandhi M.K. 1965: vol 16: 305-306) Such a bargain he thought was demeaning to both sides. Gandhi had agreed to chair the public conference session on November 24. Accordingly, he was able to announce from the chair that he could not allow the question of cow-slaughter to be discussed; it was a separate issue, to be considered separately on its own merits. Gandhi admitted that despite the desire of several of his friends that the issue be discussed, the conference acquiesced before his wishes and it was not.

Similarly, from his position in the chair, Gandhi was able to prevent a second issue being discussed at the conference. Several Hindu supporters of the Khilafat movement felt that mass Hindu support could not be gained for the campaign, unless the question of the atrocities in the Punjab was combined with the Khilafat issue. Gandhi – who at the time of the conference was heavily involved in the conduct of the Congress inquiry into the Punjab events and who had also, along with the nationalist leadership generally, received some satisfaction from the government by the appointment of the Hunter Commission to investigate these events – was strongly opposed to any attempt to combine these two issues. He argued that the Khilafat question was an international issue relating to the terms of the peace treaty to be signed by governments at the end of the war; whereas the Punjab question was an internal matter. On the Khilafat question, no significant concessions had been won, whereas, on the Punjab, further protest action should await the results of the two inquiries. (Gandhi M.K. 1965: vol 16: 310-311, 320-321)

Again, from the chair, Gandhi's veto was respected by the conference, despite strong feelings that his decision was a mistake. Gandhi was fully convinced of his right as chairman to take this action. As he commented in Navajivan at the time:

"Many had looked forward to (these questions) being discussed. My ideas on both had been already formed. If I allowed the issue of cow protection to be discussed, the cause would be harmed. If I threw open the Punjab issue for debate, both the Punjab and Khilafat causes would suffer. I could not let this happen. My position, therefore, was extremely delicate. I had to take upon myself the responsibility of causing pain to people whom I knew. " (Gandhi M.K. 1965: vol 16: 319)

Judith Brown quotes from a Bombay police report on the confrontation between Gandhi and his critics over the question of linking the Khilafat and Punjab issues:

"Gandhi maintained his veto. The opposition then said that the principle of deciding by majority vote had been admitted at the meeting on the 23rd and should apply to this question as well. Gandhi replied by a categorical statement of his intention to resign the whole campaign if any attempt was made to call for votes or even if any amendment to his decision was suggested. This threat cowed his opponents into submission." (Brown 1972: 319)

We see here Gandhi's way out of a dilemma in which he had placed himself. He had assumed the role of a satyagraha leader attempting to lead supporters and colleagues who were not convinced upholders of the satyagraha doctrine, or who were simply less well-versed than he was in the practice of it. Where he had made up his mind and was convinced that any concession by him would damage the method of satyagraha and hence the cause for which he was fighting by this method, he would insist on having his own way, or resign the campaign. Given his desire to lead non-believers in satyagraha in campaigns conducted according to the rules of satyagraha, he probably had no other choice. Thus the principle of authority became increasingly explicit in Gandhi's campaigns, and an important part of preparations for them. He, the foremost exponent and practitioner of satyagraha, must be given decisive authority in the direction of satyagraha campaigns.

What we see here also is yet another example of Gandhi's "particularist" method. Muslims and Hindus should work together both to defend the Khilafat and to end cow-slaughter; but each issue deserved support on its own merits, not as part of a bargain between the two communities. Support offered in expectation of a reward, he said, was "mercenary" and undermined the integrity of a campaign and its supporters. (Brown 1972: 308) In principle, as we have noted, Gandhi disliked pacts secured on the basis of mutual advantage. In his view, they bred suspicion and recrimination when one side felt the bargain had not been kept. If Hindu support was offered to Muslims unconditionally on the Khilafat question, then Muslims were in practice more likely genuinely to examine and change those of their practices which offended Hindus. Similar high-mindedness motivated Gandhi on the question of linking the Khilafat and Punjab issues. While the Khilafat question demanded an immediate and fierce campaign and the willingness to make the utmost sacrifices, it would be wrong to whip up feelings against the government on the Punjab question when this was already the subject of two inquiries.

Thus Gandhi was willing and indeed determined to sacrifice the apparent political advantage of automatic Hindu support, which could be gained by combining the Khilafat issue with the question of cow-slaughter, or of the Punjab. Such scrupulous insistence on tackling each issue in its own right would protect the movement from the criticism of being

191

opportunist. Under the theory of satyagraha, it should even startle and disarm the opponent (in this case, the British Raj) who finds that the satyagrahis are not playing politics by the usual rules but are governed and sustained by a strict code of ethical conduct which will not be compromised for the sake of immediate advantage. (Shridharani 1962: 84-85)

On a third issue at the Delhi Khilafat conference, Gandhi also partly had his way. As the need for a serious Muslim struggle short of violence to challenge the Raj had become clear, several Khilafatists had begun to call for a boycott of British goods. Gandhi, as we have seen from our discussion of the Swadeshi Sabha, had already given this matter a great deal of thought and was strongly opposed to boycott. His position focused primarily on two elements: firstly, the importance of sustaining a sacred vow once made, and the impossibility of sustaining a generalised boycott of British goods; secondly, the negative feelings aroused by a boycott campaign. His approach was to be *positive* by promoting Indian manufactures; to be selective by choosing a particular vital area for Indian peasant economic life, clothing; and to avoid specific hostility against the British by promoting *a general boycott of all foreign clothing*.

At the private meeting he attended on November 23 a resolution to boycott British goods was debated at the subjects committee, which met in the afternoon to draft the resolutions, and at the general meeting in the evening. On both occasions, Gandhi was invited to speak against the resolution and on both occasions, despite Gandhi's opposition, the resolution was carried. On the following day, however, in the public session over which Gandhi presided, the resolution in favour of boycotting British goods was not put before the meeting, and Gandhi spoke from the chair asking the Khilafatists to reconsider the decision they had taken the previous day! Judith Brown comments that at this public session Gandhi's influence over the Khilafatists was "carried to the point of dictatorship". She also notes that by the positions which Gandhi took, especially on the question of boycott, he helped to secure the position within the all-India Khilafat alliance of some prominent Bombay Muslim businessmen who were in danger of being outflanked by more extreme voices from north India. (Brown 1972: 203)

Nevertheless, despite his willingness as part of the preparation for satyagraha to use his personal authority and his position in the chair to get his own way, Gandhi was profoundly influenced by the militants at Delhi. Hasrat Mohani, Gandhi's most stringent critic on the question of the boycott, had pointed out that "mere boycott of foreign cloth" could not have the type of immediate impact on the British which was needed. Gandhi in struggling for a mode of action consistent with his satyagraha principles which would bring significant pressure to bear on the British government and channel the energies of the militants, hit upon the concept of withdrawing cooperation from the government. Boycott, which punished the far away British people for the actions of their government in India, was a mistaken tactic in his view; withdrawal of cooperation from the British Raj in India by individual Indians who propped up their rulers by numerous actions in their daily lives was a quite different proposition. The one was remote and crude; the other was direct and precise.

In his speech at the private conference on November 23, Gandhi first formulated the concept of noncooperation. He repeated this from the chair at the public session the following day. (Gandhi M.K. 1965: vol 16: 309-310, 318-319, 321-322) One of the resolutions at the private session had set up a subcommittee to consider further the questions of boycott and "noncooperation". Preparation of a workable programme of noncooperation became a major concern of Gandhi's in the months that followed. Judith Brown notes that, within six months, Gandhi had parted company with several of the Bombay Khilafat moderates. She comments:

"By May he was no longer prepared to act as a shield for the Bombay moderates against the stronger policies of the leaders from northern India. The reasons behind this shift of position can only be conjectured. It seems most probable that, having made an emphatic stand against violence and boycott, Gandhi realised that he must produce a viable counter-plan in order to retain Muslim support." (Brown 1972: 212)

This is undoubtedly correct. In his *Autobiography* Gandhi states explicitly that he was forced by the arguments of Hasrat Mohani – and implicitly by the strength of opinion which Mohani represented – to devise a programme going beyond "mere boycott of foreign cloth". (Gandhi M.K. 1982: 432-433; Gandhi R. 2007: 219)

Prior to the Delhi conference, in August, Gandhi had begun calling for the Viceroy and the Secretary of State for India to resign if they were unable to persuade the British cabinet to secure the wishes of the Indian Khilafatists at the peace conference following the war. He wrote in Navajivan:

> "We believe that Mr Montagu and Lord Chelmsford owe it, as a duty, to see that the Muslims get the justice to which they are entitled, or, as a mark of protest against the injustice, to give up their posts as Secretary of State for India and the Crown's Representative (in India). " (Gandhi M.K. 1965: vol 16: 105, 151-152, 207)

He continued to hammer away at this theme, arguing that the government should "make common cause with the people". (Gandhi M.K. 1965: vol 16: 228-229) When the government announced that "peace celebrations" were to be held across India to mark the end of the war, Gandhi's response was firm:

> "I venture to think that His Excellency the Viceroy can, if he will, tell His Majesty's ministers that Indians cannot participate in the celebrations, so long as the Khilafat question remains unsettled. And I do hope that His Majesty's ministers will recognise the necessity of securing and publishing an honourable settlement of the question before advising us to take part in peace celebrations". (Gandhi M.K. 1965: vol 16: 270-271)

There was therefore no difficulty for Gandhi in supporting a resolution brought before the Delhi conference in November that the Viceroy should be asked to postpone the peace celebrations "until such time as the question of the Khilafat was satisfactorily settled"; and that, failing that, "no Indian would be able to take part in the Peace Celebrations". (Gandhi M.K. 1965: vol 16: 322-323) This proposal for a boycott of the celebrations due to take place on December 13, 1919, was the main immediate result of the Delhi conference and a first act of noncooperation. Gandhi lent his powerful support to it and, with Muslim feelings rising in many parts of India, another nationwide hartal, similar to the Khilafat Day on October 17, was staged, though without much time for preparation. Police reports estimated that the protests "gave great prominence to the Khilafat question throughout India". (Brown 1972: 203-204)

Thus at the end of December 1919 when the annual session of the Indian National Congress was held in Amritsar, Gandhi was a significant figure among the leaders of a growing agitation among Indian Muslims, as well as the principal organiser of a bold challenge to the Raj through the Rowlatt Satyagraha earlier in the year. Although he had already begun pointedly to call for the resignation of the Viceroy and the Secretary of State, Gandhi was still at an early stage in preparing Muslim and Hindu support for a nationwide Khilafat agitation. Similarly, on the issue of the Punjab, Gandhi was personally involved in a detailed investigation into the events of April and May 1919, but not willing to launch a major protest agitation. This helps to explain both the uncertain status which he possessed at the Congress session and the influence in favour of moderation which he exercised during its proceedings.

During 1920, the Khilafat movement became a major political force in the country. Decisive events included the release of the Ali brothers and Maulana Abul Kalam Azad from detention as part of an amnesty staged by the British to mark the end of the war. Each of them threw themselves wholeheartedly into the Khilafat struggle alongside Gandhi. Peace terms unfavourable to Turkey and the Khilafat were published in May and were consolidated in the Treaty of Sevres in June. In India, a campaign by the Khilafatists to get the terms of the treaty revised was launched in June. At the end of May, the Hunter Commission's report on the Punjab was published. It totally failed to satisfy Indian nationalists' demands and expectation – and from this point on the basis for linking the Khilafat and Punjab issues was patent. Finally, there was the holding of a Special Session of Congress at Calcutta in September 1919 where India's principal nationalist forum would consider the programme of noncooperation being promoted by Gandhi and the Khilafatists.

Gandhi, as a champion of the Khilafat cause and the principal organiser of the Khilafat campaign, concentrated during the year on four basic problems. Firstly, to devise an effective programme of noncooperation capable of bringing decisive pressure to bear on the Raj. Secondly, to win the support of the Hindu population for the Muslim struggle. Thirdly, to develop in the nation as a whole, and particularly in the Muslim population, the necessary discipline to sustain a major nonviolent struggle, preparation which had been lacking in April 1919. Fourthly, to preserve and improve his direct links with the Raj, the British government and British public opinion, so that they would take up the case for the Khilafat and get the terms of the peace treaty revised.

It was in tackling this fourth problem that he was least successful – and this led him substantially to re-conceive and broaden the programme of noncooperation later in 1920. Preparations for satyagraha were evolving under the pressure of events.

Evolution of the Programme: November 1919 - August 1920

As we saw, Gandhi first proposed a programme of noncooperation with the Raj when told that the sanctions he had in mind would not be effective. Noncooperation was at first a vision, a largely theoretical notion: the subject withdraws his or her support from the government in India, thus compelling its submission. Gandhi's key theoretical distinction was that a boycott of British goods, the idea favoured by his critics within the Khilafat movement, would punish British workers who had nothing to do with the terms of the peace treaty; whereas withdrawal of support for the government in India would persuade the Raj's representatives to bring pressure to bear on the British cabinet in London responsible for negotiating the peace terms. (Gandhi M.K. 1965: vol 16: 322)

The actual form which noncooperation was to take involved an assessment of the specific forms by which Indians cooperated in their own subjection under the British crown. It took many months to prepare a programme for how they could withdraw their support. Khilafat conferences between November 1919 and March 1920 established a succession of subcommittees, each with Gandhi as a member to work out the programme. It was not until July 1920, eight months after the initial proposal that the final subcommittee came up with the detailed programme Gandhi was to apply in August 1920 when Noncooperation was first launched on the Khilafat issue. The programme evolved much further when Congress took up the campaign.

Table 6.1 shows some of the main steps taken in the preparation and propaganda phase of Noncooperation between October 1919 and August 1920 (when it was launched by the Khilafat movement) and December 1920 (when Congress decided to support it as well).

Table 6.1: KHILAFAT SATYAGRAHA: PHASES 1 AND 2

Date	Event
1919	**PHASE 1: PREPARATION AND PROPAGANDA**
17 October	**1st Khilafat Day.** Gandhi helps organise. Widely supported.
23/24 Nov.	**2ⁿᵈ All-India Khilafat Conference (Delhi).** Gandhi's call for boycott of "foreign cloth" criticised. Proposes concept of "noncooperation". Joins subcommittee formed to examine the idea.
13 Dec	National boycott of Raj Peace Celebrations
1920	
7 March	Gandhi publishes Khilafat "manifesto". (1) No violence in thought, word or deed. (2) No boycott of British goods. (3) Adopt minimum demands and pursue without rest. (4) Keep Khilafat issue separate.
11-14 March	**Central Khilafat Committee (CKC) (Bombay).** Four stages of noncooperation agreed (but not made public until May). (1) Relinquish honours. (2) Council members resign (3) Govt employees resign (4) Resign from Army and Police. Prior to launch, focus on propaganda.
19 March	**2ⁿᵈ Khilafat Day.** Gandhi helps organise. Well-supported.

12 May	**CKC (Bombay).** Gandhi's modifies proposal for four progressive stages: (1) Relinquish honours. (2) Govt employees resign (3) Resign from Army and Police (4) Refuse taxes. This is agreed and made public.

Note: Council resignations dropped; refusal of taxes added.

1-3 June	**CKC (Allahabad).** Support for the 4 stages. Noncooperation subcommittee appointed with Gandhi as "adviser" and as link with nationalist Hindus. Message to Viceroy announces launch of Noncooperation on August 1.
Late June-early July	**CKC (Bombay).** Gandhi advocates "progressive nonviolent noncooperation". Stage (1) now hugely expanded into five items: (a) Renounce honours; (b) Boycott legislatures; (c) Withdraw students from government schools and colleges; (d) Lawyers give up their practices; (e) Decline all invitations to government functions. To start on August 19.

Note: No focus in stage (1) on resignations from government service, including police and army, nor on tax refusal; Council boycott added.

PHASE 2: LAUNCH

1 August	**3rd Khilafat Day.** CKC launches Noncooperation with hartal.
4-7 Sept.	**Special All-India Congress (AIC) Session (Calcutta).** Special Congress recommends Nagpur annual session in December to take up Noncooperation on 3 issues: (a) Punjab, (b) Khilafat, plus (c) Swaraj.

Note: Boycott of foreign goods also added to programme.

26-31 Dec.	**All-India Congress (Nagpur).** Congress takes up Noncooperation, five months after its launch on the Khilafat issue by the Central Khilafat Committee.

Note: Aims are broadened to include issues of Punjab and Swaraj.

Maulana Azad, a Muslim nationalist from Bengal, describes his reaction in January 1920 as a member of one of the noncooperation subcommittees:

"As soon as Gandhi described his proposal I remembered that this was the programme which Tolstoy had outlined many years ago. In 1901, an anarchist attacked the King of Italy. Tolstoy at the time addressed an open letter to the anarchists that the method of violence was morally wrong and politically of little use. If one man was killed another would always take his place... Tolstoy advised that the proper method to paralyse an oppressive government was to refuse taxes, resign from all services and boycott institutions supporting the Government. He believed that such a programme would compel any Government to come to terms... I said without a moment's hesitation that I fully accepted the programme. If people really wanted to help Turkey, there was no alternative to the programme sketched by Gandhiji." (Azad 1959)

Azad quickly decided to support Gandhi, but the others on the subcommittee wanted more time to make up their minds. It took months to persuade the Central Khilafat Committee itself to adopt the programme and even longer to win the approval of the principal nationalist leaders in Congress.

Perhaps the most important point about Noncooperation is that it was not a programme of civil disobedience. (Gandhi M.K. 1965: vol 18: 78-79, 139; vol 17: 389, 393)[28] While Tolstoy and Thoreau might have conceived of a withdrawal of cooperation being centred in a campaign of tax refusal, Gandhi had already tried to launch a campaign of civil disobedience in April 1919 and had failed. Gandhi accepted the criticism of the Rowlatt Satyagraha, that he had launched civil disobedience prematurely before supporters were ready to maintain nonviolent discipline. Thus he conceived noncooperation as a programme building up in stages, the first acts involving direct or indirect withdrawal of services from the government but not a breach of the law. Gandhi's nervousness

---

28. "It should be clearly understood that this is not a movement of civil disobedience." (Gandhi M.K. 1965: vol 18: 78-79)

about moving to direct confrontation with the police and army by launching civil disobedience led him to place all sorts of restrictions on this type of action. It is a mark of his ingenuity as a strategist and organiser that he was able to outline and initiate in 1920 a programme of noncooperation that was markedly different from the programme of civil disobedience which he had intended to follow during the Rowlatt Satyagraha only a year previously. Tax refusal, the mass civil disobedience stage of noncooperation, was never reached between 1920 and 1922.[29] In the event, Gandhi did not return until a decade later to the aggressive civil disobedience on a national scale he had planned against the Rowlatt Acts in 1919.[30]

Consideration of Council Boycott

In November 1919, Gandhi first formulated noncooperation as the right to refuse to serve government by declining to accept titles or employment from it. (Gandhi M.K. 1965: vol 16: 321) The idea of noncooperation fitted well with the immediate plans of the Khilafatists for boycotting the Raj's peace celebrations. But in December, just before the Amritsar session of Congress, Gandhi was totally unprepared to consider, as a further extension of Noncooperation, a proposal for a boycott of the Raj's new reform Councils. In an article in Navajivan, he agreed that Council boycott would have been "the best remedy" for combating the Rowlatt Act and tackling the Punjab issue, but pointed out that absolutely no preparations had been made for launching such a campaign and none of the deputations to England to press for alterations to the Reform Bill had warned the British about such a boycott. Therefore he opposed the idea: "It must be admitted that the nation is not yet ready for such rejection", he wrote; "it has not had the required political education". (Gandhi M.K. 1965: vol 16: 331-342)

---

29. Except some talukas in Andhra in northern Madras, including Guntur, which took the initiative themselves without Gandhi's full agreement. See Chapter 9.

30. With the Salt March in 1930, civil disobedience began at Dandi and a few days later at the Dharasana salt works, as part of a national campaign. Civil disobedience in 1928 at Bardoli was a local struggle.

However, it is clear that within the Khilafat movement itself some Muslims were calling for withdrawal from the Councils as part of Noncooperation. Early in March, Gandhi began to shift his position a little when he said at a public meeting on the Khilafat question in Bombay:

"If this question in not settled satisfactorily and if our Muslim brethren resign from the Councils I can tell you with confidence that my brethren, the Hindu representatives, cannot but follow their example." (Gandhi M.K. 1965: vol. 17: 68)

On March 7, 1920, Gandhi tried to put some closer definition on his ideas for Noncooperation by publishing what was called a "manifesto". In this pronouncement, in response to a growing militancy in the Khilafat movement, especially in Bengal, he concentrated on "what we may not do", while remaining vague on the specific programme. Itemising four separate points, he emphasised firstly that there should be no violence "in thought, speech or deed"; secondly, there should be no boycott of British goods; thirdly, they should set their "minimum" demands and, having set them, "there should be no rest"; and fourthly, there should be no combination of the Khilafat issue with other political issues. He went on to support the call for a second Khilafat Day on March 19, but his public proposals for Noncooperation were not spelt out:

"Those who are holding offices of honour or emolument ought to give them up. Those who belong to the menial services under Government should do likewise... Advice to soldiers to refuse to serve is premature. It is the last not the first step... We must proceed slowly so as to ensure retention of self-control under the fiercest heat." (Gandhi M.K. 1965: vol 17: 73)

In private, more detailed discussions were going on. The Central Khilafat Committee meeting in Bombay from March 11 to 14 followed Gandhi's advice to concentrate on propaganda before attempting noncooperation; but it also considered and adopted a detailed plan drawn up by a subcommittee of which Gandhi was the principal member. Judith Brown writes:

"This plan suggests several stages of noncooperation, starting with the relinquishing of titles and honours, followed by the resignation of council members, the withdrawal of private servants and government employees, including the police, the withdrawal of Muslims from the army and culminating in a refusal to pay taxes." (Brown 1972: 207-208)

During March, serious discussions began in private between Muslim and Hindu political leaders to consider Noncooperation as a practical proposition for the nation. Doubts began to be expressed by conservative Muslim elements as well as by the established Hindu politicians. The most pungent criticisms were expressed by the Liberal, Srinivasa Sastri, and by Annie Besant. Both feared a repetition of Gandhi's loss of control in April 1919 and many other negative consequences. Gandhi's principal response was that of course there was a risk of violence but if they succeeded in "defeating the scheme of noncooperation" the risk was much greater; and he challenged them to suggest an alternative method of satisfying Muslim grievances. (Gandhi M.K. 1965: vol 17: 356) Eventually, on May 5, he was drawn to spell out in public the four-stage plan for Noncooperation agreed privately in March:

> "Perhaps the best way of answering the fears and the criticisms as to non-cooperation is to elaborate more fully the scheme of non-cooperation. The critics seem to imagine that the organisers propose to give effect to the whole scheme at once. The fact however is that the organisers have fixed definite, progressive, four stages."

Firstly, the giving up of titles and resignation of honorary posts – that is, no action involving the sacrifice of people's livelihoods. Secondly, if this failed, they would move to the second stage involving "much previous arrangement". This was to invite all government employees in the civil service to resign – though "all the classes of servants will not be called out at once" and no undue influence would be brought to bear on people to resign. This second stage was bound to be successful in forcing the government to capitulate, "if the response is at all on an adequate scale". Therefore, the third stage of withdrawing from the police and army was "a distant goal"; and the fourth stage, refusal to pay taxes was "still more remote". Gandhi added:

"The organisers recognise that suspension of general taxation is fraught with the greatest danger. It is likely to bring a sensitive class in conflict with the police. They are therefore not likely to embark upon it unless they can do so with the assurance that there will be no violence offered by the people. " (Gandhi M.K. 1965: vol 17: 389-392)

This four-stage programme of Noncooperation was "finally" adopted by the Central Khilafat Committee at its meeting in Bombay on May 12, prompting the resignation of several of its more conservative members.

It will be noticed that in his May 5 spelling out of the four stages, Gandhi made no reference to boycott of the councils. In fact, later in the month, Gandhi clearly envisaged supporters of the national movement standing for the new legislatures and he advised readers of *Navajivan* on who they should vote for. (Gandhi M.K. 1965: vol 17: 416-418) However, during May, the peace terms unfavourable to Turkey and a huge blow to Indian pan-Islamism were published and so was the report of the Hunter Commission on the Punjab. These two affronts to Indian national opinion shocked and outraged all sections of the national movement. Early in June, Lala Lajpat Rai – a leading Hindu politician in the Punjab, who had attended a joint meeting with Muslim Khilafatists in March and had joined a sub-committee with Gandhi and others to work out the programme of Noncooperation (Brown 1972: 209) – announced that, in protest against British behaviour in the province, he would withdraw from the forthcoming elections to the Punjab provincial council. Gandhi immediately took up the suggestion; he incorporated it as a proposal for a national boycott of the councils in the Noncooperation programme. (Gandhi M.K. 1965: vol 17: 521-522)

Combining the two issues: Khilafat and Punjab

At this point too Gandhi switched from insisting that the Khilafat and Punjab issues should be treated as two separate campaigns and took the opposite view that protest on the two questions should be combined in a single movement of noncooperation. In addition to this fundamental change in his position, he was persuaded by the anger of the Khilafatists that the time had come to move directly from the propaganda and preparation stage of the agitation to direct confrontation with the Raj. (Nanda 1989: 217-221)

On May 18, on publication of the "Turkish terms" Gandhi called them "a staggering blow to the Indian Mussulmans". He went on to call for their revision and stated his view that "they are capable of being revised" if noncooperation was faithfully followed. He called also for a joint conference of Hindus and Muslims to consider what to do next. (Gandhi M.K. 1965: vol 17: 426-427) On May 30, Gandhi attended a meeting of the all-India Congress Committee at Benares where he invited the Committee to support the Khilafat demands and the programme of noncooperation. This they declined to do, but they did announce that a special session of the Congress would be held in Calcutta in September to consider the question of noncooperation. (Krishna 1966: 50-52)

A joint conference of Muslims and Hindus to consider how to respond to the peace terms was held in Allahabad from June 1 to 3. To the consternation of some of the pan-Islamists present, most of the Hindu leaders attending were unwilling to endorse noncooperation and opted to wait for the Congress special session. But, after a fiery discussion, the Khilafat Committee confirmed its support for the four stage programme of noncooperation and appointed a new subcommittee to implement it. (Nanda 1989: 216-218) This Committee came to be known semi-seriously as the "martial law committee" of the Khilafat movement and Gandhi as its "dictator". Its members included the Ali brothers, A.K. Azad and Hasrat Mohani. (Gandhi R. 2007: 227)

On June 9, following the publication of the Hunter Report, Gandhi first argued publicly in *Young India* that the nation should take up noncooperation on the Punjab issue. He recognised, however, that the preparative stages of complaint and petition in accordance with the rules of satyagraha were not exactly the same with the two issues; he proceeded to organise for direct confrontation with the Raj on the Khilafat issue, but stayed his hand a little on the Punjab question. On June 22, he wrote to the Viceroy, Lord Chelmsford, inviting him to lead the Muslim agitation against the peace terms in order to avoid noncooperation. A few days later he announced in Navajivan that noncooperation on the Khilafat issue would begin from August 1. And on July 4, in Navajivan, he spelt out on behalf of the noncooperation sub-committee of the Central Khilafat Committee their revised programme of action.

Addition of the "Triple Boycott"

The reality of moving into open noncooperation with the Raj seems have been one factor leading the Committee to expand greatly the programme in the first of its four stages. Without delay, supporters were to decline to take up new government loans and they were to withdraw from recruitment into the armed forces and the civil service. Also, Indian troops should refuse to serve in the Middle East. From August 19, the first stage of Noncooperation was to begin as follows:

"1. Titles and honorary positions will be renounced.

2. Legislatures will be boycotted.

3. Parents will withdraw their children from Government schools.

4. Lawyers will give up practice and help people to settle their civil disputes among themselves.

5. Invitations to Government functions, parties etc. will be politely refused, non-cooperation being given as the sole reason for doing so. " (Gandhi M.K. 1965: vol 18: 4-7)

This insertion of a boycott of the councils, of schools and of the law-courts – items 2, 3 and 4, which came to be called the "Triple Boycott" – completely transformed the noncooperation programme. It was now substantially different from what had been outlined at the beginning of May. The resignation of civil servants from Government employment, that is, the second stage, was not mentioned specifically. Neither were the third and fourth stages, resignation from the police and army and refusal of taxation. Gandhi, faced with the reality of trying to organise and lead a nationwide confrontation with the British, requiring immense discipline and self-sacrifice, had switched the programme of noncooperation it its first stage to something closer to his own ideal prescription for Indian society.

In his testament published in 1906 in South Africa, *Hind Swaraj* or Indian Home Rule, Gandhi had shown that he had no love for legislatures or for the legal profession. At his ashram, he had been experimenting in devising a form of education suitable to Indian conditions rather than implanted by the Raj. In proposing a first stage of noncooperation which followed Tolstoy's advice to "boycott institutions" that were "supporting the government", Gandhi was favouring his own social and religious prescriptions for Indian society. This step was in opposition to the expectations and interests of the majority of Indian political leaders who saw the Raj's influence on Indian society as beneficial.

In drawing in to his programme boycott of the legislatures, schools and law courts, Gandhi was by implication broadening out the very programme of swadeshi he had been advocating since April 1919. However, instead of focusing on cloth as an area of life in which Indians should favour the local product in preference to that from further afield, he was now promoting swadeshi in politics, in education and in personal disputes. Indian political workers should forsake the legislatures and go out to work with the masses; schools should teach pride in Indian culture and language rather than ape the British; disputes should be settled by the time-honoured Indian method of arbitration rather than an expensive legal system.

I have seen no satisfactory explanation of why Gandhi chose to take such an extraordinary risk in broadening the programme of noncooperation in July 1920. Conservative Muslims on the Central Khilafat Committee were resigning; prominent Hindu politicians had shown themselves to be lukewarm about the programme and were awaiting a special Congress where they were likely to oppose the scheme; Gandhi's earlier efforts to promote his ideal programme through the Swadeshi Sabha had met with limited support. Presumably an explanation lies in a set of decisions Gandhi must have taken in late May at about the time of the Benares meeting of the all-India Congress Committee, followed by the Central Khilafat Committee in Allahabad at the beginning of June. This was just after publication of the peace terms and of the Hunter Report on the Punjab events.

Since the established nationalist leaders in the Congress were not going to agree easily to noncooperation he would have to go ahead and organise the campaign whether or not he had their support. In order to sustain a campaign of satyagraha – at base a social and religious as well as a political movement reliant on self-sacrifice and voluntary suffering – it was necessary for the educated classes who were most active in nationalist politics to take the lead in making sacrifices as an example to the rest of the nation. Thus Gandhi pitched his programme so as to challenge through boycott of the councils, the schools and the law courts, the self-interest and willingness to sacrifice of the very groups who were involved in Congress politics. In this he was throwing down the same challenge to Congress as he had thrown down earlier to the Home Rule Leagues – more than bitter speeches and angry demonstrations were needed if they were seriously to oppose the Raj. He was also challenging the "limited politics" of the Liberals whose petitions and speeches within the councils had failed.

But as a signal of his determination to direct a major satyagraha struggle whether or not he had the support of Congress, noncooperation was scheduled to begin on August 1, over a month before the special Congress was to meet at Calcutta. In other words, if Gandhi was to take the lead and direct noncooperation across India on his own initiative then it had to be with a programme which satisfied his own criteria for a satyagraha struggle. Hence the expanded programme of noncooperation was brought in at the point when Gandhi decided to "go for broke" and lead the struggle in his own way. This may be part of an explanation.

Following the ultimatum to the Viceroy, Noncooperation did begin on August 1, 1920, with a third Khilafat Day. The Noncooperation Committee of the Central Khilafat Committee made no mention of the Punjab issue in its instructions for the day of action circulated from Bombay, though Gandhi did raise the Punjab grievance in his second personal letter to the Viceroy. (Gandhi M.K. 1965: vol 18: 78-79, 104-106) Noncooperation was to begin with 24 hours of fasting and prayer, accompanied by the suspension of business and by public meetings. Gandhi, as part of the series of tests of the Khilafatists' readiness to take up satyagraha, was beginning to get more confident about organising large public demonstrations – but there were still to be no processions. At these public meetings, resolutions were to be passed calling for a revision in the terms of the peace treaty. It was also expected that resignations by title-holders, honorary magistrates and council members would begin on August 1.

In the event, Noncooperation began quietly with an all-India day of fasting and hartal, accompanied by a smattering of resignations by title-holders. On this, the third Khilafat Day, the Noncooperation Committee renewed its call for the boycott of the courts, the schools and the councils – the triple boycott – and Gandhi began hammering away at his theme that across the nation people should prepare themselves for acts of great self-sacrifice.

Progressive Nonviolent Noncooperation

In working between November 1919 and August 1920 as the predominant member of a series of Khilafat committees which devised the programme of Noncooperation, Gandhi's main preoccupation appears to have been to devise a strategy for a mass nonviolent movement which would bring effective pressure to bear on the Raj but would not involve the use of civil disobedience, at least in the early stages. The collapse of civil disobedience against the Rowlatt Act only a few months earlier left him with little option but to try new tactics. Working from a theoretical concept to a practical programme, Gandhi at first envisaged a programme involving the resignation of honorary positions, the withdrawal of those directly employed by the government and the non-payment of taxes. Quickly, for practical reasons, it became clear that all parts of the programme could not be launched at once. Gandhi therefore conceived of what he began to call "progressive nonviolent noncooperation", a movement building up in stages. Noncooperation was to be progressive in at least three and perhaps four senses.

Firstly, progressive nonviolent noncooperation involved moving from acts of small sacrifice to acts of greater sacrifice – that is, from resigning honours, to resigning jobs, to refusing taxes. (Gandhi M.K. 1965: vol 18: 96, 181)[31] It was to move from what are sometimes called "symbolic"

---

31. "The first stage of Noncooperation was... arranged so as to involve minimum of danger to public peace and minimum of sacrifice on the part of those who participated in the movement." (Gandhi M.K. 1965: vol 18: 96)

actions, challenging the Raj's view of itself and denting its status in the eyes of the governed, to more direct actions directly crippling its ability to function.

Secondly, the progressive noncooperation was to begin with the most privileged of the educated classes, those who had been honoured by the Raj, moving to the educated classes generally, then to everyone in government employment, and finally to the masses. Only by privileged classes making the greatest sacrifice did Gandhi imagine he could launch and build a mass movement (Gandhi M.K. 1965: vol 18: 68, 140, 149-150); only by this gradual widening of the circle of involvement did he imagine he could educate the masses in nonviolence and sustain mass nonviolent discipline.

Thirdly, as involvement broadened from the "classes" to the "masses" so there was greater risk of public disorder, particularly as the later stages would involve confrontation with the authorities. (Gandhi M.K. 1965: vol 18: 142)[32]

Fourthly, it was through this progressive build-up of the campaign that Gandhi imagined they could raise the necessary funds to sustain noncooperators who had resigned their jobs and develop in every town and village the necessary organisational structure to coordinate a mass movement. (Gandhi M.K. 1965: vol 18: 284, 447-448)

However, there was a problem with progressive nonviolent noncooperation as at first envisaged. The first stage, involving the resignation of honorary positions, did not involve a wide enough circle of people, and the second stage, the resignation of government jobs, involved asking a conservative body of people to make too great a sacrifice at too early a stage. Therefore, Gandhi had to find a way of expanding and extending the first stage – expanding so as to widen the numbers of the educated classes being

---

32. "I am resorting to noncooperation in progressive stages because I want to evolve true order out of untrue order. I am not going to take a single step in noncooperation unless I am satisfied that the country is ready for that step, namely noncooperation will not be followed by anarchy or disorder". (Gandhi, M.K 1965: vol 18:142)

asked to make sacrifices, extending so as to delay the moment when the government employees were asked to join the programme. Gandhi's solution was to expand vastly the first stage of the movement, so that it included not only the resignation of honours received from the government but also the boycott of institutions which supported the government. By this means the demand for sacrifice in the first stage of the campaign was aimed directly at the educated class who constituted the political elite of the nation and whose participation in noncooperation from an early stage was essential if the movement was to succeed. Hence the idea of council boycott – and more problematically, the schools boycott and the law-courts boycott.

Through this, the triple boycott, Gandhi was able in the first stage of noncooperation to damage the credibility of the Raj's reform programme and to put pressure on "collaborators" with the Raj; to draw school and college students into full-time work for the movement; and to pressure some of the most prestigious lawyers in the country, who were also the political elite in Congress, to give up their practices and turn to full-time political organising. This need to expand dramatically participation in the first stage is a second explanation for his sudden introduction of the triple boycott.

But this, obviously, is looking at noncooperation with hindsight. In July 1920, when Gandhi first proposed the expansion of the first stage to include the triple boycott, his proposal was looked on with incredulity. Indulal Yajnik describes the reaction of political workers in Gujarat and across India in July and August when Gandhi was preparing to launch Noncooperation on behalf of the Khilafat Committee alone, and when he proposed the boycott of schools and courts:

> "A hue and cry... arose from every quarter of India against Mr Gandhi's plan of this double boycott of Schools and Courts and it then appeared nearly impossible that he would be able to carry the Congress or the large majority of the masses with him in the novel plan that he was seeking to foist on them."

Political workers like Yajnik knew of Gandhi's views – "his thesis of philosophical anarchism as contained in his book on Indian Home

Rule" – but they had "time and again expressed the utmost opposition to them". Lawyers seemed to be the group least likely to respond to Gandhi's programme; schools boycott would be a disaster for many thousands of children, leaving school and not knowing what to do next.

Nevertheless, in Yajnik's account, some of the workers were "speedily" converted to Gandhi's viewpoint as he spelled out his "full plan of building up constructive national institutions in proportion as the Nation was weaned from the sinful Government institutions."

"Thus he asked us not to be merely satisfied by weaning voters from the polling booths, but to mass them in the Congress fold with a view eventually to organise and develop the Congress machinery and its activities as the National Government of the land... We were led to dream of setting up a chain of national arbitration courts under the aegis of the Congress... Regarding the boycott of schools... [t]he Congress would help the same teachers or draft new ones to organise National Schools... We were thus persuaded that the Congress would be readily enabled by the vast amount of popular support behind it to build up hundreds of arbitration Courts and thousands of Schools... and that apart from a few days or weeks of inevitable confusion the measure of success achieved in both these boycotts would be automatically reflected in the creation of parallel non-official institutions. We thus saw that the whole programme of Non-co-operation, even in its first stages, was [not] only not conceived in a spirit of emotional negativism, but was really designed to inspire the political workers of the country to build up a system of parallel National Government." (Yajnik 1933:114-115)

Yajnik and others who had worked with Gandhi during the Rowlatt agitation and before, but were sceptical about the Khilafat agitation, moved strongly in his support in the weeks before the special Congress. Building up the institutions of a new national government was not "philosophical anarchism", of course, but perhaps only a philosophical anarchist who was also a pragmatist could have dreamed up such a scheme. Gandhi's belief in moving forward gradually according to his assessment of the capacity of the Indian culture and its political leadership to deliver and sustain momentum, is strongly evident here. Gujarat workers called their own provincial Congress, which endorsed Gandhi's programme, and across India other provincial Congress gatherings approved the idea of Noncooperation in principle – though with many reservations about the details. (Brown 1972: 251-261)

Gandhi made it absolutely clear that he and the Central Khilafat Committee would go ahead with noncooperation on the Khilafat issue whether or not they achieved the backing of the Congress. (Gandhi M.K. 1965: vol 18: 149) But in winning the support of the special Congress session at Calcutta and then having this confirmed by the annual session in Nagpur, Gandhi was forced to modify the programme of Noncooperation yet again. In part, this was in response to the continuing pressure for a boycott of British goods. In part, it was because Congress would support a movement as drastic as noncooperation only if the goal of the movement was swaraj, independence itself, rather than two specific grievances, however important, the Khilafat and the Punjab. (Gandhi R. 2007: 232-234) The broad strategy and detailed programme of Noncooperation was nevertheless worked out almost entirely by Gandhi in collaboration with the Khilafat movement in the months prior to September. The Khilafat issue, coupled with the need for Hindu support if the Khilafat movement was to succeed, catapulted Gandhi into his bid to lead Congress into Noncooperation late in 1920.

Winning Hindu Support for a Muslim Struggle

A second issue which preoccupied Gandhi in preparing for Noncooperation was the need to draw in Hindu support for the Khilafat campaign. There was no overwhelming reason why Hindu nationalists should support the Khilafat struggle. It concerned a religious issue for many Muslims in India that had no direct bearing on Hindus or the nationalist demand for political independence. Why would they sacrifice themselves and their families on an issue of no concern for them?

We have seen that at the second All-India Khilafat Conference in Delhi in November 1919, Gandhi took an unusual, even bizarre, position on this question. Using his pivotal position as the Hindu leader most identified with the pan-Islamic Muslims, he employed all his influence to stop discussion between Muslim and Hindu politicians of a deal over cow-slaughter and the Punjab. He ruled out the most obvious basis on which Hindu support for the movement could be attracted. As a result, he faced himself with having to develop an alternative means of making the restoration of the Khilafat a national demand. (Nanda 1989: 221-224)

Gandhi's fundamental argument was in terms of the nation:

"It is impossible that one of the four limbs of the nation be wounded and the rest of the nation remain unconcerned. We cannot be called one nation, we cannot be a single body, if such a wound has no effect on us."

This he wrote in *Navajivan* in September 1919. (Gandhi M.K. 1966: vol. 16: 104) In October, in the same journal when he was seeking support for the first Khilafat Day, his argument was similar:

"A mother suffers when her only son dies. She has no desire for eating. A nation is born when all feel the same sort of grief at the suffering of any one among them; such a nation deserves to be immortal". (Gandhi M.K. 1965: vol 16: 230)

This was a moral argument on the grounds of patriotism; but when he began seriously to engage with nationalist Hindus and was striving to convince the political activists to join him, Gandhi was equally willing to argue the same point in terms of political expediency. On accepting the presidency of the All-India Home Rule League in May 1920, he wrote in *Navajivan*:

"So long as there is no unity between Hindus and Muslims I think swaraj will remain a mere dream. I should like, therefore, to extend all help to the Muslims in their fight on the Khilafat issue and thus win them over for ever." (Gandhi M.K. 1965: vol 17: 370)

Gandhi's argument here was very similar to his reason for supporting recruitment to the British Army in 1918 – that helping Britain in its hour of need was bound to help India to freedom… Later in May (though this is one sentence from a larger argument) he was even more blunt:

213

"...by helping the Mohammedans of India at a crucial moment in their history, I want to buy their friendship." (Gandhi M.K. 1965: vol 17: 460)

Gandhi was also to present other arguments which were purely expedient. In the course of his association with the Khilafat movement, he became convinced that Indian Muslims would turn to violence and attempt to make a "bloody revolution" if no nonviolent alternative that promised to be effective could be developed. (Gandhi M.K. 1965: vol 17: 91-92, 102) In May 1920 he argued in *Navajivan*:

"I am convinced that had there been no move for noncooperation violence would long since have broken out. It is noncooperation which has prevented violence. The Muslims are boiling over but they have kept their patience in the belief that the Hindus are with them." (Gandhi M.K. 1965: vol 17: 415-416)

To his critics like Annie Besant and Srinivasa Sastri who argued that noncooperation was bound to lead to violence just as the Rowlatt Satyagraha had, he replied:

"I urge those who talk or work against noncooperation to descend from their chairs and go down to the people, learn their feelings and write, if they have the heart, against noncooperation. They will find, as I have found, that the only way to avoid violence is to enable them to give such expression to their feelings as to compel redress. I have found nothing save noncooperation." (Gandhi M.K. 1965: vol 17: 390)

Again and again he challenged his critics to produce an alternative to Noncooperation, one designed to win Indian Muslims their demands without violence. When the terms of the Peace Treaty hostile to Indian Muslim opinion were announced, talk began to circulate that Khilafatists would support an invasion of India from Afghanistan. Moreover, within a few weeks thousands of Muslims began to leave the country in a mass exodus known as hijrat, quitting British India for life under an Islamic ruler in Afghanistan. Gandhi felt vindicated. In June, he argued:

"In my opinion, the best way to prevent India from becoming the battleground between the forces of Islam and those of the English, is for Hindus to make noncooperation a complete and immediate success, and I have little doubt that if the Mohammedans remain true to their declared intention and are able to exercise self-restraint and make sacrifices, the Hindus will 'play the game' and join them in the campaign of noncooperation." (Gandhi M.K. 1965: vol 17: 484-485)

Here we see Gandhi spelling out the balancing position from which he could direct the movement; on the one hand, Muslims would exercise restraint if Hindus joined them in noncooperation; on the other hand, Hindus would join Muslims in noncooperation if Muslims would show restraint. In July, Gandhi again challenged his critics to suggest an alternative:

"And may I draw the attention of those who are opposing noncooperation that unless they find out a substitute they should either join the noncooperation movement or prepare to face a disorganised subterranean upheaval whose effect no one can foresee and whose spread it would be impossible to check or regulate". (Gandhi M.K. 1965: vol 18: 77)

By July, Gandhi had found his clinching argument on grounds of expediency, which though not explicitly spelt out, was that he alone with the support of the other Khilafat leaders and through the movement of noncooperation, could control Indian Muslims. As he wrote publicly to the Viceroy at the end of June when warning him that noncooperation would soon begin:

"I venture to claim that I have succeeded by patient reasoning in weaning the party of violence from its ways. I confess that I did not – I did not attempt to – succeed in weaning them away from violence on moral grounds but purely on utilitarian grounds. The result for the time being at any rate has been to stop violence. The school of hijrat has received a check if it has not stopped its activities entirely. I hold that no repression could have prevented a violent eruption, if the people had not had presented to them a form of direct action..." (Gandhi M.K. 1965: vol 17: 504)

It was an exaggeration to say that he had not attempted to persuade Muslims against violence on moral grounds but there is no question that the practical arguments were the ones he found effective. Gandhi fully recognised that Indian Muslims were entitled by the authority of the Koran to rise in violent rebellion against the Raj. On March 19, the second Khilafat Day, he went so far as to move a resolution which reserved to Muslims the right to resort to violence "in the event of the failure of the joint movement" of noncooperation. (Gandhi M.K. 1965: vol 17: 99 fn2) In his speech to a mass meeting in Bombay he commented on the resolution:

> "...it commits the joint movement to a policy of nonviolence in the course of the struggle. But Mohammedans have special Koranic obligations in which Hindus may or may not join. They, therefore, reserve to themselves the right, in the event of the failure of noncooperation cum nonviolence, in order to enforce justice, to resort to all such methods as may be enjoined in the Islamic scriptures. I venture heartily to associate myself with this resolution." (Gandhi M.K. 1965: vol 17: 100, 102)

Gandhi put himself in a box where he was promising to deliver to the Khilafatists both Hindu support and an effective nonviolent strategy. If he failed, they would be released from their commitment to follow the discipline of nonviolence. His task during 1920 was to try to make the broad nationalist movement party to this agreement too.

Probably the bulk of Gandhi's vast journalistic outpouring and his many speeches on the Khilafat did not concern itself with making an expedient case for the movement, however. As a polemicist of great skill he wrote article after article in his two newspapers arguing with all-comers the merits of the Khilafat grievance as a genuine affront to India's Muslims.[33] If he had not believed the cause to be a just one, then the expedient arguments would not have counted with Gandhi. (Gandhi M.K. 1965: vol 16: 308) Because of his belief in the movement, he set out to build a campaign the nationalist movement could not afford to ignore.

---

33. A number of these articles are collected in a volume of his journalistic writings selected from *Young India*. (Gandhi M.K. *Young India*, 1919-1922, Madras: S. Ganesan. 1922)

In addition to his journalistic output and his extensive speechmaking tours, he took part in joint dialogues between Hindu and Muslim leaders. But through the Central Khilafat Committee he was helping to build an independent political movement across the country. When he joined the All-India Home Rule League, he was able to bring this, the most active of the nationalist organisations affiliated to Congress, under his influence. Finally, with the publication of the Hunter report in the summer of 1920 and widespread outrage against the Raj, he at last agreed to extend the scope of Noncooperation to include a wider range of issues than just the Muslim grievance.

There appears to have been no explicit deal that Muslims would help Hindus on the Punjab question in return for Hindu support for Muslims on the Khilafat.[34] Rather there was widespread outrage in both communities against the behaviour of the Raj. The Khilafat movement, by building a network of support and the momentum to start noncooperation against the Raj, was offering the only method apparently available for expressing this fury and exerting effective pressure against the government. Thus by building the plan of noncooperation and then launching the movement on August 1, before most nationalist Hindu leaders had made up their minds on what to do, Gandhi effectively compelled Hindu support for the Khilafat campaign. However, the decisive argument for nationalist Hindus was not a deal over cow-slaughter or the Punjab. It now seemed that if they did not join the noncooperation movement, they would be cast aside by the new forces which Gandhi's activities and the Khilafat agitation had brought into nationalist politics. Gandhi's decisive argument was that he was succeeding in building a movement which nationalist Hindus could no longer ignore. (Brown 1972: 271, 300-304)

Developing Nonviolent Discipline

"Fear of violence as a side-effect of his satyagraha campaigns", writes Judith Brown, "was very near the surface of Gandhi's mind after the

---

34. Both Subhas Chandra Bose and Indulal Yajnik suggest that there was such an agreement. This may have been the way political workers at the time perceived the Hindu-Muslim collaboration, but I have seen no direct evidence for it.

debacle of the Rowlatt Satyagraha and his caution attracted many Hindus who had similar fears." (Brown 1972: 208) With few exceptions, the pan-Islamist Muslim leaders of the Khilafat campaign were never committed to nonviolence in principle.

Even so, especially after a Khilafat deputation led by Mohammad Ali had returned from an extended visit to Britain and Europe where they experienced complete failure, the Khilafat leadership committed itself to seeking independence for India as the only means of securing self-determination for their community. (Hamid 1967: 240) The pan-Islamists were ready to pursue an entirely different course from the long-standing approach of Muslim leaders in India, which was to rely on the Raj to advance their position amid a majority Hindu nation. Gandhi's scheme of noncooperation seemed to be the most feasible way of bringing effective pressure to bear on the Raj with the support of nationalist Hindus. Hence the Khilafatists were drawn into a tactical alliance with Gandhi, openly acknowledged by both sides, which included a tactical commitment to nonviolence.

In his "manifesto" on noncooperation issued to the press on March 7, 1920, Gandhi stated:

> "The power that an individual or a nation forswearing violence generates is a power that is irresistible. But my argument today against violence is based upon pure expedience, i.e. its utter futility. Noncooperation is therefore the only remedy left open to us...
>
> "I will cooperate wholeheartedly with the Muslim friends in the prosecution of their just demands so long as they act with sufficient restraint and so long as I feel sure that they do not wish to resort to or countenance violence. I should cease to cooperate and advise every Hindu and for that matter everyone to cease to cooperate the moment there was violence actually done, advised or countenanced." (Gandhi M.K. 1965: vol 17: 75-76)

Moreover, after the launching of Noncooperation on August 1, in a series of speeches and commentaries during a tour of the Muslim areas of Madras he conducted with Shaukat Ali, Gandhi was extraordinarily frank about the nature of their alliance:

"He (Shaukat Ali) believes that one can kill an enemy and, for doing so, even deceit can be employed. I believe on the contrary that in killing an enemy, one falls from one's true nature as a human being... Despite this, we have joined hands, since he has understood that the people have no strength of arms; that they lack unity and qualities like firmness, courage and capacity for self-sacrifice; and that till they acquire them they cannot wield the sword. He says that, whereas his car needs good roads, my cart can move, whatever their condition. Hence, for the present, he has accepted my way... [Having] accepted it, he is trying to cultivate the qualifications necessary for success in it and pleads with the people to do likewise... He tells the people frankly that, at the present time, my way is the best for them. If the Muslims are peaceful, it is because of his firmness." (Gandhi M.K. 1965: vol 18: 210, 146, 158)

This passage, published in *Navajivan*, reveals part of Gandhi's strategy for holding the Muslim community in India to nonviolent discipline. He would need to convert and hold the Muslim Khilafat leaders to a firm conviction that nonviolent action was the only possible method to adopt in the circumstances of 1920; then they would be able to control and discipline the Muslim masses. In April, in a reply to Annie Besant and to an editorial in *The Times of India*, he claimed he had no fear of noncooperation leading to violence "because every responsible Mohammedan understands that noncooperation to be successful must be totally unattended with violence." (Gandhi M.K. 1965: vol 17: 352) When criticism grew that the Noncooperation Committee appointed at Allahabad in June to direct the movement was unrepresentative of Muslim opinion in the country, Gandhi candidly agreed that this was so because the committee did not contain "doubting elements".

"It has been purposely restricted to those who are able to give their whole time and attention to the work of organised noncooperation and, in the process, of ensuring obedience to instructions, other discipline and nonviolence. It is therefore a committee of workers ... It contains those only who have the largest faith in noncooperation and who although they swear by it, yet will not force the pace to the breaking point but will endeavour to carry the nation with its programme, in so far as it is practicable, and who whilst doing so will not themselves be deterred from taking the boldest steps and will seek out those who are prepared to do likewise." (Gandhi M.K. 1965: vol 17: 505)

Here we have the same formula that Gandhi had employed in all his earlier campaigns, from Champaran to Rowlatt, gathering round him to direct the struggle a group of the most committed "whole-timers" who accepted his leadership and for whom he was willing to accept responsibility. In the committee, whose principal members beside Gandhi were the Ali brothers, A.K. Azad, Hasrat Mohani and Saifuddin Kitchlew (who had invited Gandhi to the Punjab in April 1919 and been expelled at the same time as Gandhi was externed), he conveniently had with him those "extremist" Muslims most likely to try to launch a campaign of violence. These men he had convinced to join him in a nonviolent experiment.

As we have seen, in the run-up to Noncooperation the first means of trying to prepare the Muslim community and the whole population for an all-India satyagraha was the selection of special days of prayer, fasting and hartal, the Khilafat Days. A correspondent critical of Gandhi commented in April that hartal was becoming a "powerful political weapon for uniting the educated and the uneducated" and that it was teaching direct action. (Gandhi M.K. 1965: vol 17: 405) Three Khilafat Days were held, in October 1919 and March and August 1920. In addition, there was a hartal in opposition to the peace celebrations in December 1919; and two days of the week-long commemoration of Rowlatt events in April were devoted to the Khilafat. Thus, in ten months, Gandhi was involved in four all-India days of hartal and prayer on the issue of Khilafat, and two more days dedicated to it.

Gandhi thought that the success of the first Khilafat Day hartal was "proof" of the acceptance of satyagraha, however slightly, however unconsciously, both by the rulers and the ruled. (Gandhi M.K. 1965: vol 16: 259-260) The second Khilafat Day, in March, he called "a great success and a complete triumph of satyagraha" because in Bombay on the day of the hartal no canvassing for people to close their businesses had taken place; it had been completely voluntary. All that was necessary for the people's hopes to bear fruit was to add "the spirit of self-sacrifice" to the discipline and self-restraint they had shown. "The spirit of prayer was abroad and it dominated the people rather than the spirit of revenge, anger, excitement..." In Bombay, the vast public meeting had been conducted without applause "or any other effusive demonstration". He continued:

> "The organisers deserve the warmest praise for having introduced the ancient peacefulness, quiet, determination and orderliness in the place of modern fluster, excitement and disorderliness. The one develops just the qualities that make for satyagraha, the other inevitably leads to violence."

Gandhi felt after the second Khilafat Day that an "exemplary patience, self-restraint and orderliness... are evolving in our midst". (Gandhi M.K. 1965: vol 17: 111-113) His tests of the readiness of Khilafat supporters to engage in satyagraha were proving satisfactory.

The third Khilafat Day in August of course was used to launch the movement of Noncooperation. By then he had moved from developing discipline and calm in the conduct of the campaign to a more specific focus on the question of organisation:

> "But the greatest thing in this campaign of noncooperation is to evolve order, discipline, cooperation among the people, coordination among the workers. Effective noncooperation depends upon complete organisation. Thousands of men who have filled meetings throughout the Punjab have convinced me that the people want to withdraw cooperation from the Government, but they must know how…"

There was a danger that out of anger, citizens would attack persons representing the government or supporters of the government who refused to join the movement. "Disorderliness comes from anger, orderliness out of intelligent resistance." Those who wished to make noncooperation a success in the shortest possible time "will consider it their first duty to see that in their neighbourhood complete order is kept." (Gandhi M.K. 1965: vol 18: 93)

The Khilafat Days and other hartals and public meetings were proving the strength of support and mobilising new groups. They were building and exercising a network of organisers, educating supporters in the issues of the campaign, training them in nonviolent discipline and developing what might become a unified campaign across India.

In response to the criticisms of Annie Besant and others who feared that noncooperation would break down in violence, Gandhi began to spell out more of his strategy:

> "These writers have assumed... that the advocates of noncooperation do not know their job. The latter do not intend to climb to the last step of the staircase of noncooperation all in one jump. If they proceed step by step there will be very little fear of their falling." (Gandhi M.K. 1965: vol 17: 372-373)

"Progressive" nonviolent noncooperation had been introduced, that is, the division of the campaign into four stages, "because of doubts whether we would remain blameless". (Gandhi M.K. 1965: vol 17: 494) Gandhi frequently drew on the analogy between the conduct of this campaign and that of an army. Referring to an order by the Delhi government in May 1920 restricting public meetings, Gandhi insisted that the order be obeyed until the civil disobedience stage of Noncooperation was reached.

> "If, in this movement, even a single worker follows his own judgment, he will do it much harm.
>
> "There is no difference between those who join this fight and the troops in an army. In an army the individual soldier cannot act on his own responsibility but must await orders from his superiors, and this is also true of the Khilafat struggle... If we can acquire full control over the people, victory will be ours this very day." (Gandhi M.K. 1965: vol 17: 392-393)

In July, he went so far as to say publicly that if riots broke out as a result of noncooperation he would not hesitate "for the time being" to help the government control the disorder. (Gandhi M.K. 1965: vol 18: 96, 99) When in August it was clear that supporters of the movement in Delhi and Sind had obeyed government restrictions on their activities, Gandhi was pleased. He commented in a newspaper interview:

"I consider that people are better disciplined now than they were before. In this I include even the masses whom I have had opportunities of seeing in large numbers in various parts of the country."

However, he made it clear that in the first stage of noncooperation, even though he believed he had the support of the Muslim masses, he was not working for a "complete severance of cooperation" with the government. His aim was simply to make the government realise "the depth of popular feeling" on the Khilafat and Punjab issues. (Gandhi M.K. 1965: vol 18: 139) In general, Gandhi argued that the delay in launching Noncooperation between May and August, when the peace terms were announced, and the fact that in those two and a half months Indian Muslims did not erupt in violence, was itself a demonstration of the discipline that was being evolved in that community. (Gandhi M.K. 1965: vol 17: 433, 504) When, in May, while preparations for the campaign were in progress, some supporters of the Khilafat movement acted prematurely and renounced titles and honorary positions, Gandhi was publicly critical:

"I think this is a hasty step. Before taking the momentous step of noncooperation it is very necessary for people to make petitions for a reconsideration of the peace terms and give public expression to their feelings ... I hope, therefore, that people... will not act individually and will take no steps without instructions from the central body." (Gandhi M.K. 1965: vol 17: 446)

A further aspect of Gandhi's effort to develop discipline in Muslim supporters and to draw in Hindu support was his insistence that Muslims should take the lead in noncooperation on the Khilafat issue. (Gandhi M.K. 1965: vol 17: 485) Gandhi was convinced that if the Muslim community could discipline itself in a major nonviolent struggle then Hindus would join it too. His own presence as a Hindu on the central committee of Muslims directing the struggle was something of an anomaly he addressed by calling himself an "adviser" only – in recognition of his special qualifications in satyagraha. (Gandhi M.K 1966: vol 17: 504) Muslims taking the lead in a satyagraha struggle he thought would help make the community and its leaders conscious of setting an example to their fellow Indians. By launching Noncooperation on August 1, a month before the special Congress met in Calcutta, the Central Khilafat Committee fully acted on this principle. Muslims did take the lead. (Gandhi M.K 1965: vol 17: 510; vol 18: 5)[35]

Through his constant touring, speeches and writings, Gandhi also worked prodigiously to try to develop an understanding of nonviolence and the need for discipline among the Muslim population. In July, before launching noncooperation he undertook a major tour of Muslim areas of Northern India in Punjab and Sindh. In his speeches he emphasised the martial qualities of the Muslims, often employed by the British Army. In Rawalpindi he called for an "unarmed, swordless army":

> "The Punjabis know how to draw the sword, but I call their sword mercenary... Your sword is unavailing against anyone who can employ his more skilfully than you... I have found a way by which you can fight while keeping your swords sheathed." (Gandhi M.K 1965: vol 18: 64-65)

In Karachi he said that the movement needed "soldiers with spiritual power"; "I want you all to be soldiers with such force of will that you will stand in your place and never retire." (Gandhi M.K 1965: vol 18: 81) Before the special Congress in September, Gandhi conducted a second major speaking tour of Madras in South India. There, speaking to a Muslim community, he placed more emphasis on the religious basis of noncooperation and its value for changing the lives of individuals:

> "I call it a spiritual weapon because it demands discipline and sacrifice from us... [T]he promise behind every religion that I have studied... is that there is no spotless sacrifice... which has not carried with it its absolute adequate reward ... It is a spiritual weapon because it brings out the best in the nation and it absolutely satisfies individual honour if a single individual takes it [up]..." (Gandhi M.K 1965: vol 18: 182)

It was in August in *Young India*, when he was using all his skills as a journalist to win supporters for noncooperation that Gandhi published

---

35. Gandhi applied the same logic to the Punjab question. He publicly proposed Council boycott across India only after Lajput Rai, a prominent Punjabi politician, had called for a boycott of council elections in the Punjab.

his famous article, "The Doctrine of the Sword". Correspondents, he said, were informing him either that noncooperation would inevitably lead to violence and he must not interfere with this, or that they admired his clever tactics of publicly planning a nonviolent struggle while secretly intending to promote violence at the appropriate moment. He wrote:

"In this age of the rule of brute force, it is almost impossible for anyone to believe that anyone else could possibly reject the law of the final supremacy of brute force...

"Such being the hold that the doctrine of the sword has on the majority of mankind, and as success of non-co-operation depends principally on absence of violence during its pendency, and as my views in this matter affect the conduct of a large number of people, I am anxious to state them as clearly as possible.

"I do believe that where there is only a choice between cowardice and violence I would advise violence...

"But I believe that nonviolence is infinitely superior to violence, forgiveness is more manly than punishment. ('Forgiveness adorns a soldier.')...

"Strength does not come from physical capacity. It comes from an indomitable will...

"I am not a visionary. I claim to be a practical idealist. The religion of nonviolence is not meant merely... for saints. It is meant for the common people as well. Nonviolence is the law of our species as violence is the law of the brute...

"(B)eing a practical man I do not wait till India recognises the practicability of the spiritual life in the political world. India considers herself to be powerless and paralysed... And she takes up noncooperation out of her weakness. It must still... bring her delivery from the crushing weight of British injustice if a sufficient number of people practise it.

"Meanwhile I urge those who distrust me not to disturb the even working of the struggle that has just commenced by inciting to violence in the belief that I want violence..." (Gandhi M.K 1965: vol 18: 131-134)

This famous article, published on August 11, 1920, just after the Khilafat Committee had launched Noncooperation and before the Calcutta Special Session, has been quoted ever since to show Gandhi's conditional support for violence. Whereas it was written with just the opposite intention, to spell out that India had "better work to do, a better mission to deliver to the whole world". (Prasad D. 2012: 44-62)[36]

Within the article, however, Gandhi did recognise that India was taking up noncooperation "out of her weakness" rather than a belief in his satyagraha philosophy. And this brings us to a final point about Muslim adoption of noncooperation in 1920. In March, Gandhi learned from Hasrat Mohani, that "nobody believes in noncooperation. But it has been taken up merely to conciliate me". (Gandhi M.K 1965: vol 17: 293) Gandhi hurriedly called the principal Khilafat leaders to spend the Satyagraha Week in April (commemorating the Rowlatt Satyagraha) with him in Bombay – but it is not clear how many attended and what was decided. Later in April, he wrote about Muslims active on the Khilafat issue:

"I do not say that they are free from hatred but I am sure that joining my love with their hatred I can diminish the intensity of that hatred. I also believe that, if my method is followed by a large number, their hatred can be counteracted altogether." (Gandhi M.K 1965: vol 17: 320)

When Shaukat Ali made a wild speech in May in support of Noncooperation, Gandhi repeated the same point:

"I do admit that all the Muslims do not view noncooperation in the same light as I do. But there is a clear understanding with them that there can be no violence side by side with noncooperation. Besides, though Muslims may adopt nonviolence in a spirit of retaliation, we can produce a happy result from it and save

---

36. For Gandhi, violence was not a last resort turned to when nonviolence failed. Nonviolence (satyagraha) was superior to violence. For others, who found nonviolence too difficult, or who had not prepared themselves to use it with courage and competence, he would prefer they took up violence rather than acquiesce before injustice. But nonviolence was always the superior option.

ourselves from an outbreak of violence. All good actions, by whatever feelings prompted, yield some fruit." (Gandhi M.K 1965: vol 17: 369)

Later in August, Gandhi wrote that Shaukat Ali followed "the law of nonviolence with hatred in his heart", but "even so" Ali supported noncooperation because there was "no other effective method of upholding the honour of his faith". (Gandhi M.K 1965: vol 18: 158) On this rather tenuous basis, Gandhi launched Noncooperation in August 1920 with Indian Muslims in the vanguard.

At this stage, Noncooperation rested firstly on the pledged word of the principal Khilafat leaders that they would maintain nonviolent discipline and, secondly, on the enormous efforts that this group had made to plan and build a phased struggle conducted according to Gandhi's rigorous conditions. It is remarkable that the alliance held throughout Noncooperation and that little violence did ensue from Muslim areas. It is also interesting and important to recognise that Gandhi did propose nonviolence as a tactic to the Muslim community; he saw their adoption of nonviolence as likely to attract Hindus and therefore to promote Hindu-Muslim unity and the growth of the national movement. He also believed that, on that basis, the nation could compel concessions from the British on the Khilafat issue; and that through the experience of nonviolent action, some Muslims might be drawn to adopt the satyagraha philosophy.

Preserving Good Relations with the Raj

A major consideration for Gandhi in helping develop the Khilafat struggle was how to manage the relationship with the Raj. In September 1919 he first called for the resignation of the Viceroy, Lord Chelmsford, because of his handling of the Khilafat issue, and also for that of the Secretary of State for India, Edwin Montagu. But Gandhi's reputation with the British was already severely dented. As the author of the Rowlatt Satyagraha, he was blamed for the riots following the April hartal. The fact that he had helped in restoring order in Bombay and Ahmedabad mitigated the offence in the eyes of the Raj; but the ban preventing him from leaving the Bombay Presidency was not lifted until October.

Once he was permitted to enter the Punjab, Gandhi immediately threw himself into the unofficial inquiry the Congress was conducting there into the Amritsar massacre and other events in the Punjab. The Congress inquiry was a rival to the official Hunter Commission. Then in November, at the first Khilafat Conference in Delhi, he called for noncooperation against the Raj.

Gandhi was thus occupied during 1919 with two of the major grievances of Indian nationalists against their rulers and he was calling openly for a new movement of nonviolent rebellion on one of them, the Khilafat question. At the Delhi Khilafat Conference he refused still to permit the linking of the Khilafat and Punjab issues and, at the Amritsar Congress in December, he aligned himself consistently with the moderates who wanted to collaborate with the Raj. Also, he was instrumental in securing Congress support for the Montagu-Chelmsford reform proposals and achieved the passage of a resolution thanking Montagu for his efforts. No clearer example could be found of Gandhi's "particularist" method, his determination to pursue issues separately, one at a time. For the Raj, though, his stance must have been confusing.

Three months later, in March 1920, Gandhi revealed that his attitude to the Raj was altering drastically. In a "manifesto" on the Khilafat question, sent as a letter to the press and published in *Young India*, he began:

> "The Khilafat question has now become the question of questions. It has become an Imperial question of the first magnitude…

> "I trust that the Hindus will realise that the Khilafat question overshadows the Reforms and everything else." (Gandhi M.K 1965: vol 17: 73)

Gandhi was changing his priorities probably as a result of the dismissive response received by a deputation to London on the Khilafat issue undertaken by Indian Muslims, including Mohammad Ali. (Hamid 1967:140; Nanda 1989: 211-213) In April, Gandhi was pressed to join the deputation in England because of the short shrift they were getting from British politicians. He sent a telegram to the Viceroy's Private Secretary:

"… as one desiring welfare of Empire I feel I owe it to ministers and British Public to acquaint them disastrous consequences if decision hostile to just Muslim sentiments and to tell them that such adverse decision must result in complete withdrawal of cooperation from government… " (Gandhi M.K 1965: vol 17: 313-314)

He also telegrammed Montagu in London in similar vein:

"Before taking any serious step I would like personally place before ministers my feelings in this important matter and understand ministers' viewpoint."

This was the classic Gandhian stance, not only to forewarn the opponent, but also to gain clarity and insight for the struggle ahead, through "understanding the ministers' viewpoint". However, conscious of the hostility he expected to meet in England and, we may guess, at an early stage of his preparations for noncooperation in India, Gandhi placed a condition on his visit. He asked Chelmsford to give his "approval" to his mission. When this was not forthcoming, he made the same approach to Montagu:

"…am unwilling proceed without encouragement from government in difficult task. Could you please favour me ministerial view." (Gandhi M.K 1965: vol 18: 317)

Thus, in April, Gandhi was still attempting to get support for the Khilafat campaign from the British ministers in Delhi and London responsible for India. It may be that his failure to get this approval was a particular cause of his bitterness against Chelmsford and Montagu. (He will not have known that the Khilafat concerns of India's pan-Islamists had been recognised and taken up strongly and persistently by Montagu as a minister in the British cabinet – and equally strongly rejected by the prime minister.)[37]

37. B.R. Nanda describes how Chelmsford and Montagu were extremely concerned about the impact of the peace terms on India's Muslims. Montagu argued the case strongly in the British Cabinet and at the peace conference itself – to the intense irritation of the Prime Minister, Lloyd George. (Nanda 1989: 212-213) Frequently, Gandhi compared Montagu with General Smuts in South

By the end of April, Gandhi had decided not to go to England. As he wrote to Abdul Bari: "Organisation must start immediately", and a few days later in another private letter he put it more clearly: "Without perfect organisation here, our going would be worse than useless." (Gandhi M.K 1965: vol 17: 350) In other words, ignorant of the dispute in the British cabinet, Gandhi took the view that he would be listened to in London early in 1920 only if he had the support of the British government representatives concerned with India. Without that, there was no argument he could make which would be taken seriously. He therefore had to turn to organising the country in order to demonstrate over the heads of the Raj's representatives, India's abhorrence of the peace terms. As a result he had to sacrifice his desire – which was strictly a requirement of the satyagraha method – to "personally place before ministers" his feelings on the Khilafat and, in return, be enabled to "understand ministers' viewpoint".

He now called on the Viceroy to place himself at the head of the Khilafat agitation and to fight on India's behalf. In an ambiguous passage which indicated that noncooperation was to be conducted in stages, Gandhi also seems to have suggested that one of the last stages, refusal by soldiers to obey their orders, should not be attempted until "the Viceroy, the Secretary of State and the Premier" (that is, the British Prime Minister, Lloyd George) had resigned to lead the Khilafat struggle. (Gandhi M.K 1965: vol 17: 76)

Perhaps Gandhi did seriously believe that the power of satyagraha would persuade leading British politicians in the later stages of Noncooperation to resign in support of the Khilafat campaign; or perhaps he was taking a formal step required by the satyagraha process. If no favourable response was received, then the next step was to withdraw allegiance from the Raj. In a June letter announcing that Noncooperation would soon commence, he repeated his request to Chelmsford to "lead the agitation yourself". (Gandhi M.K 1965: vol 17: 504; Gandhi R. 2007: 227-229) The Central Khilafat Committee also called on the Viceroy in its separate warning letter to "make common cause with the people of India".

Africa, and Chelmsford with an earlier Viceroy, Hardinge. Smuts and Hardinge had both responded to Gandhi's satyagraha campaigns.

Britain's representative in India should press his case "even to the point of resignation" if British ministers failed to secure revision of the peace terms. (Gandhi M.K 1965: vol 17: 586) In June 1920 Gandhi still seems to have sustained a view that British politicians might be persuaded to support Noncooperation.

Later in June, however, Gandhi hinted at a second grand strategy where the British were concerned. He agreed in an article in *Young India* that Noncooperation might not compel revision of the peace terms. If it did not, but Noncooperation was effective, then Britain would have to choose between either its control of India or its "usurpation" of Turkey. He continued:

> "I have enough faith in England to know that at that moment England will expel her present jaded ministers and put in others who will make a clean sweep of the terms in consultation with an awakened India, [and] draft terms that will be honourable to her, to Turkey and acceptable to India." (Gandhi M.K 1965: vol 17: 521)

This fallback position – where Britain's "jaded ministers", having failed to respond to India's demands, were to be kicked out by the British public – appears to have been the perspective with which Gandhi went into Noncooperation in August. In a private letter in June, he admitted that he "thoroughly distrusted" Lloyd George, was "prejudiced" against the "deceitful" British diplomacy in the Middle East, and found the Viceroy's pronouncements on the Khilafat full of "insolence and hypocrisy". (Gandhi M.K 1965: vol 17: 499) Publicly, in July, Gandhi accused Lloyd George in regard to Turkey of choosing "the crooked course of secret treaties, duplicity and hypocritical subterfuges." (Gandhi M.K 1965: vol 18: 17) At the beginning of September, Gandhi admitted in *Young India* that he had lost faith in Lord Chelmsford's "probity and capacity to hold the high office of Viceroy of India." (Gandhi M.K 1965: vol 18: 217)

A complete breakdown in his trust that India's Muslims could get "justice" from the British leaders marked a serious crisis for Gandhi's Noncooperation strategy. If there was to be no likelihood that Britain would concede on the Khilafat issue, then it became necessary to challenge the legitimacy of British authority itself. At this point his determination to take one issue at a time, spelled out in his March "manifesto", (Gandhi M.K 1965: vol 17: 73) was significantly undermined. It became difficult for him to resist the argument – as Yajnik puts it in his comparison of Gandhi with Tilak – that the "trunk" of British imperialism must be tackled as well as its branches.

Within a few months, swaraj itself was added as an objective of Noncooperation. But Gandhi still retained his instinct for moving one step at a time, that is, not mobilising the people to fight for something beyond their capacity (nor beyond the capacity of the opponent to yield). Having admitted to himself that Britain's representatives in London and Delhi were not going to respond to the demand for a revision of the peace terms (and becoming more disillusioned with their response on the Punjab), Gandhi went into Noncooperation strongly proclaiming his loyalty to the British Empire and the British Constitution. His "disaffection", he said, was from the Imperial and Indian governments. "I can no longer retain affection for a Government so evilly manned as it is nowadays." The "present representatives" of the Empire, he added, "have no real regard for the wishes of the people of India and they count Indian honour as of little consequence". (Gandhi M.K 1965: vol 18: 89)

Having not gone personally to England to warn his opponent, Gandhi had formally prepared the Raj for Noncooperation on the Khilafat issue five weeks before the start of the campaign with his first public letter to the Viceroy. On August 1, in his second formal letter to Chelmsford to mark the birth of Noncooperation, he added the Punjab issue as a grievance. (Gandhi M.K 1965: vol 18: 104) However, ironically, at the special Session of the Congress in September, when Swaraj was added explicitly as a third objective of the programme, critics argued that insufficient warning had been given to the Raj for Congress itself to launch noncooperation. A Congress deputation to England was proposed.

Ideally, Gandhi almost certainly would have wished to take the revised demands to Britain before launching into council boycott, the most specific and pointed affront to the Raj. But elections to the new councils were due to take place within a few weeks in November and the Khilafat movement had already commenced Noncooperation. He could not afford to lose the momentum of the struggle by accepting a postponement. As a matter of principle he had personally, in his own eyes, more than adequately warned the British that noncooperation was coming; as a matter of tactics it made no sense to hold up the struggle. (Gandhi M.K 1965: vol 18: 251) Thus in both April and September 1920 Gandhi concluded that the pressing needs of organising Noncooperation in India precluded a visit to London to confront his opponents in person.

The public response during this period of the British officials in London and Delhi to Gandhi's noncooperation proposals was essentially to do nothing. Montagu and Chelmsford were in a difficult position because the Foreign Office in 1915 had indeed concluded secret agreements with Britain's war partners to divide up the Ottoman Empire once the victory was achieved. The India Office in London was in no position to ensure that its warnings were taken heed of by the British government, let alone the peace conference.

If the two men had followed Gandhi's advice, of course, they would have resigned. In January, a deputation of Khilafat leaders including Gandhi had met with Chelmsford; they were received with courtesy but gained no satisfaction. In June the Raj began to consider prosecuting Gandhi but came to the conclusion that it would be hard to gain a conviction until the later stages of Noncooperation were reached. They were also anxious not to provoke the sort of upheaval which had followed Gandhi's temporary detention in April 1919. Moreover, by tactful handling of him they hoped to retain the support of the Indian moderates who were critical of Gandhi and who were intending to stand for the new councils and make the reformed constitution work.

In July, Montagu said in the House of Commons that Gandhi could not expect to be treated as leniently as he had been after the Rowlatt Satyagraha. This provoked Gandhi in *Young India* to stronger criticism of the British. But in October Chelmsford was still inclined to believe that noncooperation was not "a practical policy" and thought that it would not be taken up. Provincial governments were authorised to arrest subordinate leaders of the campaign, but the policy of the Raj towards the main leader was to wait and see. (Gandhi M.K 1965: vol 18: 65-67, 88-90)

Overall, then, Gandhi went into Noncooperation with deep mistrust of the British on his side; while on the part of the Raj there was a stiffening resolve to hold him at arm's length, watch him carefully and not make any mistakes. In October, Gandhi published his letter "To Every Englishman in India":

> "You can repent of the wrongs done to Indians. You can compel Mr Lloyd George to redeem his promises... You can compel the Viceroy to retire in favour of a better one... You can compel the Government to summon a conference of the recognised leaders of the people...

> "But this you cannot do unless you consider every Indian to be in reality your equal and brother." (Gandhi M.K. 1965: vol 18: 373-375)

This was now a long-term struggle he was engaged in – to challenge the basic attitude of the British towards the Indians, to change the nature of the relationship between Britain and India.

In this deepening and broadening challenge to the Raj, we have a third and probably decisive explanation for Gandhi's sudden introduction of the triple boycott of councils, courts and schools into the Noncooperation programme in July 1920. During the extended preparation phase, he had been promoting the plan of noncooperation in face of widespread opposition from leading nationalist Hindu figures. Therefore, as we argued earlier, once the decision to go ahead was made, he no longer needed to bend to the arguments of the established nationalist leaders and could choose to pursue something closer to his ideal satyagraha programme. Also, secondly, the first stage of noncooperation needed broadening and lengthening. As proposed in May, it did not yet demand the involvement of a wide enough spectrum of the educated classes. With limited participation, it would lead into the second stage too quickly. Now, thirdly, the intransigence of the Raj appears to have prompted Gandhi to deepen and extend his programme and to contemplate swaraj as an explicit goal for the movement.

Summary

1. There is a direct continuity between Gandhi's promotion of the swadeshi concept through the Swadeshi Sabha and his later formulation of the programme of Noncooperation – in opposition to economic boycott – as a positive programme to signify India's growing independence from and dissatisfaction with the Raj.

2. In attempting to offer leadership to what was effectively a rebellion of Indian Muslims against the Raj, Gandhi sacrificed the opportunity to build up "a company of true believers" through developing the Swadeshi Sabha or reviving the Satyagraha Sabha. Joining the Khilafat movement, he entered into a tactical and strategic alliance with Muslim political leaders who were not believers in nonviolence and who could not be guaranteed to hold their followers to nonviolence. Gandhi's reasoning, included some of the following elements:

(i) the Khilafat cause was just;

(ii) Indian Hindus must support their Muslim brothers in their hour of need;

(iii) the opportunity to secure Hindu-Muslim unity through support for the Muslims would not recur for generations;

(iv) through his personal direction of the Khilafat campaign it might be possible to restrain the movement from violence;

(v) Muslims following the discipline of nonviolence for tactical reasons might come to embrace nonviolence at a deeper level; and

(vi) a tactical alliance between the Khilafat movement and the Indian National Congress at this moment would greatly strengthen Indian nationalism.

3. In offering leadership to the Khilafat movement on condition that it maintained nonviolent discipline under his direction, Gandhi made a variety of practical decisions. He would need to:

(i) ensure that the Koran did not expressly forbid the adoption by Muslims of nonviolent action on a life and death issue;

235

(ii) exercise arbitrary authority in rejecting proposals for a deal between the two communities over cow-slaughter and the Punjab question;

(iii) assemble and organise a reliable company of Muslim "lieutenants" who would accept the discipline of nonviolence and ensure that this code was followed by Khilafat supporters;

(iv) devise a programme of nonviolent action consistent with his satyagraha principles, which would be seen as an effective challenge to the Raj – in face of strident calls from Muslim voices for their idea of a nonviolent programme, which was for economic boycott of British goods;

(v) demonstrate that under his leadership the movement could secure major support from the Hindu population; and

(vi) publicly accept that, if the nonviolent movement failed, Muslims had the right to resort to their "traditional" sanction of violent rebellion.

4. Gandhi did succeed in securing the allegiance to his leadership of a key group of Khilafat organisers who took responsibility with him jointly for touring Muslim parts of India and promoting the Khilafat cause from a common platform, including commitment to nonviolence. Through the Central Khilafat Committee he had the authority and organisational base for developing a major nonviolent campaign on an all-India basis.

5. The first actions promoted by Gandhi on behalf of the Central Khilafat Committee were three hartals at five-month intervals plus a boycott of the Raj's Peace Celebrations. These hartals were again mass religious observances, preparing supporters in personal discipline for nonviolent action.

6. Noncooperation as conceived by Gandhi was no programme of civil disobedience. Fearing that "collective" civil disobedience might get out of hand, he formulated the concept of "progressive nonviolent noncooperation" in stages, with the moment for mass civil disobedience long-postponed. Noncooperation was progressive in at least four senses:

(i) it involved moving from acts of small sacrifice – resigning honours – to acts of greater sacrifice – resigning jobs – and so on;

(ii) it was to begin with the most privileged individuals – those who had been honoured by the Raj – and move through the educated "classes" and then to the "masses";

(iv) it would begin with actions least likely to risk breakdown into violence and develop with actions involving greater risk; and

(iv) through the progressive build-up of the campaign it was assumed that money would be gathered and organisation developed to support "noncooperators" who had resigned their jobs and were working full-time on the campaign.

7. Gandhi had the greatest difficulty in securing the support of Hindu politicians for his noncooperation programme on a religious issue for India's Muslims. But the freedom from constraint this gave him may paradoxically be part of an explanation for his decision to incorporate into the programme something close to his own "ideal" prescription for Indian society – the triple boycott. It also contributed to his decision to launch the Noncooperation movement one month before the Indian National Congress held a special session to discuss it.

8. His persistence, thoroughness and ingenuity in working with the Central Khilafat Committee were exceptional. He was flexible and inventive, continually redefining the proposed programme of noncooperation in response to Muslim and Hindu objections and changing circumstances.

Conclusion

By taking up the Khilafat issue and advocating noncooperation, Gandhi moved firmly outside his base in Gujarat and the Bombay Presidency. The Central Khilafat Committee was able to mobilise support among Muslims in north and south India and elsewhere, and the idea of noncooperation appealed to social classes in different parts of India who were being drawn into nationalist politics for the first time.

The established politicians, whose interests were directly affected by the proposal for the triple boycott and who hesitated to support both the

Khilafat campaign as an issue and noncooperation as a method, were taken by surprise by the swiftness with which noncooperation won popular support in the late summer of 1920. They failed to organise adequately against Gandhi's movement. It was the Khilafat movement which catapulted Gandhi to the centre of Indian politics and greatly aided his efforts late in 1920 to capture the Indian National Congress and organise noncooperation as a campaign sponsored by the principal nationalist organisation in India.

But in the Khilafat movement we see Gandhi as an organiser for the first time obliged to enter into real political compromises. He had directed his local struggles, in Champaran, Ahmedabad and Kheda, with complete personal authority. The Gujarat Sabha when he joined it was immediately transformed to carry out Gandhi's own social and political programme. The Rowlatt satyagraha was taken up by different groups in different parts of India, but it was initiated in Bombay by a self-selecting group who formed the Satyagraha Sabha, with Gandhi as its undisputed leader. However, the break-up of the Satyagraha Sabha in the summer of 1919, and the simultaneous failure of the Swadeshi Sabha, caused Gandhi to look beyond organisations over which he had absolute authority.

His link-up with the Central Khilafat Committee was a true political coalition, a marriage of convenience, albeit unconventional because of the terms Gandhi imposed. Gandhi was accepted by the Khilafat leaders as the "dictator" of the movement, with a significant degree of arbitrary power to develop and direct the programme of Noncooperation. Gandhi in his place had to accept that the Muslim leaders were not satyagrahis according to his conception. They had adopted nonviolence and embraced him as leader for tactical reasons only.

Thus Gandhi, in moving so decisively to promote nonviolence at a national level by taking up the Khilafat campaign and providing the movement with a feasible programme for nonviolent action, was also vulnerable. The movement which took him to the leadership of the Indian National Congress was committed to nonviolence only as a tactic. With hindsight, his need is clear. He still lacked a national organisation truly embracing his principles and following from conviction the disciplines of satyagraha.

CHAPTER 7

CAPTURING THE CONGRESS: "PROGRESSIVE NONVIOLENT NONCOOPERATION" TAKES SHAPE

The programme of Noncooperation for the Khilafat campaign was structured and restructured over many months as the seriousness of a forthcoming major confrontation with the Raj came to demand a practical and effective programme. Preparations for Noncooperation were led by Gandhi in collaboration with a section of the Indian Muslim community, the pan-Islamists; but he failed to get support from the main Hindu politicians and from the principal organisation of Indian nationalism, the Congress. If Noncooperation was to be successful in a confrontation with the Raj, it needed to be taken up by Congress.

Accordingly, Gandhi was now involved not only with launching Noncooperation on behalf of the Khilafat movement but also with campaigning for Congress to adopt his radical method of confrontation too. At this moment the Raj's handling of the two Punjab inquiry reports angered politically active Hindus to the point where a satyagraha on the Punjab issue became a realistic possibility. Other grievances too were also generating widespread dissatisfaction in different parts of India. (Brown 1972: 307-349; Sarkar 1983: 198-204) But the response of Congress was always in doubt. Most Hindu politicians questioned satyagraha as a suitable method for national struggle and were reluctant to consider Gandhi, seen as a religious man, as a pre-eminent national political leader.

His work during this period led him into fundamental dispute with the Raj, but this was matched by an intense and difficult struggle to win over his political opponents, particularly the Hindu leadership of Congress.

CASE STUDY 6: THE "PUNJAB SATYAGRAHA"

A Report for Congress

Congress prior to 1921 was not an active body. The president, appointed annually, had the assistance of three secretaries and would call quarterly meetings of the All-India Congress Committee to discuss important issues. Between the annual sessions of the Congress in December, the provincial Congress committees were virtually moribund, coming together just before the annual session to elect delegates and to debate policy. The "extremist" leaders, Tilak and Besant, formed their Home Rule Leagues to carry on active propaganda and organising between Congress sessions. The Leagues were affiliated to the Congress. Despite Annie Besant's election to the presidency in 1918, Congress remained a part-time organisation, basically an annual get-together for the nation's political elite through all the events of 1919 and 1920. (Owen 1968)

In 1919, Gandhi with other leading politicians began a campaign to get an official government inquiry into what had happened in the Punjab between March and June, when civil order had broken down, the Amritsar massacre took place, and martial law was imposed. Confined as he was to the Bombay Presidency by the banning order, he used the columns of his newly acquired journal, *Young India*, to maintain a steady questioning as new offences to due process of law and to Indian dignity became known in the Punjab.

By the end of May 1919, he proposed to the Satyagraha Sabha that they should take up the Punjab question in addition to their campaign against the Rowlatt Act. In June, he announced that he would resume civil disobedience unless the Rowlatt Act was withdrawn, an inquiry was held into the Punjab events and a Punjab journalist was freed from jail. After discussion with the Bombay governor, however, he retreated from this proposal for civil disobedience, when he received an assurance that a government Punjab inquiry would be undertaken and that Kalinath Roy, the jailed Lahore journalist, was to have his sentence substantially reduced.

The All-India Congress Committee announced in June 1919 that it was intending to conduct its own inquiry into the Punjab events with the object of bringing evidence before the government-appointed Hunter Commission. Two of the leading figures in Congress, Madan Mohan Malaviya and Motilal Nehru, went personally to the Punjab to begin their preliminary investigations, together with Swami Shradhanand, who had been the leader of the Satyagraha Sabha in Delhi. Most of the prominent Punjabi politicians were in jail. In October, however, as soon as his ban was lifted, Gandhi went himself to the Punjab and was immediately co-opted on to the inquiry committee. Within a short period, despite the involvement of a third major Congress figure from Bengal, C. R. Das, Gandhi seems to have taken charge of its work.

When the Punjab government refused to release on parole, for the period of the Hunter Commission's examination in Amritsar, those political leaders in the city who had been jailed under martial law, the Congress committee announced that it would boycott the Hunter Commission's investigation. An office was opened in Lahore and Gandhi organised the work of an independent Congress inquiry, conducted in parallel with the Commission's work, though by different procedures. (Brown 1972: 230-249) At seventeen centres in the martial law areas, public meetings were conducted at which people were invited to submit statements: 1,700 were received of which about 650 were included in appendices to the final report. (Gandhi M.K. 1966: vol 17: 39-41)

During this work Gandhi attended the first Khilafat conference in Delhi and it was at this conference that he refused to permit the linking of the Khilafat and Punjab issues. Referring to the Raj's peace celebrations proposed for December 1919, he said:

> "Personally, I feel that whatever the sufferings of the Punjab, we cannot on a local issue dissociate ourselves from a celebration

which concerns the whole Empire. We have other means by which to publicise the wrongs of the Punjab. Nor can we dissociate ourselves from the celebrations on the ground that justice has not been done in the matter of the Punjab because we still hope for justice. It is for this purpose that the Hunter Commission is sitting and our commissioners are working. We may abstain from the Peace Celebrations only if we have any cause for dissatisfaction or doubt arising directly from the peace terms. The Khilafat is the only issue of this kind." (Gandhi M.K. 1966: vol 16: 320)

Here then we see Gandhi, having taken charge of the Punjab investigation, insisting that the issue be pursued according to the principles of satyagraha. The government had conceded an inquiry into the Punjab events and until that investigation was completed and the results known, it would be unprincipled to whip up agitation on the issue.

At this time, Gandhi did have strong hopes for "justice" on the Punjab question. No doubt there were parallels in his mind with the success of the Champaran inquiry in 1917 and the partial victory in Kheda in 1918. It seems probable that when he returned to Lahore to continue his investigation, and a few weeks later to nearby Amritsar to attend the annual Congress session, it was with the view that the Punjab issue was being tackled according to the rules of a satyagraha struggle. It was thus in a conciliatory spirit that he went to Amritsar ready to make a gesture towards the Raj on an issue which he did not consider to be vitally important, namely, the question of the new reformed constitution. (Gandhi M.K. 1982: 434) When he saw that the "extremist" leadership, Tilak and Das, were proposing to reject the Montagu-Chelmsford constitutional reforms, but still to take their places in the new reformed councils, he decided to challenge them openly in the Congress session. This moment, as Gandhi comments in his *Autobiography*, marked his "real entrance into the Congress politics". (Gandhi M.K. 1982: 437)[38]

The job of writing the main section of the Congress report on the Punjab events also fell to Gandhi. This document, which occupies 178 pages in

---

38. Gandhi used the same observation to describe his role on the committee preparing a revised constitution for the Congress. (Gandhi M.K. 1982: 439)

the Collected Works, took him weeks to prepare, involving the sifting and collating of evidence from so many witnesses. Returning to the Sabarmati ashram near Ahmedabad, and later in Lahore, he worked with an intensity that staggered his friends and colleagues. Yajnik records:

"He worked then at the rate of nearly twenty to twenty-two hours a day, practically leaving him only two to four hours for food and sleep ... And the very sight of his extraordinary absorption and his sustained industry served only to feed the fires of our faith in his miraculous powers..." (Yajnik 1933: 98)

When the report was finally finished at the end of February Gandhi met with his colleagues on the Congress Committee, who included Das, to decide on its recommendations. Their choice on the principal issue was between calling for the prosecution of the leading British civil and military figures in the Punjab events, Lieutenant-Governor Sir Michael O'Dwyer, General Dyer and a few others, or for their dismissal.

In *Young India* in 1921, Gandhi wrote publicly about the discussion between the members of the committee on this point:

"The recommendation was hotly debated among them and they came to the unanimous conclusion that India could only gain by refraining from prosecution. Mr Das in a notable speech at Patna recently referred to the compact then made between the Commissioners that, whilst and if they reduced their recommendation[s] to a minimum, they must solemnly resolve to enforce them at the risk of their lives." (Gandhi M.K. 1966: vol 19: 428)

Thus not only may we assume that Gandhi persuaded his colleagues to follow the rules of satyagraha and pitch the Congress demands at the minimum, rather than the maximum. He also appears to have secured a solemn compact between the four of them that they would fight "at the risk of their lives" to ensure that this demand was met. (Yajnik 1933: 98) Such a pledge, to persist to the extent of risking one's life or livelihood, is another tenet of satyagraha. A further important recommendation of the report was that the Viceroy, Lord Chelmsford, be recalled.

The Congress Report was published on March 25, 1920. With its description of the indignities and injustices committed by the British rulers, the report created an inevitable sense of outrage in India. Gandhi, however, did little to channel or orchestrate these feelings except to promote a fund to purchase, as a permanent national memorial, the piece of enclosed land, the Jallianwala Bagh, where the Amritsar massacre had taken place. In his letters published at the end of April and beginning of May accepting the presidency of the All-India Home Rule League and outlining his programme, Gandhi mentioned the Khilafat issue but not the Punjab. In common with other nationalist leaders, he was waiting for the publication of the Hunter Commission's report. Meanwhile, Gandhi noted the progress the memorial fund was making:

"If we wish to measure the increase in popular awakening during the last year we can do so from the contributions being received from all quarters for the Jallianwala Bagh memorial."

Emphasising the willingness with which Gujarati villagers of all classes were giving to the fund he added characteristically:

"From this fact another inference may also be drawn, that it is easier to carry on national work in villages than in cities; it would, therefore, be natural to make a start with village swaraj and thence to proceed to swaraj for the whole country." Gandhi M.K. 1965: vol 17: 373-374)

Reaction to the Hunter Commission's Report

The Hunter Commission report, together with responses to it from the Government of India and the Secretary of State in London, was not published until May 28. Two weeks before, the terms of the peace treaty affecting Turkey had been published (the Treaty of Sevres), also with a commentary by the Viceroy. The publication of both documents within a few days – one addressing the Punjab grievances, the other on the future control of Muslim holy places in the Middle East – was an unfortunate coincidence for the Raj. Both caused bitter anger and dismay among all sections of nationalist opinion.

At a meeting of the All-India Congress Committee held in Benares on May 30 to discuss the Congress report (and also the call for noncooperation on the Khilafat issue) the assembled nationalist leaders went beyond the recommendation of their sub-committee and demanded the prosecution of O'Dwyer and Dyer. It is unlikely that Gandhi argued at the meeting for noncooperation to be taken up by Congress on the Punjab issue, but the AICC was unwilling in any event to endorse noncooperation on the Khilafat question. It decided instead to hold the Calcutta special Congress to discuss noncooperation on that issue. (Gandhi M.K. 1965: vol 17: 513-514; Brown 1972: 238, 244; Gordon 1973: 137,139)

On June 9, in his first public comment on the Hunter Report, Gandhi described it as "an attempt to condone official lawlessness" and he ended with a vague call for noncooperation on the Punjab issue too:

"Appeal to the Parliament by all means, if necessary, but if the Parliament fails us and if we are worthy to call ourselves a nation we must refuse to uphold the Government by withdrawing co-operation from it." (Gandhi M.K. 1965: vol. 17: 483)

On June 23, having despatched his letter to the Viceroy the previous day announcing that Noncooperation would begin on the Khilafat issue on August 19, Gandhi published an appeal in *Young India* for the Punjabi political leaders to stir themselves and take the lead:

"I am sure that if they will only begin a determined agitation they will have the whole of India by their side." (Gandhi M.K. 1965: vol 17: 508-510)

In a public speech in Bombay on June 26, Gandhi reluctantly moved a resolution calling for the prosecution of O'Dwyer and Dyer, but added:

"If I could have my way, I would bring in a resolution advising noncooperation and satyagraha against this, for that is the only way to succeed in our aim." (Gandhi M.K. 1965: vol 17: 513)

Finally, in a press statement published on June 30, he linked the Khilafat and Punjab issues for the first time. Lala Lajpat Rai, the leading Hindu nationalist politician in the Punjab, had called for a boycott of the reformed councils in the province. Gandhi took up the suggestion, deemed it to constitute support for the whole noncooperation programme, and suggested that council boycott be applied across the whole of India:

> "The issue is clear. Both the Khilafat terms and the Punjab affair show that Indian opinion counts for little in the councils of the Empire. It is a humiliating position. We shall make nothing of the Reforms if we quietly swallow the humiliation. In my humble opinion, therefore, the first condition of real progress is the removal of these two difficulties in our path. And unless some better course of action is devised nolens volens noncooperation must hold the field." (Gandhi M.K. 1965: vol 17: 521-522)[39]

Had Gandhi by linking the Khilafat and Punjab issues "reversed" the stand he had taken so forcefully seven months earlier at the first Khilafat conference in Delhi? (Brown 1972: 245) Undoubtedly there was a considerable mutual advantage for both religious communities in coming together in a single campaign on the two "difficulties". But it is unlikely that Gandhi had changed his mind in favour of an opportunistic deal, a quid pro quo. A stronger case can be made that he had not, for Gandhi's handling of the Punjab issue constitutes in many ways a classic satyagraha struggle:

- Firstly, he called for an official inquiry, announcing civil disobedience if it was not granted.

- Then when an official inquiry (the Hunter Commission) was announced by the Raj, he suspended civil disobedience.

- When the procedures of the Hunter Inquiry proved unsatisfactory, he was party to launching a parallel unofficial Congress investigation. This investigation included gathering hundreds of witness statements.

- While the Hunter inquiry was going on he was unwilling to challenge the good faith of the Raj by supporting criticism of its constitutional reforms. During both inquiries he sought to prevent a major agitation being started.

---

39. *Nolens volens* is a legal phrase which in the context means "whether we like it or not". There were many who didn't like noncooperation; Gandhi argued they had no other option.

- By taking on much of the drafting himself, he succeeded in getting the unofficial report published before the official one.[40] Publishing first gave Congress the initiative.

- The recommendations in the Congress report followed the satyagraha principles of pitching demands low (no prosecutions) and pursuing them with absolute determination.

- Finally, when the official report failed to match the findings and the demands of the unofficial one, but was supported by the Indian government, Gandhi was ready to campaign for noncooperation on the Punjab issue.

- He waited, however, for a call for direct action from the Punjab itself before doing so. And then worked tenaciously for Congress to take up Noncooperation on the issue of the "Punjab wrong".

It was logical, therefore, in terms of a "particular" satyagraha campaign on the Punjab issue, to call for noncooperation in June 1920 and not before. The fact that Gandhi's "particularist" method led him to call for noncooperation on a new issue at the same time as he was calling for noncooperation on another issue (Khilafat) was a coincidence. Admittedly, both issues by this time illustrated for Gandhi a deeper issue, "that Indian opinion counts for little in the councils of the Empire". But both, from Gandhi's viewpoint, demanded the adoption of the noncooperation programme by the Indian National Congress. Moreover, the method of noncooperation itself – in particular, boycott of elections to the new legislative councils – effectively linked the two issues. (Gordon 1973: 141) It would have made little sense to run separate, simultaneous campaigns of council boycott supported by much the same people.

From Gandhi's perspective, only through working through each issue separately by the painstaking "particularist" method of satyagraha had

---

40. Gandhi had often contrasted his style of politics with that of Tilak, the "extremist" leader who, from his base in Maharashtra, had founded one of the Home Rule Leagues. Tilak did not support satyagraha. Gandhi, in Tilak's eyes, "had taken too long over the Congress inquiry into the Punjab affair, and ruined its propaganda value by making the report much too judicial". (Nanda 1989: 229) Tilak considered an immediate "vigorous agitation" was necessary and an opportunity had been missed.

it become possible to prepare the common people for action on them both – and to demonstrate the fundamental link, the contempt of the Raj for the wishes of its people. Also, what he had previously called an internal matter, the "local" issue of the Punjab, had become a "national" issue, when the British and Indian governments failed to respond to the reasonable demands of the Congress. (Gandhi M.K. 1965: vol. 16: 310-311, 320-321)

The New Aim: To Capture Congress

But Gandhi's discovery in 1920 that British imperialism was not as amenable to his "particularist" campaigns as he had thought, left him in a difficult position. Having failed to persuade the All-India Congress Committee to endorse a campaign of noncooperation at Benares in May, he was effectively forced to aim at capturing the leadership of the Congress itself at its special session in September and its annual session in December. This new campaign to win Congress was not a "particular" struggle to gain the verdict on a particular issue of principle. As a "general" campaign, it would need to be constructed in a different way and with aims more practical and ambitious than those associated with previous protest actions in support of calls for swaraj.

It is interesting to speculate on what would have happened had Gandhi been able to launch noncooperation on a single issue like the Punjab. As it was, he was faced with a campaign focusing on three distinct issues – the Khilafat, the Punjab and swaraj – and the need to fashion it so as to challenge the Congress and, if successful, change it into a campaigning organisation.

CASE STUDY 7(A): NONCOOPERATION IN PREPARATION

Moving from a Particular Issue to a General Issue

Over the next few months (from August to December), the "Punjab satyagraha" was still in the preparation phase with the campaign to get large numbers of delegates, sympathetic to noncooperation, to the special and then the annual sessions of Congress. Noncooperation on the part of the Khilafat campaign was already under way, and a key part of the Muslim effort was to secure the support of the Congress for its struggle. Success at the annual session of Congress in late December finally saw the two campaigns brought together behind the three aims and the Noncooperation programme.

The new policy argued loyalty to the British connection, but promised progressive nonviolent noncooperation with the Empire's "present representatives". It made particular demands on Gandhi as a strategist. His view, which he stated often enough over the next few years, was that India must not swallow the "humiliation" of its opinion counting for so little "in the councils of the Empire." (Gandhi M.K 1965: vol 18: 12) Britain must no longer insult India by calling her a partner and ignoring her feelings. Lloyd George would not have dared to treat Canada, Australia or South Africa in this way: "Let her [Britain] treat India as a real partner". (Gandhi M.K 1965: vol 18: 17) To get to this point, there would have to be "a change of heart" on the part of the British officials, who must have it proved to them "that we are their equals".

Gandhi of course was confident that in progressive nonviolent noncooperation India had a weapon to compel respect from the British:

"Equality attained by means of physical force is of the lowest kind, it is the way of the beast; for the Hindu, especially, it is

249

a policy ever to be shunned. For thousands of years past our training has been in a different direction altogether.

"It is my firm belief that the British can be won over by moral force. I have, indeed, written strongly and bitterly against the injustices perpetrated by British officers but I believe all the same that no European nation is more amenable to the pressure of moral force than the British..." (Gandhi M.K 1965: vol.18: 57)

At the beginning of July, Gandhi announced the much-broadened programme of Noncooperation. It included in the first stage the boycott of councils, courts and schools. This was an attack on three of the key institutions by which, through the collaboration of the educated classes, the British secured their prestige in India; and it marked the shift in his objectives for Noncooperation. From a campaign focused solely on the Khilafat issue, objecting additionally to the Raj's handling of the Punjab events meant Noncooperation was being geared explicitly to challenge the nature of British rule in India.

From what we know of Gandhi's thinking as an organiser of previous nonviolent struggles, there was a problem with this new strategy. Instead of appealing directly to the imperial and Indian governments on a specific issue or issues, the struggle now tended to be displaced into building a broad movement to develop the identity and potential for self-government of the Indian nation. In so far as Noncooperation proved to be successful in mobilising India, the British might then be forced to rethink on the Khilafat or Punjab issues or even constitutional reform. But in the summer of 1920, the Raj was far from being conciliatory. It did not take the proposed movement of noncooperation seriously. Gandhi was thus put in the position of having to "prove" to the British their mistake.

The task was enormous. Gandhi had not conducted his nonviolent experiments on such a vast scale before – at least not a sustained struggle across the whole of India. Inevitably, his most pressing concerns became organisational, internal to the movement. Relations with the Raj became a subsidiary issue, not to be tackled again until the movement had proved its strength. In some respects, once he had lost confidence in the representatives of the Raj, Gandhi also lost control of this key aspect in nonviolent struggle, the relationship with the opponent.

Swaraj as a goal, establishing a quite different relationship with the British rulers, was on the face of it remote. This was the goal which the Home Rule Leagues had pressed in their agitation previously and which Gandhi had refused to take up because he believed it led Indian political activists into empty posturing and their supporters into continual frustration. (Gandhi M.K 1965: vol 18: 55-57) He had made it clear time and again that he preferred intermediate or single-issue objectives, the successful resolution of which brought forward the substance of swaraj. But now the "particularist" approach on the Rowlatt, Khilafat and Punjab issues had been rebuffed, he was effectively forced to move over on to the ground he had earlier rejected. While he did call mildly on August 1 for the Raj to sponsor a conference of "recognised leaders" to resolve the Khilafat and Punjab issues, the major demand of Noncooperation, which emerged in subsequent months and was toyed with up and down the country, was for "Swaraj in One Year".

Such a result was inconceivable by any conventional yardstick – and the failure to achieve it damaged Gandhi for several years afterwards. Gandhi himself had opposed a campaign proposed in December 1919 to boycott the new legislative councils on two grounds. Firstly, that the nation had not been prepared for it by a campaign of "political education" and, secondly, that the British had not been forewarned by a deputation to London. (Gandhi M.K 1965: vol 16: 341) Six months later he reversed his views, presumably partly on the grounds that both the Indian people and the British rulers were now better prepared. But events were also running away with Gandhi and he was seeking to shape and control them.

"Swaraj in One Year" was a rallying cry designed to channel the emotions of a mass movement and to shake the Raj. It was not the sort of objective enabling Gandhi easily to maintain cordial relations with the Viceroy, nor could it be expected to appeal to the British people. Yet Gandhi professed to have immense faith in the power to work changes of his nonviolent methods. Satyagraha as a spiritual weapon introduced into the realm of politics, could, he believed, work a break-through not bound by the normal limits of politics, the art of the possible. He thought that a movement engaged in acts of truly disinterested self-sacrifice would generate immense spiritual power, and so work a political miracle. (Gandhi M.K 1965: vol 17: 474-477, 493-495, 521) By arguments such as this, mystical in the sense that he believed that a spiritual awakening could be triggered on the satyagrahis' behalf if the sacrifice for a true and just cause was pure enough, Gandhi appears to have reconciled himself to his failure to maintain friendly dialogue with his opponents. However, the historian Sumit Sarkar comments that the "vagueness and lack of realism" of this risky promise, "Swaraj in One Year", aroused "soaring millenarian hopes". (Sarkar 2013:199)[41]

A major part of his alternative programme for achieving swaraj was to give practical tasks to the nation's politically active groups, undertakings demanding of them great sacrifices to help draw in the masses in support. Swaraj for Gandhi required the construction of a national movement engaged with remoulding some of the fundamental institutions of British India. Constructive programme, an indirect response to the Raj, the building up of the internal strength of the Indian nation, grew directly out of the triple boycott announced by Gandhi in July 1920. It developed through all the years that followed as a major part of Gandhi's effort to take on the issue of swaraj and build a movement to oblige the Raj to accept change. The thoroughness of his preparations for Noncooperation with the Khilafat movement had led him, by way of continually evolving proposals for practical action, to a bold new programme of rebellion.

But first it was necessary to win the support of Congress. The last months of 1920 saw him applying satyagraha principles to a political campaign, which would transform the role of India's principal nationalist organisation. It was an enormous task to persuade critics and opponents in the Congress to suspend or abandon their previous expectations as politicians, and to take up forms of campaigning unfamiliar and alien to

---

41. Sarkar refers explicitly to religious excitement in the Muslim community (for instance, "it was time for the advent of the Mahdi", the redeemer of Islam), but he clearly means to include Hindu religious (and nationalist) fervour, too.

most of them. However, his energy and skills – as well as his reputation as a new radical leader – had already established a strong position for him within the organisation. He had worked hard for Congress as an investigator, lawyer and draftsman in producing its report on the Punjab events. In addition, he had been invited in 1919 to help draft a new Congress constitution.

Moreover, Congress politicians were not immune to the unrest in many parts of the subcontinent. Under the heading "pressures from below", Sumit Sarkar refers to the real emotion and anger aroused by the Khilafat and Punjab issues, which swayed the Congress leaders, as well as self-interested calculations. Sarkar quotes the lawyer and politician Motilal Nehru from a letter he sent in June: "My blood is boiling over since I read the summaries [of the Hunter report] you have sent. We must hold a Special Congress now and raise a veritable hell for the rascals". Sarkar adds that, as well as the "popular groundswell" virtually forcing more radical courses on both Khilafat and Congress leaders, labour unrest and organising and peasant awakenings were taking place across the subcontinent during this time.

Drafting a New Congress Constitution

At the Amritsar Congress in December 1919 – that is, after the Rowlatt hartal and the Amritsar massacre, and when he had already joined the Congress inquiry on the Punjab – Gandhi was entrusted with this new responsibility. His brief was:

"1. To examine the Congress constitution and consider necessary changes in it.

"2. To examine and consider the financial transactions of the different departments of the Congress.

"3. To make suggestions for the next year's session of the Congress."

The report was to be submitted before June 30, 1920.

Gandhi makes it clear in his autobiography that he was the principal figure on a subcommittee of five appointed to do the job:

"My other aptitude which the Congress could utilise was as a draftsman. The Congress leaders had found that I had a facility for condensed expression ... I undertook the responsibility of framing a constitution on one condition. I saw that there were two leaders, viz. the Lokamanya and the Deshabandhu (Tilak and Das) who had the greatest hold on the public. I requested that they, as the representatives of the people should be associated with me on the committee for framing the constitution. But since it was obvious that they would not have the time personally to participate, I suggested that two persons enjoying their confidence should be appointed along with me ... This suggestion was accepted..." (Gandhi M.K. 1982: 438-439) (See also, Gandhi M.K 1965: vol. 16: 463-464)

Yajnik in particular emphasises the importance of this step for Gandhi's political career. At the end of 1919, he writes, Gandhi had placed himself "at the head of the revolutionary mass struggle" by three distinct moves. Firstly, he had "secured the adhesion of the most virile and militant elements" in Indian nationalism by his prosecution of the Rowlatt Satyagraha. Secondly, by taking up the Khilafat cause he had "caught the real lever which would eventually secure him the following of the vast millions of comparatively backward Mohammedan masses". Thirdly, "he made a humble approach to organisational leadership" by being appointed to this committee to redraft the Congress constitution. (Yajnik 1933: 102) There can be no question that, by the end of 1919, Gandhi was beginning to think seriously about how to organise through the principal organisation of Indian nationalism.

The problem with the structure of the Congress, in Gandhi's words, was as follows:

"The question had been coming up year after year. The Congress at that time had practically no machinery functioning during the interval between session and session for dealing with fresh contingencies that might arise in the course of the year ... The Congress was too unwieldy a body for the discussion of public affairs. There was no limit set to the number of delegates that each province could return. Some improvement upon the existing chaotic condition was thus felt by everybody to be an imperative necessity." (Gandhi, M.K. 1982: 438-439)

With his absorption in the Khilafat campaign, his responsibilities for preparing the Punjab report, and numerous other commitments, it is not surprising that Gandhi found it hard to conduct the affairs of the constitution committee properly. In fact, the subcommittee never met, though Gandhi claimed that four out of the five members had some hand in its preparation. Gandhi's first draft was completed in June 1920, revised, and then circulated at the special session in September. His final draft was submitted to the All-India Congress Committee later in the month, published in the press and brought before the annual Congress session at Nagpur in December. (Gandhi M.K. 1965: vol 18: 428; vol 17: 487)

A novel feature in the preparation of the draft constitution was that because the members of the subcommittee could not agree on several issues, Gandhi adopted the unusual procedure of submitting his own *minority* proposals to the AICC, indicating the points on which the majority disagreed with him. He justified his action in *Young India*:

"It must be stated ... that it does not pretend to be the unanimous opinion of the members. Rather than present a dissenting minute, a workable scheme has been brought out leaving each member free to press his own views on the several matters in which they are not quite unanimous." (Gandhi M.K. 1965: vol 18: 428)

The principal issue on which the committee members were divided was the question of the number of delegates permitted to attend the annual sessions. Gandhi originally favoured limiting the number to 1,000, while other members wanted no limit to be set. (Gandhi M.K. 1965: vol 18: 3) In his minority proposals to the AICC, Gandhi appears to have increased this figure to 1,500; but at Nagpur Congress it was expanded to 6,000 (or 1 to every 50,000 of the adult population). Gandhi personally was unhappy with this figure, thinking it too large, but the other members still apparently objected to any limit. (Gandhi M.K. 1982: 450; Gandhi M.K. 1966: vol 19: 207)

Disagreement focused on the nature and purpose of the annual Congress, whether it was a business session, or a great national demonstration. Gandhi argued that the two aspects could be combined if the area to be occupied by the delegates was clearly demarcated and additional spaces made available for "visitors" and "guests". He was anxious to secure an annual business session which could not be swamped by the importation of unrestricted numbers. Writing of himself to the AICC, he said:

> "Mr Gandhi... considers that the restriction is essential in order to give the Congress a truly representative character and to make it a proper deliberative body. He thinks too that the Congress demands will become irresistible when it scientifically represents the whole people of India with an effective and proportionate voice in its deliberations and when every resolution has been considered with precision."

The majority of the committee, on the other hand, while recognising the "unwieldy nature" of the existing arrangements felt that their benefits outweighed the costs. (Gandhi M.K 1965: vol 18: 3, 288-290)

A second issue provoking dissension was Gandhi's proposal to change the Congress creed, that is, the statement of aims of the organisation. This did not so much divide the subcommittee; but they knew it would create a major stir among nationalist politicians. At the Congress session in Nagpur, the proposed alteration in the creed was separated from the rest of the draft constitution and a whole day's debate given over to it.

The two questions at issue are familiar from many accounts. Firstly, there was the proposal to delete any reference to the British connection; secondly, the suggestion that the means of achieving swaraj should be stated as "legitimate and peaceful", rather than "constitutional" as hitherto. Gandhi's argument was that Congress should seek independence for India within the British Empire, if possible, but it was demeaning to make a fetish of the British connection. Moreover, since it might be claimed that a movement demanding complete independence was unconstitutional, it was necessary to change the description of the means by which swaraj would be sought. In answer to fierce newspaper criticism of the proposed changes – when the draft constitution was published before the Nagpur Congress – Gandhi replied uncompromisingly in *Young India*:

"... the extraordinary situation that faces the country is that popular opinion is far in advance of several newspapers which have hitherto commanded influence and have undoubtedly moulded public opinion. The fact is that the formation of opinion today is by no means confined to the educated classes, but the masses have taken it upon themselves not only to formulate opinion but to enforce it. It would be a mistake to belittle or ignore this opinion or to ascribe it to a temporary upheaval. It would be equally a mistake to suppose that this awakening amongst the masses is due either to the activity of the Ali brothers or myself. For the time being we have the ear of the masses because we voice their sentiments. The masses are by no means so foolish or unintelligent as we sometimes imagine. They often perceive things with their intuition which we ourselves fail to see with our intellect. But whilst the masses know what they want, they often do not know how to express their wants and, less often, how to get what they want. Herein comes the use of leadership, and disastrous results can easily follow a bad, hasty, or what is worse, selfish lead." (Gandhi M.K. 1965: vol 18: 429)

Insofar as national opinion could be brought to bear inside the Indian National Congress, Gandhi appears to have been absolutely convinced, late in 1920, that the Indian nation was ready to define a role for itself, if necessary, outside the British connection. Moreover, he implied, the determination of the more conservative elements in Indian national opinion to resist this change reflected their own ''selfish'' interest in preserving the British link, whereas the "masses" had no such interest, and to thwart or ignore them could have "disastrous results". At Nagpur, Gandhi's formula was accepted. It was the midpoint between loyalist demands to retain the British connection and republican demands to sever it completely.

Other important changes in the constitution included the expansion of the All-India Congress Committee from 180 to 350 members; the creation of a new executive of fifteen, the Working Committee, to conduct day-to-day business of the Congress; and an increase in the number of provincial Congress committees from 12 to 21 by a redrawing of provincial boundaries. What Gandhi as the principal author of these changes had in mind was a representative organisation much like the British parliament, with the AICC as the House of Commons and the Working Committee as the Cabinet. Through redrawing the boundaries of the Congress provinces on a linguistic basis, Congress business could be conducted in the vernacular languages, making possible mass participation in its affairs for the first time. (Krishna 1966: 415-430; Gandhi M.K. 1966: vol. 19: 190-191)

Brown notes the decisive change in the organisation of Congress these innovations were to bring:

"By enlarging the AICC... and relegating it to a secondary place beneath a small group of men who could act as the Congress spearhead, the Congress turned itself into an active organisation instead of a shambling federation of local groups who met annually for discussion. The creation of the working committee repeated what Gandhi had done in the Gujarat Political Conference and the Khilafat movement: it bore the stamp of his leadership which placed a premium on single-minded action and a central control which verged on dictatorship." (Brown 1972: 298)

Gopal Krishna, in an outstanding paper, "The Development of the Indian National Congress as a Mass Organisation, 1918-1923", emphasises, however, the distinction between the rigorous discipline demanded of office-holders and the exceptionally wide freedom of opinion and action permitted to Congress members. "The Indian National Congress", he writes, "represented a broad national front and not a tightly organised party." By creating a working committee bound, like the British Cabinet, by a firmly applied doctrine of "collective responsibility", Gandhi "attempted to meet the need for a compact and disciplined executive to direct a loosely-knit mass movement which necessarily had to remain a broad coalition of divergent elements." (Krishna 1966: 413-430)

In June 1921, just before the first AICC elected under the new constitution met to appoint the first working committee, Gandhi described how the executive body should operate:

"...its members must be those who command the greatest respect of the All-India Congress Committee and the nation. It dare not take any hasty decisions, and it must be a homogenous body. It cannot have two policies or two or three parties within itself. Its decisions have largely to be unanimous. When a member cannot pull on with the rest, he can resign, but he may not obstruct or affect the deliberations of the Committee by an open discussion of its deliberations in the Press." (Krishna 1996: 415)

Gandhi, then, in the redrafting of the constitution, was out to build "parliamentary swaraj". Challenged by critics, including the Governor of Bengal, who were reading his early testament, *Hind Swaraj*, and assumed that he was trying through Noncooperation to "foist" his personal crusade against "modern civilisation" on the nation, Gandhi made his famous rejoinder:

"But I would warn the reader against thinking that I am today aiming at the swaraj described therein. I know that India is not ripe for it. It may seem an impertinence to say so. But such is my conviction. I am individually working for the self-rule pictured therein. But today my corporate activity is undoubtedly devoted to the attainment of parliamentary swaraj in accordance with the wishes of the people of India." (Gandhi M.K 1966: vol 19: 277-278)

Gandhi believed that the constitution which he had helped devise for the Indian National Congress was itself one of the immediate instruments by which this swaraj could be achieved. As he wrote in *Young India* in March 1921:

"The last Congress has given a constitution whose working is in itself calculated to lead to swaraj. It is intended to secure in every part of India representative committees working in conjunction with, and under willing and voluntary submission to, a central organisation – the All-India Congress Committee... If... it is honestly worked, and commands confidence and respect, it can oust the present Government without the slightest difficulty." (Gandhi M.K 1966: vol 19: 491)

His vision of how this could be done, he explained in another article in the same terms that had so excited Yajnik in the summer of 1919:

"It is necessary for us to understand the meaning of the Congress constitution. This constitution has been so drawn up that we may be able to win swaraj at an early date. If in accordance with that constitution we can form a Congress Committee in every town, and succeed in having the name of every man and woman of twenty-one years (and over) on our register, it will mean Congress authority respected in everything simultaneously with the Government's. The latter is maintained by force. When in one and the same place, another authority comes to be voluntarily respected by the people, the authority of the Government, if it is not accepted by the people, will not last even a moment. That is to say, if we can see the Congress constitution functioning on a country-wide scale we may take it that swaraj will have been established that very day." (Gandhi M.K 1966: vol 19: 461-462)

But while Gandhi saw the implementation of the new Congress constitution as, in itself, "a peaceful and bloodless revolution" which with determined organisation could be accomplished in one year, (Gandhi M.K 1966: vol 19: 219) it was not the social and spiritual revolution which was the deeper reason for his intervention in the political world. "In so far as I can see", he wrote in December 1920, "swaraj will be a parliament chosen by the people with the fullest power over the finance, the police, the military, the navy, the courts and the educational institutions." The only part of the programme of *Hind Swaraj* "which is now being carried out in its entirety is that of nonviolence". Swaraj, as pursued by the Congress, "means the swaraj that the people of India want". (Gandhi M.K 1966: vol 19: 79-81, 277-278)

Did Gandhi really have this vision in his mind at the Amritsar Congress in late 1919 when he accepted his "humble" commission to draft a new constitution for the organisation? The likelihood is that this extraordinary organiser did. Certainly, in the late summer of 1920 when the final draft was being prepared, we may assume that Gandhi insisted on presenting his minority proposals to the AICC, because he knew that they represented what he called then "a workable scheme".

Brown points to a second aspect of the constitution drafted by Gandhi in 1920 and implemented in subsequent years. The reorganisation of the

Congress provinces on a linguistic basis and the allocation of delegates to these new provinces shifted the balance of power within the organisation. Whereas the "backward" areas previously had been swamped in Congress by the presidencies – Bombay, Bengal and Madras, from which the majority of the western-educated leaders came – the new constitution opened Congress up to new sources of power. "For the first time," says Brown, "power in Congress through voting rights came within the reach of men whose outlook and interests differed from those of the men who composed and controlled Congress in its first forty years." She adds that many of these "new Congressmen", brought into the organisation in the latter half of 1922, came precisely from those groups which Gandhi's activities – and those of the Home Rule Leagues – had helped to mobilise for the first time. (Brown 1972: 298-300) As a result of this change, Congress was able to represent and direct the upsurge of political activity taking place especially in the rural areas of India. The composition of the AICC, for example, changed by 1922 to an organisation dominated by members from rural districts, where previously most members had come from the cities and provincial towns. (Krishna 1966: 422-423)

Gandhi's drafting of the Congress constitution, then, his "real entrance into the Congress politics", (Gandhi M.K 1982: 439)[42] was in many respects an achievement of conventional politics, not a task that reflected his deeper social and spiritual aims. He fashioned for the Congress an organisational structure enabling it to adapt to the rising tide of Indian nationalism at the point when mass political organisation became possible and necessary. In this, he did the job of the other nationalist politicians for them. For Gandhi, the dilemma he faced by his failure in 1919 to build a true satyagraha movement to further his aims in India, he solved by adopting a "stages theory" of political development. The first step was the achievement of parliamentary swaraj. Of first priority was the construction of a movement to challenge the temerity of the British in refusing justice on the Khilafat and Punjab issues. His deeper social and spiritual goals were to remain "personal" and subsidiary.

---

42. Earlier Gandhi had described his contribution to the Amritsar Congress in December 1919 with the same phrase. Either one makes sense.

The All-India Home Rule League
(or Swarajya Sabha)

While his work on the constitution, the Punjab inquiry and the Khilafat issue were still ongoing, Gandhi's reputation as a rising national figure was growing. He was becoming a national leader who must be consulted by others and one whose influence and approval was increasingly sought. In 1920, Gandhi achieved control of a national organisation, affiliated to Congress, through which he could hope directly to promote his personal political and social views.

Gandhi had been consistently critical of the All-India Home Rule League, founded by Annie Besant in 1916. The League was split in the summer of 1919 on the question of civil disobedience and on whether or not to support the Raj's reform programme. Annie Besant was still president, but was rapidly outflanked by radicals dissatisfied with her leadership. (Owen 1968) Eventually, Gandhi was invited to accept the presidency and in April 1920, after consulting with a number of influential friends, he did so.

Immediately, he transformed the programme of the organisation. According to Brown there is no clear evidence of how Gandhi came to be offered the presidency of the League, though she suggests that Motilal Nehru actually invited him. (Brown 1972: 248) Gandhi himself said in a private letter to Srinivasa Sastri that the "demand" had come from people with whom he had worked before, presumably referring to the group of Bombay Home Rulers with whom he had launched the Satyagraha Sabha. In his letter to Sastri, which was circulated privately to other friends, Gandhi stated the conditions he placed on joining the League:

> "I have told them that at my time of life and with views firmly formed on several matters I could only join an organisation to affect its policy and not to be affected by it".

He went on to list five conditions, the first of which was a pointed rebuke to what he saw as the political opportunism practised previously by the nationalist movement:

"1. (The) highest honesty must be introduced in the political life of the country if we are to make our mark as a nation. This presupposes at the present moment a very firm and definite acceptance of the creed of Truth at any cost."

Only a few weeks earlier Gandhi had engaged in a public exchange with Tilak, leader of the other Home Rule League, on the question of truthfulness in politics. "Politics," Tilak had said witheringly, "is a game of worldly people and not of Sadhus (holy men)". (Gandhi M.K. 1965: vol 16: 490-491 fn2)

Gandhi's second condition of acceptance was swadeshi: "swadeshi must be our immediate goal". Thirdly, he wanted the adoption of Hindustani "in the immediate future" as a national language.[43] Fourth was the principle of redistributing the provinces of India on a linguistic basis. Fifthly, he demanded support for Hindu-Muslim unity as an "unalterable article of faith"; this would include in the official programme of the League "vigorous" promotion of the Khilafat cause.

Here were all the articles of Gandhi's social programme as developed at that stage, but he also made it clear that he would not press the League into more contentious areas of his programme: "I will not think of asking for official recognition of my creed of civil disobedience". (Gandhi M.K. 1966: vol. 17: 96-98) Gandhi insisted that his social programme in practice was non-political and should be accepted by all as "non-party" activity; whereas he recognised that civil disobedience was a method inviting strong political disagreement. With his rising reputation, Gandhi was presumably an attractive prospect as a leader of the League, whatever conditions he laid down. The invitation, at any rate, was not withdrawn and at the end of April he announced that he had joined the League as its president. "It is a distinct departure from the even tenor of my life", said Gandhi in a public letter to the members of the League, "for me to belong to an organisation which is purely and frankly political." This remark is worthy of note because it shows that Gandhi was aware that he was

---

43. The difference between Hindustani and Hindi is mainly their writing script. There are slight differences in grammar when spoken. Gandhi, however, seems to have used the terms interchangeably.

taking risks as he moved towards the centre of Indian political life. The Khilafat movement was in many respects a religious movement; while the Satyagraha Sabha and the Swadeshi Sabha had been based on religious vows. The Gujarat Sabha was a civic organisation whose object was to promote the social and economic wellbeing of the people of Gujarat.

By accepting the leadership of the League, Gandhi was identifying himself with a political organisation of which he had been strongly critical. He justified his action with three arguments. Firstly, that he had already moved into the political arena by his activities at the Amritsar Congress where he "found it impossible to remain silent" as on previous occasions. Secondly, that he would not lose his independence to act freely according to his own conscience, what he called his "splendid isolation", for the League had accepted him as president in full knowledge of his views. Moreover, he would be wrong not to "utilise" the organisation for advancing the causes associated with him, for he would "gain a platform for propagating my ideas". Gandhi's third point was that the object of the League, swaraj, could be achieved most speedily by those causes which he espoused – swadeshi, Hindu-Muslim unity and the spread of Hindi: "If I succeed in engaging the League in those activities I shall feel confident of our being able to achieve swaraj at an early date". (Gandhi M.K. 1965: vol 17: 347-349, 369-372)

In a reiteration of the views he had expressed in his "Swaraj in Swadeshi" article the previous December, (Gandhi M.K. 1965: vol 16: 335-337) Gandhi made it clear that he thought the political reforms being introduced by the British were of secondary importance to the programme of social reforms he was inviting the League to take up. In July he was to issue a direct challenge to the nation's educated when – on behalf of the Khilafatists – he announced the triple boycott of the councils, the courts and the schools. But he had made the same challenge to the League members, less dramatically but equally clearly, three months earlier in April. He announced then a reform programme for the League, not of pressure to get the rules for the forthcoming elections changed, nor of propaganda to get a Gandhian faction elected to the councils. Typically, he wanted to get the nationalist activists of the League out of the legislatures and into the villages. "We are to work with the millions and

264

influence them," he said. (Gandhi M.K 1966: vol. 17: 348; Tendulkar: 1951: vol. 1: 288-290)

Once in control, Gandhi set out immediately to convert the League's members to his views. As president he was in a position now to direct a national network and develop a body of support independent of, and additional to, the Khilafat movement. (Gordon 1973: 134) Leadership of the League gave him the opportunity to explore publicly the question of how swaraj could be achieved by his methods – and move himself into the centre of nationalist agitational politics. In particular, his advocacy of linguistic provinces recognised growing movements for autonomy within the old presidencies. Even so, his main preoccupation was still with the Khilafat movement and the developing noncooperation campaign – and it was perhaps inevitable that the Home Rule League became not a politicised reinvention of the Swadeshi Sabha, as he seems to have intended, but an important vehicle for Gandhi's drive to win the nation to Noncooperation.

Richard Gordon, in his study of council boycott and noncooperation, states that:

"Gandhi planned to capture Congress by a pronged attack: through the All-India Home Rule League, the Khilafat Committees and such support as he could muster in the Congress Committees themselves."

Moreover, at the special session of the Congress in Calcutta, when it was still unclear whether the subjects committee would support noncooperation, Gandhi is reported to have called a meeting of the League to discuss what to do in case he lost. (Gordon 1973: 141, 145) Once the special session had agreed to support noncooperation, Gandhi still did not have full support from the All-India Congress Committee, which directed the affairs of Congress between the annual sessions. He was thus obliged, for example, to send out a circular letter to branches of the Home Rule League drawing to their attention the Congress resolution in support of noncooperation and requesting them "for the next two months" to concentrate their attention principally on the boycott of the reformed councils. (Gandhi M.K. 1966: vol. 18: 285-286, 287) The letter contained the wording of a "form" which voters were to be asked to sign, stating that they did not desire to be represented in the councils.

Between the special session in September and the annual session at Nagpur in December, Gandhi remained dependent for the organisation of Noncooperation on the Central Khilafat Committee and the Home Rule League. (Gordon 1970: 134) During October, however, the League was hit by a number of prominent resignations, including that of Jinnah, at that time a leading moderate nationalist Muslim and a former president of the League branch in Bombay. The contentious issue was that Gandhi had had the constitution of the League changed, including its name, which was to be Swarajya Sabha. In this move, Gandhi was quite clearly using the League as a lever to influence the Congress session at Nagpur, just as he had used the Gujarat Political Conference in August to nudge the special Congress into support for Noncooperation. The aim of the new Sabha was to be independence with or without the British connection. The means of achieving this aim were to be "peaceful" and "legitimate". These were precisely the changes in the Congress constitution Gandhi advocated successfully later at Nagpur.

Jinnah argued that Gandhi had acted unconstitutionally; he said that the meeting in Bombay which took the decision, was attended by only 61 members out of an all-India membership of 6,000. Gandhi, who had already been blocked once by similar charges after an earlier meeting in September in Calcutta, (Dalal 1971: 32 fn10) replied that the meeting was legal and he added:

> "...the country is moving so fast now that our leaders cannot keep pace with it. In such circumstances, no matter how much we are pained, we must go ahead. India will not have such an opportunity for a century. We cannot afford to miss it. We may only hope that when the leaders realise the value of the strong popular current, they will not hesitate to join it." (Gandhi M.K 1966: vol. 18: 365-368, 370-372; Brown 1972: 276-277)

Gandhi's view was that Congress must question the British connection and be willing itself to launch civil obedience if it was to remain representative of nationalist feeling in the country. In this he was undoubtedly correct.

Nevertheless, in endeavouring to keep pace with this current, Gandhi was using the Swarajya Sabha for a quite different set of objectives than he had outlined when he accepted the presidency of the League only a few months earlier.

In particular he had stated in April that he had no intention of drawing the League into civil disobedience, whereas in October he now admitted that the new creed of the Sabha would "cover" civil disobedience. (Gandhi M.K 1965: vol 18: 367) Gandhi's "utilisation" of the League for his own purposes did not stop there, however, for once his second victory at Nagpur confirmed that he could work through the organisation of the Congress itself he appears to have dropped the Swarajya Sabha altogether. Brailsford quotes a prominent nationalist Hindu on the affair:

"Some resentment was felt because Gandhi, before he was sure that he could win Congress, had entrenched himself within the Home Rule League, which he renamed the Swarajya Sabha. This rival organisation, when he no longer needed it, died a peaceful death." (Brailsford 1949: 138)

Gandhi's capture of the All-India Home Rule League was thus a temporary phenomenon lasting only eight months until he achieved control of the Congress. Again we see his belief that with superior political insight and experience he was entitled to force the pace and set the programme for the League as long as its members had confidence in him. Again, as with the Satyagraha Sabha, we see strong political disagreements with colleagues operating from different political principles causing splits in the organisation when Gandhi chose to follow his own lead.

Although through the Home Rule League Gandhi had arrived at the leadership of the national Congress, he had done so by using it for a far more "political" purpose than he had promised when taking over as president. Instead of creating a "non-political" organisation, which would substitute for and extend the work of the Swadeshi Sabha, he appears to have done what he said he would not do, recruit from the Home Rule League a "party" organisation which helped his rise in the Congress. (Gandhi M.K. 1966: vol. 17: 97, 348) This meant that Gandhi, at the height of his power in India, with the Indian National Congress under his direction, still did not control an all-India organisation committed to his principles of satyagraha. Gandhi in taking on the leadership of the Indian National Congress took on the leadership of a coalition of political interests, which like the Khilafat movement had its own expedient reasons for accepting his lead. But his own base of support, for the full satyagraha programme he was advocating, was thin.

Thus he embraced the leadership of Congress in much the same way as he had accepted the leadership of the League and the Khilafat movement, hoping by directing the membership into a nonviolent programme to do some good and to recruit from out of the experience some new converts to his position. But within the Congress coalition, Gandhi was operating on a far vaster scale on a larger issue and on a larger range of issues and with more formidable political figures as colleagues than ever before. Thus again he was vulnerable to losing control.

Two Campaigns Become One: Five months to win Congress

We have seen how the linking of two campaigns – on the Khilafat and Punjab issues – was eventually to bring together two satyagraha struggles to be pursued by the same progressive nonviolent programme. That programme had to be taken up and adopted by Congress, with Congress as the vehicle for taking it forward. It had also to take on a much larger agenda when the demand for swaraj was added as a further aim. Noncooperation was launched in August by the Khilafat committee; but was still at the preparatory stage on the Punjab issue.

Gandhi's achievement in constructing the new Congress constitution reflected not so much his aptitude as a draftsman as his profound awareness of how the new political forces emerging in India could be harnessed. In the late summer of 1920 his ability to have the constitution agreed and implemented in full depended largely on whether Congress at its special session and then annual session would take up Noncooperation. His triumphs at Calcutta and Nagpur enabled his "workable scheme" to be attempted.

When the Gujarat Political Conference acting as a provincial Congress committee voted in favour of Noncooperation in August 1920 and then proceeded to implement the programme without waiting for the verdict of the special session, Gandhi came under a lot of public and private pressure to "play the game" and wait for the national body's decision. He replied with characteristic audacity:

"In my humble opinion, it is no Congressman's duty to consult the Congress before taking action in a matter in which he has no doubts. To do otherwise may mean stagnation.

"The Congress is after all the mouthpiece of the nation. And when one has a policy or a programme which one would like to see adopted, but on which one wants to cultivate public opinion, one naturally asks the Congress to discuss it and form an opinion. But when one has an unshakable faith in a particular policy or action, it would be folly to wait for the Congress pronouncement. On the contrary, one must act and demonstrate its efficacy so as to command acceptance by the nation.

"My loyalty to the Congress requires me to carry out its policy when it is not contrary to my conscience. If I am in a minority I may not pursue my policy in the name of Congress. The decision of the Congress on any given question therefore does not mean that it prevents a Congressman from any action to the contrary, but if he acts he does so at his own risk and with the knowledge that the Congress is not with him." (Gandhi M.K 1965: vol 18: 112-113)

According to Krishna, the fact that Gandhi continued to maintain this doctrine after he had captured Congress meant that the degree of latitude permitted to dissenters in the now mass organisation was ''exceptionally wide''. (Krishna 1966: 428; Gandhi M.K 1966: vol. 19: 185-186)

Between August when the Khilafat campaign launched Noncooperation and December when the issue was brought before the annual Congress session for its decision, Gandhi undertook a number of major speaking tours in different parts of India, travelling mainly by train. The first for 10 days in August was in the *south*; he travelled widely across the Madras Presidency. Much of September was taken up with visiting Bengal in the *east* for the special Congress in Calcutta. In October, he went *north* for 15 days, visiting Delhi and the Punjab. In November, he toured the *west* for 12 days throughout the Bombay Presidency. Then later in November and early December, he travelled in the east again, going back to Delhi, and then on to the United Provinces, Bihar and Bengal, a tour of 26 days; before finally arriving in Nagpur for the Congress, where he arrived 10 days or so before the annual session began.

At many of the cities, towns and villages visited, public meetings were held. Some of them were huge gatherings. Describing this period, Nanda says:

> "Gandhi's meetings in 1919-1920 were attended by fifty or even a hundred thousand people from all walks of life. Since there were no loudspeakers, Gandhi's speeches had to be repeated or translated by local leaders. But for most of the audience it was enough if they had a glimpse of the Mahatma".

Nanda adds that the direct emotional link between Gandhi and the people was something new in Indian politics: "It gave him a distinct advantage". Inducting semi-literate and illiterate masses into the political arena was not something the former "moderate" Congress leaders would have attempted; and the "extremist" leaders of the Home Rule Leagues spoke mainly to the "white-collar class". (Nanda 1989: 247)[44]

A far from comprehensive selection of topics Gandhi covered in his speeches during the five months of touring prior to Nagpur, shows that all were linked with his social and political programme. A number of the towns were "off the beaten track" and would not normally receive a visit from a leading politician. He opened national schools in Surat, Bombay, Cawnpore, Delhi and Calcutta; and laid the foundation stone for a national school in Hajipur. Students were advised by him to leave their schools in Ahmedabad, Surat, Aligarh, Amritsar, Lahore, Benares

---

44. Nanda compares Gandhi's ability to draw crowds in 1920 with the numbers attending Tilak's meetings in Bombay a few years previously: "Even at the height of the Home Rule movement, Tilak's meetings… were attended by no more than three or four thousand people, largely from the white-collar class".

and Patna. In Madras he spoke on the beach on non-cooperation and later addressed "a meeting of labourers". In Salem he opened "a free water service for the poor". In Bezwada, there was a meeting with "peasants and labourers". In Ahmedabad he spoke about the grievances of untouchables. He addressed "meeting(s) of women" in Dakor, Ahmedabad, Nadiad, Broach, Poona, Satara, Chikodi, Belgaum, Delhi and Patna. He met "merchants and students" in Poona; laid the foundation stone of a free reading room in Sangli; and in Bombay attended a meeting of Muslims "to consider boycott of legislatures". In Delhi he opened a swadeshi handloom factory, and attended a conference of Muslim clerics (ulemas). He talked in Allahabad on noncooperation; addressed lawyers in Dacca; and attended a conference of weavers in Nagpur. Gandhi addressed Muslims and Hindus on these tours. On the first, to Madras and the south, he was accompanied by one of the Ali brothers, Shaukat, who again toured Bengal with him in December. (Dalal 1971:32-35)

Noncooperation led by the Khilafatists began on August 1 with the call for a nationwide hartal. This was well supported, particularly by Muslims, in some of the northern provinces like Sind, but did not attract major activity elsewhere. Even so the response made clear that "his programme had percolated throughout India". (Brown 1972: 252)

By September, when the Special Congress was held in Calcutta, the political classes, predominantly Hindu, whose strategy for decades had been to press for reforms within the elected Councils of the Raj, were still undecided.[45] They tended to adopt the expedient position of supporting noncooperation in principle, but objecting to specific parts of the programme. Gandhi was faced with convincing political opponents understandably reluctant to gamble with open rebellion; but also aware of the strength of feeling in the sub-continent that the Congress needed to make a major challenge to the Raj.

---

45. Moderate Muslims had pursued much the same strategy of seeking political advancement within the Raj's consultative structures. But some felt forced into support for Noncooperation by the Raj's failure to defend their co-religionists in the Middle East.

September 1920: Calcutta Special Session votes for Noncooperation

Gandhi made his bid to win Congress support for Noncooperation at the special session at Calcutta.[46] Over 5,800 delegates were registered, of whom over 2,700 voted. (Brown 1972: 266 fn) Of those taking part in the Calcutta vote, the largest number came from the Bengal presidency, where the Congress was being held. Sizeable delegations attending from the Bombay and Madras presidencies were matched by those from formerly "backward" provinces like Punjab, United Provinces, and Bihar. Gujarat was included in the Bombay delegation. (Brown 1972: 270)

All the leading nationalist figures opposed Gandhi – perhaps because most of them had spent months in 1920 building up electoral organisations and wished to contest the new elections to the provincial councils. They were unwilling to support council boycott. Debate centred around whether noncooperation could be carried on within the new councils by a determined policy of obstruction, rather than wholesale boycott of the elections. But Gandhi won a narrow verdict in the subjects committee – the preliminary meeting of elected representatives from provincial delegations to decide what resolutions should be brought before the Congress – and then a substantial victory in the open session.

Commentators agree that Gandhi's opponents had underestimated him. The principal reason why he won the verdict in the subjects committee is that his efforts at mobilising support prior to the special Congress (through the networks of the Khilafat movement, the All-India Home Rule League and the provincial Congress committees) had succeeded. Not only had supporters from the newly politicised areas like Gujarat, Bihar, Punjab and the United Provinces been drawn to the Congress, but also significant numbers of Muslims were attending for the first time. In addition, Noncooperation was beginning to undermine the presidency

---

46. The following discussion of the special Congress session in Calcutta and the annual session in Nagpur is based largely on Brown (1972: 250-304), Gordon (1973: 123-153) and Nanda (1989: 227-249). In particular it is addressed to Gordon's argument that, at Nagpur, Gandhi capitulated to Das.

politicians on their home ground as new social groups responded to Gandhi's militant programme.

Congress opponents of Gandhi had been thrown into disarray by the death in August 1920 of the outstanding "extremist" leader from Bombay presidency, Tilak; and Annie Besant from Madras in the south had lost her influence. Moreover, recognising that Gandhi had captured a new mood in the people, a key figure like Motilal Nehru (Jawarhalal Nehru's father) may also have calculated that the chances of his local Congress organisation winning a majority in the elections in the United Provinces were slim. In the course of the special Congress, Nehru and others defected to Gandhi's side. This was the specific turning point giving Gandhi victory.

The concessions Gandhi had to make to achieve this extraordinary result were few, but significant. At Nehru's suggestion, proposals for schools and courts boycott were watered down, so that Congressmen were committed only to a "gradual" adoption of them. This meant effectively that Gandhi's opponents, if they chose to, could delay taking a personal decision on these for three months until the annual Congress session met to debate them at Nagpur.

To Gandhi's publicly stated embarrassment, a second compromise was that the proposal for economic boycott was reintroduced into the programme, despite his often-stated opposition to it. Between Gandhi's reluctant acceptance of a boycott of *foreign cloth* and his opponents' determination to press for a boycott of *British goods*, a compromise was found in favour of a boycott of *foreign goods*. Both sides were also able to agree to Gandhi's suggestion to add the propagation of swadeshi to the programme. (Gandhi M.K 1965: vol 18: 248-249, 250, 262)

A third significant change was the addition of "swaraj" as an aim of Noncooperation. The preamble to the Noncooperation resolution carried at Calcutta now read:

"This Congress is of the opinion that there can be no contentment in India without redress of the two aforementioned wrongs

(Khilafat and Punjab) and that the only effectual means to vindicate national honour and to prevent a repetition of similar wrongs in future is the establishment of swarajya." (Gandhi M.K 1965: vol 18: 230)

During the debate before the subjects committee, Gandhi still stuck to his preference for pursuing specific grievances. His argument was reported as follows:

"He accepted the amendment regarding full self-government in his proposal not on the ground that the Khilafat question was subservient to the question of swaraj. To him the Khilafat and the Punjab were greater than swaraj…

"…[H]e was clear that he wanted to go to every elector and ask him to boycott elections for the insult offered to the country by the Punjab and Khilafat questions. He would not use his appeal to them on the question of swaraj. To him swaraj was only a means to an end and he, for his part, was prepared to exchange swaraj for any other system of government if, in his opinion, it was for the good of the country." (Gandhi M.K 1965: vol 18: 233-234)

But in his speech moving the resolution before the open session of the special Congress on the following day, Gandhi had begun to expand the concept of swaraj so that it was more in line with his own thinking, now being advanced through the Home Rule League, on the necessity of developing national self-reliance and self-confidence. Placing greater emphasis therefore on the demand for swaraj, he said:

"If there is a sufficient response to my scheme [that is, the full noncooperation programme of council, schools and law-court boycott] I make bold to reiterate my statement that you can gain swarajya in the course of a year."

Gandhi's use of the word "you" is surely significant – "you can gain swarajya". He had not yet fully accepted this new objective for Noncooperation. He went on:

"Not the passing of the resolution will bring swarajya but the enforcement of the resolution from day to day in a progressive

manner due regard being had to the conditions in the country."
(Gandhi M.K 1966: vol. 18: 247)

Nevertheless, when pressed by moderate critics of his programme to justify the addition of the demand for swaraj to the Noncooperation campaign, he went back to his earlier position that swaraj was a subsidiary demand, made necessary by the other two. It was on this basis that he rejected the strongly-advanced argument that, before Noncooperation was launched on the issue of swaraj, British public opinion and the British government itself had to be prepared by propaganda, warnings and attempts at negotiation. (Gandhi M.K 1965: vol. 18: 251) Despite the changes, in its essentials the Noncooperation resolution approved at the special session in Calcutta described the same programme Gandhi had outlined at the beginning of July.

It is notable that of the 12 provinces represented at the special Congress, ten voted in favour of Gandhi's resolution. The greatest support came from the United Provinces (90%), Bihar (87%), Delhi (87%) and Andhra (83%). The two where support was withheld were Central Provinces (48%) and Berar (15%). The three presidencies (with the longest history of involvement in Congress) were also for Gandhi, though less decisively: Bombay (73%); Bengal (58%) and Madras (54%).[47]

Following this extraordinary achievement at the Calcutta special Congress, however, Gandhi was by no means in control of Congress supporters across the subcontinent. The presidency politicians had to make up their minds quickly on whether to accept the special Congress decision on council boycott, and reluctantly most of them did. But they were unwilling to accept even the "gradual" boycott of schools and courts as a practical political programme, and this remained largely a project of Gandhi's immediate Gujarat and Khilafat colleagues, prior to the projected "showdown" at Nagpur.

---

47. This information is calculated from Table 5 in Judith Brown's study. (Brown 1972: 270)

December 1920: Nagpur Annual Session Endorses Noncooperation

In October, after the special session had recommended in favour of Noncooperation but before the Nagpur annual Congress had approved it, the elections to the Raj's new reformed councils took place. Of course, Noncooperation had already started for the Khilafatists and in Gujarat. India's politicians had to decide whether to acknowledge the new policy by joining the boycott before it was finally determined by Congress, or resist it and risk isolating themselves. Nanda comments: "Noncooperation was put to its first serious test after the Congress [special] session" and adds: "But most Congress leaders decided not to defy the verdict of the Congress. The tide of opinion was clearly moving in the direction of Gandhi's campaign." (Nanda 1989: 237)

Prominent Congress leaders withdrew from the elections in Bengal, Bihar, Bombay, Central Provinces and Madras. Nanda says:

"Most of those who boycotted the elections did so reluctantly, against their better judgement. But they sensed the mood of the party and the country, and preferred to toe the party line to being swept into political oblivion." (Nanda 1989: 237)

However, Council boycott ceased to be a seriously divisive issue once the elections to the reformed councils were completed in November 1920. The nationalists then felt free to address the remainder of Gandhi's Noncooperation programme.

The main opposition to Gandhi's plan of action in the weeks prior to the Nagpur Congress in December was from the Bengal Presidency, where C.P. Das and B. C. Pal tried to fashion an alternative approach to Noncooperation and to rouse other nationalist leaders defeated at Calcutta in their support. Their two main objections were, firstly, that the schools and courts boycott was being launched without adequate preparation and, secondly, picking up on the argument maintained consistently by Hasrat Mohani since November 1919, that in Gandhi's programme economic boycott was grossly under-stressed. In response to the schools and courts boycott, therefore, they did not oppose it, but outlined more detailed proposals for establishing national schools, arbitration courts and means of support for noncooperating students, teachers and lawyers. In addition, they wanted the aims of Noncooperation revised, so that "swaraj", added by his opponents at Calcutta and treated as an afterthought by Gandhi to his principal concern with the Khilafat and Punjab issues, would become the principal demand. Also, they called for a vigorous new Congress organisation to be developed as part of Noncooperation, geared especially to social groups brought newly onto the provincial electoral rolls, and a major fund-raising drive to support this effort.

Gandhi's dominance at Nagpur is demonstrated by the Congress agenda itself. Following elections to the subjects committee on the first day and the president's opening speech, the second and third days were devoted in the subjects committee and then in open session to discussion of the new Congress creed proposed by the constitution subcommittee. Similarly, the fourth and fifth days were used to discuss the programme of Noncooperation; and the last day was occupied with the constitution subcommittee's proposals for totally reorganising the Congress structure. In other words, he had generated all the significant Congress business.

After fierce debate in the subjects committee, Gandhi's compromise formula for a change in the creed was seconded in open Congress by the Bengali leader, Pal, and accepted without alteration. On the Noncooperation resolution itself, a great deal of horse-trading in the subjects committee brought a success for Gandhi too. Gandhi's other leading Bengali critic, C.R. Das, rose in the open session to propose support for the Noncooperation programme and, with Gandhi seconding, the resolution was carried without difficulty. On the last day, again, the resolution to change the constitution went through "calmly" with, according to Gandhi, the single alteration (which he deplored) of increasing the number of delegates to the annual session from 1,500 to 6,000.

None of the changes to the Noncooperation resolution moved by Das constituted a fundamental concession by Gandhi, except perhaps the revised aim of the movement as stated in the preamble. This now read:

"Whereas in the opinion of the Congress the existing Government of India has forfeited the confidence of the country; and

"Whereas the people of India are now determined to establish swaraj: and

"Whereas all methods adopted by the people of India prior to the last Special Session of the Indian National Congress have failed to secure due recognition of their rights and the redress of their many and grievous wrongs, more especially with reference to the Khilafat and the Punjab; ... (Gandhi M.K 1966: vol. 19: 576-578)[48]

It meant that the "general" aim of swaraj now took decisive precedence over the two "particular" grievances, Khilafat and the Punjab, which were merely illustrative of the need to achieve swaraj. Gandhi had the support of the Muslim Khilafat leaders in accepting this change; but it marked a substantial shift in his position from Calcutta and posed problems as we have suggested for his strategy as an organiser.

At Nagpur, however, Gandhi appears not to have been in the least embarrassed by this change. It seems clear that Gandhi considered the revision of the Congress creed achieved in the first three days of the Nagpur session freed him to link Noncooperation decisively and solidly to the demand for swaraj. (Gandhi M.K 1966: vol. 19: 159-162, 164-168, 187, 206-207) In other words, taking over the Congress organisation in order to launch such a momentous and critical struggle for the future of India made it inevitable and necessary that he should gear the campaign to the achievement of the Congress's principal goal, which was swaraj. Moreover, the fact that the creed had been revised meant that it was now possible to do this: whereas at Calcutta and afterwards, Noncooperation, particularly its later confrontational stages, had been deemed by several leading Congressmen to be contrary to the organisation's creed. (Gandhi M.K 1966: vol. 18: 489)

There were other changes too. The section in the revised Noncooperation resolution congratulating Congress supporters on their boycott of the

---

48. For Gandhi's original draft of the resolution, see Gandhi, M.K. 1966: vol 19: 182-185.

polls in November and calling for the resignation of those who had defied the boycott and been elected to the councils, omitted to mention whether the next round of elections in 1923 should be boycotted. (Gandhi M.K 1966: vol. 19: 577) Also Gandhi's statement in the resolution that swaraj should be "established within one year" was heavily underlined. This was taken to mean by many that the Triple Boycott was to be enforced for one year only. It also gave Das a let-out for contesting the 1923 elections, which in the event he took.

Again, Das's proposal to include the development of the Congress organisation as part of the Noncooperation programme was a particularly important innovation in line with his and Gandhi's own proposals to reform the Congress through the revised constitution. Moreover, Das's proposal to establish a band of national workers, the Indian National Service, and to finance them and other activities by a special fund, the Tilak Swaraj Fund, had been foreshadowed by Gandhi's own proposals to the All India Congress Committee in September, which had been accepted in October. (Gandhi M.K 1965: vol 18: 284) So there was no reason for disagreement there.

Another change in the Nagpur resolution on Noncooperation was the proposal by Das to strengthen alternative arrangements for people taking part in the schools and courts boycott. Yet this was balanced by a clear commitment by the nationalist politicians to "make greater efforts" to carry out these boycotts. The word "gradual" had been withdrawn. This was therefore a major success for Gandhi, made all the greater by endorsement in the Nagpur resolution of all four stages of the Noncooperation programme, including tax refusal: whereas at Calcutta only the first stage had been explicitly supported.

The inclusion of economic boycott in the programme was a decisive defeat for Gandhi, which did embarrass him: but that defeat occurred at Calcutta and not at Nagpur. At Nagpur, he appears to have been reconciled to promoting a boycott of foreign goods by which he meant foreign cloth. (Gandhi M.K 1966: vol 19: 239-242, 184, 204, 208) In principle what he could not accept was a boycott of British goods – and he prevailed on that.

This, then, was what is often called the Das-Gandhi Pact.[49] The Bengali politicians, in acquiescing before Gandhi, may have seen that they could turn Noncooperation (and the fervour it was arousing in Bengal and elsewhere) in their own interests by going out to build through it a mass, agitational and ultimately electoral machine. They also appear genuinely to have accepted their defeat and to have sought from their own perspective, which was not that of satyagraha, to make the Noncooperation programme workable for them. (Brown 1972: 296, 299-300; Broomfield 1968: 168) Gandhi seems to have understood what their objectives were by his statements later that he was working for "parliamentary swaraj" and by his argument that the enrolment of millions of members in the Congress would constitute a parallel government, which could itself establish swaraj . He may have thought, though, that the Congress itself would constitute the swaraj parliament; rather than becoming, as it did, an organisation through which the nationalist politicians could contest elections to the councils of the Raj. Gandhi also is known to have agreed, as part of the bargaining in Nagpur, that the Bengali leaders should have autonomy directing Noncooperation in the Bengal presidency. (Brown 1972: 297 fn)

The price that the Bengali and other nationalist leaders had to pay for their agreement with Gandhi was a large one, however. They had to accept Gandhi himself, with his unconventional views on the conduct of politics and his insistence on discipline at the top. He was to be the dominant leader in national politics and the "general" in whose hands the conduct of the national struggle would largely rest. Against the better judgment of most of them they were committed to calling the students and teachers out of government schools, colleges and universities and to finding somehow the resources and the staff to found new national educational institutions. Several of the leading Congressmen like Nehru and Das were extremely wealthy lawyers who, having accepted Gandhi's programme, were obliged to resign their practices. These acts of self-sacrifice by veteran nationalist figures caused a great impression and were seen as a particular triumph for Gandhi. (Bose 1935: 55-65)

---

49. Most of my assessment of the evidence above runs contrary to Gordon's interpretation of the agreement. (Gordon 1973: 150-151)

Finally, and most important of all, with Gandhi at the helm, they were obliged to join him in the boldest satyagraha experiment he had yet attempted, a deadly serious adventure in taking politics to the masses and challenging the power of the Raj. No-one could know what the results of this unprecedented gamble would be. While it was not the satyagraha of *Hind Swaraj*, the nationalists were committed by the Noncooperation resolution at Nagpur to the development of a wholly nonviolent movement "in word and deed". Gandhi, having first taken the Khilafat movement into Noncooperation, had now forged a second major tactical alliance with the main body of Hindu nationalism. As a result he could attempt to conduct his first sustained experiment in nonviolent civilian resistance on an all-India scale.

In the long run by aligning themselves with Gandhi the nationalist politicians were able to avoid splitting the Congress organisation and then to participate in its transformation into a major national instrument for governing the country. In the long run, Gandhi lost control to more conventional political leaders who were able to utilise the Congress for purposes more limited than he had in mind.[50] But in the short run and indeed throughout his career Gandhi was to have an extraordinary influence over the politicians who joined him in Noncooperation and in later projects. Their self-sacrifice as they followed him in simplifying their lives and taking up civil resistance to the Raj, was often exemplary and heroic. (Kaushik 1964)

How Gandhi Addressed His Indian Opponents

Gandhi's Indian opponents who had resisted the take up of Non-cooperation included Muslim public figures. Among politicians of both the main religious backgrounds, there were "moderates" sympathetic to much of Gandhi's social programme, in particular, who fundamentally disagreed with taking politics out of the long-established system in which they co-operated with the Raj. Equally sceptical were former "extremists" who agreed with Gandhi's rhetoric against the British and

---

50. This I take to be the underlying thrust of Gordon's argument, which I think is sound.

for Home Rule, but who had little faith that Noncooperation was the right programme to succeed in a major struggle. Some of the moderates passively or actively sided with the British. They continued to participate in the Raj's institutions and publicly attacked Gandhi's programme. Often, at the same time, they expressed personal regard for Gandhi's motives and sincerity.

Gandhi's aims and conduct in this complicated competition for the future of the Indian nationalist movement were effectively those of a conventional politician, but pursued in his own way at a time of unusual opportunity. His particular advantage was having a practical programme of radical activity to offer, based on the satyagraha method, at a time when the nationalist movement wished to express their outrage against the British and no other programme seemed practical.

Unity was needed in the national movement to build an effective campaign. Even though outnumbered at the highest leadership levels in the Congress by his opponents, he was able eventually to achieve majority support in Congress by calm, rational argument and dignified persistence, showing the courage to engage outspoken and angry opponents in extensive public debate. Indulal Yajnik, who had worked with Gandhi in the early days in Gujarat but was a persistent critic, recalled that his reply to the noncooperation debate at Calcutta was "the ablest and the most convincing masterpiece of Gandhi's oratory". (Nanda 1989: 234) Of course, he would not have achieved that majority without also showing the energy and persistence to build organised nationwide support through his tours, writings, and speeches; and ensuring that these supporters attended the Congress from many parts of the country in large numbers.

He pursued the same satyagraha principles in debate and negotiation with his fellow nationalists as he would with direct opponents. Those principles included his determination to stick to "one step at a time", which we have discussed in terms of the separation of the Khilafat and Punjab issues until both were capable of generating mass support. He was determined also to keep demands as low as possible so as to maximise the chances of compromise, show understanding of the opponent's position and reduce the necessity for outright conflict and breakdown. Here, for example, the take up of "swaraj" as a goal was at first resisted by Gandhi, but then accepted and adopted when he decided that a form of "parliamentary swaraj" was potentially achievable – and of course that he would need to take on this "general" objective in order to get political agreement behind Noncooperation. "Swaraj in one year" was a huge gamble. Gandhi was willing to compromise if that was consistent with progress towards fundamental objectives as he saw them.

A major factor in the relationship between Gandhi and his Indian opponents was the personal regard felt by many for him. Commentators have spoken about the charisma which enabled Gandhi to gather huge crowds, often unable to hear him speak, but happy to have a glimpse of him and to become his supporters. Among his political followers, this reputation helped inspire a loyalty – amounting virtually to surrender – to his vision, determination and sense of mission. But for his political opponents in Congress and outside, Gandhi's legal and rhetorical skills, his calm, clarity and vision, together with a charismatic hold on loyal supporters, made Gandhi a formidable adversary, whose sincere motives they recognised.

As a result, and in the unsettled conditions of India at the time, Gandhi was able to sweep all before him. His Indian opponents were forced to move onto the ground his vision had helped prepare and to hang on to see what would happen. His British opponents on other hand were confronted with a rebel of unusual sincerity and a cleverly pitched programme of action, someone they were reluctant to touch until he made a wrong move.

How Gandhi Approached His Opponents: The Raj

Gandhi's sense of betrayal over the treatment of India's Muslims' religious feelings and the failure to express remorse and make redress for the outrages committed in the Punjab, caused him (in common with many other nationalists) to lose faith in Britain's representatives in India and the India Office in London. By focusing on the resignation of its "present representatives", he was clearly trying not to argue for a complete break with British rule. But the Congress demand for swaraj was already causing him to step beyond this "minimum" goal to a potential call for complete independence.

Unknown to Gandhi, the Secretary of State for India, E.S. Montagu, and the Viceroy, Lord Chelmsford, had unsuccessfully supported the Indian Muslim position during discussions in London preparing the British Government's position for the Middle East negotiations. Montagu maintained this pro-Muslim position at the Sevres treaty negotiations, which he attended as part of the British delegation. However, the British prime minister, Lloyd George, bluntly opposed the Khilafatist argument and any compromise with it. Montagu probably damaged his political career by stressing the importance, for the sake of harmony in British India, of quietening Muslim concerns about the Middle East settlement.

Gandhi had consistently argued to the British that his advocacy of Noncooperation was strongly motivated by a desire to head off probable violent rebellion by India's Muslims. So both sides in India were occupying much the same ground, except that the Raj's British officials were unable to deliver the Treaty concessions which they, the Khilafatists and Gandhi wanted, and the British of course would not tolerate a campaign of civil disobedience against them.

The rhetoric of refusing to co-operate with the British rulers in India amounted virtually to sedition. Despite this, in practice, the early stages of the Noncooperation programme did not involve civil disobedience. They included symbolic acts of propaganda (returning medals, resignations, boycotting festivities) and more direct affronts to British institutions (boycotting elections, leaving schools, withdrawing from the legal system). The Khilafatists and Congress were walking close to the line, but there was nothing here that would constitute justification in law for wholesale arrests of noncooperators, or prosecution of Gandhi. Moreover, Gandhi was at this moment so popular and the agitation on the Khilafat and Punjab issues so strong, arresting Gandhi might trigger more serious disturbances. The Raj continued to bide its time, but did evolve a strategy of gradually arresting and jailing less significant figures as the agitation persisted. When Gandhi was due to begin his speaking tour of Madras in August, prior to the special session of Congress, the governor of Madras asked for permission to extern Gandhi from the presidency. The government of India refused this request on the grounds that to do so might stir up more support for him. (Brown 1972: 261)

Earlier, Britain's senior representatives in India were also deeply critical of the Punjab governor O'Dwyer and of General Dyer, who had ordered the massacre in Amritsar and other humiliations. The Delhi officials were not responsible for the actions of the British House of Lords, which agreed a motion in support of Dyer, nor for a public appeal by a British newspaper, which raised over £26,000 in recognition of Dyer's service in the Punjab and presented him with a sword of honour. (Gandhi R 2005: 223-224; Brown 1972: 240-244) These racist insults to Indian opinion caused enormous offence in the subcontinent.

Congress launched Noncooperation in January 1921 and the programme of "progressive nonviolent noncooperation" was gradually escalated towards direct confrontation and civil disobedience. Gandhi's relationship with the Raj inevitably suffered increasing strain.

Summary

1. Gandhi's control and shaping of the nationalist investigation into British repression in the Punjab in 1919 is directly similar in its structure to the Champaran and Kheda satyagrahas. It can be identified as a satyagraha campaign, which late in 1920 was absorbed into Noncooperation.

2. When the Hunter report was published and largely endorsed by the government of India, it meant that the minimum demand of the Congress, for the dismissal of the British officials responsible for the Punjab outrages, had not been accepted. Gandhi, having waited for months for the government decision, then called for noncooperation on the Punjab issue and linked this with the Khilafat campaign, since both were now "national" campaigns.

3. In 1919, Gandhi, as a rising national leader, was invited by the Indian National Congress with others to draft a new constitution for the organisation. Gandhi assumed the main burden of this work. He fashioned an organisational structure for Congress capable of capturing

and representing mass support and with the aim that it could become an instrument for the achievement of swaraj.

4. The structure Gandhi helped create – as with all organisations in which he was involved – assumed an active, tightly-disciplined leadership at the top and a much looser organisation below.

5. The Home Rule Leagues had been established a few years earlier by nationalist leaders concerned that Congress as a body was unwilling to move into agitational politics. In 1920 Gandhi accepted the leadership of one of the Home Rule Leagues. He did so on condition that he would be permitted to shape the organisation according to his own views on how to achieve Home Rule – that is, through promotion of swadeshi, Hindu-Muslim unity, the Hindustani language and linguistic provinces. However, he undertook specifically not to lead the League into civil disobedience.

6. Nevertheless, in his campaign to win Congress support for the Khilafat programme of noncooperation, Gandhi controversially used the League as a lever. He argued that his critics were out of tune with the country's mood. When Gandhi, in less than a year, achieved control of the Congress organisation, the two bodies had much the same objectives and programme, and the Home Rule League was allowed to die.

7. The peace terms for the Middle East negotiated by the British government at the end of the First World War dashed the Khilafatists' hopes. At the same time the Hunter Commission's report on the Punjab massacre and wider repression, which offended all Indian nationalists, was published. The double blow created the circumstances where, in Gandhi's eyes, the Khilafat and Punjab issues could be linked legitimately. Both demonstrated the failure of the Raj to respond to Indian opinion and, on both issues, national anger would lend support to a radical nonviolent assault on the structures of British India.

8. At the Calcutta Special Congress to consider the proposal for Noncooperation, Gandhi achieved a partial victory. There was support for a boycott of the legislative councils, though with strong reservations on this and other aspects of his Noncooperation programme.

9. At the annual Congress session in Nagpur, Gandhi achieved a more substantial victory. Major opponents like Das publicly endorsed the Noncooperation programme under Gandhi's leadership. His proposals for a complete reorganisation of the Congress structure and for a change in the Congress creed – which would permit nonviolent rebellion against the British crown – were accepted.

10. Organising a perilous campaign on a vast scale and losing confidence in British political leaders, Gandhi sacrificed his wish to go to England to forewarn the opponent of his intentions. Forced to adopt swaraj – a general rather than a particular objective – as a goal for the campaign, he bent his efforts to trying to build up the substance of swaraj through the triple boycott. He began to hope, too, that his message would bypass British political leaders and get through directly to British public opinion.

11. During this period, Gandhi became a pre-eminent figure in nationalist politics for the first time.

CHAPTER 8:

BOYCOTTS SPREAD, JAILS FILL AND THE VICEROY OFFERS TALKS

CASE STUDY 7(B): CONGRESS TAKES UP NONCOOPERATION

The immediate results of Gandhi's capture and reorganisation of Congress, and the impact of his taking the organisation into Noncooperation, were phenomenal. By 1922, the organisation had expanded to cover most of British India: 213 out of the 220 administrative districts in British India had district Congress committees. A drive early in 1921 to recruit 10 million members was only partially successful but, at the end of the year, paid membership of Congress was almost two million. (Nanda, B.R. 1989: 263) Fund-raising campaigns produced the most remarkable results. In three months in 1921 ten million rupees were collected for the Tilak Swaraj Fund, compared with an annual income for the All India Congress Committee (AICC) in previous years of less than 50,000 rupees. (Brown 1974: 320) In the process, Congress was transformed into a mass organisation.

Villages with five or more Congress members formed a committee to carry out the national programme. Above the village, in a conventional hierarchical structure, were often two other levels of representative units – the firka and the taluka. Above these were the district committees, which sent representatives to the provincial Congress committees. (Krishna

1966: 413-430) Mass politicisation was progressively brought into being as the Congress carried out Noncooperation.

One of the notable features of Noncooperation in practice is that Gandhi, having taken months in 1920 to construct the four-stage plan of action and to win acceptance for it, more or less threw away the blueprint during 1921 and proceeded to improvise. From his position of authority in Congress there was no one in the early months to challenge him.

"Progressive nonviolent noncooperation" did take place in principle as Gandhi had intended, that is, as a movement developing progressively in stages (from defensive to aggressive), leading to a climax of activity reached late in 1921. But the first stage, the period of mobilisation and preparation, planned to involve minimal risk of confrontation with the Raj, had been extended ingeniously for many months until August 1921, taking in several new campaigns. (See Table 8.1 below.)

The second stage, beginning as it did in the summer of 1921, had been envisaged to have more direct acts of noncooperation against the Raj, with civilians withdrawing from government employment. But at this point, Gandhi's control wobbled. Increasingly impatient Khilafatists (who by August had been engaged in their specific Noncooperation campaign for a year) initiated two stages of the individual noncooperation programme together. The controlled escalation of withdrawing from the Raj's Indian civil service was launched simultaneously with a further escalation to civil disobedience. Muslims were instructed to resign from the uniformed services, the military and the police, as a result laying the Khilafatists open to charges of sedition.

In relation to the progressive noncooperation strategy, it was a move to "aggressive" civil disobedience sooner than Gandhi would have wanted. His response was to fall in behind the Khilafatists, but to try to temper their impatience and to ensure that Congress gave its support to them. He also stepped up the programme of constructive work, particularly the foreign boycott and production of swadeshi cloth, and organising Congress volunteers. Finally, as defiance of the Raj became stronger and more widespread, what had been planned by him as the fourth stage, the moment for the "masses" to undertake refusal of taxes, was substantially

Table 8.1:

THE THREE STAGES OF ALL-INDIA NONCOOPERATION

Date	Event
1920	
	STAGE 1: MOBILISATION, AVOIDING DIRECT CONFRONTATION
26-31 December	**Nagpur Congress.** Five months after its launch by Khilafatists, Indian National Congress annual session adopts Noncooperation strategy: "Swaraj in One Year". Congress agrees a new constitution.
1921	
January	**Congress takes up Noncooperation.** First, surrender titles and medals. Then: (a) *Triple Boycott.* Withdraw from Councils/ boycott elections. Close universities/ boycott schools. Resign legal practices.
April 1	(b) *The Bezwada Programme.* Collect 10 million rupees. Enrol 10 million Congress members. Get 2 million spinning wheels into villages and homes.
July 30	(c) *Complete Boycott of Foreign Cloth by 31 October.* Huge bonfires of foreign cloth across India.
August	**But Moplah revolt.** Muslim peasants attack Hindu landlords. Gandhi and Mohammad Ali prevented from going there. Ali arrested.
	STAGE 2: INDIVIDUAL "DEFENSIVE" CIVIL DISOBEDIENCE
July and October	(a) *Solidarity with Khilafat Leaders facing trial.* Khilafat leaders call on Muslims to resign from government service, including police and military. When Ali brothers arrested, 50 Congress leaders "as individuals" on October 4 repeat the same call to all Indians.

Nov 17	*Bombay boycott of Prince of Wales' Visit.* Severe rioting and reprisals. But hartals in Calcutta and other Indian cities are successful.
November	(b) *Challenging Ban on Congress and Khilafat Volunteers.* Civil disobedients defy the Raj's ban: they (illegally) picket, sell khadi cloth and newspapers, hold processions and public meetings. Thousands of arrests. Gandhi proposes moving to stage 3, with mass civil disobedience to start at Bardoli on 23 November.
Nov 23	**Launch postponed of mass civil disobedience at Bardoli.**
Mid December	*Moderates propose talks with Viceroy.* Gandhi rejects Viceroy's terms.
Late December	**Swaraj in One Year not achieved.** Ahmedabad annual Congress adopts temporary, less confrontational strategy. To counter Raj's repression, focus on three freedoms: of speech, assembly and press.

STAGE 3: OFF-ON PREPARATIONS FOR MASS "AGGRESSIVE" CIVIL DISOBEDIENCE AT BARDOLI

1922

January	*Banned Congress volunteer groups reorganised,* major recruitment drive.
	Moderates again propose talks with Viceroy. Bardoli mass civil disobedience again postponed. Viceroy rejects Gandhi's terms.
February 1-6	*Gandhi's "ultimatum" to Viceroy dismissed.* Bardoli rebellion to begin February 11.
February 4	But *Chauri Chaura massacre.* Mass civil disobedience is suspended.
March 10	**Gandhi arrested and jailed.**

altered. Gandhi proposed and began preparations for a highly original and focused plan of "mass" civil disobedience. The proposal included tax refusal and other forms of resistance. As excitement mounted and the "swaraj year" came to an end, implementation of the Noncooperation strategy was concertinaed from four stages down to three.[51]

Stage 1: Mobilisation Avoiding Directing Confrontation, August 1920-October 1921

First, there was the long-drawn out phase of continued preparation – propagandising throughout the country, mobilising different social groups and regions, building an effective organisation, training Congress workers and supporters and educating them in nonviolence and satyagraha, testing to see if the movement was ready to move on to the next stage.

Implicit in this process was the notion that if the movement was unable to develop within itself the requisite discipline to tackle the next stage successfully, then Gandhi as the "general" in command had the authority and the duty to withdraw, or to try new tactics. In practice, though, he did not possess unlimited freedom of action. Given the nature of the political coalition he was directing, his colleagues in the leadership, both Hindu and Muslim, were not committed as he was to nonviolence as a principle and were liable to chafe under restrictions. He was effectively riding two horses, the Central Khilafat Committee and the Congress; ensuring they pulled together was often difficult. Also, the pressures of building a mass movement of newly mobilised civilians, drawn from all parts of the subcontinent, from different religions and castes, and moving in different directions according to local conditions, did not give Gandhi an easy task.

Gandhi's improvised response therefore was to prolong the first stage of mobilisation and preparation for as long as he could, taking up new

---

51. Subhas Bose quotes Gandhi as describing the programme of Noncooperation in a similar breakdown of stages to the one followed here, though the stages are not reduced to three. (Bose, S.C. 1935: 55-91)

campaigns to sustain the level of activism and to develop as far as possible what he called the "atmosphere" necessary before he would move on.

The Triple Boycott, 1 August 1920 (Khilafat Committee) and 1 January 1921 (Congress)

The first campaign was the Triple Boycott. Launched by the Central Khilafat Committee in August 1920, it began with pressure on prominent Indians to surrender titles and medals; but the initial drive was towards winning the verdict at the special Congress at Calcutta. At Calcutta, Congress agreed to support Council boycott and, with some exceptions, Congress members withdrew from the elections in November and organised a voters' boycott. Two-thirds of those eligible to vote are reported to have stayed away. (Gandhi, R. 2007: 235)

Prior to the Nagpur annual Congress session, however, it was left to Gandhi and his immediate supporters, basically the Khilafatists and the Gujaratis, to prosecute the schools boycott and the law-courts boycott. Their approaches to parents, to students, to staff and to governing bodies met with some success, especially in Gujarat; while, for example, the managing board of the Sikh Khalsa college in Amritsar took up Noncooperation and refused to accept funding from the Raj. But when Gandhi and his colleagues tried to engage the boards of the main Muslim and Hindu universities at Aligarh and Benares in similar acts of defiance, they were rebuffed. Undaunted, the noncooperators proceeded to establish alternative "national" institutions themselves, some of which still survive. Also, numbers of nationalist students left or didn't take up their places in order to take part in the Noncooperation struggle. (Nanda 1989: 286-288; Riar S.B. 2006: 149)

Before Nagpur, one of the senior Congress politicians, Motilal Nehru, father of the future prime minister, Jawaharlal Nehru, resigned his wealthy legal practice. By the time of the annual Congress most of the leading politicians had begun to adopt the mode of dress favoured by Gandhi, that is, the wearing of swadeshi (or khadi) cloth. Gandhi was asking for a simplification of lifestyle and a dedication to public work, just as he had with his team of co-workers in Champaran in 1917. At the Nagpur Congress, Das and other nationalist politicians were "converted" to

293

Noncooperation, and when the Bengali leaders returned to Calcutta, Das resigned his legal practice – as did several other prominent Congressmen – and took up the schools boycott. A major student strike was the result and the establishment in Calcutta of a number of mainly short-lived national schools.

Gandhi all along had argued that the schools boycott should be promoted in advance of establishing alternative institutions. He came back from Nagpur to Gujarat with a new campaign. Most of the educated "classes" who were likely to respond to the Triple Boycott had done so. While a country was at war, he said, its young people left their schools without thought for their studies, and returned having made their sacrifice when the war was over. In the national schools, instead of developing a new academic training, they should prepare for the national struggle by taking up spinning, and if they felt confident enough they should then go out to the villages to promote the swadeshi campaign. (Gandhi, M.K 1966: vol.19: 223-230, 494-495)

In practice, the task of these "public workers" was not simply to promote spinning and weaving, but as Noncooperation progressed to implement a wider constructive programme and to take up the latest drive initiated by Congress:

"Objecting to the Raj's control over their colleges, thousands of bright young men and women walked out. Many streamed into squalid villages and city slums to propagate khadi or Hindustani or Hindu-Muslim unity or the removal of untouchability or to recruit members for the Congress." (Gandhi, R. 2007: 235)

Gradually, so as to decentralise the constructive work, Gandhi's more dedicated followers were encouraged to establish ashrams across the provinces of India, particularly in rural areas. There they encouraged local people to contribute to the revolutionary struggle by taking up the constructive programme and by undertaking training in nonviolence. (Thomson 1993: 110-113)[52]

---

52. But despite his enthusiasm, he appears to have accepted that there were limits to what could be expected directly from peasants taking up constructive

The Bezwada Programme, April 1921

The second campaign in the first stage of Noncooperation (known as the "Bezwada Programme") was launched at a meeting on 1 April 1921 of the All India Congress Committee in Bezwada, Madras. Under the new Congress constitution, the expanded AICC – the "parliament" of the new movement – was to be elected by June 30, 1921; at its first meeting it was to appoint the new working committee. Other targets were set: for example, February to elect new district Congress committees and March to form new provincial committees; and Gandhi announced that by the time the new Congress organisation was in place three additional organisational drives should be completed. (Gandhi M.K. 1966: vol 19: 196, 217-220)

The three new targets for Congress workers under the Bezwada Programme, to be achieved by June 30, were:

- collection of ten million rupees for the Tilak Swaraj Fund;
- enrolment of ten million members;
- introduction of two million spinning wheels "in working order" into villages and homes.

Gandhi was reported as saying at the meeting:

"The awakening of the masses was phenomenal and while the masses were fully alive to the urgent need of realization of swaraj the leaders were lagging behind. It was therefore necessary to give form and shape to the aspirations of the masses. Their aspirations for swaraj were based upon the very definite perception that without swaraj their condition could not improve and the direct means of improving their condition was to enable them to clothe and feed themselves. It was for this purpose that he felt the charkha (spinning-wheel) movement was full of the utmost potentialities in the winning of swaraj." (Gandhi M.K. 1966: vol 19: 494)

---

work. He advised the "public workers" that civil disobedience was a discipline reserved for those "saturated with the spirit of truth and nonviolence and ready for the utmost sacrifice".

295

The background to the Bezwada Programme was the revised Congress constitution and the new creed adopted at Nagpur. Gandhi was trying to adapt Noncooperation so as to prepare the Congress movement for nonviolent struggle and he was also attempting to shape his methods to a "general" issue like Swaraj. His principal slogan "Swaraj in One Year" had become the rallying cry for the whole movement and excited enormous expectations. Gandhi said he had adopted the slogan specifically to distinguish Noncooperation from previous campaigns by the politicians – especially, one may assume, the Home Rule Leagues – for swaraj. From his perspective, this was not an empty slogan, to be mouthed from public platforms but not acted on. It was a commitment to build an organisation within a certain time period, so as to change the lives of Indians and compel the achievement of swaraj. (Gandhi M.K. 1965: vol 18: 247; Tendulkar 1951: vol. 2: 74)

Swaraj, Gandhi argued repeatedly, could be realised through the fulfilment of almost any "particular" aspect of the Noncooperation programme. In the concrete achievement of new levels of organisation and discipline – through getting spinning wheels into every home, for example, or developing the Congress organisation in every village – lay the essence of swaraj. (Gandhi M.K. 1966: vol. 19: 239-242) We go back to December 1919 and Gandhi's argument that swadeshi was more important than the reforms, because the swadeshi programme, if properly carried out, would demonstrate "powers of organisation and industry" which would then enable the nation to undertake everything else necessary "for its organic growth". (Gandhi M.K. 1965: vol 16: 335-337) If this could be done, then it would compel respect and recognition from the Raj of a new Indian capacity and dignity and it might not even be necessary to engage in the risk and sacrifice of civil disobedience. If the targets were not achieved, no harm would have been done and the effort would have prepared and disciplined the people for further struggle.

The Bezwada programme was a partial success. Large sums were raised for the Tilak Swaraj Fund, particularly in Bombay city and Gujarat, a feature being the involvement of educated women for the first time, donating jewellery, and of some sections of the merchant classes. But there were also the contributions from vast numbers of the poorer class and caste groups particularly in rural areas. Such collections established the role of "honest" Congress public workers – they had to be trusted – bringing the Congress programme down to the villages and creating reliable networks.

The huge Tilak Swaraj Fund, says Krishna, "made it possible to expand Congress activity on a scale hitherto inconceivable." (Krishna 1966: 427) Each of the new Congress provinces had its particular target of money to be raised – and a similar allocation was made for the membership drive and distribution of spinning wheels. The money was spent as it was raised, Gandhi objecting to the establishment of a permanent fund. Provincial Congress committees were thus enabled to finance the spinning-wheel campaign, to promote swadeshi cloth, Hindu-Muslim unity and national education, to tackle problems of untouchability, depressed classes, famine and flood relief, and to support various picketing campaigns, the volunteer organisations and general propaganda. (Nayar 1994: 490)

The second two targets were not reached but, as we have noted, the major expansion of Congress membership was achieved and the spinning wheel programme led many of the "public workers" or "national workers" to change their lives and take on the role of "whole-timers" in the villages. (Bose, S.C. 1935: 66; Shridharani 1962: 155-156) The Congress goal of "Swaraj in One Year" – together with the new target of June 30 for completion of the Bezwada Programme – excited tremendous enthusiasm. At first, Gandhi's prophecy was expected to be fulfilled by 11 August 1921. This was one year after the partial launch (by the Khilafatists) following the Calcutta special Congress. Later, it was shifted to 31 December, twelve months after Congress had fully endorsed Noncooperation at Nagpur.

Expectations of "swaraj" were expressed in different parts of India according to local conditions. A temperance movement began in the Central Provinces and spread to several other provinces. Boycotting liquor stores badly hit government excise revenue from sales – and won Gandhi's approval because of its character as a campaign of moral improvement as well as of practical benefit. Sikhs in the Punjab began a movement for the reform of their shrines; in Champaran, in Bihar, peasants campaigned to establish their rights to graze cattle on waste lands; in the United Provinces, a peasant movement began a campaign of tax and rent refusal against government and landlords; and in Assam, workers on the British-owned tea plantations went on strike, encouraging strikes in sympathy from Bengali ship and rail workers. Gandhi was reluctant to take up several of these campaigns, largely because of his fear of violence. (Brown 19: 315-316, 322-327; Broomfield 1968: 212-219) He emphasised – as in the Rowlatt satyagraha and throughout 1920 – that noncooperators should obey the law and all police instructions until civil disobedience was authorised. (Gandhi M.K. 1966: vol. 19: 497)

Incidents of rioting and even killings – including at Malegaon in Bombay Presidency, the murder of police officers who had arrested some noncooperators – marked the difficulty of holding Noncooperation across the whole subcontinent to the nonviolent discipline and of keeping the different local and regional centres of the movement in phase with each other. (Bamford 1974: 32-33, 56-65) In May, just over a month after his arrival, rising tensions moved the new Viceroy, Lord Reading, a former Lord Chief Justice in Britain, to accept a request from Gandhi to meet with him.[53] They met at Simla in the north of India for a series of six informal talks, said to have occupied up to 13 hours over six days. Gandhi was able to talk widely about the key issues troubling Indian nationalists, including the Punjab and Khilafat grievances, the relationship between India and the Raj, his ideas for swaraj, and the satyagraha principles underpinning the Noncooperation campaign. Reading focused on violence and nonviolence, and the danger of the Khilafat agitation slipping over into violence, as evidenced by some of the statements of the Ali brothers.

Clearly, one purpose on both sides was to "know your opponent". From Gandhi's point of view, to be taken seriously by the Raj was a huge step forward and part of the process of conversion at the heart of his nonviolent method. Reading wrote privately to London that he was impressed by Gandhi and "liked him". But Reading (unsurprisingly) was manipulative. At the Viceroy's prompting, Gandhi agreed to advise the Ali brothers to make a statement confirming their commitment to the

---

53. The invitation was arranged through the good offices of a political moderate and long-term friend of Gandhi's, Madan Mohan Malaviya. Malaviya consistently opposed Noncooperation.

nonviolence of the Noncooperation movement. Gandhi drafted this, with some revisions proposed by Reading. The Ali brothers then stated, "we never imagined that any passages in our speeches were capable of bearing the interpretation put on them"; but they accepted the force of the argument that the speeches could be interpreted in that way. They also pledged themselves to nonviolence "only so long" as they were associated with the movement of Noncooperation.

The Viceroy then presented the brothers' statement as an "apology". He also claimed privately in letters to London that he had driven a wedge between Gandhi and the Khilafat leaders, weakening both and, as a result, "the bridge… between Hindu and Mohammedan".

Some of Gandhi's colleagues felt he had bungled. But Gandhi considered that the episode in fact had helped demonstrate the Ali brothers' continuing public commitment to nonviolence. It also confirmed to Gandhi that the "system which [Reading] is coming to administer will not permit him to do what is right". As for the Ali brothers, they did not find it necessary to moderate their criticisms of the Raj. (Nanda 1989: 301-305)

By the end of June, when the target date for completion of the Bezwada Programme arrived, Congress workers generally were expecting Gandhi to move on to the next stage of Noncooperation. They expected the mobilised Congress movement to be directed into open nonviolent confrontation with the Raj. However, while Gandhi was still deliberating on how to translate this growing pressure into action, the Central Khilafat Committee meeting in Karachi in the second week of July, passed a resolution which effectively began to move Noncooperation from the first to the original third stage, and beyond. The resolution proclaimed:

"…it is in every way religiously unlawful for the Muslims at the present moment to continue in the British Army or to induce others to join the army, and it is the duty of all the Mussulmans in general and Ulema [mullahs] in particular to see that these religious commandments are brought home to every Muslim in the army, and if no settlement is arrived at before Christmas regarding our campaign, Indian republic will be declared at the Ahmedabad session of the Congress." (Tendulkar, 1951: vol 2: 70)

Gandhi, however, did not directly take up this call. In line with his policy of a slow build-up to full confrontation, he waited to see how the Raj would respond.

Later in July, the first meeting of the AICC called under the new constitution was expected to be the symbolic moment when the next phase in the struggle would be announced. But Gandhi apparently asked the Ali brothers not to press the Khilafatists' call for resignations from the Army; and no resolution to this effect was presented. (Yajnik 1933: 184, 190) Instead, he launched a new campaign, extending the first and less confrontational stage of Noncooperation.

Complete Boycott of Foreign Cloth, July 30, 1921

The third campaign Gandhi announced at the expanded All India Congress Committee gathering in Bombay was for the complete boycott of foreign cloth. The next day in Bombay, he personally set alight a massive bonfire of foreign clothing, including many luxurious items, and this action was later imitated in hundreds of locations across India.

This AICC meeting brought together for the first time a balanced representation of delegates from the newly-formed twenty-one Congress linguistic provinces. Gandhi proposed a new target date of September 30 for the achievement of the complete boycott of foreign cloth, a deadline later extended to October 31. Another campaign announced at the Bombay meeting was for a hartal across India when in November the Prince of Wales (the future Edward VIII) would arrive from England on an official visit. A boycott of the visit was proposed across all parts of British India.[54]

Gandhi stated clearly what he was doing in an article published at the time:

---

54. The Raj was taking a risk. The Prince's tour lasted four months, taking in many Indian cities. It was part of an eight months' excursion to fly the flag in Britain's imperial possessions across Asia (and parts of Africa, including Egypt), also taking in Japan and the Philippines.

"Civil disobedience is on the lips of every one of the members of the All-India Congress Committee. Not ever having really tried it, everyone appeared to be enamoured of it, from a mistaken belief (that) in it was a sovereign remedy for our present-day ills. I feel sure that it can be made such if we can produce the necessary atmosphere for it. Mass civil disobedience... can only be tried in a calm atmosphere.

"We have too long been mentally disobedient to the laws of the state and have too often surreptitiously evaded them, to be fit all of a sudden for civil disobedience. Disobedience to be civil has to be open and nonviolent.

"Complete civil disobedience is a state of peaceful rebellion – a refusal to obey every single, state-made law. It is certainly more dangerous than an armed rebellion. For it can never be put down if the civil resisters are prepared to face extreme hardships. It is based upon an implicit belief in the absolute efficacy of innocent suffering... A full grasp of the conditions of successful civil resistance is necessary at least on the part of the representatives of the people before we can launch on an enterprise of such magnitude. The quickest remedies are always fraught with the greatest danger and require the utmost skill in handling them. It is my firm conviction that if we bring a successful boycott of foreign cloth, we shall have produced an atmosphere that would enable us to inaugurate civil disobedience on a scale that no Government can resist. I would, therefore, urge patience and determined concentration on swadeshi upon those who are impatient to embark on mass civil disobedience." (Tendulkar 1951: vol 2: 52-53)

The bonfires of foreign cloth helped to capture the mood of resistance spreading among the Congress workers and also to channel the urge towards violence. As Gandhi wrote in reply to criticism:

"India is racial today. It is with the utmost effort that I find it possible to keep under check the evil passions of the people. The general body of the people are filled with ill will because they are weak and hopelessly ignorant of the way to shed their weakness. I am transferring the ill will from men to things." (Tendulkar 1951: vol 2: 55)

The bonfires also neatly symbolised, as the collections for the Tilak Swaraj Fund had done, the willingness of the wealthy classes to make sacrifices of valuable belongings in the interests of swaraj – and of course endeavoured to unite all classes in the promotion of swadeshi and the cult of the spinning wheel. Moreover, by focusing on one "particular" aspect of the constructive work – not national schools, or arbitration courts, or Hindu-Muslim unity, or the membership drive, but swadeshi – Gandhi put to the test his theory that in the achievement of one aspect of the programme lay the essence of swaraj. (Tendulkar 1951: vol 2: 60)

However, the dilemma soon caught up with Gandhi of trying to restrain a mass movement actively mobilised in many parts of the subcontinent and to bend leaders of the Noncooperation coalition to his will. In August, a rebellion against the British by Muslim peasants along the Malabar coast in Madras led to repressive intervention by the British army and to the murders of Europeans, many Hindu landlords and money-lenders, and the forcible conversion of some Hindus to Islam. There was no doubt that the rising had been stirred by the spread of Noncooperation activity, some as part of the drive to give Congress a presence in every province.

In September, when Gandhi and Mohammad Ali arrived in Madras presidency on their way to the rebellious area, Ali was arrested by the Raj for the July Khilafat statement calling on Muslims to resign from the army. The British authorities prevented Gandhi from proceeding to the area where what is known as the "Moplah Revolt" was going on. Gandhi argued that preventing him from going there, denied Congress the opportunity of getting the situation under control. The Raj's intervention also helped determine his opinion that relying on British troops to suppress communal disturbances was demeaning and should not be supported by Indian nationalism.

However, Gandhi did not defy the ban as he had done in Champaran and during the Rowlatt campaign. Instead, he decided that the time for civil disobedience had not arrived and he must devote even greater efforts to promoting the swadeshi campaign. Touring Bengal and now Madras was showing him that the take-up of the hand-made cloth campaign in much of India was much worse than he had realised. In his many public speeches he upbraided his audiences for their failure to do more. The best response that noncooperators could make to the arrest of Mohammad Ali, he thought, was to redouble their efforts to promote across the subcontinent spinning and weaving and the destruction of foreign cloth. As the end of the swaraj year approached, noncooperators should concentrate intensively and exclusively on the swadeshi campaign. The deadline for complete boycott of foreign cloth was extended by a month to the end of October.

A week after Ali's arrest, Gandhi made the startling announcement, broadcast through his newspaper, that he would reduce his clothing to a loin-cloth. He also proceeded to shave his head. During his many public meetings on this tour, Gandhi had been challenged by the argument that bonfires of foreign cloth were depriving poor people of clothing they could use, and that the demand for khadi cloth could not be met by Indian homespun production. (Gandhi, M.K. 1966: vol 21: 181, 225; Tendulkar 1951: vol 2: 60; Yajnik 1933: 187-188) In an article in *The Hindu*, he explained his change to minimal clothing:

"...Millions are too poor to buy enough khaddar to replace the discarded cloth... Let them be satisfied with a mere loin-cloth... Let there be no prudery about dress. India has never insisted on full coverage of the body for the males as a test of culture.

"... I adopt the change because I have always been hesitant to advise anything I may not myself be prepared to follow, also because I am anxious by leading the way to make it easy for those who cannot afford to change [by] discarding their foreign garments. I consider the renunciation also to be necessary for me as a sign of mourning and a bare head and a bare body is such a sign in my part of country. That we are in mourning is more and more being brought home to me as the end of the year is approaching and we are still without swaraj...

"...If only we can go through the course of organising manufacture [of khadi cloth and boycott of foreign cloth]... during the month of October, abstaining all meetings and excitement, we shall produce an atmosphere calm and peaceful enough to embark on civil disobedience..." (Gandhi, MK 1966: vol. 21: 180-181)

His action was in some respects similar to the moment in the Ahmedabad workers' strike when the strikers' morale began to weaken and Gandhi announced his fast. This time – in addition to his concerns about the poor take-up of the swadeshi campaign – there was the threat to Hindu-Muslim unity and to the doctrine of nonviolence posed by the Moplah revolt. And the Ali brothers and four other Khilafat leaders had been jailed. Gandhi needed to reassert his leadership and control within the Hindu-Muslim coalition by some dramatic statement; his choice of method was a visible self-sacrifice.[55] Incidentally, he insisted that his immediate colleagues should not copy his example.

But the arrests of the Ali brothers and other Khilafat leaders effectively signalled the end of the prolonged first stage of Noncooperation – without the activities of the Triple Boycott, the Bezwada Programme or the foreign cloth boycott having achieved swaraj. Gandhi's argument that if those "constructive" activities were pursued with enough dedication then swaraj could be gained without the necessity for direct confrontation with the Raj, had been found wanting – or at best unproven. What he, the Congress and the Khilafat movement had achieved as the end of the "swaraj year" approached, was the mobilisation of large numbers of "noncooperators", increasingly ready to take part in more confrontational forms of action. There was a new Congress structure and organisation behind them, as well as the Khilafat committee and its network.

There was also, in parts of Gujarat, an evolution from boycotting national schools to taking control of municipal councils and announcing

---

55. Simplifying his clothing and shaving his head – most obviously religious symbols of penitence and humility – may also be seen as the pragmatic acts of a leader who needed to do something. Gandhi's own preferred course of action – to defy the ban and commit civil disobedience – he could not allow himself, because the moment did not fit with his strategy of progressive build-up; and Rowlatt had shown what could happen if he mis-stepped. Alarmed at the way events were moving, he wanted a stronger response on swadeshi from noncooperators. He took the dilemmas of the situation onto himself in an act of personal sacrifice when he could find no better means of capturing the attention of his followers and the wider public. It was also of course a symbol of identification with the poorest people and a claim on their loyalty.

plans to run the schools themselves. Ahmedabad, Nadiad and Surat rejected government control of their education departments. (Gandhi, M.K. 1966: vol 21: 363; vol 22: 29, 183-185) The boycott of provincial councils remained.

Most British officials were scathing publicly and privately about Gandhi's activities, seeing his social programme as "trickery": though some also had a grudging respect for him. Certainly the Indian moderates, who were crucial to the Raj's plans at this time, respected Gandhi's constructive programme, if not his linking it with civil disobedience and with a directly political campaign for swaraj. Also the Raj was reluctant to arrest Gandhi, not least because he was seen by so many as a mahatma, a holy man; and his energy, fearlessness for his own safety and dedication to constructive work added to the regard in which he was held.

Stage 2: Individual Civil Disobedience ("Defensive"): July-December 1921
Solidarity with the Khilafat leaders facing Trial, October 4, 1921

The second stage of Noncooperation was effectively launched on October 4, 1921, when fifty Congress leaders – acting "in our individual capacity" – issued a manifesto in solidarity with the jailed Khilafat leaders, stating that it was contrary to national dignity for Indians to serve the Government. (Tendulkar 1951: vol. 2: 60-61)

While focusing on a final effort with the swadeshi campaign, Gandhi was involved too in organising and publishing the manifesto. It repeated the words of the July Khilafat resolution, rendering all the signatories liable to prosecution, and read:

> "In view of the prosecution of the Ali brothers and others... we the undersigned, speaking in our individual capacity, desire to state that it is the inherent right of every one to express his opinion without restraint about the propriety of citizens offering their services to, or remaining in the employ of the Government, whether in the civil of the military department.

We, the undersigned, state it as our opinion that it is contrary to national dignity for any Indian to serve as a civilian, and more especially as a soldier, under a system of government which has brought about India's economic, moral and political degradation and which has used the soldiery and the police for repressing national aspirations, as for instance, at the time of the Rowlatt Act agitation, and which has used the soldiery for crushing the liberty of the Arabs, the Egyptians and the Turks and other nations who have done no harm to India. We are also of the opinion that it is the duty of every Indian soldier and civilian to sever his connection with the Government and find some other means of livelihood."

This statement was swiftly endorsed by the Congress working committee and repeated by hundreds of individuals from numerous platforms. However, despite it being a straightforward challenge, the government took no immediate action. (Tendulkar 1951: vol 2: 81-82)

Through the initiative of the Khilafat leaders, Congress had taken up the second and third stages of Gandhi's original outline plan for Noncooperation. But it did so, not so much as a signal to the country to take up the campaign and bring pressure to resign on all Indian employees of the Raj. Rather, Gandhi and the working committee recast their action as a civil liberties issue. They argued that Indians had a right to demand the resignation of their compatriots serving such an intolerable government and that India's Muslims had a religious duty to do so. This was "defensive" civil disobedience, focused on the right to call for resignations, rather than a strong "aggressive" campaign to spread disaffection from the army. The working committee added that it had not called for such resignations before because the Congress was not yet ready to support those who had no other means of livelihood. (Bamford 1974: 36-38)

Some resignations from government employment did take place, including police and probably soldiers too (Brown 1972: 310; Bamford 1974: 34-35, 56, 171-173) – but the relatively small response may be related to the fact that the Congress did not launch a high profile and protracted campaign on the issue. What was launched, with the individual statements of solidarity, was "individual civil disobedience", the second stage of Noncooperation as it evolved in practice.

Individual civil disobedience, according to Gandhi, could be launched before the country was organised and disciplined. As a "defensive" action, it was about asserting one's rights peacefully in face of an oppressive government. Mass civil disobedience, on the other hand, was "aggressive" and could only be tried "in a calm atmosphere". (Gandhi M.K. 1966: vol. 22: 360-362; Tendulkar 1951: vol. 2: 52; Dhawan 1957: 242-246)

Mass civil disobedience, Gandhi said later:

> "...is like an earthquake, a sort of general upheaval on the political plane. Where the reign of mass civil disobedience begins, there the subsisting Government ceases to function. There, every policeman, every soldier, every Government official must either leave the place, or enlist in the service of swaraj. The police stations, the court offices etc. all shall cease to be the Government property and shall be taken charge of by the people... But although the opposition to the Government must be so determined in character, the essence of civil disobedience is that it must be undertaken in a spirit of perfect composure."
> (Tendulkar 1951: vol 2: 66)

At the October working committee, Gandhi secured the passage of a resolution stating that mass civil disobedience could not be attempted in any district until it had achieved complete boycott of foreign cloth and self-sufficiency in the production of cloth by hand-spinning and hand-weaving. Later in the month, concerned that the swadeshi campaign was not making enough progress, he made a new personal vow. He would spin daily for half-an-hour; and forego an evening meal when he failed to spin, "except during journey or sickness". (Dalal, C.B. 1971: 43)

One of the problems for Gandhi at this time, as Yajnik points out, was that not only had none of his colleagues engaged in mass civil disobedience as he described it, neither had he! On the other hand, since he was vastly more experienced in the theory and practice of civil disobedience, they felt themselves effectively obliged to accept his leadership, his definitions and his conditions, at least until, in a matter of months, the "swaraj year" was out. (Yajnik 1933: 192)

Visit of the Prince of Wales, Ban on Congress and Khilafat Volunteer Organisations, and Civil Disobedience against the Ban, November 1921

Once the Khilafat leaders, including the Ali brothers, were sentenced at the beginning of November to two years rigorous imprisonment, pressure built up further for Congress to reply with more aggressive action.

Bamford, deputy director of the Raj's intelligence bureau and author of the official government history of Noncooperation published in 1925, writes about the next meeting of the AICC in Delhi on November 4 to 5:

"The feature of this Delhi session was the restiveness displayed by a large proportion of the delegates against Gandhi's shyness of declaring mass civil disobedience immediately... It seems correct to say that the Committee gave a grumbling assent to the scheme, mainly out of personal regard for Gandhi and a feeling that he should be allowed to have his own way in his own movement till the end of the year within which he had promised "Swaraj". It seemed clear that after that time Gandhi would have served his turn and if he failed to produce Swaraj as promised he would have to make way for other leaders and other methods." (Bamford 1974: 40)

Taking as his text the fact that "the Nation had demonstrated its capacity to observe complete nonviolence over the arrest of the Ali brothers", Gandhi's scheme (to which the committee gave its "grumbling assent") was to authorise provincial Congress committees to launch both individual and mass civil disobedience. (Gandhi, M.K, 1966: vol. 21: 412-413)

But over the months of November and December the narrative becomes complicated.

- The Raj stubbornly brought the Prince of Wales to India on a leisurely royal visit across the subcontinent, met by hartals everywhere he went.

- Several provincial governors banned and attempted to suppress through prosecutions and aggressive policing the volunteer organisations driving Noncooperation.

- Indian moderates, who were not supporters of Noncooperation, were nevertheless outraged at the number of arrests and the treatment of those arrested and jailed; they called for the Raj to begin negotiations with the Congress.

- Gandhi, occupied with all these events, was also drawing up plans for an escalation to mass civil disobedience, as Noncooperation moved into its third, decisive stage.

The Noncooperation year came to an end amidst intense excitement and uncertainty.

Hartals and The Prince of Wales' Visit

Before the mass civil disobedience at Bardoli backed by Congress was due to begin, the Raj staged as a sign of its confidence in British rule, a royal visit by the Prince of Wales. The future Edward VIII arrived by sea at the city of Bombay on 17 November to start his lengthy tour. Hartal was proclaimed across India, and in part was remarkably successful. Gandhi proposed that noncooperators should arrange hartals on the Prince's arrival:

> "Certainly not for the sake of impressing him, certainly not for the sake of demonstration. But I would use the occasion of his imposed visit for stimulating us into greater activity." (Gandhi M.K, 1966: vol. 21: 379)

A hartal was arranged in Bombay to coincide with the Prince's setting foot on Indian soil and Gandhi sent a briefing message to a public meeting beforehand listing the conduct he expected. It began with "If you wish to bring glory to Bombay…" and continued with ten points. No-one, he advised, "not even a child", should attend any celebration in the Prince's honour, nor any entertainment; no-one should "go out of curiosity to see what was happening"; and nobody should stir out of their house, unless unavoidably. Everyone should stay at home and spin, or learn to spin; and sing "devotional songs", or pray.

The briefing continued: When the Prince has landed, a bonfire of foreign cloth should be lit (on open ground away from the procession route) and foreign cloth collected for it. But the message then revealed some apprehension on Gandhi's part. No passengers should be "forcibly dragged out of trains"; workers should not stop work without leave from their employers.[56] The briefing ended with a statement: "We can be fit for swaraj only if everyone is free to do what he chooses..." Presumably Gandhi meant that people in disagreement with the hartal should not be prevented from acting as they wished. (Gandhi, M.K. 1966: vol 21: 435-436)

As the Prince arrived, a huge bonfire was lit and a public meeting held at which Gandhi spoke. The Bombay crowds did stay away from the official procession of welcome in what Sushila Nayar calls a "complete hartal". However, elsewhere in the city, serious rioting broke out. It lasted for several days and led to the deaths of 53 people, including policemen and Congress and Khilafat volunteers. Some minority groups ("co-operators") trying to attend the celebration were harassed or attacked, and their foreign garments forcibly taken. Some tramcars and liquor stores were set on fire. Nayar also comments: "It seems that Parsis, Christians and Jews had joined to welcome the Prince. This angered Khilafat and Noncooperation volunteers, who had therefore taken to violence." And in subsequent days these minorities, including Anglo-Indians, retaliated with violent reprisals against Muslims and Hindus. It was these reprisals apparently which accounted for the bulk of the casualties. (Nayar 1994: vol 5: 364-366)

When Gandhi went immediately to the scene from the foreign cloth bonfire, it was to find at that point that much of the violence was in his name and in the name of Noncooperation. (Gandhi M.K. 1966: vol 21: 462-465) Mortified, he announced he would not eat, and would drink only water, until the "noncooperators have made peace with the cooperators". Three days later, the ugly retaliations in both directions that were part of the communal violence ended: in the presence of local community and religious leaders, Gandhi felt able to break his fast.

A particular embarrassment for Gandhi was that, by provoking the communal violence, he thought the noncooperators had behaved worse

---

56. For a helpful short discussion of Gandhi's views on class struggle, see "Gandhi, Socialism and the Doctrine of Trusteeship" in Hardiman, 2003: 81-85.

than the cooperators. He added that Congress volunteers had done commendable work in restoring peace "even at risk of their lives"; whereas he was much less content with the Khilafat volunteers, who lacked an understanding of nonviolence. He thought the disparate volunteer groups were lacking overall discipline and should be brought together in one organisation. He also addressed a letter to "hooligans" regretting that he had failed to get his message across.

On November 23, the Congress working committee, meeting in Bombay, agreed to postpone the launch of mass civil disobedience at Bardoli. A few days later, Gandhi took another personal vow to fast for 24 hours every Monday "till swaraj is attained". (Tendulkar 1951: vol 2: 94)

More Hartals and a Ban on Nationalist Volunteer Organisations

On the same day that Bombay saw such fierce rioting, successful hartals were called in major cities and towns across India, in particular Calcutta.

The shut down in Bengal's major city was managed so effectively by the Congress and Khilafat volunteers that the police were seen not to be in control. The streets were empty. All markets and mills were closed; also courts and government offices; and a lawyers' boycott closed the high court. No trams and vehicles were on the streets; railway stations were deserted. Doctors visiting patients got permits from the Congress office to attend emergency cases by car. (Nayar 1994: vol 5: 366) Calcutta's daily paper for Europeans, *The Statesman*, commented: "…it must be admitted that the Indian city of Calcutta spent yesterday under the Gandhi Raj". Another Calcutta paper, the nationalist daily *Amrita Bazar Patrika*, added "…writ large on the hartal of Calcutta is – Revolution". (Nanda 1989: 328)

Alarmed by the growing strength and visibility of the Noncooperation campaign and its volunteers, the Raj advised provincial governors to use powers against sedition and under criminal law to monitor and if necessary ban the volunteer organisations. The Government of Bengal immediately declared the Congress and the Khilafat volunteer organisations "unlawful associations" and banned political meetings. Police raided Congress and Khilafat offices and banned all public assemblies and processions. Enrolment as a volunteer was made illegal. To wear a Gandhi cap or a suit made of home-spun cloth became an offence; noncooperators were arrested for shouting pro-Gandhi slogans. A group of prominent women were arrested for selling khadi cloth at the bazaar. In Calcutta, thousands of noncooperators signed a manifesto calling on people to enrol in the banned Bengal volunteer corps. Within a matter of days, the governments of Punjab and the United Provinces, Bihar and Assam followed suit and imposed similar bans.

C.R. Das in Calcutta and numbers of leaders and noncooperators elsewhere were arrested and jailed. (Nanda 1989: 327-328; Nayar 1994: 366-367) Defiance of the bans amounted to a second campaign of individual civil disobedience and was taken up in much of India, especially Bengal. Over the next few days and weeks, 30,000 civil disobedients were arrested as they defied the government bans and engaged in picketing, selling khadi cloth or uncensored newspapers, or holding meetings and parades. Virtually all the prominent leaders in these provinces were arrested and jailed, including Lajpat Rai, Motilal Nehru, A.K. Azad and Jawaharlal Nehru. (Tendulkar 1951: 71-72)

Voluntary suffering was often described by Gandhi as the essence of satyagraha and the source of its power. He based this claim partly on his religious beliefs, but also on a pragmatic reading of what mobilises public opinion most effectively in support of a cause. His view was that, in the real world, the innocent, normally law-abiding person, resisting repressive violence bravely, peacefully and without retaliation, best dramatises injustice and attracts support, and in time undermines the oppressive government's self-confidence.

Gandhi had read and published in India in translation Thoreau's essay "On the Duty of Civil Disobedience", but claimed that he had invented his own interpretation of this method of rebellion. Commenting just before the wave of arrests took place, he wrote that imprisonments

"... are not courted with the object of embarrassing the government, though as a matter of fact they do. They are courted for the sake of discipline and suffering. They are courted because we consider it to be wrong to be free under a Government we hold to be wholly bad. No stone should be left unturned by us to make the Government realize that we are in no way amenable to its control... [T]he only safe and honourable place for us is the prison... [W]hen imprisonment comes to us in the ordinary discharge of our duty, we must feel happy because we feel stronger, because we pay the price of due performance of duty. And if exhibition of real strength is the best propaganda, we must believe that every imprisonment strengthens the people and thus brings swaraj nearer." (Gandhi, M.K. 1966: vol 21: 378-379)

Of particular note is the culture of civil disobedience coming into being at this time, promoted by Gandhi: no anger, no mourning, but happiness and (quiet) celebration. On hearing of the arrest of four of the leading noncooperators in the United Provinces, including three of the Nehru family, Gandhi wrote that "it filled me with joy" (Gandhi, M.K. 1966: vol 21: 550). On rumours of the arrest of C.R. Das, the leader in Bengal, he wrote "[w]e should rejoice... if Deshbandu Das has been arrested, feel enthused rather than despondent and have hope that the hour of victory is near... [A]nyone who serves when outside the prison serves better still if, though innocent, he is imprisoned." (Gandhi, M.K. 1966: vol 21: 565)

Pleasure at being jailed, and enthusiastic congratulation if a friend or relative suffered imprisonment, became a feature of the satyagrahi culture. Gandhi extended this doctrine of positivity and compliance to include the sentencing and penalties for noncooperators as well as their conduct in prison. Prison was an honour to be welcomed.

As a former lawyer, Gandhi had thought through his position on civil disobedience extremely carefully. So long as he accepted the legitimacy of British rule, the purpose of civil disobedience was to correct injustices as a loyal citizen: it also meant pleading guilty and seeking the severest penalty. Now that he flatly denied the right of the British to remain in India, he still advised noncooperators to accept the right of the state to exact a penalty from them for their voluntary civil disobedience. In both cases, the jailed noncooperators would accept imprisonment gladly and follow prison rules without complaint, while peacefully refusing to tolerate treatment demeaning to their dignity. (Gandhi, M.K. 1966: vol 21: 382, 455-457, 539; vol 22: 19-20, 28-29, 108-110, 125-127, 188-189)

His thoughts of course included tactical considerations. Whether to offer civil disobedience was not solely a matter of principle. A calculation was made whether it was the right moment to make this powerful statement of dissent and disaffection. (Gandhi, M.K, 1966: vol. 21: 389) The banning by provincial governors of legitimate peaceful campaigning activities by noncooperators provided such a moment.

On 1 December, despite the arrests of significant figures, another successful hartal was staged when the Prince visited Lahore in the Punjab. In mid-December when the Prince arrived in Allahabad in UP (United Provinces) there was a further peaceful hartal. His arrival in Calcutta on 24 December was a source of much anxiety to the Raj, prompting the advice to governors to begin the suppression of the volunteer groups. However, Calcutta staged another peaceful hartal. There were celebrations welcoming the Prince in the European area of the city, but elsewhere shops were closed, blinds drawn and streets deserted; and no traffic on the streets. (Nayar 1994: vol 5: 377)

However, on 13 January, following his visit to Burma, the Prince visited Madras. Here, Brahmins and Muslims boycotted the Prince's welcome, but non-Brahmins celebrated it. Caste differences had split political affiliations in the Hindu community. Non-Brahmins tended to support the government and go onto the streets to welcome the British Prince; Brahmins and Muslims stayed at home. But co-operators joining the procession were barracked and stoned, pedestrians and cars attacked, streets barricaded and decorations torn down. Some liquor stores were looted and burned; some women were spat at and abused. (Nayar 1994: vol 5: 378)

Gandhi as always was distressed by the damage and destruction the Noncooperation campaign had caused and worried that the popular movement was disregarding his calls for discipline and nonviolence. He secured from the Congress working committee a further postponement of the mass civil disobedience proposed for Bardoli.

Opportunity to Negotiate with the Raj

Fears on all sides of potential public disorder accompanied the succession of hartals that confronted the slow procession of the royal visit. But Indian moderate politicians quickly became just as alarmed at the Raj's repressive response, the jailing of thousands of Indian "noncooperators". The moderates were "cooperators" on whom the government was relying – by their participation at the highest levels of government – to ensure the credibility of its reform programme. However, leading moderates began pressing the new Viceroy, Lord Reading, much more strongly than he had expected: 1,000 signed a manifesto urging him to seek a truce with Congress and call a conference to find "a reasonable settlement". (Nayar 1994: vol 5: 373-374)

Reading agreed to explore this possibility, apparently anxious in early December to ensure that the Prince of Wales' visit to Calcutta later in December would be hartal-free. He seems to have been willing – despite powerfully-expressed objections from his provincial governors in India and from the British cabinet in London – to grant a round table conference at which increased participation of Indian representatives in the Raj's ruling councils might be "on the table". (Nanda 1989: 328-331; Nayar 1994: vol 5: 374-375)

According to the historian D.A. Low, Lord Reading was seriously troubled by the revolt he was facing and wanted to avoid a situation where his only option was to suppress an incipient uprising. The Raj's policy of slowly incorporating Indian nationalists into its ruling councils should not be jeopardised by losing the goodwill and participation of the moderate politicians.

Das and Azad were in jail in Calcutta, where they were visited by a key moderate politician, Madan Mohan Malaviya, acting as the Viceroy's envoy. Their representatives then travelled to visit Gandhi and pressed him to agree to Reading's conditions; these were simply for Gandhi to call off Noncooperation prior to the proposed conference and, in particular, to cancel the upcoming hartal in Calcutta, by then due within a few days. (The sounding out of Gandhi began on 18 December, just six days before the Prince's visit.) Reading was apparently willing to have the ban

315

on Congress volunteer organisations lifted and the prisoners jailed under those bans freed; however, he was unwilling to release the Khilafat leaders jailed previously for their call for resignations from the Indian Army.

Gandhi, in response, did not refuse to attend the round table conference, but did decline to call off Noncooperation in advance and before a date for the conference had been set. He also made no move to cancel the Calcutta hartal. His other condition was the release of the Ali brothers. With time so short, the negotiations – more accurately, perhaps, "talks about talks" – failed. (Low D.A. 1966: 241-259; Nanda 1989: 329-333; Nayar 1994: vol 5: 375-376)

Whether such a conference could have succeeded with more time for preliminary talks is debatable. Gandhi, as we have seen, had lost faith completely in the Raj and its "present representatives"; and his, as yet incomplete, preparations for mass civil disobedience, plus the shock of the Bombay hartal, had convinced him that the national movement was not yet ready to face the Raj in negotiations from a position of sufficient strength. From his point of view, the move to initiate a negotiation was premature: he thought "a Conference at which the Government is represented will be useful only when the latter has tried the non-co-operators to its satisfaction and measured their strength in quantity and quality." (Gandhi, M.K. 1966: vol 22: 68) This reaction may sound like a lust for battle, but more accurately it showed an understanding that the Raj was unwilling to yield very much.

The moderates strongly disagreed, as did many of Gandhi's colleagues and supporters. Das, in jail, was furious and is said from this point to have "abandoned the Mahatma as a profitable ally". (Brown 1972: 339) Das's objections were essentially tactical. He is reported to have commented that, so close to the end of the Swaraj year, something had to be achieved "to save the face of the Congress and fulfil the Mahatma's promise"; and then explained:

> "If a settlement was made before December 31st and all the political prisoners are released, it would appear to the popular imagination as a great triumph for the Congress. The Round Table Conference might or might not be a success, but if it

failed... the Congress could resume the fight at any time..." (Nanda 1989: 333)

What neither Das, nor Gandhi, knew was how strongly the British government in London, in secret communications, had objected to Lord Reading's proposal for the conference, and had refused to authorise him, if one did take place, to make any concessions. (Nanda 1989: 331)

Again, from Gandhi's perspective, the tactical issue was to keep alive the sympathy of the moderates and their pressure on the Viceroy, while developing the Noncooperation movement to the point when real power could be exercised for swaraj through escalation to mass civil disobedience. Achieving a worthwhile settlement required a negotiation between equal partners that would recognise Indian dignity and sovereignty. For him, it was not a matter of persuading the far-away imperial Parliament in London to legislate increased electoral representation for Indians in their own country. Far from seeking more places for India's leaders on the Raj's advisory councils, India should be seeking dominion status within the "commonwealth of nations", similar to other former British colonies such as Canada, Australia, New Zealand, and South Africa; or perhaps, if necessary, complete independence, like Ireland. He also thought that the transfer of power should be a democratic process, with possible consideration of a constitution for swaraj similar to the one he had drawn up for the Congress, that is, based on linguistic provinces and with voting rights extended to all who could pay the 4 annas membership fee. (Nayar 1994: vol 5: 386; Gandhi M.K. 1966: vol 22: 198, 217)

Commenting in January, he wrote:

"Swaraj scheme is undoubtedly a matter on which there will be as many minds as there are men and women... The adoption of the Congress Franchise is my own suggestion but what I have laid down as the guiding principle is really unassailable. The scheme of Swaraj is that scheme which popular representatives frame." (Gandhi M.K. 1966: vol 22: 218-219)

It is clear that at the end of 1921, the "parliamentary swaraj" which Gandhi favoured as an immediate objective was for the "popular representatives" of the Congress themselves to exercise sovereignty and decide their constitutional arrangements. (Gandhi M.K. 1966: vol 22: 18-19; 141)

Even so, despite such radical views, Gandhi was at one with those of his fellow politicians who felt that full swaraj could not yet be achieved. (Gandhi M.K. 1966: vol 22: 68, 198-199, 218) Whereas his colleagues were keen to test what Reading might offer at a round table conference, Gandhi expected little from the Raj and preferred to step up and strengthen the Noncooperation campaign for swaraj and to refocus it.

Gandhi of course had been persuaded at the Nagpur annual Congress in 1920 to commit to the goal of swaraj in one year. The coalition he had ingeniously helped pull together, based on the two issues, the Khilafat and the Punjab, had gained enthusiastic backing when swaraj was added as an overriding objective too. But little discussion had taken place, and no agreement had been reached, on how they would proceed if they got into negotiations. Gandhi's tactical alliance was with politicians who disagreed with him not only on nonviolence but also on the aims of their collective nonviolent rebellion.

Moreover, Gandhi stated publicly his belief that, at a round table conference, the British should be "penitent" for the enormous harm their conquest and domination of India over several centuries had done the country and its people. If they were "truly penitent" then they would recognise their fault and a negotiation between equals would be straightforward: "…No matter how you repress us, we shall one day wring reluctant repentance from you…" (Gandhi M.K. 1966: vol 22: 103; see also 33, 35, 54, 69, 179) (But, of course, the British were very far from penitent and were unlikely to change their attitude of entitlement.)

Gandhi's critics saw his approach as idealistic and impractical. Gandhi, occupied as he was throughout the swaraj year with marshalling the Noncooperation campaign, had not determined with his political colleagues what version of swaraj they should take into negotiation. (Gandhi M.K. 1966: vol 22: 219) The opportunity for negotiation arrived suddenly and probably sooner than he expected.

At the annual session of Congress held in Ahmedabad in December, Gandhi won the crucial votes, but most of his most senior colleagues who might have advised or challenged him were in jail. There was considerable unease from a minority of Khilafatists who wanted to press on immediately to mass civil disobedience and with a demand for complete independence.

New Priorities for Noncooperation

Effectively, as 1921 came to an end, Gandhi was drawn in to pursuing two new priorities. They pulled in different directions, were hard to manage and perhaps confusing for noncooperators to follow. On the one hand, he planned to move on to stage 3 of progressive nonviolent noncooperation by launching mass civil disobedience. On the other, he wanted to lower the temperature so as to keep open the door for a possible round table conference and not lose the support of the moderates as key allies.

The first priority required escalation to "aggressive" civil disobedience, but in a defined, small area of the sub-continent where the noncooperators were fully prepared. At the same time, the rest of India should stay calm and pursue only "defensive" civil disobedience, or indeed suspend civil disobedience altogether.

Thus a de-escalation for a temporary period was his second priority and appeared to make sense while preparations for mass civil disobedience took place. Gandhi wanted to overturn the narrative of the Viceroy that the Raj's volunteer bans and mass arrests were necessary to combat the lawlessness of the noncooperators. He argued the opposite. The Raj's policy was one of repression and denial of civil liberties. Bans and mass arrests of nonviolent noncooperators were unjustified because it was legitimate and peaceful Congress activities that were being outlawed and suppressed. The Raj had effectively introduced martial law "without the odium of the name". (Gandhi M.K. 1966: vol 22: 213) Peace could be restored instantly if the bans were lifted and the prisoners released:

"…[W]e are not the aggressors. We have not got to stop any single activity. It is the government that is to stop its aggravatingly offensive activity aimed, not at violence, but at

319

lawful, disciplined, stern, but absolutely non-violent, agitation. It is for the Government of India and for it alone to bring about a peaceful atmosphere if it so desires." (Gandhi M.K. 1966: vol. 22: 89)

Gandhi's expectation was that the moderates would defend noncooperators against attacks on their civil rights. He thought activists had a right to continue with their campaigning activities as long as these actions were "defensive" and non-threatening, and while noncooperators were prepared to accept peacefully imprisonment as a consequence of defying the unjustified bans. Moderates should recognise the violation of civil liberties constituted by the Raj's bans on speaking freely from public platforms, attending public meetings or picketing liquor stores, and publishing plain-speaking articles in nationalist newspapers. Gandhi even went so far as to say that defending free speech and assembly and freedom of the press should for a temporary period replace the Khilafat and Punjab issues and swaraj itself as the immediate objective of Noncooperation, until mass civil disobedience could be launched. (Gandhi M.K. 1966: vol 22: 89-90, 125, 141, 142-143, 177; Nayar 1994: vol 5: 382-383)

Effectively, concentration on non-aggressive civil disobedience would extend stage 2 of Noncooperation even further. But Gandhi's manoeuvre of calming the combative spirit in the rest of the country and re-directing it onto civil liberties' issues – while preparing it simultaneously to focus on the struggle for swaraj in just one small district – was extraordinarily difficult to manage. A two-speed campaign was to take place at a moment when much of the country was aroused and expecting escalating confrontation.

The moderates, on the other hand, were still tempted by the round table conference and far from convinced that Gandhi had been right to decline the opportunity to attend. Gandhi may have underestimated the fears of the moderates who wanted a truce and a suspension of Noncooperation. They were reluctant to one-sidedly criticise the Raj's repressive measures.

One Year After Nagpur: Ahmedabad Annual Congress Session

In late December, Ahmedabad hosted the first annual session of Congress held under the new constitution. The twenty new "linguistic" provinces are recorded as sending 4,726 delegates (out of 6,173 eligible to attend). This attendance was impressive, given so many Congress leaders and activists, particularly from northern provinces, were in jail. Noncooperation had stimulated enthusiasm across the entire nation.

Delegates occupied a temporary township and attended sessions dressed in white khadi, sitting "Indian fashion" on the ground rather than, as previously, benches and chairs. All provinces were represented and most took up close to the full number of delegate places allotted them under the constitution. There was no clapping and "the strings of resolutions" and oratory associated with previous Congresses, were missing. For the first time women delegates and a specific women's conference were included and Hindi and Urdu spoken as well as English. (Nanda 1989: 333-334; Nayar 1994: vol 5: 381-382; Gandhi M.K. 1966: vol 22: 166-167)

The Ahmedabad reception committee had planned for 100,000 visitors to attend the annual session as well; but reportedly up to 200,000 actually came. (Nayar 1994: vol 5: 379)

Having failed to deliver swaraj, or negotiations with the Raj, or to begin mass civil disobedience, Gandhi was subject to strong criticism. It might have been fiercer if colleagues like Das had been present at Ahmedabad, but one of the leaders of the Khilafat movement, the Muslim cleric, Hasrat Mohani, pressed vehemently not only for the goal of complete independence immediately, but also for an amendment to the Congress's creed. He argued that the creed should permit the use of violence. However, the impatient Khilafatists were defeated by a substantial majority, as Congress agreed to endorse the original Noncooperation resolutions from a year earlier at Calcutta and Nagpur. The annual session followed Gandhi's advice on most issues.

Gandhi was the dominant figure, set most of the agenda and drafted the main resolutions. One notable feature was his determination to act on

321

lessons learned following the vicious communal fighting in Bombay after the hartal in November. Constructive programme in future, he proposed, should cover not just unity between Hindus and Muslims but include all religious communities, like the minorities of Parsees, Christians and Jews. Moreover, management of the Congress and Khilafat volunteer groups needed to be brought into a single framework, co-ordinated by central boards set up by provincial Congress committees, with the individual volunteers trained to a much higher standard.[57]

The main resolution castigated "the repression started by the Government of India... by way of disbandment of Volunteer Corps and forcible prohibition of public and even committee meetings in an illegal and high-handed manner..." The repression, it said, including the arrest of many Congress workers in several provinces, was clearly intended to stifle all Congress and Khilafat activities. It continued:

"... this Congress resolves that all activities of the Congress be suspended as far as necessary and appeals to all, quietly and without any demonstration, to offer themselves for arrest by belonging to the volunteer organizations to be formed throughout the country..." (Gandhi M.K. 1966: vol 22: 100)

No one was to be accepted by the provincial boards as a member of the new National Volunteer Corps who did not sign an eight-point declaration "with God as witness". This pledge was to be the centrepiece of Congress activity for the immediate future and all people over the age of eighteen were eligible to sign. The text stated that, while a member, the signatory would remain nonviolent in word and deed and "earnestly endeavour to be non-violent in intent".

Members were to pledge their belief in communal unity, swadeshi and the removal of untouchability – all key items in the constructive programme – and promise to take practical steps to promote them. Volunteers' duties would include preservation of order and regulation of meetings,

---

57. Both the Congress working committee and the All India Congress committee had approved the proposal previously in November. The annual Congress was being asked to confirm it.

hartals and processions. They were also to provide help in emergencies. The declaration required discipline from the volunteer in carrying out instructions from superior officers, together with all regulations "not inconsistent with the spirit of this pledge" as prescribed by the provincial boards or other Congress bodies. The volunteer also vowed "to suffer imprisonment, assault or even death… without resentment" and, in the event of imprisonment, not to claim financial support from the Congress.

Formation of the national volunteer corps was just part of the lengthy resolution, which was approved. Within a defiant challenge to the Raj was included suspension of "offensive" aspects of the Congress's programme. Gandhi was not happy with the quality of existing volunteers following the Bombay hartal and a number of other incidents, and he had formed the view that volunteers elsewhere (such as Bengal) did not really believe in nonviolence or parts of the constructive programme.

At a meeting with delegates from Bengal he justified the much stricter terms for membership of the volunteer corps quite straightforwardly:

"In spite of the non-violence that has been observed in Bengal to an enormous extent, I still doubt whether your minds are nonviolent."

He also told them: "In Bengal today I know that there is a great deal of impatience and therefore intolerance…" (Gandhi M.K. 1966: vol 22: 111-112) Picketing in some cases had become too aggressive; much campaigning too confrontational. It was not possible to match the oppressive power of the Raj with the disabling power of Congress's nonviolent noncooperation, except by developing a more dedicated, disciplined and better-organised volunteer corps.

Signing up volunteers to a new national volunteer organisation showed open defiance of the Raj's crackdown. Joining the volunteers was an act of "defensive" civil disobedience, legitimate and non-threatening, while the Government bans lasted. It also provided the essential preparation for an escalation to mass civil disobedience when the country was ready. Gandhi's resolution contains a fine statement of the case for civil disobedience (defensive and aggressive, individual and mass) at this time:

"This Congress is … of opinion that civil disobedience is the only civilised and effective substitute for an armed rebellion, whenever every other remedy for preventing arbitrary, tyrannical and emasculating use of authority by individuals and corporations has been tried, and, therefore, advises all Congress workers and others, who believe in peaceful methods and are convinced that there is no remedy save some kind of sacrifice to dislodge the existing Government from its position of perfect irresponsibility to the people of India, to organise individual civil disobedience and mass civil disobedience, when the mass of people have been sufficiently trained in the methods of non-violence…" (Gandhi MK 1966: vol. 22: 101)

But it was a risk to re-organise the volunteer groups (and tighten the conditions for membership) at a moment when the hartals, picketing and rallies had severely shaken the Raj. To re-prioritise the Congress's main campaigning goals, if only for a temporary period, also risked confusing supporters.[58]

Introduction of the 8-point pledge shows Gandhi's determination to persist with his political agenda and methods, and it underlines the interdependence of constructive programme and civil disobedience in his preparations for the next stage of Noncooperation. The pledge also demonstrates the demands Gandhi felt able to make as a political organiser. Provincial Congress committees were required to form a more tightly disciplined, hierarchical volunteer organisation; the volunteer must show a willingness to make life-changing sacrifices; and Congress, not wishing to deceive its volunteers about the seriousness of their commitment, made a hard-headed disavowal of compensation for those volunteers and their families who might suffer injury in the struggle.

At Ahmedabad, Gandhi was given "sole executive authority" to lead the campaign in the event of communication between the Congress leadership being disrupted by arrests. But it was not quite the confirmation of his

---

58. Later Gandhi was to criticise severely the poor preparation of volunteers, especially reluctance to take up the swadeshi vow. (Gandhi M.K. 1966: vol 22: 464; see also 146, 152, 273)

"dictatorship" that is sometimes suggested. It was proposed and agreed as a contingency, in case arrests made the normal functioning of the working committee and other Congress bodies impossible.[59] (Gandhi M.K, 1966: vol. 22: 102, 122)

Congress was now gearing up for the final stage of Noncooperation, under Gandhi's direction. His focus was on mass civil disobedience; but the very success of Noncooperation so far – and fears that further escalation was a risky step – meant that other Indian politicians were continuing to contemplate a settlement.

(A summary of the key events of this chapter is included at the end of Chapter 9.)

---

59. If Gandhi himself were arrested, he would have the "sole executive authority" to appoint his successor, the next leader the same, and so on. In the event, Gandhi did not exercise this power formally, because the working committee and the AICC continued to make decisions with him. Or perhaps more accurately: they continued to discuss and authorise Gandhi's proposals for what Congress should do next. It is clear, for example, that Gandhi was consulting with members of the Congress working committee about what concessions he should offer throughout and after the moderates' conference held two weeks' later. (Gandhi M.K. 1966: vol 22: 196)

CHAPTER 9

WAITING FOR MASS CIVIL DISOBEDIENCE

Case Study 7(C): NONCOOPERATION AT ITS PEAK

Stage 3: Off-On Preparations for Mass Civil Disobedience ("Aggressive")

Following the Ahmedabad conference, Gandhi was faced with a number of initiatives still outstanding when the swaraj year came to an end. Ongoing projects had their origins in work begun months earlier. Mass civil disobedience had been postponed partly because of the proposal from the Viceroy, prompted by the moderates, for a round table conference. Also the successive hartals and their impact – including the bans imposed by provincial governors and the resulting eruption of Congress volunteers offering themselves for arrest – had contributed to a further upsurge in activism and captured the attention of the political classes.

Enthusiasm from the moderates for a round table conference did not go away, at the same time as Congress preparations for mass civil disobedience, begun the previous November, were revived. Gandhi was occupied with both. His plan of progressive nonviolent noncooperation was essentially a simple but flexible plan of escalation, gradually preparing for a showdown with the Raj. Negotiations for a settlement were problematic for him and even a diversion, given that the movement was not quite ready to launch mass civil disobedience. But he felt unable to ignore the call from the moderates and some noncooperators to explore what might be on the table.

More Talks about Talks

Although the Viceroy had rejected Gandhi's terms, the moderates wanted to try again. Malaviya was the moderate leader who had acted as envoy from the Viceroy earlier in December. He attended the Ahmedabad annual conference, where he moved a resolution asking the Congress to welcome a round table conference and to reject mass civil disobedience. (Gandhi M.K. 1966: vol 22: 97-99) The resolution was defeated.

Gandhi said that he "attached not the slightest importance" to such a conference. He added nevertheless that it might be worthwhile if the Raj could give some prior indication of "a change of heart" and of a successful result leading from it; but he had seen no evidence for that. He said later:

> "If [Lord Reading] wants a table at a conference where only equals are to sit and where there is not to be a single beggar, then there is an open door and that door will always remain open." (Gandhi, M.K. 1966: vol. 22: 104)

Despite Gandhi's rebuke to the Viceroy, Malaviya and other leading moderates were not discouraged. Two weeks later in Bombay, they convened a "leaders' conference" mainly of moderates, attended by up to 300 people. Gandhi was invited and made an opening statement on behalf of Congress, but declined to contribute to the resolutions from the meeting. His aim, he said, was to win the support of those attending for the civil liberties campaign, to act as an adviser, and to listen. (Gandhi M.K. 1966: vol 22: 178-181, 195-199, 233)

What he heard showed that he did not have the support he had expected (Gandhi, M.K. 1966: vol 22: 214). The moderates' main purpose was to get Congress to meet the Raj's pre-conditions for a round table conference. They wanted Congress to call off mass civil disobedience and to suspend Noncooperation campaigning. If it did, then moderates would be more likely to support the Congress pre-condition that the volunteer bans be lifted and the bulk of prisoners released.

Gandhi refused to call off preparations for mass civil disobedience, but did agree to postpone its launch by two weeks, as a concession "to enable the committee appointed by this conference to enter into negotiations

327

with the Viceroy". (Gandhi M.K. 1966: vol 22: 196) Also, instead of adamantly insisting on removal of the bans and release of almost all the Congress prisoners, he agreed to let prisoner release be adjudicated by representatives of the moderates and of the Raj, or by an umpire chosen by them. He further agreed to suspend "hostile picketing".[60] None of these concessions was to take effect until the Raj had agreed to go ahead with the round table conference and at the point the conference was due to take place.

Gandhi did not relax his insistence that government repression must stop, while the signing up and training of volunteers in preparation for the launch of mass civil disobedience would continue. Also, at any round table discussion, the Congress would call for the Raj to take action on the long-standing Khilafat and Punjab issues and press for dominion status for India.

> "There is no open mind about the Khilafat. There is no open mind about the Punjab. The irreducible minimum has been before the country for a long time." (Gandhi M.K. 1966: vol 22: 98)

All the issues were simple as far as Gandhi was concerned. On the Khilafat, where the Raj could not reasonably be expected to dictate what happened in the Middle East peace settlement, the British government simply had to show good faith, doing their utmost to represent the interests of India's Muslims fully in the treaty negotiations. On the Punjab they had to show respect for outraged Indian opinion. That meant censoring General Dyer and the Punjab governor, O'Dwyer, for the Amritsar massacre and other atrocities, rather than allowing the British Parliament and imperialist opinion in Britain to celebrate their actions. Also the two should be deprived of their medals and pensions.

On swaraj the Raj simply had to treat Indians as equals and allow Indian opinion to determine the country's future constitutional arrangements.

---

60. There was some evidence that picketers were "aggressive" in some parts of India, but suspending all pickets, as he did, meant withdrawing some that were following "defensive" nonviolent discipline to the letter. (Gandhi M.K. 1966: vol 22: 197-198)

(Gandhi M.K. 1966: vol 22: 260-261) But on swaraj he went further and repeated the insistence on full dominion status, with the precise form of the new Indian constitution to be determined by representatives of the Indian people themselves. They should be elected under the Congress franchise:

"Every Indian adult, male or female, paying 4 annas and signing the Congress Creed, will be entitled to be placed on the electoral roll."

Thus Gandhi, in 1922 at the Bombay moderates' meeting, was stating publicly that women in India should have the vote on terms of equality with men; he also was assuming that Congress would remain committed to its nonviolent creed and that those principles would decide who determined the new Indian constitution. (Gandhi, M.K. 1966: vol 22: 217) Gandhi freely admitted that his call for full independence was probably premature and that there were other views of swaraj to be discussed: but he thought the nature of swaraj should be debated at the round table conference.

A committee of 20 drawn from the moderate leaders present – and advised by Gandhi – drew up the resolutions to be submitted to the Viceroy. They went a long way to supporting the Congress position, while maintaining the moderates' consistent opposition to civil disobedience. The moderates' first resolution described the bans, arrests and imprisonments as "an unwarranted encroachment upon the elementary rights of citizenship, of the freedom of the press and liberty of speech and association". It went on to suggest that they "ought to be reversed without delay".

The second said that the civil disobedience being undertaken by Congress "ought not to be resorted to". Their third resolution supported the proposal for a round table conference and added that the banning orders should be withdrawn and those jailed under them released. (Nayar 1994: vol 5: 383-384) No link was proposed between the release of the prisoners and the holding of the round table conference – but a link was implied by inclusion of both proposals within the same resolution. A further resolution went so far as to suggest that the British government "should clothe the Viceroy with authority necessary for the purpose of arriving at a settlement". (Nanda 1989: 335) The Malaviya committee then submitted its recommendations to the Viceroy.

A few days later, the Congress working committee met in Bombay and considered the results of the moderates' discussions. It agreed to postpone the launch of offensive civil disobedience until 31 January, pending the result of the Malaviya negotiations. It also linked suspension of hartals, picketing and civil disobedience with a simultaneous cancellation by the government of the bans on volunteer groups; release of nonviolent Noncooperation prisoners; and the calling and commencement of the round table conference. (Gandhi M.K. 1966: vol 22: 210-211) Gandhi had succeeded in bringing the moderates to a closer understanding of the Congress position. Nevertheless, he concluded that "the mind" of the moderates seemed to be "centred more on a round table conference than upon asserting the right of the people" to the civil liberties which are "three-fourths of swaraj". (Gandhi M.K. 1966: vol 22: 214)[61]

Later in a strong defence against fierce criticism that Congress should not have engaged in these discussions with the moderates, Gandhi stressed how important it was for noncooperators to win the public argument:

"And if the Viceroy or a party [such as the moderates] desires a conference, it would be foolish for non-cooperators not to respond. The case of non-co-operators depends for our success on cultivation of public opinion and public support. They have no other force to back them." (Gandhi M.K. 1966: vol 22: 219)

Within a few days, resolutions were tabled by leading moderates in the Raj's central councils in support of a revived round table initiative, but they were defeated. It then quickly became clear that the Raj's response to the moderates' efforts would be negative. The Viceroy's private secretary replied to them on January 26. He regretted that the Viceroy was unable to discover in the proposals of the Bombay conference any "basis for a

---

61. His unorthodox role as an "adviser", helping with the wording of the Malaviya resolutions, is reminiscent of his part in the Champaran inquiry. As a protagonist for one side, he was nevertheless trusted to play a part in finding a solution.

profitable discussion on the subject of a round table conference" and that no useful purpose would be served by further talks. (Nayar: 385-386)

B.R. Nanda comments:

> "The Moderate leaders, the sponsors of the Conference, did not, of course, know that the Viceroy's wings had been clipped by the British Cabinet; that he was in no position to make any concessions to Gandhi and the non-cooperation movement." (Nanda 1989: 335)

Thus Gandhi had been diverted from preparing for mass civil disobedience by the possibility of a round table conference that was no longer in prospect. Even so, he was becoming increasingly convinced that the overall campaign of Noncooperation needed to be reined in so as to maintain contact with moderate opinion, and so as to calm the atmosphere for the next stage of the struggle.

Preparations for Mass Civil Disobedience

The months either side of the Ahmedabad Congress are frequently seen as the highpoint of Noncooperation. (Brown 1979: 359; Nanda 1989: 398-399; Sarkar, 1983: 203) Provincial governors in different parts of India were beginning to be seriously worried that the Raj might lose control. Noncooperation in several areas was beginning to move from the "classes" to the "masses". The educated who had responded originally to Gandhi's call for noncooperation, were being joined in activism by a wider range of caste and class groups from urban and some rural areas.

Increasingly, the devolution of campaigning to provincial Congress committees meant that local issues were coming to the fore. In many areas much of the activism was devoted to issues from the specific programme and priorities that Gandhi had set; in others Noncooperation provided the inspiration and framework within which campaigners pursued their own agendas. The success of moves towards engaging the peasantry, including expectations of mass civil disobedience and swaraj, meant that as the movement grew and as local leaders gained in confidence, Gandhi and his co-workers were more remote from much of the activism generated, and less in control.

331

One extraordinary campaign was the Akali reform movement within Sikhism in the Punjab. It involved a series of prayer marches to Sikh shrines and their surrounding lands, including nonviolent invasions. Protests moved from one site to the next over a period of five years. The aim was to gain control of shrines where the established priests, supported by the British authorities, were seen as or known to be corrupt. Thousands of Sikh peasants were involved; some were ex-soldiers who had fought for the British army in the Middle East. Participants were highly disciplined, organised into small bands, walking forward in prayer to be confronted by police or British troops. Before launching the action they would take a vow promising to remain nonviolent "in thought and deed" and resist assault without any retaliation. Some wore khadi. Large numbers were brutally beaten, before being arrested and jailed, where again they might be beaten; many were killed. After 5 years, with a significant number of shrines including the Golden Temple at Amritsar ceded to the Akalis, legislation was passed in the Punjab parliament giving legal title to the reforms. (Nayar 1994: 443-444, 476-480; Sarkar 1983: 210-211, 228)

Gandhi expressed his enthusiastic support for the movement, which was linked at first to Noncooperation. He wrote in December 1921:

"Their resolute behaviour, their religious fervour, their calmness and their suffering command my highest admiration. One sees in everything that is happening in the country the throes of a new birth. May God grant no hasty action, no outbreak of violence impedes our unmistakeable progress towards our destined goal!"

He was deeply impressed by the Akalis' disciplined and consistent refusal to retaliate against appalling brutality; but he was also unable to throw off some scepticism about how non-threatening the civil disobedience of the movement really was, and said so. (Nanda 1989: 405; Brown 1974: 325-326, 325 fn 4)

Another significant campaign, closer to home, was the attempt, particularly in Gujarat, to promote non-cooperation through political control of municipalities and local boards. The controversial boycott of Councils was located at the provincial level in opposition to the Raj's limited reforms. At municipal level, there was no boycott and it was a matter for noncooperators themselves to decide whether, through their engagement with these local bodies, they were serving the Raj or defying it. In Ahmedabad, Nadiad and Surat, all in Gujarat, noncooperators seized on the opportunity the control of the education function by municipalities gave them to support the creation of national schools. They proceeded to close government schools and reopen them as national schools. This campaign had considerable success and continued until 1922 when the government took direct control of the three authorities. (Gandhi 1966: vol 21: 363-365)

Sarkar writes of growing "waves" of urban and rural activism during 1921 and into 1922, a "groundswell" which, particularly in Bengal, showed "a repeated tendency to burst Gandhian bounds". (Sarkar 1983: 220-221) Gandhi was regularly enthused and then dismayed as, alongside reports of the spread of scrupulously nonviolent acts of resistance in different parts of the country, came news too of riots and attacks on landlords and police. "It is difficult to distinguish between hooligans and noncooperators," he wrote following the trouble associated with the Madras hartal, "when hundreds or thousands take part in smashing cars, swearing at innocent passengers or threatening a cinema keeper." (Gandhi M.K. 1966: vol 22: 257)

He considered "quiet" in the rest of the country to be essential, as Noncooperation moved towards the experiment with mass civil disobedience in one small area. He began to write regularly about the difference between "civil" and what he called "criminal" disobedience. (Iyer 1973: 275-292)[62]

As a lawyer trained in London, Gandhi presented a lawyer's justification for civil disobedience. He believed that civil disobedience was a precious nonviolent weapon available only to those who normally were law-abiding and conscientious citizens. If they chose deliberately to break a

---

62. Raghavan Iyer in his classic book on Gandhi's philosophy, *The Moral and Political Thought of Mahatma Gandhi*, primarily uses as examples of Gandhi's thinking on civil disobedience, his speeches and articles published during Noncooperation in 1921 and 1922. As a political philosopher, Iyer discusses what Gandhi meant by "individual" and "mass", and "defensive" and "aggressive", civil disobedience. He also explains "civil" and "criminal" disobedience.

law, it must be because they considered that law or its use to be immoral. Also, the "civil" side was the most important part of civil disobedience:

> "We must... give... full... and greater value to the adjective 'civil' than to 'disobedience'. Disobedience without civility, determination, discrimination, non-violence is certain destruction." (Gandhi M.K. 1966: vol. 22: 137)

He warned that those who undertook civil disobedience without the training that would enable them to understand civility – and without having taken the volunteers' vow that would help them to maintain civility under the severest pressure – might easily stray into "criminal" disobedience, and that would damage the Noncooperation movement.

As tension mounted in 1922 and as Gandhi was distracted by the Madras hartal and other outbreaks of disorder and violence, the distinction became increasingly important to him. He was dissatisfied with the quality of training of Congress volunteers and insisted that conditions for membership be tightened. He came close to suggesting that civil disobedience would be "criminal" which did not match the criteria he had laid down.

The Raj's second rejection of a round table conference meant it had opted for confrontation. Its tougher policy towards the noncooperators included a clear view of how to treat Gandhi. Despite the intense pressure from London and from provincial governors, Lord Reading had decided not to arrest immediately the man planning and driving Noncooperation. He was waiting until Gandhi made a decisive step into illegality by launching mass civil disobedience. Gandhi was frustrated that so many of his leading colleagues had been arrested while he was left free, but he knew that the Raj was wary of any hasty move against him. With the clamour for a round table conference ended, his efforts were now mainly concentrated on the final stage of progressive nonviolent noncooperation.[63]

---

63. In these pages I have described aggressive, mass civil disobedience as the final stage of Noncooperation. Raghavan Iyer, though, highlights Gandhi saying that "noncooperation excludes civil disobedience of the severe type" (Gandhi, M.K. 1966, vol. 19: 466) and he uses the distinction to structure his discussion of both

Gandhi had been visiting different parts of the country, particularly in his home province of Gujarat, assessing their readiness for large-scale civil disobedience. He was focused on selecting an area to launch the action, testing its capability to fulfil the huge responsibility he planned to place on it. At the same time, he was trying to assess the atmosphere in the country as a whole, the readiness of other areas to watch the developing nonviolent struggle against British rule unfold, as well as prepare for joining the struggle themselves when their time came.

The final stage of Noncooperation was of course tax refusal. Gandhi was understandably nervous of this "do or die" moment. He had never stopped stressing the danger that an outbreak of violence could derail the experiment. However it is necessary to go back to early November 1921 to trace the preparation of the detailed plan for mass civil disobedience itself and how he proposed to address the problem of derailment.

Readiness to engage in mass civil disobedience

Work preparing for mass civil disobedience had begun before the swaraj year ended –and before the gift to the noncooperators of the Prince of Wales' visit transformed the situation and triggered the hartals. Gandhi spelled out his vision as part of a remarkable article:

"...If one district can be found where ninety per cent of the population have completely boycotted foreign cloth and are manufacturing all the cloth required by them by hand-spinning and hand-weaving, if the whole of the population of that district, whether Hindu, Muslim, Parsi, Sikh, Christian or Jewish, is living in perfect amity, if the whole of its Hindu population is purged of the sin of untouchability and if at least one in every

civil disobedience and noncooperation. But the distinction Iyer quotes appears in a statement Gandhi made in 1920, before the later stages of Noncooperation had been reached. In practice, Gandhi clearly came to see civil disobedience, especially mass civil disobedience, as the culmination of the Noncooperation campaign: non-cooperation was crucial to preparations for civil disobedience and an essential part of the campaign surrounding and supporting it. (Iyer 1973: 275-292]

ten of its inhabitants is capable of suffering imprisonment or even mounting the gallows, and if while that district is civilly, peacefully and honourably resisting the Government, the rest of India remains non-violent and united and prosecutes the programme of swadeshi, I hold it to be perfectly possible to establish swaraj during this year. I shall hope that there are several ready. In any case the method now to adopt is for workers to concentrate on and develop their own districts without reference to the rest." (Gandhi M.K. 1966: vol 21: 382)

On 4 November, the all-India Congress committee authorised every provincial Congress committee "on its own responsibility to undertake civil disobedience including non-payment of taxes". One condition the AICC specified for endorsing mass civil disobedience in a chosen area was that "a vast majority of the population" was fulfilling the tighter membership rules for volunteers: that is, making and wearing swadeshi cloth, showing belief in Hindu-Muslim unity, opposition to untouchability and commitment to nonviolence. (Gandhi M.K. 1966: vol 21: 412-413)

Gandhi asked provinces not to exercise their autonomy "till he gave the lead" from his home area of Gujarat and they could see how he was building the civil disobedience campaign. On seeing the result, "they should follow his example which should open the eyes of the world..." He went on:

"He knew that at present mass civil disobedience was impossible and he would be quite satisfied if in such a big continent only one 'tahsil' or district fully prepared should practise it rather than that the whole unprepared masses should partake in it." (Gandhi M.K. 1966: vol 21: 396)

Gandhi warned that mass civil disobedience was a gigantic step. Nothing should be done without recognition of the realities; there could be no turning back. In an article in his newspaper *Young India* he wrote:

"... so far as I can judge at present, it will be best for every part of India scrupulously to respect all orders and instructions while one part is deliberately taking the offensive and committing a deliberate breach of all the unmoral laws it possibly can. Needless to add that any outbreak of violence in any other part of India must necessarily injure and may even stop the experiment." (Gandhi M.K. 1966: vol 21: 416)

Provinces had been asked to nominate districts to begin the mass civil disobedience campaign on behalf of the nation, and potential names were put forward. Gandhi's approach in November 1921, having spent the previous months touring the country promoting Noncooperation and the swadeshi campaign, was sceptical and indeed critical, doubting that the candidates were close to meeting the hugely demanding criteria he had set. The AICC praised the "tremendous headway" that progressive nonviolent noncooperation had made over the previous 10 months but it added that, so far as the preparation was actually ready to deliver swaraj, it "falls far short of requirements". Even so, gradually the process threw up three areas in Gujarat that might be suitable and some others. It is clear that Gandhi favoured Gujarat because he wanted the honour to fall to his province, and he wanted the location to be reasonably close to Ahmedabad so that he could direct the campaign personally. (Gandhi M.K. 1966: vol 21: 396-397, 422)

In the event, a district of Gujarat was chosen. Gandhi proposed that mass civil disobedience should begin on November 23 in the Bardoli taluka in the Gujarat district of Surat. His enthusiastic rhetoric was accompanied by a warning:

"When the swaraj flag floats victoriously at Bardoli, then the people of the taluka next to Bardoli, following in the steps of Bardoli, should seek to plant the flag of swaraj in their midst. Thus, district by district, in regular succession, throughout the length and breadth of India, should the swaraj flag be hoisted. If, however, while the movement is on, there is the slightest outbreak of violence in any part of the country, then it would not be safe or advisable to prosecute the campaign any further." (Tendulkar 1951: vol 2: 89)

Gandhi consistently spelt out his fear that violence breaking out elsewhere in India would damage the image he hoped would be projected, of ever-extending civil disobedience capturing the whole country.

With his usual thoroughness Gandhi requested a survey. Each taluka (administrative area within a district and including numbers of villages) that wished to be chosen for mass civil disobedience should prepare a separate register for every one of the villages in its area, covering thirteen different questions. The questions included its name, its distance from the area's Noncooperation headquarters, and its total population with a breakdown of the numbers of men and women, and children under 16, and a breakdown by religious and non-caste backgrounds. In relation to the constructive programme, the register should cover the number of spinning-wheels, hand-looms and hand-carding tools and the stock of cotton. Other topics included whether it had a school and how many pupils; the number of policemen and "other marks of British authority"; the number of liquor shops; the number of persons ready for imprisonment; and the number of people, if any, who favoured co-operation with the government rather than Noncooperation. (Gandhi M.K. 1966: vol 22: 471)

Gandhi added that

"when… the fight actually begins, every satyagrahi man and every women will either be offering civil disobedience [by] courting imprisonment or will be spinning or weaving or carding or ginning cotton. No one, without exception, can sit idle even for a moment, whether he be rich or poor."

He talked of the civil disobedients as an army, with a village council in every village. The "army" should have a "representative leader" and be divided into batches of 20, each with their own leader. These leaders themselves should be grouped into 20 with one of them appointed as leader, thus creating a disciplined structure. As far as possible the groups should not be based on distinctions of any kind, such as Hindus and Muslims. Gandhi saw this organisation as a means of "educating" public opinion in the village. The process of collecting data on every village and of organising its civilian "army" was also a useful measure for him of readiness:

"I shall expect full information on all these details in the taluka to which I may be invited to go." (Gandhi M.K. 1966: vol 22: 471)

But then the momentum was suddenly stopped. The serious communal fighting, including fatalities, which broke out in Bombay following the November hartal, was a shattering blow. From Bombay, while engaged in the fast, Gandhi wrote to two of the leading organisers in Bardoli[64] and put arrangements for mass civil disobedience on hold: "In this condition, how can I go there?" (Gandhi, MK 1966: vol. 21: 461)

Gandhi was in despair as his fast for communal harmony began, and for some days questioned his entire strategy. At a Congress working committee in Bombay on 23 November when mass civil disobedience had been due to begin, he announced its postponement. (Nanda B.R, 1989: 327) Gandhi then apologised to the people of Bardoli and Anand for suspending the launch of the campaign. (Anand, in nearby Surat, was another taluka under consideration.) But within a short time his confidence was returning. He asserted: "No irretrievable harm has been done. We are still in the game", and went on to counsel patience. He even suggested that the delay was a positive thing because it gave more time to the thwarted satyagrahis to remedy faults in their preparedness. (Gandhi, M.K. 1966: vol. 21: 489-492) In his Gujarati newspaper he explained his thinking:

---

64. The principal organisers in Bardoli were Kunverbhai Mehta and Dayalji Desai. Kunverbhai and his brother Kalanjyi, had supported Gandhi since the Kheda and Rowlatt satyagrahas, when they were joined by Dayalji. Kunverbhai had his ashram in Surat District and brought together a group of 40 active workers who concentrated their efforts particularly in Bardoli. From the start of non-cooperation, "they toured the countryside, opening national schools, propagating khadi, exhorting abstinence from liquor, appealing for settlement of disputes through private arbitration rather than through British courts." (Nanda B.R. 1989: 336-337) Two other brothers, Vallabhbhai and Vithalbhai Patel, significant figures in Gujarat and Congress, also came from the Surat District and were closely involved with Gandhi. Both had worked with Gandhi during the Kheda satyagraha. Vallabhbhai was a leading figure with the Ahmedabad municipality and became one of his most important colleagues in the Congress. Vithalbhai, also prominent in Congress, had recommended that Gandhi choose Bardoli as the taluka to launch mass civil disobedience, and he became the chair of the committee preparing to lead the civil disobedience campaign.

"If we start civil disobedience in Bardoli and Anand and consequently Bombay turns violent, a little reflection is enough to show that not only will Bombay not help us, but that actually it will harm the cause. Undisciplined disobedience is nothing but the fullest co-operation with the Government. Have we still to learn that this Government is kept in power by our weakness, our habit of breaking laws at will and our violence?" (Gandhi M.K. 1966: vol 21: 492-493)

The next step was to visit Bardoli and assess how far it was matching up to his criteria.[65]

The choice of Bardoli

The verdict was mixed. At the end of his two-day visit of inspection with a colleague at the beginning of December, Gandhi reported back at a public meeting in typically painstaking detail. He praised Bardoli for its progress in "removing the bar of untouchability from your minds", noting that non-caste groups were now attending public meetings and sharing the use of wells. But he thought the noncooperators could go further, visit untouchables' homes and help ensure their children attended national schools.

---

65. Gandhi had not fully developed a plan for what to do if the impact of mass civil disobedience was countered or undermined as a result of violence breaking out in another part of India. He certainly anticipated the problem and pursued a partial solution of prevention – promoting nonviolence and the constructive programme constantly through resolutions and instructions circulated within the structures of the Congress and volunteer organisations. The same message was contained in speeches everywhere he went and in countless articles and interviews. In practice, the response he made and encouraged in other Congress leaders and with Congress volunteers was to go to the scene and attempt to calm things. Gandhi would also call off an action and blame himself by staging a fast as an act of penance, with the effect of putting pressure on colleagues and opponents to stop the violence. At this time Congress organisation was not robust enough for a reliable response to breakdown of nonviolent discipline in Gandhi's home region. In a remote part of India the problem would be more difficult.

As for swadeshi, the take-up of hand-spinning was excellent, but there was a lack of hand-looms and weavers, so the strength and quality of the thread produced were uncertain because it had not been tested by weavers. Khadi cloth used was mostly from outside the village and this was "a disqualification". Progress on boycotting government schools and creating national schools, as well as boycotting liquor stores, was good, but could be achieved through verbal persuasion rather than more intense forms of nonviolent pressure. Even so, Bardoli should not think him disappointed. He had not known any other taluka "as well prepared on the way to civil disobedience." Only a little yet remained to be done. (Gandhi M.K 1966: vol 21: 517-518)

In articles in his Gujarati and English language papers, Gandhi used his 13-question survey to give a picture of the taluka being readied to engage in struggle. Bardoli had a population of about 100,000 people, made up of about 140 villages. There were 65 government schools, of which 51 had been nationalised, most in the last few months. There were 6,000 pupils in the national schools, of which several hundred were girls; while numbers in the remaining government schools had hugely declined. Spinning was compulsory in national schools, but there were not yet enough instructors. Most men were dressed in khadi, and others complained about not being able to get hold of it. Ironically, the staple crop of area was cotton, but it was all exported. Hindu-Muslim unity was good. A peaceable atmosphere had been maintained while the changes in the area were being carried through, including with co-operators and with government officials and during the boycott of government schools. (Gandhi M.K. 1966: vol 21: 532-534) Gandhi reported that the key organiser, Kunverbhai Mehta, estimated that they could remedy the shortfalls "in a month"; while some of his co-workers said "six months".

Gandhi concluded his reports with an interesting aside:

"The reader will see that I have not discussed the question whether or not the people have the capacity to suffer, to go to jail or to face bullets. I have not even inquired of anyone. It is my experience and my faith that, when a person does his duty faithfully, he soon gets the strength to suffer. Bardoli, moreover, is making all this effort in order to be fit to go to jail... At this

341

time, going to jail is a difficult thing… If a person does not spin, does not wear khadi, is not honest or polite, has ill will towards all and refuses to mix with [untouchables] will anyone ask such a person to go to jail? A taluka which clings to the practice of untouchability will never be invited to court imprisonment. I, therefore, do not at all doubt Bardoli's courage or its readiness to go to jail." (Gandhi, M.K. 1966: vol. 21: 562-563)

Perhaps translation from the Gujarati has disturbed the logic here. The obvious unfitness for Gandhian civil disobedience of those who refuse to carry out the Bardoli self-disciplines does not prove the fitness of those who do. However, Gandhi's experience at this time had convinced him that, for a community-wide struggle to succeed on such a fundamental issue as swaraj, the discipline of living by his rules was essential. To him, the challenges of changing to this way of life were enough to toughen the individual for the risks of "aggressive" mass civil disobedience and for enduring its penalties.

A few days later, buoyed by the successful defiance of the bans and willingness to face imprisonment of Congress volunteers, he expressed the hope "conclusively" that "Bombay's aberration was an isolated instance in no way symptomatic of the general condition of the country." He added in support of this assessment: "A year ago it would have been impossible for the Government to arrest so many leaders of the front rank in so many parts of the country leaving the people absolutely self-controlled." (Gandhi, M.K. 1966: vol. 22: 13) In addition to Bardoli, two more talukas were asked to prepare for mass civil disobedience – Nadiad and Anand – both in Gujarat. Gandhi began to formulate the idea that, if the nominated talukas were not ready, then individual civil disobedience could take its place, though it "may mean some delay" in achieving swaraj. (Gandhi, M.K, 1966: vol. 22: 41-43)

Growing Pressure to Launch Mass Civil Disobedience

As the swaraj year ended and Ahmedabad prepared to stage the Congress annual session, Gandhi took up preparations in Bardoli again. The twin successes by then of the peaceful Calcutta hartal and the individual civil disobedience campaign, had helped put progressive nonviolent noncooperation back on track. The Viceroy's move towards a round table conference and the pressure to join negotiations from the moderates and some leading Congressmen, brought mass civil disobedience into focus as the ultimate sanction: Gandhi needed the expectation of mass civil disobedience as the next step for the extra pressure it would bring on the Raj. At the Ahmedabad Congress, the launch date was re-set for January 25.

By mid-January Gandhi was worrying that in Nadiad, some nonviolent fighters were so far from ready that they were prepared to take violent revenge on anyone who bought their confiscated property at auction. He asked Bardoli and Anand to provide assurances by 20 January that they were fit and ready. He also asked noncooperators who were proposing to stop paying revenue, to do it that day, rather than pay up just before the tax boycott began: "I hope the residents of the taluka will not first pay up and then declare they are ready for the fight." (Gandhi M.K. 1966: vol 22: 191-193)

The Congress working committee met in mid-January. No response had yet been received from the Viceroy to the latest proposals from the moderates group for a round table conference. The working committee agreed to postpone the launch of mass civil disobedience at Bardoli till January 31. (Gandhi M.K. 1966: vol 22: 210)

At the same time, Gandhi came under pressure from another province to permit a taluka to take the lead. Andhra, in southeast India, a province in the Madras presidency, had already taken up a no-tax campaign and the Congress leaders in Andhra wished the taluka of Guntur to be chosen to lead the nation's nonviolent revolt. Gandhi through the AICC had issued an invitation in November for provinces to submit bids if local communities in their area were ready to lead according to the conditions the working committee and AICC had laid down, and he had made his personal preference for Gujarat and Bardoli clear.

He responded cautiously and negatively to the request from Andhra, querying whether they were ready to sustain mass civil disobedience when they had not yet reached the specified targets on untouchability, non-violence or production of khadi cloth. However, he reluctantly conceded when the leader, Konda Venkatappayya (who was a member of the AICC), responded with great enthusiasm pointing out that there was considerable progress on untouchability and over 60% were wearing khadi. Moreover, to advise payment of taxes when some had already refused and were suffering distrainment of property and facing down military pressure, including armoured cars, would seriously jeopardise the provincial Noncooperation campaign. Gandhi replied: "You are the best judges of the situation. If conditions… are satisfied… I have no right to interfere. Godspeed… Keep me daily informed." (Gandhi M.K. 1966: vol 22: 211-212, 228, 228 fn1, 263)

Shortly before the Bardoli launch was due, Gandhi returned to check progress in the taluka and prepare to direct the nonviolent revolt. There he met what he called "the real workers", about 50 Congress volunteers who had been organising in the villages, and also with the president of the campaign, Vithalbhai Patel, and a few other workers. They agreed that another two weeks were needed to complete preparations.

With postponement in mind, he addressed a meeting of about 4,000 khadi-wearing "representatives" of the taluka, and stressed the lack of progress in two particular areas: untouchability and swadeshi. Failure to persuade untouchables to bring their children to join classes in the national schools he described as "negligence". Also, despite an increase, the number of hand-looms was still too few and Bardoli was not producing enough khadi cloth and clothing of its own, while the quantity of hand-spun yarn was insufficient and the quality variable. Not enough time was being devoted to spinning. After this rather negative opening, he said he was considering delaying for another 15 days.

However, according to Gandhi, the "brave and earnest workers of Bardoli would not listen to the postponement". He decided to take them through each of the "essential" conditions for starting mass civil disobedience. The conditions, bound by a vow, were reformulated as "beliefs". After outlining each one, he asked them to raise their hands to show they understood and agreed:

1. "As explained by me, do you regard promoting friendship of the Hindus, Muslims, the Parsis and the Christians as your sacred duty?

2. "Those who believe that, looking to India's present condition, only one method, that of non-violence, can bring us swaraj and secure justice, in regard to the Khilafat and the Punjab, may raise their hands.

3. "Those who believe that the country cannot reach her goal without adopting swadeshi and those brothers and sisters who have decided to give up the use of foreign or mill-made cloth and have resolved that they will not use khadi made outside the Bardoli taluka, may raise their hands.

4. "Do you believe that the practice of untouchability is contrary to dharma? Further are you ready to let [untouchable] children sit with yours in national schools?

5. "Without minding it if your crops, your cattle and property are seized and you are reduced to beggary, are you ready to lose your all and to go to jail – and all that without getting angry – for the sake of the country's honour?" (Gandhi M.K. 1966: vol 22: 294)[66]

Each belief was endorsed strongly by the crowd. Gandhi said later that the frankness shown to him by the representatives in Bardoli and the progress the taluka had made in preparing itself, persuaded him that it should be trusted with leading the nonviolent rebellion on behalf of the nation. (Gandhi M.K. 1966: vol 22: 287-294; 295-297; 333-334)

A meeting of the Congress working committee in Surat on 31 January approved the decision at Bardoli and requested the rest of the country not to embark on mass or individual civil disobedience unless explicitly endorsed by Gandhi.

---

66. Gandhi's Collected Works contains two versions of these conditions. This one, a translation of the original, was spoken to the crowd and published in Gujarati in Gandhi's paper *Navajivan*: it shows Gandhi seeking some reflection on the reason for the condition before asking for consent to it. The other, written in English for his paper *Young India*, is more formal and structured to appear like a conference resolution. (Gandhi M.K. 1966: vol 22: 296) (In so much of what he did, Gandhi was speaking to a number of audiences.) The questions in this translated record are of course "leading questions" and it may well have been hard to express dissent. However, as we shall see, a similar crowd in Bardoli was quite capable of expressing flat disagreement with Gandhi too.

Exchange with the Viceroy: the "Ultimatum"

Gandhi's next steps were to call for the resignation of all the village heads (patels) in Bardoli and to write to the Viceroy. Many of the *patels* had expressed interest in resigning their posts, an official position in each village under the Raj. Gandhi wished them to remain in their posts, at least for a temporary period. He asked them to place their letters of resignation in his hands, because he still had not lost hope that the government might have a change of heart. Once civil disobedience was announced, he would forward their letters to the government. He expected every patel to hand over their letter without delay. (Gandhi M.K. 1966: vol 22: 298)

Gandhi then drafted a letter to the Viceroy announcing his intention to launch mass civil disobedience in Bardoli, but delayed by 7 days to give the Raj time to reconsider its policy of "repression". (Subsequently it has been called his "ultimatum" letter.) (Gandhi M.K. 1966: vol 22: 302-305) It was a curious mixture of defiance, rebuke and blunt language; and also courtesy, admission of weakness, and limited demands. His letter was extraordinary in its underlying assumptions and the arguments he developed from them. He later called it his "manifesto". Effectively the gist of the "ultimatum" was as follows:

- The Raj should return to a position of "neutrality" while India was engaged in determining its own future by nonviolent means. The Viceroy (by the unjustified use of widespread repression) should not stand in the way of Indian public opinion working out its own future. And the Raj should permit the nonviolent Noncooperation campaign to continue its propaganda work of peaceful public speeches and meetings, demonstrations and picketing. It should allow the press to publish articles freely too.

- And it should also free the prisoners already wrongly jailed.

- If the Raj would show this change of heart, then Gandhi would suspend "aggressive" civil disobedience and discuss with the prisoners released from custody how best to proceed with Noncooperation.

When he explained the "ultimatum" to his Gujarati newspaper audience

346

a week later, he repeated a similar message. (Gandhi M.K. 1966: vol 22: 328-331)

- The government by adopting a policy of repression has introduced a smokescreen preventing the Indian public from seeing the real issues of swaraj, Khilafat and Punjab. This smokescreen created by repression needs to be cleared away.

Gandhi calls his ultimatum letter a "peace offer" and adds that the main aim of the planned action at Bardoli is to force an end to the repression.

"In the peace offer which has been dispatched from Bardoli... the demand that the Government should stop repression is given the first place... The task before Bardoli today is to secure the release of our fighters and compel the government to give up repression. If Bardoli achieves this, it will have done its job fully." (Gandhi M.K. 1966: vol 22: 331)

Gandhi was following his usual practice of keeping demands low and within the power of the opponent to concede. He is focused on the limited issues of civil liberties, rather than the goals of swaraj, Khilafat and Punjab. It was a key part of his method to use the strongest nonviolent methods in pursuit of a limited goal.

If Gandhi had succeeded in winning support throughout Congress and the Khilafat movement for this approach it might have had a powerful effect, but it is doubtful if the reasons for the leader lowering the demands were understood by the majority of members, nor agreed by them. The several postponements of mass civil disobedience and the adoption of this civil liberties campaign in preference to a focus on swaraj, were giving rise to the criticism that Gandhi was constantly changing his mind about the objectives to be pursued and the right method to use. The frequent changes were likely to have sown confusion in the volunteers.[67]

---

67. There is an interesting confirmation of the disruption caused by new initiatives from Gandhi's own ashram in Ahmedabad. The manager, Maganlal Gandhi, a cousin, was a dedicated constructive worker interested in technical innovation and training, particularly in agriculture. He complained that his work was regularly broken up by Gandhi's frequent changes of campaigning priorities,

This lowering of demands may also reflect Gandhi's original reluctance to launch Noncooperation on "the main issue" of swaraj; he preferred the confrontation to be on carefully chosen lesser issues, easier to win. His "bargain" with the Congress at the Calcutta special session had made swaraj the goal, but he was finding it hard to complete delivery of the plan of campaign. In his letter to the Viceroy he partly confirms this assessment, admitting that the movement does not have the strength to compel compliance from the Raj.

But Gandhi's "ultimatum" does not read like a peace letter. He complains that the Viceroy himself, by endorsing the brutal enforcement of the provincial bans on Congress volunteer organisations, has retreated from his earlier position of "neutrality". Previously, according to Gandhi, the Viceroy had permitted the Noncooperation campaign to develop without interference, provided it remained peaceful. Gandhi suggests this was an agreement the two of them had reached privately when they met for several days in Simla in May (and discussed Reading's complaint against the Ali Brothers). Making personal criticism of the Viceroy is of course contrary to the satyagraha principle of separating the person from the action to be condemned. Gandhi later defended his letter, not entirely convincingly, as follows:

> "It was not without deep thought and prayer that I wrote the letter to His Excellency the Viceroy. It is not a threat because every word in it is meant. It is a heartfelt prayer to the tyrant to desist from evil. Lord Reading is not the tyrant. The system of which he is himself the unconscious and helpless victim is the tyrant. But every system becomes embodied in a person. Today it is personified in Lord Reading, no matter how unconscious he is of it." (Gandhi M.K. 2016: vol 22: 368)

His statement that the "ultimatum" was not a threat addresses another criticism. As Gandhi saw it, the notification was not an attempt at intimidation but simply a forewarning of what Congress would do next. The Raj was being given a few days to change its policy and avoid confrontation.

---

taking the ashram inmates away from constructive projects to contribute to political campaigns. (Thomson 1993: 114-115)

Gandhi of course did not know that the British government had ordered Reading to make no concessions at all to the Noncooperation movement. If Reading had previously agreed to remain "neutral" while the Noncooperation movement remained nonviolent (which Gandhi clearly was convinced he had), he was no longer in a position to maintain that policy, even if he had wanted to. Gandhi, it seems, was reluctant to go ahead with mass civil disobedience, his long-promised "do-or-die" moment. He feared, as he effectively admits to the Viceroy, that noncooperators generally were insufficiently trained or prepared to follow the conditions he had prescribed. Later he remarked that the nonviolent pressure exerted by civil disobedience would accordingly be weaker. We also know that he feared the risk that aggressive civil disobedience accompanied by British repression might trigger widespread violence in other parts of India. He remains uncertain whether to use the Guntur taluka in Andhra as a second centre for the rebellion. He tells the Viceroy that he may ask the working committee to authorise "at once" mass civil disobedience in 100 villages in Guntur, "provided they can strictly conform to the conditions of nonviolence..." (Gandhi M.K. 1966: vol 22: 304)

Gandhi was going ahead in Bardoli rather against his better judgement. Perhaps, not having the control he wanted but committed to the next and final step, he found himself and the Noncooperation movement in a position where he could not turn back. Gandhi seems torn in the ultimatum letter between needing to justify employment of the most extreme weapon in his nonviolent arsenal, and a realistic expectation that, in a nonviolent rebellion against the crown, swaraj was not achievable at this point. It is not the letter of someone who expects to find a compromise. Anticipating a rejection of his letter, Gandhi decided to go ahead with the Bardoli revolt. (Gandhi, M.K. 1966: vol 22: 302-305, 331; Nanda, 1989: 339)

Gandhi was now committed and planning his next steps. A no-tax campaign would involve mainly the owners of land from higher castes, the Patidar farmers of Bardoli, who paid land taxes: the lower caste and non-caste groups were not greatly involved. Bardoli would have to do more to remedy this and the volunteers should ensure that the lower castes and untouchables were brought into the active movement. (Gandhi M.K. 1966: vol 22: 334-335) Also, he issued the first of a proposed series of leaflets to the people of Bardoli. In it, he advised that even though the government had the legal powers to confiscate land, he doubted that it would be uncivilised enough to do that. He also noted improvements in the admission of untouchables to an additional 16 national schools. (Gandhi, M.K. 1966: vol. 22: 336-337)

Reaction to the ultimatum letter

Members of the Congress working committee, when they met and discussed Gandhi's letter to the Viceroy, at first thought that he had dropped the Congress demands for swaraj, the Khilafat and the Punjab; and that the focus on civil liberties and willingness to suspend mass civil disobedience signified a substantial change in the Congress's campaigning strategy. In an interview with the *Bombay Chronicle* he described how he reassured them:

> "There is no change of front in the manifesto, but it is simple adaptability to the exigencies of the situation. Suppose you are making for a point and an impassable barrier has been placed in your way by the enemy. Your point of attack is naturally shifted and you will concentrate all your forces upon the barrier before you make further progress. That is what I have done with the full approval of the working committee." (Gandhi M.K. 1966: vol 22: 341)

When the Viceroy's reply (Gandhi M.K. 1966: vol 22: 512-515) was received on 6 February, it rejected in a peremptory manner all his charges of repression and his proposals for a change of policy. Gandhi was affronted. He dictated an immediate response sent the following day (Gandhi M.K 1966: vol 22: 334-350). He had expected a negative reply, but not the confident repudiation and questioning of his probity that he received. Rejection of his final "peace offer" meant that, at last, the moment for launching mass civil disobedience had arrived. However, news of a tragic confrontation that had occurred elsewhere on 4 February was just beginning to reach Gujarat.

Chauri Chaura and Bardoli

Mass civil disobedience at Bardoli was all set to proceed, when the news came through to Gandhi that "twenty-two" policemen[68] had been burnt to death as a result of a riot by noncooperators at a small market town in the United Provinces. Not knowing exactly what had happened nor how working committee members would react, Gandhi wrote a confidential note asking them to give their opinion in person (or by letter, or wire) at an urgent meeting in Bardoli on 11 February, and also "to consult all the friends you meet" and bring them, if they wished to come. His own opinion was clear:

> "The civil disobedience of Bardoli can make no impression upon the country when disobedience of a criminal character goes on in other parts of the country, both for the same end. The whole conception of civil disobedience is based upon the assumption that it works in and through its completely non-violent character... I personally can never be party to a movement half violent and half non-violent, even though it may result in the attainment of so-called swaraj, for it will not be swaraj as I have conceived it." (Gandhi M.K. 1966: vol 22: 350-351)

The two issues for discussion he said were, first, whether mass civil disobedience should be suspended "for the time being"; and, second, if suspended, whether it should be discontinued for a definite and long enough period for the country to organise constructive work and establish an "indisputable" non-violent atmosphere.

On the day before the hastily convened Congress working committee was due to meet, Gandhi called a meeting at Bardoli of the volunteer workers who were about to launch mass civil disobedience on his instruction. He asked them to discuss "the propriety or otherwise" of starting civil disobedience in face of the terrible events at Chauri Chaura. A note of the meeting says:

---

68. In his outstanding survey of the peasants who participated in the Chauri Chaura massacre and the impact on their lives and on their families of the subsequent arrests and court cases, Shahid Amin shows that the correct figure for deaths is 23. Amin argues that Chauri Chaura was damned unfairly, as a counter-symbol to Bardoli, by the nationalist movement. (Amin 1995)

"He asked for the opinion of everyone present... [A]lmost everyone young and old declared... that if Mahatmaji retreated after throwing out a challenge to Lord Reading in the manner he had done... the whole country would be disgraced before the world..."

Gandhi was uncompromising, even withering, in response. He said he had in front of him some of the best workers in the country. Since most of them had failed to understand the message of nonviolence, that convinced him that the country at large had "not at all accepted the teaching of non-violence". Therefore, he must immediately stop the movement for civil disobedience. (Gandhi M.K. 1966: vol 22: 377 and 377n)

Only three members of the Congress working committee were available to attend the following day's meeting in Bardoli. The committee reluctantly supported Gandhi. They agreed two sets of resolutions. The first deplored the inhuman conduct of the mob at Chauri Chaura, suspended mass civil disobedience at Bardoli, and instructed local Congress committees to stop tax refusal campaigns immediately and all other preparations for "aggressive" activity. It also advised, among other things, the tightening up of volunteer membership lists and removal of those not following the terms of the pledge.

The second set outlined a substantially revised eight-point Congress programme. Instead of an aggressive policy designed to bring the government to its knees, an almost entirely non-confrontational list of activities was announced. Noncooperation would now focus on developing the character and discipline in Congress workers (the "indisputable" atmosphere) that could support a return to more aggressive nonviolent methods at some indefinite point in the future when the preparation had been done. It was effectively a consolidation of the first two stages of Noncooperation and a restatement of various elements of the constructive programme:

1. A recruitment drive for Congress members

2. To popularise spinning and khadi manufacture

3.   To organise national schools

4.   To organise untouchables for a better life

5.   To take the temperance campaign into people's homes

6.   To organise village and town panchayats (village councils) for settling disputes

7.   To organise a social service department to offer help during illness or after accidents to all, irrespective of religion or caste

8.   To continue to raise money for the Congress through the Tilak Memorial Fund. (Gandhi M.K. 2016: vol 22: 377- 381)

These resolutions were then referred to the AICC meeting on 25 February for their approval. The next day Gandhi undertook a 5-day fast as a penance and a punishment for his burden of responsibility for Chauri Chaura.

Over the next few days and weeks, Gandhi learned that his adamant decision to stop mass civil disobedience in its tracks was an overwhelming disappointment not only to the Bardoli workers, but also to a number of his closest colleagues. Many of them expressed confusion and anger, particularly those who were in jail. Mahadev Desai was Gandhi's secretary and had worked with him for many years. From jail in Agra, he wrote to Gandhi saying that the working committee's resolutions at Bardoli had "absolutely unhinged him". Rajagopalachari, Gandhi's chief supporter in Madras, also in jail, wrote that he could not see the "logicality" of the decision. Motilal Nehru, one of Gandhi's earliest supporters and in jail, was reported to be furious; while Gandhi received a "freezing dose" from the imprisoned Jawaharlal Nehru. Das, the jailed Bengal leader, was "beside himself" with anger. Lajpat Rai, in Lahore jail, wrote about "the bitter pill of ignominious defeat". (Nanda 1989: 345-346; Nayar 1993: 394-395)

If the reaction of Congress leaders was a shock, the effect on Khilafatists was "shattering": they felt "let down, betrayed". (Nanda 1989: 357) But their anger against Gandhi was soon mitigated somewhat, or diverted, because events in the middle east were undercutting their whole position. First, the new military ruler in Turkey, Kamal Ataturk, a secular leader, was concentrating on restoring Turkey's own sovereignty and borders. He had no interest in preserving remnants of the old Ottoman empire, including the Caliphate.[69] Second, within months, the publication of official documents about the negotiations conducted at the end of the First World War showed that the Government of India and the India Office in London had tended unsuccessfully to support the Khilafat position. Consequently, the religious quarrel of the Indian Khilafatists with their British rulers lost its justification. (Nanda 1989: 362-371; 377-379)

A number of prominent Muslims remained active within the Congress and with Gandhi for some years (including the Ali brothers); others remained through to independence and beyond; but the active issue of the Khilafat cause itself ceased to be the driver, and Hindu-Muslim unity was gradually eroded.

When the AICC met in Delhi at the end of February to approve the working committee's Bardoli resolutions, opinion was overwhelmingly against them. Gandhi was forced to accept some amendments to get his proposals through. The AICC were not prepared to let all political activism be suspended. The amendments had the effect of permitting individual civil disobedience to continue, though not of course mass civil disobedience. Gandhi wrote later: "I got the votes because I was Gandhi and not because they were convinced..." He summed up, sadly: "[N]ot on... merits, but for my sake". (Nanda 1989: 345-347) Although individual civil disobedience was permitted to continue, the momentum of the movement was lost and its morale badly shaken.

Early in March, Gandhi was arrested, tried and jailed. He was charged with promoting disaffection against the state, which he could hardly deny, having argued for it consistently for months; but Gandhi of course was proud to plead guilty, arguing that his disaffection was so complete that

69. Ironically, representations from prominent Indian Muslims to the new Turkish leader, Ataturk, to preserve Muslim control of the Holy Places, were the trigger for him finally to abolish the Caliphate altogether. (Nanda 1989: 366-367)

he should be given the highest penalty. As in Champaran, the judge was placed in a difficult position, hugely impressed by Gandhi and reluctant to be too punitive. His solution was to sentence him explicitly to the same sentence that the former Indian nationalist hero, B.G. Tilak, had received in 1910: six years imprisonment. Gandhi expressed his gratitude for the compliment. (In the event, he fell ill, had a stomach operation in jail and, as a result, was released unconditionally in 1924.) For loyal Gandhians – the "no-changers" – Noncooperation continued in its revised, less confrontational form, but for many of the leading nationalists Gandhi's policy had failed and a new direction was to be attempted.

"Chauri Chaura", the name of the village where the policemen were murdered, was a symbol operating in the reverse direction to Gandhi's hoped-for symbol at Bardoli. It has achieved notoriety because, through the events there, his grand scheme of nonviolent rebellion was brought up short. The political impact of "Chauri Chaura" has caused it to be seen in the Gandhian narrative not just as an example of "criminal disobedience" but as a critical mis-step in India's progress towards independence.

Chauri Chaura was a railway marketplace, not far from the town of Gorakhpur, in the United Provinces in northern India. It had experienced Gandhi's power to mobilise large crowds a year earlier when his train stopped there and he briefly addressed a huge gathering. With Muhamad Ali as his companion during their tour promoting Noncooperation, Gandhi's train had stopped at every station. On the way back, the train passed through Chauri Chaura again before stopping overnight at another station some miles away, still in the Gorakhpur district, where again a huge and this time over-enthusiastic crowd greeted him.[70] The 1921 visit was effective in stimulating a network of Congress and Khilafat volunteer groups in the Gorakhpur district. (Amin 1995: 163-169)

---

70. The overnight stop at Salempur station in 1921 has become part of Gandhian folklore – showing the demands crowds made on him and the burden he placed on himself. While sleeping in the train, Gandhi was woken by members of a large crowd shaking him and demanding that he should get up and allow people to see him. Eventually he complied, stood in the open carriage doorway to give the crowd the glimpse they wanted, and visibly annoyed, struck his head several times in anger; the crowd eventually quietened down. (Amin 1995: 167-169)

A year later, as Congress volunteers prepared Bardoli for its decisive confrontation, the volunteer organisations in the Gorakhpur area had expanded rapidly and were actively engaged in picketing liquor stores and fish-stalls at the market near Chauri Chaura. One of the volunteers taking part was a former soldier; he was insulted and severely beaten up by a police sub-inspector. The next market day, 400 volunteers assembled from a number of surrounding villages and formed a procession, returning to the market as a protest against his treatment. One of the leading Congress volunteers recommended that the march be abandoned and, if not, be re-routed to avoid the local police station. He was shouted down. With large numbers of spectators joining in, the procession numbered 4,000 by the time it reached the police station.

The volunteers leading the procession had asked the crowd to throw away any sticks or *lathis* (batons) they were carrying and to remain nonviolent. However, when the procession had nearly passed the police station, the police, angered by jeering and shouting, were ordered to attack the marchers. The crowd was unarmed and it scattered, but at a nearby railway crossing stones were easily found. The police began to be overwhelmed and opened fire in the air and then into the crowd, killing two volunteers and injuring others. When their ammunition was exhausted, they retreated and barricaded themselves in the police station.

The crowd then went berserk, set fire to the building and would not allow the policemen to escape. Some volunteers tried to stop the massacre, others did nothing and some took part in the affray. Villagers from 60 villages had taken part, most from 5 villages near the police station. Later, following a massive crackdown, the Raj took its revenge and 172 villagers were sentenced to death. On appeal in Allahabad, the number acquitted was 38, while 19 had their death sentences confirmed and were hanged, 110 were transported for life and three jailed for two years. (Nanda 1989: 352-355)

The "Experiment" with Mass Civil Disobedience

As these details gradually came out (though the trials and sentencing of course did not take place until some months later), the argument of those shocked that Gandhi had called off "aggressive" Noncooperation became clearer. If Gandhi was going to suspend mass civil disobedience for such an infrequent but inevitable type of incident, then his method could not succeed. However, Gandhi was unmoved. He had said constantly that he feared such violence would upset his method. He had worked tirelessly to try to prepare the country so that this type of incident could be avoided, but too many were now occurring. What particularly concerned him was that Congress and Khilafat volunteers had played leading roles in the assault on the police station. With several hundred volunteers pledged to nonviolence in the crowd, he thought they ought to have been able to stop the march being routed past the police station and to stop the attack on it when it occurred. (Gandhi, M.K. 1966: vol 23: 1-4; Nanda 1989: 344-354.)

The nature of the method and strategy he was following at Bardoli meant it was almost inevitable that he would call off the action. Mass civil disobedience on a small scale as he had prescribed it, perhaps extending and escalating as other talukas joined in, required absolute attention and quiet in the rest of India. As the inhabitants of Bardoli suffered repression and cruelty from the forces of the Raj, so public opinion in India was to be aroused, nonviolent activism spread and the conscience of the Raj's officials and the British people touched. Ultimately, "Bardoli", the symbol of resistance, if carried through, was to have resulted in a new respect for the dignity, courage and organisational ability of the Indian people.

Probably it was an impossible scheme. Gandhi never attempted it again. But in the Salt Satyagraha in 1930, he organised a small group of seventy-nine handpicked and personally trained people to march across Gujarat and electrify the nation into support for his next national campaign of civil disobedience. While in 1928, the same taluka of Bardoli did undertake a successful tax refusal campaign – on a much more limited issue than swaraj – which helped to focus nationwide attention for the 1930 struggle.

357

"Chauri Chaura", however, has been seen by Gandhi's critics ever since, as the occasion for an enormous blunder by him. Subhas Chandra Bose commented in 1935:

"I am reminded of what the Deshbandhu (C.R. Das) used frequently to say about the virtues and failings of Mahatma Gandhi's leadership. According to him, the Mahatma opens a campaign in a brilliant fashion; he works it up with unerring skill; he moves from success to success till he reaches the zenith of his campaign – but after that he loses his nerve and begins to falter." (Bose 1935: 85)

Gandhi certainly was hesitant about launching mass civil disobedience late in 1921 and early in 1922. But the loss of nerve does not seem to be that of someone who fears to capitalise on his success. What appears to have happened is that Gandhi felt forced to change tactics and sound the retreat when a realistic assessment told him that his nonviolent civilian "army" was not sufficiently prepared and his hitherto successful method and strategy could no longer be followed. Gandhi in 1920 and 1921 was probably overconfident in his ability to organise the Indian subcontinent according to his principles of satyagraha. The painful reality became absolutely clear that mass civil disobedience would not give him and the Congress at that moment the necessary political leverage to negotiate with the Raj from a position of equality.

Gandhi was not prepared to settle for a "swaraj" which meant increased representation for Indian nationalist politicians in the provincial legislatures. As he had said consistently, the Raj's reforms did not interest Gandhi much, because he was seeking a "swaraj" which would mean real changes and improvements in the lives of the Indian "masses". This meant in parliamentary terms, for him, the achievement of full self-government at the centre "under the Congress Franchise" and with Dominion status.

By pursuing such an uncompromising vision of "swaraj", Gandhi was led to overestimate the bargaining-power that progressive nonviolent noncooperation, culminating in civil disobedience, could deliver for him and Congress at the time. He consistently presented his pursuit of satyagraha in politics as a series of "experiments". The experiment with

Non-cooperation showed that just eighteen months (August 1920 - February 1922) was too short a time to achieve across a large part of British India the "atmosphere" and discipline he considered he needed. Moreover, from surveys by Low in particular of the British willingness at this time to concede independence to India, it seems clear that Gandhi unwittingly exaggerated the possibilities for a change in British public opinion to meet his objectives. (Low 1966: 241-259)

In other words, Gandhi in 1921 was unrealistic in his hopes for swaraj. Civil disobedience was called off when he realised that the strategy he had been pursuing could not be sustained. It would have taken an even more extraordinary campaign of nonviolent pressure in 1921 and 1922 than the one Gandhi did organise, to have pushed the British remotely close to conceding his concept of swaraj. For this, India had to wait another 25 years, and even then it was not really the "parliamentary swaraj" which Gandhi had in mind.

SUMMARY (of Chapters 8 and 9)

1. Noncooperation was a partial success.

2. It did secure through the Triple Boycott, the active participation of a section of the nation's educated in a single-minded campaign to break with the Raj and build Indian institutions. It did through the Bezwada Programme raise vast sums of money and establish the Congress organisation as a viable political machine in many parts of the country. Also, it did, through the boycott of foreign cloth, draw Congress volunteers into villages across the whole country and give a tremendous boost to the swadeshi programme.

3. But the campaign was built around the slogan "Swaraj in One Year" and impatience began to grow as the year came to an end. When the Khilafat leaders finally broke ranks and called for the resignation of Muslims in government service, both civilian and military, the Raj was obliged to consider action against them. Gandhi, anxious not to lose control of Noncooperation and to maintain nonviolence, felt it necessary to devise a campaign as risky as the bonfires of foreign cloth – so as to

transfer the growing ill will "from men to things". The jailing of his allies, the Ali brothers, forced him to sanction individual civil disobedience, with repetition from public platforms of the offending words of the Ali brothers' resolution.

4. Through extensive touring of India (with the Ali brothers), Gandhi had become sceptical of the country's readiness to act nonviolently in a challenge to the Raj on a mass scale. But Noncooperation was rescued by an extended official tour visiting most of India by the Prince of Wales. Serious rioting following the hartal in Bombay led Gandhi to postpone his ingenious plan for mass civil disobedience in one small area of Gujarat, but elsewhere the national boycott of the Prince's visit was largely peaceful and effective. Government bans on Congress and Khilafat volunteer organisations were introduced in several parts of India, so as to prevent hartals and picketing of clothing and liquor stores. Thousands were arrested in a new campaign of "defensive" individual civil disobedience, especially effective in Bengal.

5. As individual civil disobedience began to spread and the Raj's bans on volunteer organisations saw large numbers of leading activists going voluntarily to jail, Noncooperation began to exert real pressure.

6. Inspired by this success, Gandhi revived plans for mass civil disobedience in a single taluka at Bardoli. But this action was postponed again as a result of pressure from moderate nationalist politicians who had information that the new Viceroy, Lord Reading, was willing to negotiate a settlement. To have achieved this offer of talks from the Viceroy was of course another significant achievement of Noncooperation. But Gandhi did not find Reading's offer acceptable and the negotiations collapsed – leading to much bitterness among Gandhi's fellow Congress leaders.

7. Progressive nonviolent noncooperation was a flexible method and could of course be scaled up or down. Gandhi considered that the Raj's "repression", with the bans on volunteers and their organisations, was preoccupying the movement and distracting non-cooperators from the goal of swaraj and the careful nonviolent programme designed to achieve it. He accordingly scaled down the demands issued to the Viceroy so as to focus on repression and the rights of free citizens denied by it –

freedom of the press, speech and assembly. This (temporary) damping down of objectives was strongly defended by him, but helped dismay and confuse Congressmen and Khilafatists alike, and the movement as a whole, who were focused on swaraj.

8. Gandhi then issued his ultimatum to the Viceroy that the Bardoli "aggressive" civil disobedience (which would be focused on the civil liberties objectives) was about to begin. But within days mass civil disobedience was called off instantly when he heard that major rioting in Chauri Chaura had resulted in the deaths of more than 20 policemen. This shattered the unity and morale of the Noncooperation movement and shortly afterwards, when Gandhi was jailed, the movement faded.

9. It seems possible that Noncooperation might have achieved negotiations with Reading late in 1921 (though not in January 1922) which might have led to increased nationalist participation in the Raj's provincial legislative councils. However, opposition from the British Cabinet in London makes this unlikely. Negotiations would have meant leaving the leaders of the Muslim supporters of Noncooperation, the Ali brothers, in jail – and increased representation in provincial councils was not at all what Gandhi meant by "parliamentary swaraj".

10. Faced with the symbolic warning of Chauri Chaura, which implied a spreading movement of violent outbreaks as against the spreading movement of nonviolence he had hoped to initiate at Bardoli, Gandhi had little option but to suspend mass civil disobedience. Not to have done so would have gone against the whole strategy which he had so painstakingly constructed since first formulating the concept of "progressive nonviolent noncooperation".

11. Like the Rowlatt satyagraha, Noncooperation collapsed but never formally ended; many "noncooperators" continued the struggle unceasingly until 1945. Within the Congress movement there were serious disputes about the "noncooperation" strategy to be followed – in particular whether "noncooperators" could enter the legislative councils of the Raj and engage in obstruction from within. The movement of progressive nonviolent noncooperation launched by Gandhi in 1920, was revived in a new form in 1930 and again in 1941.

12. Wound through the whole of the Noncooperation campaign was a strong thread of constructive programme, designed to pull the coalition of noncooperators together and provide a sound base for civil resistance campaigns.

POSTSCRIPT

Noncooperation was constructed on two "grand bargains":

(1) That the nationalist movement, promoted largely by the Hindu population, would, as an act of Hindu-Muslim unity, support India's Muslim population in insisting that their British rulers must defend the Muslim holy places in the middle east. Within that bargain, Gandhi sought and got agreement from key Muslim leaders that it was not against the teachings of the Koran for them to embrace a practical commitment to nonviolence.

(2) That the political leadership of the nationalist movement would support Gandhi's noncooperation programme for one year, despite their lack of experience with nonviolence (and disbelief in the satyagraha philosophy) and their reluctance to withdraw from the political councils of the Raj. Within that bargain was a commitment to nonviolence and agreement that the objective must be swaraj.

Once the swaraj year was over, Congress support for the Noncooperation programme was renewed by a resolution of the Ahmedabad annual Congress in 1921. However, despite that decision, some Muslim noncooperators took the view that they had pledged themselves to the nonviolence of the campaign for one year only; while many Hindu politicians thought similarly that a crucial part of the Noncooperation programme, their boycott of provincial councils, would need to be re-examined.

During the swaraj year and beyond, both groups had honourably followed Gandhi's programme and put themselves directly in the firing line by voluntarily seeking arrest and in many instances going to jail. Both groups had been willing to support, and were indeed impatient for, the move to aggressive civil disobedience in the final stage of Noncooperation, to be launched at Bardoli. Its abrupt suspension allowed Muslim leaders to withdraw from their conditional pledge of nonviolence; and it deprived leading Congressmen of the cutting edge which encouraged them to believe that Gandhi's programme could best advance their ambitions for political power and eventually swaraj.

We have briefly noted the deflating effect on the Muslim non-cooperators and their Khilafat campaign of the settlement, ignoring their wishes, reached by the western powers in the middle east. With no progress on the Punjab issue either and independence as far away as ever, many congressmen decided Congress now needed a new spine or focus for its campaigning. The solution was to go back to the councils and continue there the challenge to the Raj.

With Gandhi in jail, Congress divided into two main factions. There were those, the "No-changers", the convinced Gandhi supporters, who decided to follow the 8-point noncooperation programme Gandhi had outlined as the next step and to carry out his proposals, principally for constructive work and for strengthening the Congress and volunteer organisations. The other group favoured "council entry". The latter formed their own party, the Swarajists, who before long took the leadership of Congress and campaigned for political reforms within the Raj's system as a route to independence.

When Gandhi came out of jail, he rejoined his supporters and toured the country promoting his social programme; but Congress, including members of the Swaraj Party, continued to seek his advice and eventually invited him back to lead a new campaign.

PART IV

CHAPTER 10

GANDHI'S METHOD IN THE WEST

From the Margins

In most of the years reviewed in this book, Gandhi was not yet the established national leader who could command automatic attention and veneration. This makes his activities particularly interesting because, for this short period, he was more nearly in the position of other nonviolent political activists who do not command the allegiance of masses of people and a political machine, but who are at the margins of political life looking for a way in.

As a newcomer to Indian politics with a distinctive political philosophy Gandhi found his place in the nationalist movement at a time of economic and political turmoil. The consequent uncertainty made it possible for a novel political doctrine like satyagraha to be introduced as a bright new strand in Indian political life. But this impact for Gandhi's "experiments" with nonviolence was not achieved without much effort and skill. Practical choices faced him as an organiser about what issues to take up, which groups to involve, what methods to pursue and to what lengths he should go in order to achieve the results he was seeking.

Many Indian nationalists were to be captivated by Gandhi's ideas and proposals; many more adopted some aspects of the satyagraha programme while it was the policy of the national movement or while it was fashionable to do so. As a result Gandhi became a pre-eminent national figure with unprecedented authority. From this position, Gandhi continued with his satyagraha "experiments" apparently no more afraid to take personal risks than before. His unusual position at the centre of political life, however, gave him the opportunity as a political organiser to experiment increasingly with methods of nonviolent action which only someone in his place could have attempted.

The remarkable fasts of his later years to influence his fellow countrymen on questions of Hindu-Muslim unity and the abolition of untouchability can be repeated in most situations only by national political leaders of similar prominence. Quite probably a symbolic march, like the Salt March which Gandhi led in 1930, would require a personality of his renown at its head to command the attention and precipitate the mass imitative action which that demonstration did. Thus the years in India before Gandhi had achieved his position as "Father of the Nation" are particularly worthy of attention for students of nonviolent action who want to know how a nonviolent movement, which had a major impact, was planned and organised by someone on the edge of the political mainstream.

The case-material presented in this book can be grouped broadly into three periods. The first period, up to 1918 and including the Champaran, Ahmedabad and Kheda satyagrahas, was the period when he was searching for ways to introduce his ideas and methods into Indian politics. The actions he attempted were principally local in their scope and focused on particular issues or grievances. His successes brought him and his movement to prominence in Gujarat. The second period sees Gandhi in transition to national leadership and is pivotal to this study. Gandhi attempted in 1919 from his base of support in Gujarat and Bombay city to initiate a national campaign on the particular issue of the Rowlatt Bills. As a mass action this lasted for less than a month and as an ongoing campaign it survived only six months before petering out. Shaken by the rioting and repression which Rowlatt catalysed, Gandhi rethought his approach and began casting around for other ways to launch nonviolent action on a mass scale.

In the summer of 1920, the third period begins with Gandhi's decision to initiate a second national satyagraha campaign, combining two particular grievances, the Khilafat and Punjab issues, and quickly taking on the general issue of swaraj. A key contention in this book is that Gandhi's principal response to the Rowlatt debacle was to devise an additional method of mobilising civilians on a mass scale, which fell short of civil disobedience and other methods of civil resistance. This was to initiate a co-ordinated programme of constructive work, including the Triple Boycott and then the Bezwada Programme, which can be seen to have evolved later into the constructive programme.

Organising Methods

In addition to this fundamental question of the balance between civil resistance and constructive work in Gandhi's method, a number of other related themes have been explored. These include how his methods as an organiser changed as he moved from local to national campaigns. Also, how he adapted his method of organising on particular issues to the problem of launching a mass movement on the general issue of swaraj. Again, how he adapted his approach when he came to lead coalitions of political activists most of whom were not convinced upholders of his satyagraha ideology.

Two other features of Gandhi's method have been noted. In the early campaigns in Gujarat we saw the fundamental importance to his campaigning of the religious vow – this was one of the principal techniques he employed for introducing the religious spirit into politics. The other is the distinction he made in 1920 and 1921 between aggressive and defensive civil disobedience. These tactics were pursued within a gradually worked out plan of "progressive nonviolent non-cooperation".

For followers of Gandhi in India, most of these points are familiar. In particular, the contention that Gandhi's method employed a careful balance between negative and positive – between campaigns of civil resistance and constructive programme – with the priority given to constructive work, is wholly unexceptionable. Several of the other points are also widely reported in works by Dhawan (1957), Diwakar (1946), N. K. Bose (1947), and so on.

However, in the west, the principal authorities on nonviolent action have neglected practically all these aspects – with the partial exception of the vow. In particular, the fundamental point that nonviolent action as a method and technique focused just as much on constructive work as campaigns of civil resistance, has been virtually ignored. Yet Gandhi's successes as an organiser cannot be understood unless it is recognised that at the base of every campaign of civil resistance – especially at the national level – was a programme of constructive work.

Looking at his method narrowly as a conflict technique, there's a tendency to abstract the conflict experiments from the overall package and lose a full appreciation of how it was done. Looking at Gandhi as an organiser, and seeking to identify all the resources and methods he employed and how he utilised them, we can get a better idea of how his campaigns worked.

The Purpose of Constructive Work

Faced with the problems we have indicated, Gandhi turned to a programme of constructive work almost as a panacea. (Dhawan 1957: 190-208) Constructive work was designed to discipline the people prior to civil disobedience. It was to provide tasks some of which could be taken up by the poorest peasants and give them a place in the national movement. It was designed to provide a link between the national political elite and the peasantry and to take active nationalists out of the Raj's legislatures to the "real" politics of India, tackling poverty and injustice in the villages. It was used too not only as a preparation for civil disobedience but also as a delaying tactic. Until the targets were reached and the "capacity" of the nation demonstrated, civil disobedience could or should not be launched

Again, promotion of constructive work helped Gandhi deal with the problem of scale, moving from a local level where he could preserve face-to-face contact to a national level where he could not. If it was impossible to rely on inexperienced satyagraha leaders to launch civil resistance campaigns across the subcontinent, what he could do with much less risk was to invite them to introduce the nation to campaigns of constructive work.

Constructive work too helped Gandhi to deal with the problem of campaigning on a general issue rather than a particular issue. Before

367

Quit India in 1942, he insisted on launching "do-or-die" struggles on limited, particular issues capable of achievement. Swaraj, full political self-government, was a general goal not likely to be achieved in 1920. However, re-interpreted in Gandhi's concept as the development of a nation organised, united, self-reliant and capable of solving its own economic and social problems, swaraj could be approached as a general issue by a programme of constructive work.

Again, moving solidly into the political arena when he entered political organisations like the Congress and the Home Rule League, Gandhi knew he would be unable to find unity at the highest levels behind his distinctive satyagraha ideology. Accommodation with the nationalist elite was buttressed therefore by mass constructive campaigns, which (after the Triple Boycott) were in significant respects politically uncontentious or innocuous and designed to develop unity in the mass movement at the base. They served in effect to undercut opposition to Gandhi at the top.

Scholars in the West: Bondurant

Satyagraha as a method has been the subject of a number of scholarly studies published in the west. The best known of these originally were published during Gandhi's lifetime or within 20 years of his death – Richard Gregg's *The Power of Nonviolence* (1960), Krishnalal Shridharani's *War without Violence* (1962), and Joan Bondurant's *Conquest of Violence: The Gandhian Philosophy of Conflict* (1965) – and developed a common theme expressed by the subtitle of Bondurant's work. This is that in satyagraha Gandhi demonstrated a method and a philosophy of engaging in conflict, which can be developed as an effective substitute for political violence. Shridharani and Gregg go further and urge that nonviolent conflict can replace war as a method of settling disputes between nations, a theme taken up subsequently by Gene Sharp and a number of other scholars.

When scholars make such claims for their interpretations of Gandhi's method it is extremely important that they present them in a way that makes it possible to understand how he used and developed the technique in practice. Bondurant comes very close to the explanation

368

of Gandhi's method developed in this book when she defines satyagraha as "a technique for social and political change"; or again "an instrument of struggle for positive objectives and for fundamental change". Clearly this is more than a conflict technique in her eyes. (Bondurant 1965: 3-4)

She states too in one section:

> "The constructive program was an essential component of the Gandhian revolutionary struggle for Indian independence. It was the constructive program which gave content to the satyagraha framework and applied Gandhian principles to the Indian circumstance." (Bondurant 1965: 180)

Nevertheless, the balance of her especially valuable study of satyagraha is overwhelmingly on the conflict side. "I have tried only", she writes, "to attack a problem inadequately explored in political theory by abstracting from the Gandhian experiment a theoretical key to the problem of social and political conflict." (Bondurant 1965: xiv)

The place of constructive programme within her analysis is understated and ambiguous. She tends to see it as an ideal goal or a prescription for moral conduct, rather than as a method of mobilising people for social change. Primarily it is presented as a subsidiary discipline and necessary demonstration of social rectitude to be taken up for the duration of a direct action campaign, rather than as an autonomous part of the satyagraha method, to be followed and organised for its own sake.

Gregg, Shridharani and Sharp

Richard Gregg, as we have seen, was personally a satyagrahi in the full Gandhian sense – one who believed that the essence of the technique is to apply a number of disciplines in one's own life and to build out from there a political movement. In *The Power of Nonviolence* he devotes the final portion of the book to the type of "training" needed to engage in nonviolent resistance. He also repeats his prescription for taking up manual work and social service projects. (Gregg 1960: 141-175) There is, though, a complete divorce between the idealised proposals in Gregg's concluding argument and the powerfully presented case studies of nonviolent resistance with which the book begins. His abstract presentation, unrelated to the historical examples, fails to show how constructive programme was an integral part of the method of satyagraha developed by Gandhi. Also, constructive work is seen as a personal discipline for individuals and small groups rather than a programme of campaigns to be waged on social issues as part of a larger political struggle.

Shridharani took part personally in the Salt March in 1930 and his book, *War Without Violence,* first published in 1939, remains an inspiring and persuasive argument for learning from Gandhi's campaigning methods. (Shridharani 1962) His work includes a chapter on "organisation" which describes in outline the Congress machinery for conducting satyagraha campaigns. But the dynamic process of Gandhi actually organising satyagraha, that is, making decisions as an organiser, is still missing from his account. Gene Sharp rightly claimed Shridharani as a pioneer of the "technique approach" to nonviolent struggle – by which Sharp meant nonviolence as a technique for engaging in conflict divorced from any necessary connection with Gandhi's philosophy of life. (Sharp 1979: 315-318)

Sharp himself has been overwhelmingly the most important theoretician of nonviolent action in the west and made it a life's work to establish the technique on a body of case-material and theoretical argument which separates it from Gandhi's particular philosophy and beliefs. He was not however in any way hostile to Gandhi and remained profoundly respectful of him. A collection of essays he published, *Gandhi As a Political Strategist,* (1979) demonstrates successfully that Gandhi himself was willing to make a distinction between nonviolence as a philosophy and nonviolence as a policy or expedient, and that Gandhi organised his satyagraha campaigns fully understanding that most of those who supported him did so as a temporary and sometimes unwanted discipline for the period of the struggle only. The collection includes an excellent short summary of Gandhi's satyagraha method and a brief, accurate representation of the importance of constructive programme in Gandhian theory. (Sharp 1979: 219-221)

What Sharp signally failed to do, however, in his enormous compendium of theory and case-material, *The Politics of Nonviolent Action,* is describe adequately how Gandhi's method of action worked in practice. (Sharp 1973) The reason is that Sharp did not look at Gandhi as an organiser, a politician making strategic choices and tactical decisions about how to shape the campaigns he is directing. Where Sharp considers strategy and tactics it is in the context of a pre-existing nonviolent struggle. How Gandhi found himself as leader of mass campaigns of noncooperation or civil disobedience is outside Sharp's brief, which is essentially to analyse how nonviolent struggles were conducted once they started. In particular, the place and role of constructive programme in Gandhi's method, is almost entirely missing.

Each of these major theoreticians of nonviolent action did understand Gandhi's method fully and then chose to tailor their presentation of it to what they thought was most significant in his achievement. They also followed Gandhi's broad principle of "*swadeshi*" (cultivating that which is local) by attempting to translate satyagraha into terms which are assimilable for readers whose background is in the political and social culture of the west.

Bondurant explains the basis on which she selected from his method as follows:

"It is essential rigorously to differentiate satyagraha as technique of action from those specific considerations of right living with which Gandhi also concerned himself." (Bondurant 1965: 12)

Sharp draws attention to the personal battles he had to endure with "dogmatic" Gandhians and pacifists over many years, as he maintained his revisionist attitude to the Gandhian method. (Sharp 1979: 251fn)

The studies of these scholars are in my opinion as important historically as their authors claim because they do demonstrate that there is another way of fighting and of exercising power not based in violence, a perspective which is not readily recognised in political theory and practice. However, by presenting Gandhi's method for a western audience with such a single-minded emphasis on conflict – particularly war and the takeover of state power – they narrowed the focus of their analysis in such a way that, unfortunately, it is difficult to understand how Gandhi's campaigns were built up and sustained. Methods of engaging in conflict have been separated from methods of mobilising the social and political movement equipped to engage in conflict.

This is not an argument for taking over Gandhi's beliefs wholesale before engaging in nonviolent struggle. But Bondurant is surely mistaken when she says that it is necessary rigorously to differentiate satyagraha as a technique of action from Gandhi's hobbyhorses regarding "right-living". It helps us to understand Gandhi's technique if we see it as a method of social struggle informed by strongly held positive values, with rules about how we approach people and present ourselves and with a vision of how life could be better, virtually all of which may some have relevance for us. It appears to me that the attempt to separate the technique of action from the background of beliefs and social initiatives which supported it, has diminished our understanding of the technique.

Strategic nonviolence

After Sharp published *The Politics of Nonviolent Action* in 1973, his voice was the predominant one in discussion of nonviolent action, not least because he continued to publish prolifically, but also because a number of succeeding scholars have built their work from the foundations he provided. They have tended to move even further away from Gandhi's "principled" method. Partly this can be explained by the many decades now separating us from the years when Gandhi was alive and active. But another explanation is the desire to compare nonviolence with violence and to present the former as a method more effective than violence in some or many situations. As we have seen, Gandhi himself made this comparison, consistently arguing that nonviolence was the most realistic option for Indian nationalists under the Raj.[71] However, for western scholars, a necessary part of validating nonviolent action came to be the downgrading or disavowal of principled nonviolence.

---

71. He claimed consistently to British officials that his advocacy of nonviolence was restraining the Indian national movement from much worse disruption and breakdown of civil order – and convinced the Khilafat leaders, and then the Congress itself, that they would not succeed if they turned to violent uprisings, but could if they followed his methods.

A key text from Peter Ackerman and Christopher Kruegler in 1994, *Strategic Nonviolent Conflict: The Dynamics of People Power in the 20ᵗʰ Century,* makes a point of separating their arguments from principled nonviolence (Ackerman and Kruegler 1994: x, xii):

> "As behavioral phenomena, nonviolent sanctions are not equivalent to or synonymous with any of the philosophies of principled nonviolence, such as pacifism or satyagraha... Nonviolent sanctions as behaviours are different from the value systems of the people who may occasionally engage in them". (Ackerman and Kruegler 1994: 4)

They note that their studies have found few examples of strategic nonviolent conflict where principled nonviolence was followed.

The result is that they take their presentation of strategic nonviolence even further away from Gandhi's methods, despite a case study of the Salt Satyagraha of 1930-1931. Their interest is in conflict and a focus on better ways of confronting state power and ousting unjust or repressive regimes. Where Gandhi's strategic aim, at least in theory, would be win-win (where both parties go away satisfied), they are adamant that the strategic objective is win-lose (where one side is victorious and the other is defeated). The win-lose philosophy is probably not a good starting point for understanding what Gandhi was doing and how he went about it. (Ackerman and Kruegler: xx, 4, 5, 9,14)

The authors follow their predecessors by endeavouring at a strategic level to separate out those elements of satyagraha they deem useful. For example, they accept that "constructive work" can play a part in enhancing "the environment in preparation for waging conflict". (Ackerman and Kruegler 1994: 49) They then add a footnote:

> "Our use of the phrase 'constructive work' is compatible, but not precisely synonymous with, Gandhi's usage. In his philosophy, a constructive program was a voluntary effort outside the aegis of the state, which had the dual purpose of redressing material inequalities and training the participants to be more competent and self-reliant. We refer to positive actions that can be taken primarily with a view to improving the material situation in

which a conflict may be developed." (Ackerman and Kruegler 1994: 53 fn 18)

Such a limited presentation leaves the reader short of understanding the contribution Gandhian constructive programme can play in strategic nonviolent method.

The authors acknowledge Gandhi for the outstanding exponent of a strategic approach to nonviolent conflict he was, and do at one point capture the argument of this book when they observe: "Satyagraha is both a form of principled nonviolence and a technique of political action" (Ackerman and Kruegler 1994: 162). They fault Gandhi correctly too for taking too much onto himself when he should have acted more closely with colleagues to share the burden of key decisions. However, because the authors are unwilling to engage with Gandhi's method of satyagraha on its own terms, they disable themselves from seeing its complexity and promise.

The Place of Principled Nonviolence

In the 21st century, studies on nonviolent action began to move even further away from Gandhi's example. This development was not because the attempt was still being made actively to distinguish principled from pragmatic nonviolence, but because it appeared to be taken for granted that principled nonviolence was largely irrelevant.

For example, in the enormous sweep of their valuable and influential book, *Why Civil Resistance Works: The Strategic Logic of Nonviolent Conflict*, Erica Chenoweth and Maria Stephan mention Gandhi just once (2011: 56). Their central focus is on a statistical analysis of several hundred historical case examples between 1900 and 2010 of violent and nonviolent uprisings. It demonstrates that nonviolent campaigns are more likely to succeed than violent ones. A key theme is that nonviolent insurgencies tend to secure the "participation" of a larger proportion of the population in "antiregime" and "antioccupation" campaigns [note: these are the authors' spellings] than violent ones, and may polarise society less: "barriers to participation are much lower for nonviolent resistance than for violent insurgency". (2011:10)

This finding of course accords with the assessments Gandhi made of India's position in face of the Raj (taking up violence was not a realistic option) and of how to mount an effective campaign that repudiated violence (involve as activists and supporters the largest numbers of people and groups). But Chenoweth and Stephan do not mention constructive programme.

Towards A More Balanced Approach

Another current scholar who favours pragmatic over principled nonviolence is the political sociologist Kurt Schock. He is not one, though, who excludes consideration of the principled approach altogether. In his book, *Unarmed Insurrections: People Power Movements in Nondemocracies*, Schock presents principled nonviolence straightforwardly as one approach with a role to play, even if it is unlikely to be the dominant one. (Schock 2005: xv, xvii, 11, 36-37, 122) His case studies include uprisings in the Philippines, Burma and Nepal as well as China, Thailand and South Africa. His balanced approach is refreshing and may help encourage greater interest in the methods of those who have favoured a principled approach.

Schock is an advocate for Sharp's presentation of nonviolent conflict, but not uncritical. At one point he claims that Sharp "undertheorises… as a technique of nonviolent action" the development of "alternative structures… to promote social and political change". He adds:

"Autonomous structures may gradually develop…or… may be consciously established through establishing constructive programs, developing autonomous organizations, appropriating existing organizations and, more generally, extending the sphere of oppositional civil society". (Schock 2005: 45)

More recently, Sharon Erickson's Nepstad's textbook, *Nonviolent Struggles: Theories, Strategies and Dynamics* provides evidence that Gandhi's method may be regaining its place in nonviolent scholarship alongside Sharp's pragmatic nonviolence. (Nepstad 2015: 4-22). She describes the beginnings in the 1920s of academic study of Gandhi's achievements, followed by Sharp's work over several decades starting in the 1950s; and shows how Gandhi's ideas and methods were "diffused" to North America with the US civil rights movement. She outlines Gandhi's strategic approach to developing nonviolent campaigns in India, and recognises the importance of constructive programme:

> "While civil resistance is aimed at the opponent, constructive programs are aimed at building one's own community". (Nepstad 2015: 54)

She also makes comparisons between the two approaches to nonviolence associated with Gandhi and Sharp and begins with a table showing the distinctions between them (Nepstad 2015: 5) as shown in Table 10.1.

The table is useful in suggesting some key distinctions between the two approaches, but I find myself uneasy with it. It is designed to highlight key distinctions, but in practice goes further as if it is contrasting main points in the methods of both. Sharp drew hugely on the Gandhian model in formulating his "pragmatic" nonviolence and decided to jettison points such as those listed in the left-hand column. But still a large amount of practical Gandhian nonviolent action remained. If the table was indeed making a comparison between the two approaches, much of what is shown on the right should properly be shown in the left column too.

When I look down the Sharpian column, of the nine attributes given to pragmatic nonviolence, arguably seven could be allocated in whole or in part to Gandhian nonviolent action. From each of the case examples I have discussed, for example, it is clear that he always asked himself "what will work?" and he regularly argued that violence was ineffective. It is true that he always hoped to change hearts and minds, but he was obliged to settle most often for a change in behaviour.

And of course it is inconsistent with what we have seen in the case studies to suggest that Gandhi was interested simply in "personal and social transformation" (by implication, an over-idealistic and remote goal), but not in transforming specific social institutions. He was interested in specific transformations of institutions such as the British Raj's legal, education and land-tax systems or, slightly differently, its callous racism in failing to express remorse for the Amritsar massacre. It is true that Gandhi was not much interested in pursuing limited reforms to the

Table 10.1: Distinctions between Pragmatic and Principled Nonviolence

Principled (Gandhi)	*Pragmatic (Sharp)*
MOTIVE	MOTIVE
1. Ethics: violence is wrong; nonviolence is the most ethical response to conflict	1. Practicality: violence is ineffective or too costly
2. Often has a religious or ideological basis	2. Secular basis
3. Key question: What is the moral way to respond?	3. Key question: What will work?
GOALS	GOALS
4. Changing the opponent's heart and mind	4. Changing the opponent's behaviour
5. Personal and social transformation	5. Transformation of a social institution
6. Ending all violence and establishing social justice	6. Ending all violence and establishing social justice
7. Seeks a win-win solution; opponents are seen as partners in the struggle to meet the needs of all parties	7. Is satisfied with a win-lose outcome: opponents are seen as antagonists with incompatible interests
TECHNIQUES	TECHNIQUES
8. Avoids coercion, emphasises persuasion and understanding	8. Willing to use nonviolent coercion
9. Moral jiu-jitsu: suffering is means of transforming self and others	9. May try to avoid suffering but emphasises political jiu-jitsu

constitutional arrangements for India permitted by the Raj, but he devoted huge energy to a specific project to completely remodel the Congress organisation and its constitution.

Gandhi as an idealist did not necessarily expect his ideals to be realised in the real world, nor in his lifetime, but attempted to discipline himself and his followers to do the very best they could. I have identified his pragmatism in all the case studies. It consisted in finding the most appropriate solution without compromising fundamental principles. My argument has been that separating Gandhi's values and vision from pragmatic nonviolence has made it hard to understand how Gandhian nonviolence actually works.[72] Fortunately, Nepstad herself does not disagree with this: she concludes:

"… [T]he bifurcated view of principled and pragmatic nonviolence does not adequately convey the areas of overlap between these two traditions. … We should not falsely characterize them as polar opposites". (Nepstad 2015: 12)

A Reviving interest in Gandhi

Two American community organisers, the brothers Mark and Paul Engler, have produced a highly original book, *This is an Uprising: How Nonviolent Revolt is Shaping the Twenty-first Century*. Its approach is different from the others cited because its focus is on day-to-day political activism. It describes how political campaigners can use lessons from local and national struggles in many settings to inform their own actions.

The Englers take Gandhi as the most important figure in the development of nonviolence: "Both [Martin Luther] King and Sharp saw themselves as standing in his shadow". (Engler and Engler 2017: 13) And they use insights and examples from the work of each of these three figures

---

72. There has been a reluctance to look closely at what Gandhi actually did, a failure to distinguish between his rhetoric and his practice, or rather to understand the role of rhetoric in his practice. His rhetoric was almost always aimed at his highest ideals, but these were placed behind his practical proposals, so the two are not in conflict with each other but mutually reinforcing.

throughout the book. They also take the work of two well-known American community organisers, Saul Alinsky and Frances Fox Piven, to provide a useful framework for how nonviolence can be developed in future. The Engler brothers look at Gandhi as an outstanding political organiser.

The brothers are most interested in mass civil disobedience, which they see as creating significantly disruptive events with the effect of making major social and political changes possible; but they also recognise the amount of work that may be needed to trigger a "whirlwind" event:

"More than the work of any other individual, it was Gandhi's experiments in nonviolent escalation that laid the foundation for the modern field of civil resistance. But to sustain his work over a period of more than fifty years, Gandhi used a full range of social movement approaches, including structure, momentum driven-organizing and the creation of prefigurative community." (Engler and Engler 2017: 277)

Examples of these "social movement approaches" can be drawn from the case studies in this book. "Structure" would include, for instance, the overhaul of the Indian National Congress. "Momentum-driven organising" includes the ratcheting up of enthusiasm and tension as a campaign like Noncooperation develops and grows. The "prefigurative community" is represented by long-term alternative projects, like a constructive programme. In a bold step (for those who know the objections so many make to the Gandhian concept of self-suffering), the Englers also include "sacrifice" and "suffering" as an unavoidable part of the conflict method they propose.

Another recent book seeks to locate nonviolence within a substantially different theoretical framework from that constructed by Sharp. In his book *A Theory of Nonviolent Action: How Civil Resistance Works* (2015), the sociologist, Stellan Vinthagen, puts a number of Gandhian values firmly back into his definition. He does not reject Sharp but draws directly from Gandhi to construct a new model of nonviolent action, which is brought up to date in the light of major developments in social theory and in the practice of nonviolent action in the years since the two, Gandhi and then Sharp, each developed their ideas.[73]

Vinthagen does not restore all Gandhi's ideas of "right living" and, quite explicitly, adapts or ignores some of his concepts. He broadens out the model of nonviolent action by including not only Sharp's key concept of the vulnerability of a dominant or illegitimate power to popular nonviolent noncooperation (termed "power-breaking"), but also adds three more aspects. These are, first, the development of social norms which reinforce nonviolence ("normative regulation"). Second, a better understanding of how dialogue can work within campaigning groups and with the opponent, so as to improve communication and potential co-operation ("dialogue facilitation"). And third, the presentation in nonviolent action of forms of utopian witness, which can give the opponent, together with the watching public, a better sense of what supporting and taking up nonviolent action might mean for them ("utopian enactment"). Each of these four strands is necessary for his theory of nonviolent action to hold and be effective, not just "power-breaking" as advocated by Sharp. (Vinthagen 2015: 300-309, 304-305 fig 8.2)

Thus nonviolence is restored as a principled or moral force to be taken up by a movement for social liberation and wholesale political change. Drawing on prominent social theorists like Habermas, Foucalt and Bourdieu, as well as Sharp's specialist contribution, Vinthagen constructs his sociological model with a new vocabulary that takes some time to grasp. He stresses that nonviolent actions must be simultaneously "without violence" and "against violence", meaning that in fighting against violence we do not use violence. At its heart the movement commits to building a free society while confronting obstacles in the present society. All actions address practical objectives in the present, geared to a long-term goal.

---

73. Vinthagen also acknowledges his debt to the Norwegian philosopher, Arne Naess, whose attempt to reconstruct Gandhian philosophy and method as a coherent doctrine for a western audience (Gandhi and Group Conflict, 1974) has long been neglected.

Drawing on his experiences with a deeply embedded nonviolent movement in Brazil, Vinthagen includes constructive programme as an important part of a nonviolent culture (Vinthagen 2015: 288-296):

"... [It] is not limited to liberal forms of protest and claims-making but is about enacting and living both the alternative and the resistance... [and]...is co-ordinated collectively like Gandhi's constructive programme..." (Vinthagen 2015: 297)

Vinthagen's analysis attracts controversy, because it proposes many challenging ideas, not least its attempt to rescue the study of nonviolence from its presentation predominantly as a conflict technique (in some respects like a martial art or an alternative option for military strategists). The nonviolence he constructs acts in society as a force to challenge illegitimate power and transform the whole society for the common good.

Taking these two very different books together there may be a willingness emerging to engage again with Gandhi and take nonviolence forward in an updated form. That is, as a social and political doctrine as well as a conflict method.

CHAPTER 11

CONSTRUCTIVE AND OBSTRUCTIVE METHODS

From the evidence of the case studies we can now derive a better understanding of how Gandhi organised his campaigns. We can also suggest some additional features to a standard description of the satyagraha method itself.

In a study which draws its case material almost entirely from only seven years of Gandhi's career in India (from 1915 to 1922), it is not possible to draw final conclusions about Gandhi's methods throughout his career. It is not possible either to attempt a detailed analysis of the place of constructive work in his method on the evidence of this early period. However, there are a number of conclusions from the study, which do appear to have resonance throughout his years of campaigning and organising.

Local and National Organising

In local struggles Gandhi was able to play a highly visible part in the action, directing many matters personally and taking much of the burden of civil resistance onto his own shoulders. When he moved onto a national scale and tried to repeat this pattern, the level of organisation proved to be inadequate and discipline broke down. As a result, Gandhi adapted his organising methods in several respects.

First, instead of relying on individuals who broadly accepted his satyagraha principles and would loyally follow his lead, he joined regional and then national organisations (for example, the Home Rule League, Khilafat campaign and Indian National Congress) not committed to satyagraha

382

as a creed. He then tried to persuade their members as far as he could to adopt his approach and methods.

Second, having joined the Congress he was instrumental in devising for it a membership structure, which enabled it to be representative of nationalist activists throughout India. Congress was a machinery for bringing most of the elements of Indian nationalism into one organisation (Gandhi likened it to a "parliament" rather than a "party") and Gandhi's followers were one faction only within it. Gandhi's principal innovation was the disinterested one of extending the Congress organisation into the villages rather than extending his own following.

Third, because of the problem of mass all-India civil resistance campaigns getting out of hand if the leaders moved too quickly to aggressive confrontation, he devised a programme for diverting the energies of the nation's political elite out into constructive work and out into rural areas. There they could consolidate the membership of the vastly expanded Congress organisation and prepare it for disciplined nonviolent struggle. At the same time, he strongly resisted attempts to launch all the proposed stages of Noncooperation simultaneously. In resisting a drive for total withdrawal of co-operation all at once, he was forced to develop the concept and then the programme of "progressive nonviolent noncooperation". Progressive build-up was to become a key principle.

Fourth, having moved to construct a national mass organisation within which his own following was a faction only, Gandhi experimented with ways of developing forms of action over which he could have personal control. These would then attract attention as the leading edge of the movement. His followers in one district (Bardoli) of rural Gujarat were selected to launch aggressive civil disobedience. Or again, as a personal action to promote the use of swadeshi cloth among the poorest peasantry, he vowed publicly to reduce his own clothing needs to match what they could afford.

In this way, by working with people of differing political viewpoints, by developing disciplined organisation, by pitching the struggle as far as possible at the level of constructive work rather than confrontation, and by devising new symbolic ways of exerting personal leadership, Gandhi adapted methods of organising from local to national struggles. But it should be said too that the "promise" which motivated large numbers of the more politically active to support his movement was the expectation that within a short time they would be moving on to a decisive moment of open conflict with the raj, through mass civil disobedience.

Gandhi himself has drawn attention to the differences between his organising methods at a local and a national level in his pamphlet, *Constructive Programme: Its Meaning and Place*, which provided the framework of discussion in Chapter 4. There he states categorically that, in local struggles, "no elaborate constructive programme was or could be necessary"; but he insists that to organise civil disobedience at a national level without securing "the co-operation of the millions by way of constructive effort is mere bravado and worse than useless". (Gandhi 1945: 35-36) The same passage has been quoted approvingly by Bose in his excellent *Studies in Gandhism* and restated by Sharp as Gandhi's viewpoint. (Bose 1947: i; Sharp 1979: 86) But neither writer has attempted to analyse this perspective further.[74]

Dhawan also notes Gandhi's conclusion, which was maintained over many years. (Dhawan 1957: 193) Subsequently, the local-national distinction seems to have disappeared from the literature on Gandhi and on nonviolence.[75]

---

74. To be fair, Sharp does suggest in one essay:
"Many questions could be raised in relation to the theory of Gandhi's constructive program; its potentialities and limitations... [E]xploratory analysis may be merited on development of constructive programs based on this broad theory for other countries including those in the industrialised West". (Sharp, 1979: 85-86)
But I am not sure that he or his co-researchers took these observations further.

75. The distinction between local and national struggles reappears in David Hardiman's commentary on Chenoweth and Stephan's *Why Civil Resistance Works*. (Hardiman 2017: 51-89) Hardiman applies their method of analysis to nine national-level nonviolent campaigns in India and two national-level violent ones; and to 34 local-level standalone nonviolent campaigns and 12 local-level standalone violent campaigns.

Working as a Member (or Leader) of a Coalition

Having failed to develop an all-India organisation of his own supporters, Gandhi was drawn into political coalitions with other nationalist leaders and factions. His skills as a political organiser are abundantly clear from his achievements.

Expediency was the only basis on which he could win consent at the highest levels of nationalist politics for his judgments, campaigns and methods. His fellow politicians backed Gandhi when his proposals seemed to be the most feasible to follow at that particular moment. None of this prevented him, however, on the public platform and in his weekly newspapers, from arguing his full political position based in satyagraha principles. As a result, within a coalition of divergent views, Gandhi was still able to recruit popular support for his more fundamental beliefs.

On many issues, Gandhi's judgment of what it was possible to achieve and right to aim for was closer to the nationalist "moderates" than to the "extremists". What distinguished him from the "moderates" was, first, his belief that real politics lay outside the legislatures in the Indian villages and, second, once he had set himself a limited aim, his determination to pit his body and soul to the struggle to achieve it. His links with the "moderates", on the one hand, and his commitment to populism and radical action, on the other, gave him a special leverage in nationalist politics. He could outmanoeuvre the "extremists" because he appeared just as committed to radical action as they and more committed to practical objectives.

The fact that Gandhi became leader of all-India political coalitions pursuing limited objectives on the basis of expediency does not mean that he compromised his satyagraha principles. He insisted, for example,

---

Hardiman finds that of the 34 local-level nonviolent campaigns he identifies in India, 18 were a "success" or a "partial success". Of the 12 local-level violent campaigns, 3 were a "partial success". Hardiman concludes as a broad observation that we should be studying the efficacy of nonviolent action "at every level" (that is, not simply concentrating on the national-level capture of state power). (Hardiman 2017: 62-89)

on nonviolent discipline in the Khilafat and Congress movements while he led them. He insisted too on the particular campaigning issues of the Khilafat and Punjab being kept separate until all avenues of compromise with the Raj had been gone down fully on both questions. He fervently opposed the boycott of British goods, rather than foreign goods.

Furthermore, strategies for achieving the limited aims of the coalition were always designed to advance the cause of satyagraha. Changing the creed in the constitution of the Congress, for example, when he assumed its leadership in 1920, ensured that civil disobedience would be permitted, but the use of violence ruled out. Adopting "Swaraj in One Year" – a dubious slogan – convinced some nationalists that they need make sacrifices for one year only, (Gordon 1973) but Gandhi attached the target to a mass programme of constructive work, which helped build the movement's organisational strength and begin to tackle the "real" problems of India as he saw them. The Triple Boycott had the startling effect of persuading thousands of members of the nationalist elite to make contact with village India.

Lacking a national organisation committed to satyagraha, Gandhi recognised that within the nationalist coalition were different levels of commitment to his ideas. At the base Congress was a very fluid organisation with considerable freedom and uncertain discipline. But at the top Gandhi created a tight working committee of a few individuals. While he retained authority from the Congress to act as leader, he insisted that the working committee follow a policy of collective responsibility (like the British Cabinet), thus speaking with one voice. In this way unity was achieved at the top behind his policy.

At a local and regional level, a nationwide organisation of volunteers was created within the Congress structure. These volunteers were obliged as a condition of membership to take a vow committing them to nonviolent discipline. (Dhawan 1957: 211) Some of them received training in Gandhian ashrams and established new ashrams from which to carry out constructive and other work. The programme of constructive work was promoted by Gandhi as an uncontentious movement of national self-improvement, which should be supported by all factions in the Congress. It was designed too to achieve unity at the base of the movement.

Thus considerations of expediency prompted other nationalist politicians to support Gandhi's leadership of Congress – a position helped by his novel balance of commitment to "moderate" views with determination to fight by radical methods. This unusual combination, together with tight discipline at the top, support for his policies at the base, and development of a network of volunteer groups broadly accepting his direction, alongside ashrams of committed workers, enabled Gandhi to enter political coalitions without sacrificing his satyagraha principles.

The principal discussion of Gandhi's acceptance of expediency as a basis for political coalition is in Gene Sharp, *Gandhi as a Political Strategist*, though he concentrates on the issue of nonviolent discipline in conflict.

Building Campaigns Around Particular Issues

We have laid considerable stress on Gandhi's consistent strategy of working for general goals by way of campaigns focused on particular, limited objectives.

During his early struggles back in India, as a less than typical loyalist who nonetheless was intending no immediate or general assault on the legitimacy of British rule, Gandhi concentrated on trying to eradicate particular "blots" on the Raj's record.[76] Even then, however, his positive aims of strengthening the Indian nation by developing self-reliance, social responsibility and moral awareness were general in scope. We can recognise, therefore, two well-known features of the Gandhian method.

First, there is the selection of a series of particular measures, "one step at a time", to advance a general goal. (Iyer 1973: 228) Second, there is the concentration on means as containing within them the essence of whatever end will emerge – hence satyagraha being a doctrine of means as much as ends. (Iyer 1973: 359-371)[77] For Gandhi, from pursuing a

---

76. The Ahmedabad millworkers strike, of course, was an exception.

77. On ends and means, Gandhi's views are sometimes assumed to be that nonviolent action is an end in itself. But this is not Gandhi's position. As this study has demonstrated time and again, Gandhi was intensely concerned about

means as general and all-embracing in its scope as satyagraha, unforeseen general benefits will result, even though the nominal aim is limited to a specific issue.

Concentrating, as Gandhi did, on the single issue assumes, among other things, that rationality and fairness can be brought to bear in politics, that both sides in a dispute can learn to understand and even respect the other's position if no side issues are brought in, and that by limiting demands to the minimum short of sacrificing principles, practical gains can be achieved. Using this method, Gandhi was able to control the pace and development of struggle precisely because it was limited in scope and objective, and also to restrict and restrain retaliatory opportunities open to the opponent. (Rothermund 1963: 64-86)

When Gandhi did move to the general issue of swaraj in 1920, we have seen that this was with great reluctance, even though by that time it had become logical to combine campaigns on two "particular" issues, which had reached the same stage of breakdown with the Raj. Gandhi's ingenious solution to this was to interpret swaraj in terms of a number of particular objectives for constructive work: such as, a Congress organisation capable of assuming the running of the country, or a nation capable of throwing off dependency on imported cloth and of supplying all its own clothing needs through the efforts of the largest number of its citizens.

Thus his "particularist" method survived Gandhi's transition to national leadership committed to the goal of independence for India. It facilitated control of the action and restraint on the activities of both sides. Within

---

goals (ends), and spent much time selecting goals that could be expressed in the means he chose. At the same time he knew that goals might not be achieved and that to focus on aspirations which were too remote in time or too sweeping in their effect could easily lead to unnecessary suffering and disappointment as well as distract attention from maintaining nonviolence, integrity and respect for the opponent. Hence, he insisted on the importance of "pure" means.

There is of course a pragmatic spirit behind his insistence on "taking care of the means". (The full slogan is "Take care of the means and the ends will take care of themselves.") As the American Gandhian teacher, Ira Sandperl, cleverly re-interpreted this injunction: "We get what we do".

campaigns on the issues selected, general advances could be achieved "one step at a time", while the nonviolent means served to bring forward a philosophy of "right-living".

These three related questions, of keeping issues separate, being satisfied with limited gains as long as the principle is won, and emphasising means as much as ends, have been widely discussed in the literature on Gandhi.

Truth-Force and the Vow

There is a fourth question, however, which must be introduced as well if we are to understand the impact of a method which employed nonviolent means for limited objectives on particular issues. This is the determination to gain a victory once a struggle has been launched without even contemplating the possibility of defeat. Gandhi continually insisted on the infallibility of his satyagraha method. In his eyes, if it failed, it was because the satyagrahis (including himself) had failed the method, rather than the method failing them.

To understand this in secular terms, it is tempting to notice how strong is the emphasis on absolute determination in Gandhi's method. Starving mill workers vow not to return to work until they have won a victory; farmers vow to forfeit their ancestral lands if necessary. When the workers in Ahmedabad weakened, Gandhi himself took a vow that he would share their conditions by starving himself until the justice of their claim, and the outstanding courage of their sacrifice in withdrawing their labour, was recognised.

Such an explanation goes only half-way to explaining Gandhi's method, however. Gandhi's absolute determination not to give in on a campaign once launched was allied to a belief that the strength to maintain the fight comes from God. Taking a religious vow to struggle until some amelioration or advantage was won was not, as cynics argue, simply an opportunist move to bind ignorant people to a course of action which otherwise they would think better of and slide out of. In the vow, and in the successful outcome of struggles where people had vowed that they would not give in, Gandhi saw the means of enabling people to bring their most profound sense of spiritual rectitude into politics. In victory, not only would their self-confidence soar, but also their belief in the power of the spirit or, as Gandhi came to express it more and more, truth.

Here then we come to the core of satyagraha – which has often been translated as "truth-force" or "soul-force". Gandhi tried hard in practice not to overemphasise the power of the human soul to force change in the political world. But on a specific, carefully-defined issue, where the objectives of the campaigners had been limited to the least they could reasonably demand, if the struggle was conducted scrupulously in a nonviolent spirit without recourse to trickery or manipulation and with a willingness to endure suffering without giving in, then the human soul could exercise power and force changes in the world of politics.

This was Gandhi's "truth-force" or "soul-force", conceived and organised as a novel experiment in political action. It was a fragile technique because it was so poorly understood and so little tried as a conscious method. Gandhi remained fascinated by this experiment throughout his life, convinced that if it was applied with enough skill and dedication it could never fail. However, as we have argued in this study, he came to realise that he had been overconfident in promoting it as a method on the conflict side in campaigns of civil resistance. Increasingly he placed stress on campaigns of satyagraha which were constructive in nature, designed to change social conditions directly, rather than set squarely in the fraught arena of conventional politics. Iyer comments, contrasting the demands of civil disobedience and noncooperation:

> "Civil disobedience was regarded as a universal human right, which in practice only a few were capable of exemplifying in a spirit of tapas or self-suffering. Noncooperation was considered to be a readily available universifiable method of social change, which made fewer spiritual demands on its users." (Iyer 1973: 281)

Numerous writers have defined truth-force. Iyer has stressed the importance of the vow in satyagraha. (Iyer 1973: 73-83) My analysis suggests that fundamental to its success was the combination of a limited issue and absolute determination. Gandhi's first conscious experiments in

India were expressly limited in their scope in order to match their chances of success to the moral strength of the satyagrahis. If this is accepted, then the problems of organising satyagraha on a national scale, particularly in its more contentious form of civil disobedience, become obvious. Where the spirit of the people cannot be concentrated on a particular issue and their struggle conducted in something approximating to the rules developed by Gandhi, then the "truth-force" method is unlikely (or less likely) to work.

There is no question that Gandhi, drawing from concepts deep in Hindu thinking about conflict, did see innocent suffering as a means to changing hearts and minds, and he felt vindicated when individual civil disobedients – who in their thousands in late 1921 were jailed and endured beatings and other injustices without complaint – acted with bravery, dignity and self-respect.

From a secular point of view, Gandhi clearly saw the willingness to risk injury and death of a conventional soldier as an example of bravery that he expected a satyagrahi to emulate. He also judged that the public emotional impact of innocent people suffering unwarranted brutality could generate shock and sympathy and spark momentum for a campaign. The Engler brothers refer to "trigger events". (Engler and Engler 2017: 181-190) In the case studies we have examined, what I have noticed is Gandhi's expectation that the satyagrahi should be willing to make sacrifice, so that the vow is a key part of recruitment and an assertion that only those who are seriously committed should consider volunteering. Vinthagen proposes much the same thing when he identifies a willingness to take the risk of suffering as a key criterion:

"One way of making the liberation activists' humanity clear is to show a kind of courage that differs from the courage displayed by the militarised people in power – the courage to die for one's belief in an egalitarian society… My interpretation of nonviolence is that activists use the risk of suffering in order to undermine enemy images, blocking and hate``. (Vinthagen 2015: 215-216)

The Slow Build-Up and Defensive Action

A final feature of Gandhi's organising method explored in this study is the change in his approach to initiating satyagraha on a national scale. Whereas in the Rowlatt Satyagraha the campaign was launched with plans for immediate, widespread individual civil disobedience, during Noncooperation the launch of aggressive civil disobedience was delayed and delayed and then finally abandoned altogether. My interpretation is that the restriction order placed on Gandhi during the Rowlatt satyagraha caused him (possibly consciously) to try to repeat the defiance which had worked so well for him two years earlier in Champaran. The disastrous results of this symbolic resistance, however, caused him to rethink his approach.

A key feature of the Noncooperation movement was its slow development and build-up, that is, progressive nonviolent noncooperation. It should be seen as a more mature example of Gandhi's method of organising at a national level. As the first sustained all-India campaign, it established his leadership of the nationalist movement. What it involved was a progressive series of steps: first, mobilising some of the nationalist elite, inviting them to break their links with the Raj by resigning positions and suspending lucrative careers, directing them to the villages where real issues for the future of India lay; second, consolidating the links achieved between full-time idealistic workers and villagers, in a programme to develop organisation and expand constructive work; third, moving onto defensive civil disobedience when the Raj tried to restrict the activities of Congress volunteers; and, fourth, preparing to launch aggressive civil disobedience in a limited area when the nation was ready.

Thus the essence of the revised method was a long drawn-out period of mobilisation and preparation, building up enthusiasm, unity and constructive achievement until the right "atmosphere" for civil disobedience had been achieved. It was no longer assumed, as Gandhi had in 1919, that satyagraha would take the people by storm. Defensive civil disobedience – in this case, the continuance of "legitimate" activity and defiance when subjected to repression by government – was permitted by Gandhi on an individual rather than a mass basis. (Dhawan: 242-247) Aggressive civil disobedience, the deliberate breaking of a law chosen by Gandhi at the right moment to escalate the confrontation, was held back as a last resort for when the movement was thoroughly prepared to support and sustain nonviolent discipline.

Defensive civil disobedience was remarkably successful. Commentators have suggested that the whole Noncooperation campaign reached its highest point in December 1921, with thousands going to jail when the Congress volunteer organisation was banned. It was the time when, for a few weeks, the British Raj was most troubled and nationalist opinion was most firmly behind Gandhi

Case examples selected by Bondurant in her classic study of satyagraha give the impression that Gandhi favoured exemplary civil disobedience as his method of mobilising a mass nonviolent movement. This was the technique employed in the only two national struggles she describes, the Rowlatt Satyagraha and the Salt Satyagraha in 1930. (Bondurant 1973: 73-102) Gene Sharp in his valuable study of the 1930-1932 movement in *Gandhi Wields The Weapon of Moral Power* also implies by his selection and treatment that Gandhi favoured aggressive civil disobedience. (Sharp 1960) In Sharp's *The Politics of Nonviolent Action* almost all his references to all-India actions organised by Gandhi are to this period, which Sharp had studied in depth. (Sharp 1973)[78]

Rowlatt and the Salt Satyagraha are the best-known examples of Gandhi's method in the west. Their reputation has, however, in my view, helped give nonviolent activists in the west a misleading impression of how Gandhi's satyagraha campaigns were constructed. The crucial point is that Rowlatt was a failure and the Salt Satyagraha followed 10 years of preparation led by Gandhi, including principally the major initial mobilisation achieved by Noncooperation from 1920 to 1922. It is beyond the scope of this study to develop this contention further – but the argument that the

---

78. It means that two of the most influential authorities on nonviolent action in the west, do not take account explicitly of the principal national struggle (Noncooperation) by which Gandhi established his position in India. I have noticed in researching this book that none of the western authors referred to, and very few of the Indian ones, discuss Noncooperation and all use the Salt March as their main case study of Gandhi.

Gandhian method places less emphasis on dramatic civil disobedience than is usually supposed, is well supported in this study.

Satyagraha in Action

In only four pages of her book *Conquest of Violence*, Joan Bondurant has summarised what she calls "The Essentials of Satyagraha in Action". Derived from earlier Gandhian scholars, this summary first published decades ago is still generally accepted as the best practical description of Gandhi's method. (Bondurant 1973: 38-41)

Bondurant herself makes no great claims for this section of her work, which outlines a possible handbook for satyagrahis following Gandhi's methods. (Bondurant 1973: 38) It is perhaps surprising that such a modest and, as the author herself suggests, incomplete presentation has not been re-evaluated subsequently. For instance, Bondurant's example of the "code of discipline" for satyagrahis is based on a single document Gandhi prepared for those undertaking civil disobedience in 1930. In the years up to 1922, Gandhi prepared a number of codes of discipline depending on the circumstances at the time.

Fundamental Handbook Rules

The other two "chapters" of Bondurant's imaginary handbook do fall more squarely within the framework of this book and demand closer examination. Bondurant's first "handbook chapter" on "fundamental rules" contains nine points. Adapted and elaborated from N. K. Bose in his *Studies in Gandhism*, these rules can be grouped under three broad headings. (Bondurant 1973: 237 fn4) They are shown in Table 11.1 in the left hand column, while the right hand column shows some additional "rules" I have derived from the case studies in this book. Probably they are not all "fundamental"; some are elaborations of rules not made explicit by Bose/Bondurant.

If we examine each of these in turn, we will see that indeed a number of important "rules" as demonstrated in this study are either underemphasised or omitted from the Bose-Bondurant list.

Table 11.1: The Essentials of Satyagraha in Action: Fundamental (and Additional) Rules

Gandhi's Rules (from Bondurant)	*Additional rules (from seven 1915-1922 case studies)*
PREPARATION FOR SUSTAINING A STRUGGLE	
1. Self-reliance at all times. Never count on outside aid.	• Orientation of the satyagrahis to face hardship and to identify with the poor • A daily discipline of constructive work. Participation in specific constructive programme projects. • Circulate a solemn pledge, committing the satyagrahis to maintain the struggle without fear for themselves
2. Initiative in the hands of the satyagrahis, pressing the movement ever forward	
3. Propagation of the objectives, strategy and tactics of the campaign as an integral part of the campaign	
4. Reduction of demands to a minimum consistent with truth, with continuous reassessment to allow possible readjustment	• The issue should be specific and practical and should not be combined with other issues for opportunistic reasons.

CONDUCT

5. Progressive advancement of the movement through steps and stages, avoiding a static condition

- Delay advancement to next stage if movement is not prepared.
- Willingness to suspend campaign if no further advance can be made.

6. Examination of weaknesses within the satyagraha group, including impatience, discouragement or breakdown of nonviolent attitude

- All actions by satyagrahis should represent the highest ideals of the movement

- Test capacity of satyagrahis to sustain struggle before it moves to the next stage

7. Persistent search for avenues of co-operation with the adversary on honourable terms: sincere effort to reach an agreement rather than triumph over the adversary

BASIS FOR SETTLEMENT

8. Refusal to surrender essentials in negotiation

- Refusal to negotiate when disrespected by opponent and without capacity to compel respect

9. Insistence upon full agreement on fundamentals before accepting a settlement

- Willingness to consider arbitration

First, at the stage of *preparation and sustainability*, there is the question of the basic orientation of those taking part in satyagraha. For Gandhi the the first question often was "Are you prepared to die?" or "Are you prepared to go to jail?" There was also the insistence that those taking part in the campaign should give up their privileges and identify with the peasantry by some forms of practical action

Second, Bondurant is certainly right to emphasise self-reliance – that is, for example, strikers supporting themselves from their own resources, rather than launching a strike fund. But in a list of Gandhian rules there should surely be an explicit emphasis on constructive work – that is, at the individual level, a daily discipline which can be a symbolic act of identification with the poor and with the national struggle itself, and an occasion for meditation and quiet; and it may also be a means of earning some money. While, as a social and political commitment and as a test of readiness for civil disobedience, elements from the constructive programme might be "required" by Gandhi. Bardoli in 1922 gives good examples, such as the creation of national schools and the admission to these schools of the children of untouchables, with specific targets for achievement set as a condition for moving on to the next stage of the struggle.

Third, the demands of the campaign should indeed be reduced to a minimum consistent with truth, but the issue itself should be specific and practical rather than general and remote. Also, the campaign should remain focused on the specific issue and not combined (opportunistically) with other campaigns for the sake of political advantage.

Finally, once the issue is defined and the demands set, satyagrahis should pledge themselves never to give in, whatever the penalty, until the principle expressed in the demand is met. This fundamental determination to act without fear of the consequences to oneself is basic to "truth-force".

The second set of rules relate to the *conduct of a campaign*. We may add, first, to the rule about progressive advancement of the movement, a corollary that where the movement has not reached the requisite level of awareness and discipline for the next stage, then ways of extending the campaign at its present level must be found.

A further corollary is that where it proves impossible to hold the movement to the requisite level of discipline and concentration for applying the satyagraha technique, but on the other hand the movement appears to be slipping out of control, then there should be a willingness to suspend the next stage of the campaign or even to call off the campaign.

Again, as a further rule, all actions of the satyagrahi are symbolic in the sense that they represent the movement and affect ultimately the reputation and fortune of the whole movement – so they must be polite and civil, determined and brave, by which Gandhi meant that they should represent the highest ideals of citizenship.

When we come to the basis for a settlement, two aspects of cooperation with the opponent should be further emphasised. One is that the opponent must show respect for the satyagrahis. If it is not shown and the satyagrahis lack the strength to "compel" respect, then it is likely that the basis for a successful negotiation is not present. A second is the willingness to surrender the campaign to third-party arbitration, where this will enable the opponent to recognise the principle in the satyagrahis' case with the least loss of face.

Steps in a Satyagraha Campaign

The third proposed "chapter" in Bondurant's handbook is derived from Shridharani's *War Without Violence* and lists nine "Steps in A Satyagraha Campaign". (Bondurant 1973: fn6) It is a descriptive classification of the stages in a satyagraha struggle to which the rules we have just discussed apply. Bondurant says that these steps are for a movement "against an established political order" but they could be adapted to "other conflict situations". They are:

1. Negotiation and arbitration.

2. Preparation of the group for direct action.

3. Agitation.

4. Issuing of an ultimatum.

5. Economic boycott and forms of strike.

6. Noncooperation.

7. Civil disobedience.

8. Usurping the functions of government.

9. Parallel government.

Perhaps the most important point in addressing this schema is to observe that it is unlikely to fit any satyagraha campaign in its entirety. To take two examples, the Champaran satyagraha began with civil disobedience (stage 7), when Gandhi refused to be externed from the area. Once Gandhi was permitted to stay and to conduct an investigation, the agitational stage (3) was entered; followed by negotiation and arbitration (1); then, in some respects, usurping the functions of government (8), and again, negotiation and arbitration (1). A settlement was reached and no further action was necessary.

Noncooperation (1920-1922) was different, however, and fits much more closely. The first four stages were gone through over a period of months in 1920 up to the first ultimatum (4) in July. Then noncooperation and economic boycott (stages 6 and 5) were begun. They were sustained for many months as the main body of the campaign. Civil disobedience (7) took place mainly defensively in defiance of restrictions on picketing, the selling of literature and rights of assembly – and the campaign was suspended without taking up aggressive civil disobedience.

Omitted from, or insufficiently emphasised in, the Shridharani-Bondurant list are

- the underlying bedrock of preparation for civil resistance in a programme of constructive work

- conscientious and comprehensive investigation to prepare a cast-iron case

- building links between different sections of the movement and mobilising support

- the important step of the pledge

- the interplay throughout a national campaign between constructive social projects and direct challenges to government authority

- progressive nonviolent noncooperation, that is, the build up from smaller and less challenging actions to more risky and defiant ones

- the distinction between defensive and aggressive civil disobedience as distinct stages in the development of a satyagraha movement.

- in a campaign which falls short of a revolutionary objective, particularly a local level struggle, the most likely outcome of a satyagraha will be a compromise, or arbitration.

There are further qualifying issues which could be explored as further "chapters" of a satyagraha handbook. One is the question of scale: is the action local, regional or national in scope? Second, if national, whether it is conducted simultaneously across the nation, or concentrated symbolically in a particular region, or one locality? Third, is it a mass action (either dispersed or concentrated); or a small group action; or action taken by individuals; or by a leader or leaders personally?

Other key dimensions concern the political orientation or sophistication of the participants. Are they full-time satyagrahis who may be living in Gandhian ashrams, or are they political nationalists who have accepted nonviolent discipline for the duration of the struggle only? Or is the campaign based around a coalition of "pure" satyagrahis and "tactical" satyagrahis?

Again, have different tactics been selected for different sections of the movement? For example, are particular actions being asked of leading members of the nationalist elite, or of the educated classes generally, or self-employed shop-keepers, or industrial owners, or mill-workers? Some caste-groups, some provincial or language groups, some classes owning land or some who are landless, some religious groups – are different tactics and programmes designed to mobilise these different elements?

All these gradations give a sense of a movement which has to be planned and organised in the real world – and which does not therefore have a uniform programme or strategy, but must be flexible and adaptable to circumstances. The point is that Gandhi was not afraid to make distinctions according to capacity or position or local issues when developing strategy and tactics for campaigns.

Other issues for the organiser of satyagraha include questions of timing. For example, how is an organiser of Gandhi's stature able to "know" when is the right moment to propose an all-India hartal or to launch a Triple Boycott? Such questions of judgment and intuition are notoriously difficult to pin down. As we have seen, Gandhi developed his method of "testing" by observing the conduct of public demonstrations, especially hartals, or the take-up of his campaigns of constructive work, or the number of signatures to a pledge, or contributors to a fund.

Again, how are the issues to be taken up selected? Gandhi, as we have seen, concentrated on limited issues rather than taking up the main issue, gearing "truth-force" to the practical capacity of the satyagrahis. Mobilising the peasantry to national self-consciousness and developing effective organisation was a major consideration. Fundamental seems to have been questions of local initiative, organisation and self-reliance. Clothing was selected as the item for boycott and for home production, rather than sugar or other goods. Production of clothing was chosen at the time as the key to mobilising on a national scale, rather than housing, or sanitation, or improvement of food production, or land-redistribution, or labour organising.

There is then much subtlety and flexibility in Gandhi's use of the satyagraha method. My purpose in comparing some of the issues raised by this study with the outline of satyagraha provided by Bondurant has been to demonstrate a principal argument. That is, by studying Gandhi as an organiser (dynamically, in his context) we can gain fresh insights into his methods and a deeper understanding of them. Also, we have seen how the move from local to national organising faced Gandhi with a number of problems, which forced him to adapt and clarify his methods. More generally, a third argument has been that the principal authorities on nonviolent action in the west have, until recently, consciously chosen to ignore the importance of constructive work in Gandhi's method. It is to the place of constructive programme in satyagraha that we shall finally turn.

The Place of Constructive Programme

Satyagraha was described neatly by Shridharani as "Gandhi's method of fighting the British". (Shridharani 1962:15) This simple recognition of conflict is the way in which the term is normally used, to describe a nonviolent fight, so that to talk of "a satyagraha" is to refer to a battle with a beginning and an end fought by nonviolent means. The term has spread into general usage in India where many campaigns not involving the use of violence have come to be called "satyagrahas". Bondurant, however, following Gandhi, has distinguished strictly between "satyagrahas" which follow the scrupulous rules for the conduct of these struggles laid down by the Mahatma and "duragrahas" or "passive resistance" where the activists do not resort to violence, but the campaign is not shaped or constrained by Gandhi's philosophy and guidelines. (Bondurant 1973: vii-ix, 41-45)

Against this, the general tendency of western scholars, most notably Sharp, has been to ease the study of nonviolent action out of the limits and some of the philosophical biases established by Gandhi. Nonviolent action, as defined by Sharp, promotes change as a result of persuasion, accommodation, coercion or disintegration. Satyagraha, on the other hand, when conducted according to Gandhi's rules, relies principally on persuasion, is reluctant to settle for accommodation and seeks always to avoid coercion. (Sharp 1973: 705-776)

What is common to both approaches – those looking at satyagraha in its "pure" principled form, and those taking a narrower view of nonviolent action – is that in focusing on the question of conflict they have neglected a large area of the technique of nonviolent action as developed by Gandhi. Satyagraha in its second widely accepted usage, refers to the broad philosophy of truth-force developed by Gandhi, a philosophy which was adopted by "life satyagrahis" who went to live in ashrams, engaged in personal religious and other disciplines, and accepted a public role as social and community workers, as well as engaging in nonviolent political campaigns when called upon. (Kumarappa 1951: iii)

Bondurant, as we have seen, says we should "rigorously" distinguish satyagraha as a technique of action from "those specific considerations of right living with which Gandhi also concerned himself". (Bondurant

1973: 12) But my contention is that not only does this distinction diminish Bondurant's presentation of the satyagraha method and make it hard to understand how it worked. Also, it seems to me, the theorists of nonviolent action who treat satyagraha as an approach unsuited to western conditions have distorted our understanding of the technique by presenting Gandhi's experiments selectively. It is not necessary to hold to Gandhi's full philosophy of satyagraha to recognise that programmes of constructive work are essential in many situations to the method of nonviolent action developed by Gandhi.

Gandhi's campaigns of civil resistance, certainly at a national scale, would have been impossible without complementary campaigns of constructive work. The two were strongly interlinked in his method of satyagraha, which should be seen as a method of making social and political change beyond its undoubted significance as a conflict technique. Thus one important conclusion of this study, from a careful examination of Gandhi's method, is that the technique approach to nonviolent action should be broadened to include consideration of methods and campaigns which had little directly to do with conflict.

The following table (Table 11.2) shows how the two sides of satyagraha were balanced during the Noncooperation campaign. The development of the Congress as an effective national organisation is not usually seen as a part of constructive programme, but it is included here because, in providing a framework for the Noncooperation campaign, it began to build a constructive alternative to the political structures of the Raj.

By studying Gandhi as an organiser we have been able to step back from one common approach, which is to look at him as a nonviolent general or warrior. The other conventional view is to see him as a philosopher of right-living, training followers in ashram disciplines and projecting for the wider society a vision of a decentralised politics based in a rural and craft-based economy. In between these views, Gandhi stands in this study as a consummate political activist and organiser, who had an original perspective on how to build and direct a movement for nonviolent social and political change.

Table 11.2: The Two Sides of Satyagraha: The Balance between Constructive Programme and Civil Resistance during Noncooperation, 1919-1922

Constructive Programme	Civil Resistance
Respect Indian institutions	Return honours etc
Develop Congress as potential parliamentary system.	Boycott Provincial Councils
Support Noncooperation against the Raj.	
Create new national educational institutions	Boycott government schools. Capture some municipal councils and support national schools in defiance of the law.
Support Indian system of arbitration	Resign legal practices
Develop hand-made Indian cloth; promote spinning and weaving (swadeshi)	Boycott foreign cloth
Replace service of the Raj with support for independence (swaraj) and Noncooperation	Resign from civil service, police and military
Take up swadeshi campaign, support Hindu-Muslim unity, practise nonviolence and oppose untouchability and liquor sales	Individual, defensive civil disobedience to challenge ban on Congress and Khilafat volunteer groups
Preparations in Bardoli include take up of swadeshi, opposition to untouchability etc	Plan for mass, aggressive civil disobedience, initially through tax refusal in Bardoli

Difficulties with Organising National Campaigns

In Chapter 4, I followed Gandhi's own distinction between organising at a local level and at a national level, arguing that it was harder to deliver an effective and sustained nonviolent campaign at the national level: consequently, somewhat different techniques became necessary, particularly the use of constructive programme in preparation. A neglected author among the many writers who have analysed Gandhi's methods is Indira Rothermund. In a brief section of her book *The Philosophy of Restraint* she goes further than I have. Looking at his whole career, she suggests that as Gandhi gained greater experience of trying to organise civil disobedience on a mass scale, he became more wary of the difficulties of maintaining nonviolent discipline and sought to develop forms of confrontation more easily controlled by him as leader.

Rothermund distinguishes between three levels of participation: Mass, Representative and Individual, where "mass" is large-scale, "representative" involves a small group or a small area acting on behalf of the campaign as a whole, and "individual" is action by the leader. This breakdown fits well with what the case studies in this book have shown. Gandhi's attempt at mass action in Rowlatt failed; he moved towards representative action during Noncooperation with individual "defensive" civil disobedience challenging the ban on Congress volunteers and with the plan for exemplary "aggressive" action in one small area only, at Bardoli, and relied on his own actions at Champaran and Ahmedabad and in the Bombay fast after the hartal. (Rothermund 1963: 64-80)

Rothermund's simple classification is useful to look at Gandhi's organising in more detail. But I prefer to change the terminology of the three types of action, as follows: "Mass", "Individual or Representative", and "Personal Action by the Leader".[79] Using these three categories we can get a clearer

79. I find confusing Rothermund's use of the term "individual" to describe Gandhi's personal satyagrahas, because the defiance of the provincial bans on Congress volunteers in late 1921 was described by Gandhi at the time as individual civil disobedience, while the Quit India Campaign during 1940 and

405

idea in Table 11.3 of how the "constructive" and "obstructive" sides of satyagraha were organised at a national level, particularly in order to gain time for preparation and training before taking up the more aggressive forms of civil resistance. But it could be that Gandhi was seeking to diversify and sustain the campaign and to control its pace. He might be straightforwardly trying to reduce the risk of violence, or to hold on to momentum. Equally on occasions he would be seeking to build enthusiasm and morale and achieve a new breakthrough in respect and reputation for the campaign. These tactics were used during Rowlatt and Noncooperation, as Gandhi sought to shape a nation-wide uprising.

What the table illustrates is Gandhi's tendency, even in a national campaign, to take the responsibility for decisions and the burden of actions onto himself, with the creation of a drama where he is often the leading player. He makes an enormous personal contribution as leader with unconventional as well as conventional initiatives, working tirelessly to achieve readiness and capability for mass participation in both "constructive" and "obstructive" campaigns. Especially important to his method is the range of exemplary activities, taken up by selected individuals, groups, districts or even regions as representatives of the movement.

At the national level Gandhi used broadly the same strategy and tactics in organising the two sides of satyagraha. There is a clear hierarchy of roles between the leader whose decision and action is awaited, the organisers and trained satyagrahis who co-ordinate and carry out the plan or convey the instructions, and the non-cooperators from towns and villages who take up the mass campaigns and promote their messages. There is a balance and an intermingling between constructive work and civil resistance in devising the preparation for and carrying out a national rebellion.

1941 is well-known for its widespread individual satyagrahas as individuals offered themselves for arrest.

Table 11.3: Organising Satyagraha at a National Level: Rowlatt and Noncooperation 1919-1922

	MASS ACTION (DISPERSED OR CONCENTRATED)	REPRESENTATIVE OR INDIVIDUAL ACTION	PERSONAL ACTION BY THE LEADER
CONSTRUCTIVE PROGRAMME	Spinning, weaving, wearing swadeshi cloth; opening khadi stores	Key leaders take up hand-spinning or wearing khadi; ashrams founded to spread campaigns	Gandhi makes speeches, writes weekly articles on swadeshi etc; sets targets; opens swadeshi stores; vows to spin daily and to wear the clothing of the poor
	Demonstration of Hindu-Muslim unity in e.g. hartals	Leaders visit each other's temples, attend each others' conferences	Debates in private with mullahs. Fasts for communal unity. Speeches; articles. Tours with Ali brothers
	School students attend national schools with new curriculum	Establish National schools. Gujarat leads the way	Presidency of Gujarat National University. Speeches; articles
	Drive to build up Congress membership, raise funds	Establishment of local and provincial Congress organisation	Writes Congress constitution. Plays active role in Congress.

CIVIL RESISTANCE			
Rowlatt hartal in Bombay and more hartals across India.	Individual civil disobedience selling banned literature.	Gandhi resists order restricting him to Bombay Presidency. Fasts after rioting in Bombay and Ahmedabad. Writes Congress report on Punjab.
Khilafatist Muslims launch Noncooperation through their own organisation	Khilafatists call for resignations from Indian military. Congress supports them	Lobbies Raj on Khilafat issue. Launches Noncooperation with Khilafatists without waiting for Congress support. Joint political tours with Ali brothers.
Boycott of elections to Raj's provincial councils	Politicians withdraw from elections; notables return honours	Gandhi leads opposition in Congress to Council entry
Boycott of courts. Students leave Raj schools to take part in Noncooperation campaign	Lawyers withdraw from courts. Teachers resign. Campaigns to close Hindu, Muslim and Sikh universities.	Speeches and articles promoting Noncooperation campaigns
Boycott of foreign cloth	Setting fire to huge mounds of foreign cloth	Publicly vows to wear only peasant clothing
Boycott of royal visit	Successive hartals across India	Fast to end communal riots
Congress volunteers defy ban on meetings and processions	Key leaders and supporters arrested and jailed for defying ban on volunteers actions	Proposes Individual "Defensive" civil disobedience. Expresses joy for those jailed

CIVIL RESISTANCE	Plans for widespread tax refusal to follow representative action	Selection of Bardoli only to launch "aggressive" mass tax refusal	Focus on his choice of Bardoli. Sends ultimatum to Viceroy. Publishes articles deemed seditious by Raj
	Districts across India preparing to follow Bardoli's lead. Instructed to suspend action.	After months of expectation, Bardoli satyagrahis reluctantly comply with suspension	Chaura Chaura causes Gandhi to suspend Bardoli action. Jailed for his published articles.

Symbolic or representative action was not simply about attracting attention, though Gandhi clearly had a talent for imaginative actions. It was also about what Rothermund calls "control of the action". (Rothermund 1963: 64-65, 71-72) Differentiation between the lesser expectations placed on a mass movement and the much greater requirements placed on a smaller, "representative" or select grouping is fundamental. The plan for Bardoli, as we have seen, was to set an example of constructive programme in support of civil resistance that could be taken up by the whole nation.

In his *The Politics of Nonviolent Action*, Sharp describes, with great perception, a key element in nonviolent strategy and tactics, which he calls "the indirect approach to the opponents' power".

> "In nonviolent action there is no attempt to combat [the government's troops, police, prisons and the like] by using the same type of instruments, as would be the case if both sides were using violence. Instead, in strategic terms, the nonviolent group counters this expression of the opponent's power indirectly, in various ways ...

> "Nonviolent struggle carries indirect strategy ... to the point where the military opponent is confronted not only with differing

strategies but with a contrasting technique of struggle and non-military 'weapons system'. Nonviolent action involves opposing the opponent's power, including his police and military capacity not with the weapons chosen by him, but by quite different means." (Sharp 1973: 452-453)

Yet Sharp makes no mention of one of the most obvious and brilliant examples of this in the strategy Gandhi pursued in India, the programmes of constructive work. These were an integral part of Gandhi's "indirect" method.

It we could learn to study Gandhi as a practical strategist immersed in the immediate political issues of his society, then we might see ways of filling some of the glaring gaps in the development of nonviolent action in the west. Gandhi didn't set out to abolish war or to find a substitute for it.[80] Gandhi's object was less ambitious. It was to offer a practical method and a vision to the people of his country so that they could improve their society and the tenor of their political activity. He was forced by the intransigence of the British to accept that their removal was a necessary focus for nonviolent struggle. He saw no limits in theory to the application of this method and philosophy (including matters of national defence) – but where it began and ended in practice was in the capacity of ordinary people to believe in themselves and to practice self-reliance. This gave him his main task as an organiser.

His achievement suggests that if we want nonviolent action to fill the great role as substitute for violence which has been claimed for it, then the most important starting point is to develop a perspective and a

---

80. Gandhi was certainly pressed in the 1930s and 1940s, by the dilemmas of the Second World War and India's transition to a sovereign state, to turn his mind to questions of war and defence, which he did. Gandhi tried to persuade the Congress unsuccessfully in 1940 to agree to pursue a nonviolent defence policy, but then withdrew because he could not convince his former colleagues. He continued to argue for it, however. Sharp, noting Gandhi's pragmatic and experimental habits of thought, suggests that his lack of a practical plan was not simply because of this rebuff, but because a defence policy against invasion, or conflict with another sovereign state, involves hypothetical threats, whereas he tended to react to immediate, practical problems. (Sharp 1979: 131-198)

programme which link it to the most pressing, immediate concerns of ordinary people. Gandhian satyagraha should be seen as a method of organising a movement for positive social change. The social programme of nonviolence precedes, complements and continues on from its use as a conflict technique. An integral part of this technique – as important to its successful development as the use of civil resistance – is constructive programme.

Acknowledgments

This book is dedicated to Howard Clark and Devi Prasad.

Howard was a friend for over 40 years. When he died suddenly, too young, in 2013 he was the hard-working activist Chair of War Resisters International (WRI) and a recognised scholar in the field of nonviolence. He had pressed me over many years to get this book finished. On his death I promised myself I would do it.

Like Howard, Devi Prasad was a former chair and secretary of WRI. Devi had been the art teacher at Gandhi's ashram. When I began the first version of this book, whenever I was puzzled or stuck, I would discuss the problem with him. It was Devi who taught me, for example, that the Gandhian interpretation of "civil disobedience" focuses on the "civil" before the "disobedience". He cannot be held responsible for my misinterpretations, though!

++++

Andrew Rigby took up the role of chivvying me to get the job done. Andrew is an expert in his own right on nonviolent action in India and elsewhere. He advised me on several chapters as well as being a great support throughout. Likewise, Carol Rank who lectures in peace and conflict studies. Carol read each of the chapters as they appeared and made many sound proposals for changes. Another long-standing friend, Martin Pierce, then kindly read the whole manuscript through to check the flow of the narrative and argument.

The historian, David Hardiman, an expert on peasant uprisings in India, has read my original unpublished manuscript and publicly recommended the analysis of Gandhian campaigns it contains. This was a great boost. Since then David has assisted me on several points, particularly in the early chapters.

A third former Chair of WRI, Jørgen Johansen, is my publisher at Irene Publishing. Jørgen has been a most reliable and generous facilitator for this book and I am especially grateful to him.

Stephen Pittam has offered me great encouragement throughout. Other friends who have read parts of the manuscript and offered helpful comments include Andrew Papworth, Andy Rutherford, Paul Wesley and Niall Fitzduff. More support has come from: Dave Webb, Frances McNeill, Colin Archer, Lisa Zychovicz, Greg Quiery, Rachel Julien and Ron Wiener.

I must not omit either my Californian friend, Lee Swenson. Lee was based at the Institute for the Study of Nonviolence near San Francisco. His enthusiasm for "alternative" projects in the Bay area stimulated my interest in constructive programme.

Other American friends who have helped shape this book at a distance include George Lakey, Joanne Sheehan, and longer ago Bob Cooney and Helen Michalowski.

Early versions of the manuscript received helpful comments from: Nigel Young, Geoffrey Ostergaard, Adam Curle, James O'Connell and Hugh Tinker. Before that I was greatly influenced by a Tolstoyan academic, Ronald V. Sampson.

I am indebted to the Nonviolence Study Group in Bradford: Michael Randle, April Carter, Walter Stein, Christina Arber, Lindis Piercy, John Brierley, Howard Clark, Andrew Rigby and Carol Rank. An early version of chapters 10 and 11 was discussed at one of its meetings.

I could not have attempted this book without the special collection of 20th century Gandhian literature in the Commonweal library at the University of Bradford. I have benefited in particular from the book donations to Commonweal from Indian publishers, such as Navajivan Press; and also the Gandhi Peace Foundation and the Government of India. I am grateful too to the Universities of Bradford and Leeds Beckett for access to their libraries.

++++

Finally I owe huge gratitude to my family. My mother, Christine, typed the original manuscript many years ago. My son, Tom, designed the splendid cover for this book and my daughter, Katie, when I was making slow progress, surprised me with a bound copy of my original thesis (a bound copy was too costly at the time it was written). My sister, Lu, and her husband, Steve, helped me think through ideas for titles and for publishing. So too did my sister-in-law, Isabel Huggan, who is a writer and writer's mentor. I am grateful for her ideas on design and promotion.

Above all, my wife and best friend, Ruth, deserves all the love and thanks I can give for endless support and encouragement.

Glossary

adivasi	Tribal people
ahimsa	Nonviolence, non-injury
akalis	Reformist Sikh group
shram	Spiritual retreat; centres of Gandhian constructive movement
bania	Member of the merchant caste
bapu	Father; used by many for Gandhi
bhakti	Worship
brahmin	Member of the priestly caste
chappal	Sandals
charkha	Spinning wheel
crore	Ten million
dalit	Down-trodden; untouchable
darshan	Viewing a virtuous person
dharma	customary observance, duty, law, underlying social morality of Hinduism; right course of action or conduct
dhoti	Loin cloth, traditional dress of Indian peasant
goonda	Ruffian, criminal
harijan	Untouchable; literally, people of god
hartal	Suspension of business; closing of shops and suspension of work, often as a sign of mourning
hijrat (hizrat}	Voluntary exile, mass emigration of Muslims from an unholy land to a virtuous one
himsa	Violence, injury
khadi, khaddar	Hand-spun cloth
khilafat	In India, first world war Muslim movement to protect the Sultan of Turkey, spiritual ruler or Caliph (Khalifa) of the Holy Places of Islam

kshatriya	Member of the warrior or kingly caste
lakh	100,000
lathi	5 foot club tipped with metal
mahatma	Great Soul
mamlatdar	Administrative head of a local district
maulana	Title of respect given to Muslim men of learning
maulvi	Islamic scholar
moksha	Liberation from earthly bondage
panchayat	Court of arbitration; originally a committee or council of 5 members, now a small local council; committee of village elders
patel	Village head man
puja	worship
sabha	Assembly, association
sarvodaya	The welfare or rise of all; Gandhi's social philosophy
satya	Truth
satyagraha	Truth-force, Gandhi's technique of nonviolent resistance
satyagrahi	One who practices satyagraha
swadeshi	Made in one's own country: a programme of economic self-reliance
swaraj	Self rule, independence
taluka, taluq	Sub-division of a district; administrative unit comprising many villages and constituting a portion of a district
taluqdar	Title of landowner
tapas	Ascetic practice; religious penance, austerity, sacrifice
thana	Police station
tinkathia	A contract in Bihar obliging peasants to grow indigo on part of their land
ulama	Muslim priest

vakil	Lawyer or pleader
varna	Caste, colour
Veth	Extortion by government officers of free services
zamindar	Landholder

PROMINENT FIGURES

Biographical Notes* on Some Prominent Figures

Ali, Mohammed. Journalist. Prominent Muslim leader of the Khilafat campaign. Kept under house arrest with his brother, Shaukat, for their anti-British writings and speeches. Close colleague of Gandhi's, he toured with him during Noncooperation. Gandhi made the Ali brothers' release a condition for settlement with the Raj.

Ali, Shaukat. Journalist. Worked alongside his brother and Gandhi drumming up support for the Khllafat campaign and Noncooperation. Both brothers were jailed for sedition.

Andrews, Charles Freer. Christian missionary from Britain. Visited Gandhi in South Africa and India. Became lifelong friend.

Ansari, M. A. Khilafat leader, supporter of Gandhi. Became Congress leader.

Azad, A. K. Prominent Muslim scholar and Khilafat leader. Supported Gandhi and later became President of the Congress.

Bajaj, Jamnalal. Loyal Gandhi supporter. Active in Congress as Treasurer. Jailed during Noncooperation and later struggles. Helped found and support Gandhian ashrams.

Banerjea, Surendranath. Leading Bengali Moderate politician. Left Congress in 1918. Helped the Raj to implement its reform programme.

* Mostly derived from Sushila Nayar, *Mahatma Gandhi, vol 5, India Awakened*, Navajivan Trust, 1994: pp 643-693

417

Banker, Shankerlal. Gujarati colleague of Gandhi's. Active in Ahmedabad mill strike, 1918. Constructive worker, khadi expert. Jailed with Gandhi in 1922.

Bari, Abdul. Muslim religious leader. Supporter of Hindu-Muslim unity, the Khilafat campaign and Noncooperation.

Besant, Annie. British Theosophist leader. Moved to India in 1895 when nearly 50. Set up one of the two Home Rule Leagues in 1917. Jailed by the British, but opposed Gandhi and Noncooperation, and supported British reforms. Founded numerous schools and colleges.

Bhave, Vinoba. Joined Gandhi's ashram as a young man in 1916. A key figure in promoting the home-spun cloth campaigns. Also engaged in civil disobedience. Known as Gandhi's "spiritual heir", he went on to lead the land-gift (bhoodan and gramdan) movements

Chamberlain, Sir Austen. Secretary of State for India in British Cabinet, London, 1916-1917.

Chelmsford, Lord. Viceroy of India, 1916-1921.

Das, C. R. Brilliant Bengali lawyer and Congress leader. He initially opposed Noncooperation until agreeing to the "Das-Gandhi pact" in 1921. Jailed for civil disobedience. Founded the Swaraj Party opposed to the boycott of elected Councils in 1923.

Desai, Mahadev. Joined Gandhi as his secretary in 1917 and served in this capacity for 27 years. Took part in and was jailed for civil disobedience campaigns. Wrote numerous articles, books and pamphlets.

Gandhi, Devadas. Youngest of Gandhi's four sons. Worked as Gandhi's assistant, investigating controversial events and reporting back. Jailed during Noncooperation. Became a professional journalist.

Gokhale, Gopal Krishna. Leading Moderate Congress politician prior to Gandhi's return from South Africa. Served on the Raj's Imperial Legislative Council. Visited Gandhi in South Africa and supported Gandhi's causes there. Named by Gandhi as his "guru in politics".

Hardinge, Lord. Viceroy of India, 1910-1916.

Horniman, B.G. British journalist, editor of the Bombay Chronicle. Actively supported Indian nationalism. Deported to England in 1919 for publishing articles on the Amritsar massacre.

Jayakar, M.R. Bombay lawyer. Main author with Gandhi of the Congress report into the Punjab massacre.

418

Jinnah, Muhammad Ali. Prominent Bombay lawyer from a Gujarati family. Moderate Muslim supporter of Congress. Consistently opposed civil disobedience. Later rejected Indian nationalism and led campaign for Pakistan, becoming first Governor-General of the separated state.

Joseph, George. Syrian Christian from south India and lawyer who gave up his legal practice to work for Congress and Noncooperation. He withdrew his children from government schools. Strong supporter of national education, cottage industries and emancipation of women.

Kitchlew, Saifuddin. Muslim lawyer from Amritsar. Involved with the Rowlatt agitation, the Khilafat Movement and Congress. Supporter of Hindu-Muslim unity.

Kripalani, J.B. Academic economist. Originally from Sind. While teaching in Bihar, he joined Gandhi in the Champaran campaign. Active in Congress, he took part in Noncooperation and was jailed. Later, he devoted his life to constructive work.

Lajpat Rai, Lala. Punjabi lawyer and journalist based in Lahore. Helped Tilak set up India Home Rule League. Opposed to Noncooperation and civil disobedience until the 1920 Congress. Then arrested and jailed. Later supported the Swaraj Party. Died in 1928 after police beating.

Lloyd, George. Governor of Bombay Presidency, 1918-1923.

Malaviya, Madan Mohan. Teacher, journalist and prominent Moderate nationalist politician, originally from Allahabad. Congress leader, close to Gandhi for his progressive social work, but opposed to civil disobedience. Member of the Imperial Legislative Council. Attempted to promote negotiations with the Raj during Noncooperation.

Mohani, Hasrat. Muslim religious leader, poet and Khilafat leader. Also, Indian nationalist and Congress supporter. Critical colleague of Gandhi, he called for complete independence and chafed at code of nonviolence.

Montagu, Sir Edwin. Secretary of State for India in British Cabinet, London, 1917-1922.

Naidu, Sarojini. She met Gandhi in London in 1914 and back in India was a prominent supporter during the Rowlatt campaign. A well-known poet, she played a leading role in his later campaigns.

Nehru, Jawarhalal. Son of Motilal, he became the first prime minister of an independent India in 1947. Supported Gandhi during Noncooperation and was jailed with his father. As a Congress politician, he worked closely with Gandhi in later years.

Nehru, Motilal. Prominent lawyer and Congress politician from Allahabad. Initially opposed civil disobedience but crucially changed his mind to support Gandhi and Noncooperation in 1920. Gave up his legal practice and adopted khadi clothing. Jailed with his son, Jawarhalal. Later founded the Swaraj Party, which ended the boycott of elections.

Pal, B.C. Bengali nationalist and leading Congress politician prior to Gandhi's emergence. Associated with Tilak. Promoted swadeshi, boycott of British goods and national education. A strong critic of Noncooperation.

Patel, Vallabbhai. (Called "Sardar" – that is, leader or chief.) Lawyer and leading Congress politician, based in Ahmedabad. Became first Deputy Prime Minister on India's independence. Met Gandhi in 1917 and became an active colleague in the Kheda campaign. Gave up western clothing. Mobilised support for Noncooperation in Gujarat. Gandhi's most trusted "lieutenant" and adviser. Strong supporter of constructive programme.

Patel, Vithalbbhai. Elder brother of Vallabbhai. Prominent Gujarati lawyer, Congressman and vigorous opponent of the Rowlatt Bills in the Imperial Legislative Council. Supported Noncooperation, particularly promotion of national schools. Later supported Swaraj Party.

Prasad, Rajendra. The first President of India after Independence, he was a Bihari lawyer who joined Gandhi more than 30 years earlier in Champaran. He supported Gandhi throughout the Rowlatt agitation and during Noncooperation withdrew his sons from the Raj's schools. Jailed several times, he was a strong advocate for the constructive programme.

Rajagopalachari, C. A gifted lawyer in Madras, he hosted Gandhi early in 1919 and shortly after gave up his legal practice. Strongly involved in the anti-Rowlatt agitation, he emerged during Non-cooperation as the leading Congress figure from South India, also dedicated to the constructive programme.

Reading, Lord. Viceroy of India, 1921-1926.

Roy, Kalinath. Lahore journalist jailed for 2 years for publishing articles criticising the government crackdown in the Punjab in 1919 under martial law. Gandhi's protests succeeded in getting his sentence reduced to 3 months. Remained editor of the *Lahore Tribune* till 1943.

Sastri, Srinivasi. "Moderate" politician favouring gradual political progress through co-operation with British reforms. Admirer of Gokhale, he gave much of his life to the Servants of India Society. He remained a personal friend of Gandhi's, but rejected civil disobedience and resigned from Congress when it adopted Noncooperation.

Shraddhanand, Swami. Punjabi lawyer and Hindu politician. Leader in Delhi of Gandhi's campaign against the Rowlatt bills, but resigned after disagreement. Later joined Arya Samaj, the pro-Hindu movement.

Tagore, Rabindranath. World renowned poet, awarded Nobel Literature Prize in 1913. Friend of Gandhi's. Resigned his knighthood in 1919 after the Punjab atrocities. Disagreed with several aspects of Noncooperation.

Tilak, Bal Gangadar. "Extremist" Maharashtrian politician, known as Lokamanya ("Beloved Leader of the People"). Jailed three times for sedition, he founded one of the two Home Rule Leagues during the first world war. Opposed the Raj's limited reforms. Died in 1920 after leading an unsuccessful deputation to Britain.

Tyabji, Abbas. Lawyer and retired Chief Justice from the princely state of Baroda. Member of the Congress inquiry into the Punjab atrocities. Active in Gujarat in the Noncooperation campaign. Later, deputised for Gandhi and led the Salt March.

Venkatappayya, Konda. Congress activist from Andhra province. During Non-cooperation, he joined the working group advising Gandhi and launched a No-Tax campaign in the Guntur district. Jailed as a result for one year. Later he was imprisoned twice more and, on release, worked on the constructive programme.

Willingdon, Lord. Governor of Bombay Presidency, 1913-1918

Yajnik, Indulal. Gujarati journalist and political activist. Early supporter of Gandhi in Gujarat involved in the Kheda, Rowlatt and Noncoopertaion campaigns. Jailed with Gandhi in 1923. Later, became a disillusioned Marxist critic but, later still, revised his views.

BIBLIOGRAPHY

Ackerman, Peter and Kruegler, Christopher. 1994. *Strategic Nonviolent Conflict: The Dynamics of People Power in the 20th Century*. Praeger.

Ackerman, Peter and Duvall, Jack. 2000. *A Force More Powerful: A Century of Nonviolent Conflict*. Palgrave.

Amin, Shahid. 1995. *Event, Metaphor, Memory: Chauri Chaura 1922-1992*. University of California Press and Oxford University Press.

Azad, Maulana Abul Kalam. 1959. *India Wins Freedom*. Orient Longmans.

Bond, Becky and Exley, Zack. 2016. *Rules for Revolutionaries. How Big Organizing Can Change Everything*. Chelsea Green Publishing.

Bondurant, Joan V. 1965. *Conquest of Violence: The Gandhian Philosophy of Conflict*. University of California Press

Bondurant, Joan V. 1973. "Introduction" in Harijan: *A Journal of Applied Gandhism*, 1933-1955, Vol 1, New York: Garland Publishing

Bose, N.K. 1947. *Studies in Gandhism*. Indian Associated Publishing Company

Bose, S.C. 1935. *The Indian Struggle, 1920-1934*. London: Wishart and Co.

Brailsford, H.N. 1931. *Rebel India*. London: Leonard Stein and Victor Gollancz Ltd

Brailsford, H.N. 1949. "The Middle Years, 1915-1939" in Polak, Brailsford and Pethick-Lawrence, *Mahatma Gandhi*. Odhams Press.

Broomfield, J.H. 1968. *Elite Conflict in a Plural Society: Twentieth Century Bengal*, Cambridge University Press.

Brown, Judith. 1972. *Gandhi's Rise to Power: Indian Politics, 1915-1922*. Cambridge University Press.

Brown, Judith. 1977. *Gandhi and Civil Disobedience*. Cambridge University Press.

Brown, Judith. 1989. *Gandhi: Prisoner of Hope*. Yale University Press.

Burrowes, Robert J. 1996. *The Strategy of Nonviolent Defence: A Gandhian Approach*. State University of New York Press.

Chandra (Bipan), Tripathi (Amales), and De (Barun). 1972. *Freedom Struggle*. New Delhi: National Book Trust.

Chenoweth, Erica and Stephan, Maria. 2011. *Why Civil Resistance Works: The Strategic Logic of Nonviolent Conflict.* Columbia University Press.

Dalal, C.B. 1971 *Gandhi 1915-1948: A Detailed Chronology.* New Delhi: Gandhi Peace Foundation.

Desai, Mahadev. 1951. *A Righteous Struggle (A Chronicle of the Ahmedabad Textile Labourers' Fight for Justice).* Ahmedabad: Navajivan Publishing House.

Desai, Mahadev. 1957. The *Story of Bardoli.* Navajivan.

Desai, Mahadev. 1968a. *Day to Day with Gandhi (Secretary's Diary) Vol 1 1917– 1919* (ed. Parikh.) Sarva Seva Sangh Prakashan.

Desai, Mahadev. 1968b. *Day to Day with Gandhi (Secretary's Diary) Vol 2 1919-1920* (ed. Parikh.) Sarva Seva Sangh Prakashan.

Devji, Faisal. 2012. *The Impossible Indian. Gandhi and the Temptation of Violence.* Hurst and Company, London.

Dhawan, Gopinath. 1957. *The Political Philosophy of Mahatma Gandhi.* Third Edition. (1st edition, 1946) Ahmedabad: Navajivan Publishing House.

Diwakar, R.R. 1946. *Satyagraha: Its Technique and History.* Bombay: Hind Kitabs

Engler, Mark and Engler, Paul. 2017. *This Is An Uprising: How Nonviolent Revolt is Shaping the Twenty-First Century.* New York: Nation Books.

Erikson, Erik. 1969. *Gandhi's Truth.* Norton.

Ferrell, Donald W. 1971. "The Rowlatt Satyagraha in Delhi" in Kumar, R. (1971)

Gandhi, M.K. 1982. *An Autobiography, or My Experiments with Truth.* Penguin Books.

Gandhi, M.K. 1945. *Constructive Programme: Its Meaning and Place.* Ahmedabad: Navajivan Publishing House.

Gandhi, M.K. 1951. *Satyagraha.* Ahmedabad: Navajivan Publishing House.

Gandhi, M.K. 1964. *Collected Works, vol 13.* Government of India.

Gandhi, M.K. 1965. *Collected Works, vols 14 to 18.* Government of India.

Gandhi, M.K. 1966. *Collected Works, vols 19 to 22*. Government of India.

Gandhi, M.K. 1967. *Collected Works, vol 23*. Government of India.

Gandhi, Rajmohan. 2007. *Gandhi: The Man, His People and the Empire*. London: Haus Books.

Gillion, K.L. 1971. "Gujarat in 1919" in R. Kumar (Ed) *Essays on Gandhian Politics: The Rowlatt Satyagraha of 1919*. Oxford University Press.

Gokhale, B.K. 1959. (Title) in Park, R.L. and Tinker, T. (1959).

Gordon, R.A. 1970. "Aspects in the History of the Indian National Congress with Special Reference to the Swarajya Party, 1919 to 1927", D. Phil thesis, St Edmund Hall.

Gordon, R.A. 1973. "Noncooperation and Council Entry 1919-1920" in Gallagher, Johnson and Seal, *Locality, Province and Nation*, Cambridge University Press.

Gregg, Richard B. 1941. *A Discipline for Nonviolence*. Ahmedabad: Navajivan Press.

Gregg, Richard B. 1960. *The Power of Nonviolence*. (First published, 1935) London: James Clark & Co Ltd

Hamid, Abdul. 1967. *Muslim Separatism in India: A Brief Survey, 1858-1947*. Lahore: Oxford University Press.

Hardiman, David. 1977. "The Crisis of the Lesser Patidars: Peasant Agitations in Kheda District, Gujarat, 1917-1934" in Low, D.A. (1977).

Hardiman, David. 2003. *Gandhi In His Time and Ours: The Global Legacy of his Ideas*. London: Hurst and Company.

Hardiman, David. 2017. "Nonviolent Resistance in India, 1915-1947" in Hardiman (ed). *Nonviolence in Modern Indian History*. Orient BlackSwan.

Hardiman, David. 2018. *The Nonviolent Struggle for Indian Freedom, 1905-19*. Penguin/Viking.

Henningham, Stephen. 1976. "The Social Setting of the Champaran Satyagraha: The Challenge to An Alien Elite", *Indian Economic and Social History Review*, 13: 59.

Hodge, J. Z. 1949. "When Mahatma Gandhi Came to Champaran", in Shukla, Chandrashankar (Ed). *Incidents of Gandhiji's Life*, Bombay: Vora and Co.

Iyer, Raghavan N. 1973. *The Moral and Political Thought of Mahatma Gandhi*. New York: Oxford University Press.

Kaushik, P.D. 1964. *The Congress Ideology and Programme 1920-1947: Ideological Foundations of Indian Nationalism During the Gandhian Era*. Bombay: Allied Publishers Private Ltd.

King, Mary Elizabeth. 2015. *Gandhian Nonviolent Struggle and Untouchability in South India: The 1924-25 Satyagraha and the Mechanisms of Change*. Oxford University Press.

Kripalani, J.B. 1946. *Politics of Charkha*. Bombay: Vora and Co. Publishers Ltd

Krishna, Gopal. 1966. "The Development of the Indian National Congress as a Mass Organisation, 1918-1923", *The Journal of Asian Studies,* vol XXV, no 3, May, pp 413-430.

Krishna, Gopal. 1968. "The Khilafat Movement in India: The First Phase (September 1919-August 1920", *Journal of the Royal Asiatic Society*, nos 1 and 2, pp 37-53.

Krishnadas. 1928. *Seven Months with Mahatma Gandhi: Being an Inside View of the Noncooperation Movement of 1921-1922, vol 1*. Madras: S. Ganesan Publisher

Krishnadas. 1951. *Seven Months with Mahatma Gandhi: Being an Inside View of the Noncooperation Movement of 1921-1922*. (Abridged and edited by Richard Gregg) Ahmedabad: Navajivan Press

Kumar, R. 1971. *Essays on Gandhian Politics: The Rowlatt Satyagraha of 1919*, Oxford University Press.

Kumarappa, B. 1951. "Editor's Note" in Gandhi, M.K. *Satyagraha (Non-Violence)*. Ahmedabad: Navajivan Press.

Lakey, George. 2018. *How We Win. A Guide to Nonviolent Direct Action Campaigning*. Melville House Publishing.

Low, D.A. 1966. "The Government of India and the First Non-cooperation Movement, 1920-1922". *The Journal of Asian Studies*. Vol XXV, no 2, February. (Reprinted in Kumar, R. 1971)

Low, D.A. 1968. (Ed). *Soundings in Modern South Asian History*. University of Carolina Press.

Low, D.A. 1973. *Lion Rampant: Essay in the Study of British Imperialism*. London: Cass.

Low, D.A. 1977. (Ed.) *Congress and the Raj: Facets of the Indian Struggle 1917-1947*. London: Heinemann.

425

Masselos, James. 1971. "Some Aspects of Bombay City Politics" (in Kumar, R. 1971)

May, Todd. 2015. *Nonviolent Resistance: A Philosophical Introduction.* Polity Press.

Mishra, Girish. 1963. "Socio-Economic Background of Gandhi's Champaran Movement", *The Indian Economic and Social History Review,* 5, no 3: 245-275.

Naess, Arne. 1974. *Gandhi and Group Conflict: An Exploration of Satyagraha.* Oslo: Universitetsforlaget.

Nagler, Michael. 2004. *The Search for a Nonviolent Future: A Promise of Peace for Ourselves, Our Families, Our World.* Inner Ocean Publishing.

Nair, Kusum. 1962. *Blossoms in the Dust: The Human Factor in Indian Development.* New York: Praeger.

Nanda, B.R. 1989. *Gandhi: Pan-Islamism, Imperialism and Nationalism.* Bombay: Oxford University Press.

Nayar, Sushila. 1994. *Gandhi: vol 5: India Awakened.* Navajivan Publishing House.

Nepstad, Sharon Erickson. 2015. *Nonviolent Struggle: Theories, Strategies and Dynamics.* Oxford University Press.

Ostergaard, Geoffrey, and Currell, Melville. 1979. *The Gentle Anarchists: A Study of the Leaders of the Sarvodaya Movement for Nonviolent Revolution in India.* Oxford: Clarendon Press.

Owen, H.F. 1968. "Towards Nationwide Agitation and Organisation: The Home Rule Leagues, 1915-18" in Low, D.A. (1968).

Owen, H.F. 1971. "Organising for the Rowlatt Satyagraha of 1919" in Kumar, R. (1971).

Panjabi, K.L. 1969. *The Indomitable Sardar,* Bombay: Bharatiya Vidya Dhavan.

Park, R.L. and Tinker T (Eds). 1959. *Leadership and Political Institutions in India.* Madras: Oxford University Press.

Payne, Robert. 1969. *The Life and Death of Mahatma Gandhi.* London: The Bodley Head.

Pouchepadass, Jacques. 1999. *Champaran and Gandhi: Planters, Peasants and Gandhian Politics.* New Delhi: Oxford University Press.

Prasad, Rajendra. 1949a. *Satyagraha in Champaran.* Ahmedabad: Navajivan

426

Prasad, Rajendra. 1949b. "Since He Came to Champaran" in Shukla, Chandrashankar (Ed). 1949. *Incidents of Gandhiji's Life*. Bombay: Vora and Co

Prasad, Rajendra. 1955. *At the Feet of Mahatma Gandhi*. Bombay: Hind Kitabs.

Riar, Sukhmani Bal. 2006. *The Politics and History of the Central Sikh League, 1919-1929*. Chandigarh: Unistar Publishing.

Ricketts, Aidan. 2012. *The Activists' Handbook. A Step-By-Step Guide to Participatory Democracy*. Zed Books.

Rothermund, Indira. 1963. *The Philosophy of Restraint: Mahatma Gandhi's Strategy and Indian Politics*. Bombay: Popular Prakashan.

Rudolph, Lloyd I. and Rudolph, Susanne Hoeber. 1967. *The Modernity of Tradition: Political Development in India, Part 2*. University of Chicago Press.

Rumbold, Sir Algernon. 1979. *Watershed in India: 1914-1922*. University of London: Athlone Press.

Sandperl, Ira. 1974. *A Little Kinder*. Science and Behavior Books.

Sarkar, Sumit. 1983. *Modern India 1885-1947*. Macmillan Publishers India Ltd.

Schock, Kurt. 2005. *Unarmed Insurrections: People Power Movements in Nondemocracies*. University of Minnesota.

Sharp, Gene. 1960. *Gandhi Wields the Weapon of Moral Power*. Ahmedabad: Navajivan.

Sharp, Gene. 1973. *The Politics of Nonviolent Action* (vols 1, 2 and 3) Boston: Porter Sargent

Sharp, Gene. 1979. *Gandhi as a Political Strategist*. Boston: Porter Sargent

Shridharani, Krishnalal. 1962. *War Without Violence*. Bombay: Bharatiya Vidya Bhavan. (First published: 1939)

Shukla, Chandrashankar (Ed). 1949. *Incidents of Gandhiji's Life*. Bombay: Vora and Co

Tendulkar, D. G. 1951a. *Mahatma: Life of Mohandas Karamchand Gandhi. Vol 1 (1869-1920)*. Delhi: Government of India, Ministry of Information and Broadcasting

Tendulkar, D. G. 1951b. *Mahatma: Life of Mohandas Karamchand Gandhi. Vol 2 (1920-29)* Delhi: Government of India, Ministry of Information and Broadcasting

Tendulkar, D. G. 1957. *Gandhi in Champaran.* Government of India.

Thomson, Mark. 1993. *Gandhi and His Ashrams.* Bombay: Popular Prakashan.

Tidrick, Kathryn. 2013. *Gandhi: A Political and Spiritual Life.* London: Verso.

Van Den Dungem, P.H.M. 1971. "Gandhi in 1919: Loyalist or Rebel?" in Kumar, R. (1971).

Vinthagen, Stellan. 2015. *A Theory of Nonviolent Action: How Civil Resistance Works.* London: Zed Books.

Watson, Francis. 1969. *The Trial of Mr Gandhi.* London: Macmillan.

Yajnik, Indulal. 1933. *Gandhi As I Know Him.* Bombay: Mr G.G. Bhat. (Second edition, Delhi: Danish Mahal, 1943.)

INDEX

Ackerman, Peter 12n1, 373-374

Ahmedabad Satyagraha 61, 65, 73, 78, 84, 143 (*see also* Fasts, Gandhi's; Strike; Vows and Pledges)

Ali, Mohammad 184, 218, 228, 290, 302-303

Ali, Shaukat 184, 218, 219, 226, 227, 271

All-India Home Rule League (Swarajya Sabha) 24, 52, 58, 98, 168, 213, 217, 244, 262-267, 272

Amritsar Massacre 124, 228, 240, 244, 253, 328, 376

"Punjab issue" 125-26, 186,190, 200, 204, 207, 232, 239, 242, 245-47, 268, 285, 363

Andhra 343-344

Ashrams 28, 32, 54, 56, 60, 66-67, 76-77, 87-88, 91, 164, 174, 178, 180, 206, 243, 294, 339, 347-348, 386-387, 400, 402-403, 407, 412

Bardoli taluka 337, 345

Besant, Annie 52-53, 55, 58-59, 69, 89, 91-92, 98, 103, 165, 168, 202, 214, 219, 222, 240, 262, 273

Bezwada Programme 291, 295-297, 299, 304, 359, 366

Bondurant, Joan 16, 73-74, 142, 147n23, 368-369, 371-372, 393-403

Boycott 14, 179, 192-1944, 196-201, 203, 205-208, 210-212, 224, 232, 234-237, 241, 245-247, 250-252, 264-365, 271-276, 278-279, 284, 286-7, 289-291, 293-294, 295, 297, 300-301, 303-305, 307, 311, 314, 332, 341, 343, 359, 360, 362, 366, 368, 398-399, 401, 404, 408

in principle 14, 168-171, 192

of British goods 168-170, 192, 196, 212, 273, 279, 386

of foreign goods, 273, 279

of foreign cloth, inc Bonfires 160, 179, 193-194, 273, 279, 290, 300-303, 335-336, 359

Boycott, Triple 205-211, 234, 252, 264, 274, 275, 279, 293-294

Councils 160, 200-203, 205, 210, 264-265, 271-276, 278-279, 293, 332

Courts 160, 275-277, 279, 280, 293, 311

Schools 159-60, 205, 206, 270, 275-276, 279, 280, 293-294, 304-305

British Raj 28, 50, 75, 79, 85, 137, 151, 183, 192-3, 376, 393

Broach Conference 59, 175

Brown, Judith 11, 61n9, 84, 125, 130-131, 134, 163-168, 182n27, 190, 192-193, 201, 217, 258, 260-262, 272n46, 275n47

Champaran Satyagraha 22, 30, 49, 75, 399

Chauri Chaura 50n7, 291, 251-253, 355-356, 358, 361

Chenoweth, Erica, 374-375

Civil Disobedience 15, 19, 31, 36-37, 48, 50, 56, 59, 60, 65, 79, 85, 90, 92-93, 95, 99, 100-105, 107-109, 112-18, 122, 125-133, 135-137, 138-50, 156, 160-162, 165, 172, 176, 180, 199-200, 208, 222, 240-241, 246, 262, 263, 267, 284-286, 295n52, 296, 298, 301, 302-303, 305-9, 311-314, 316-317, 319-321, 349-354, 357-362, 365-367, 371, 379, 383-384, 386, 390-394, 397, 412 (*see also*, Law and Criminality)

Aggressive 289-92, 306-307, 319, 320, 330, 342, 346, 362, 366, 383, 392-394, 399-400, 404-5, 409

Defensive 289-292, 306-307, 323, 328, 366, 392-394, 399-400, 404-405, 408

Individual 114, 118, 126-128, 136, 166-167, 306-7, 354, 392, 404-405, 408

Mass 114-115, 152-154, 236, 291-292, 307, 308-9, 311, 323-325, 326-347, 351-354, 392, 404-405

preparation for 108-109, 113, 154-156, 159, 340-342, 344-345

Civility 15, 205, 301, 307, 333-334

Civil Liberties 306, 319-320, 346-347, 350, 360-361, 390

Civil resistance 14, 16, 19, 132, 143, 153, 157, 159, 163, 281, 301, 362, 367, 376, 379, 383, 390, 399, 403-404, 406, 408-409, 411

Constructive 14, 17-18, 23, 406-408

Obstructive 17-18, 23, 406-408

Offensive 323

Constructive programme 14-17, 19, 22, 23, 39, 111, 126, 138-149, 153-162, 168, 175, 178, 182, 211, 252, 294, 297, 305, 322-324, 338, 340, 352-353, 362, 366-368, 369-372, 373-376, 379, 381, 384, 395, 397, 399, 401-404, 405-409, 411

Arbitration courts 78, 211, 339n64

Communal harmony 339n64

Congress, as alternative to Raj 211

Hindu-Muslim unity (and Parsee, Sikh, Christian, Jew) 185, 322, 335

Khadi cloth and stores (swadeshi) 168-180, 294, 338

National schools 39, 211, 294, 304-305

Picketing liquor stores 297, 353

Removal of untouchability 322, 340

Social care and relief 353

Spinning and weaving (swadeshi) 168-180, 294-296, 302-303, 338, 341

Untouchability 142, 144, 152, 271, 340, 342, 335, 344-345, 353, 397, 415

Vernacular languages 56, 59, 258, 286

Village councils 338, 353

Women's education 59

Das, C.R. 241-243, 254, 272, 276-277, 279-280, 287, 293-294, 312-313, 315-317, 321, 353

Discipline 14-15, 20, 25, 63, 65, 69, 76, 101, 103, 109-110, 114, 116-117, 121, 134-135, 143, 146, 148-149, 152-154, 156-159, 162, 196, 199, 205, 209, 209n32, 216-219, 221-224, 227, 235, 238, 258, 280, 292, 298, 311-312, 314, 319-320, 322-324, 328, 338, 340, 342, 352, 359, 367, 369-370, 382, 393-395, 398, 400, 403, 405

Code of discipline 102-103, 120-121, 188

Daily discipline 156-157, 397

Diet 65, 88, 430

Diwakar, R.R. 12, 17, 366

Engler, Mark and Paul 378-379, 391

Extremists 28-29, 89, 130, 163, 220, 240, 242, 247, 270, 273, 281, 385, 421

Fasts, Gandhi's 66-68, 72, 75-78, 81-83, 92-93, 95, 101, 109-110, 117, 128, 133, 135, 143-144, 149, 153, 188, 207-208, 220, 266, 304, 310-311, 339-340, 353, 365, 405, 407-408

Gandhi, Rajmohan 168, 182

Goals, campaign

General 146, 149, 152-153, 211, 231-232, 234, 248, 249, 250-251, 268, 296, 366, 388, 397 (See also, 'Swaraj in One Year')

Keeping Separate/Combining 195, 231-232, 241, 245-248, 249-250, 278, 397

Local 141-143, 149-151, 152-153, 241-242

National 139-41, 144, 145, 149, 152-153, 162, 167, 211, 285

Particular 145, 146, 150, 162, 166-167, 247-248, 251, 296, 366, 387-388, 389-391, 397

Pitched low 31, 37, 43, 72-75, 77, 81, 149-151, 243, 347, 397

Principled and Pragmatic 375-378

Godhra Conference 60-61

Gokhale 28-9, 55, 57, 418, 421

Gregg, Richard 12, 156-157, 159, 368-369, 424

Gujarat 53-60

Guntur 200n29, 343, 349

Hardiman, David 38n6, 61n9, 79-80, 161, 310n56, 384n75

Hartals 133-136, 171-173, 179, 220-222, 227, 236, 271, 291, 322-324, 326, 330, 339, 342, 360, 401, 407-408

Rowlatt 92-94, 97-103, 105, 107-110, 114-121, 124, 127, 129-131, 133-135, 171, 179, 227

Horniman 117, 119n21, 125n22, 126, 128, 136, 188

Khilafat Days 188, 195, 177-178, 208, 220-2, 236

Prince of Wales Visit 300, 308-311, 314-316, 322-324, 333-335, 342, 360

Identification with Poor 19, 36, 38, 40, 72, 83, 156-157, 159, 271, 296, 303-304, 367, 383, 395, 397, 407

Indian Home Rule League 58

Swarajya Sabha 24, 262, 266-267, 274

Indian National Congress 12, 15, 22-24, 28, 34, 53, 56, 58, 89, 91, 163, 168, 178, 185, 195, 212, 235, 239-240, 247, 257-259, 278, 285, 290, 296, 317-318, 319

Annual Session, Lucknow (1916) 31

Annual session, Delhi (1918) 91

Annual Session, Amritsar (1919) 176-178, 253

Special Session, Calcutta (1920) 265-266, 268, 271-275, 293, 297

Annual Session, Nagpur (1920) 268, 276-281, 293-294

Annual Session, Ahmedabad (1921) 321-325

All-India Congress Committee (AICC) 204, 206, 240-241, 245, 248, 255, 257-260, 265, 295, 300-301, 308, 322n57, 336-337, 343, 353-354

New Constitution (1920) 253-261, 286, 288, 296, 304, 321, 329

Punjab Report (1919) 241-245

Working Committee 257-259, 295, 306, 307, 314, 322n57, 325, 330, 339, 343, 345, 350, 351-354

Iyer, Raghavan 12-3, 15, 17, 19-20, 333, 334-5n63, 387, 390

Jail behaviour 312-313

Jinnah, Mohammad 56, 266

Khadi (see Constructive Programme)

Kheda Satyagraha 61, 69, 73, 91, 128, 339

Khilafat 23-24, 98, 145, 163-164, 176, 181-201, 201-238, 239, 245-248, 253, 258, 261-266, 268-269, 271-272, 274-278, 281-282, 284-286, 289, 292, 293, 297, 298-300, 304-306, 308, 310-312, 316, 318-319, 321-322, 328,

345-347, 350, 353-355, 357, 359-361, 362-363, 365, 378, 382, 386, 404, 408 (*See also*, Boycott: British Goods; Hartal: Khilafat Days; Noncooperation)

At Issue 98, 183-185, 195, 204, 212, 228, 230-232, 284, 286, 317, 353-354

Muslim call for resignations from military 289, 299-300, 302, 304-308

Congress call for Hindu solidarity 305-308

Cow slaughter, no deal 189-192, 213, 217, 236

Nonviolent means 186-189, 214-227, 235-236, 238, 372n, 386

Single issue 189-192, 201, 203, 244, 245-248

Law and criminality 50, 95, 129, 313-314, 333-334

Low, D.A. 315-316, 359, 424

Malaviya, Manan Mohan 68-69, 120, 166, 241, 298n53, 315, 327, 330

manliness 88

Meetings 127, 128, 129 (*See also*, Negotiations)

Moderates 28-9, 89-90, 120, 131, 137, 151, 163, 180, 193, 228, 233, 266, 270, 271n45, 275, 281-282, 291, 298n53, 305, 309, 315-317, 319-320, 325n59, 326-331, 343, 360, 385

Mohani, Hasrat 187, 193, 204, 220, 226, 276, 321

Moplah Rebellion 290, 302, 304

Nanda, B.R. 111n20, 182n27, 185, 188, 229n37, 247n40, 270, 272n46, 276, 331

Negotiations, 31-32, 42-43, 44, 45, 78-81, 137, 318 (*See also*, Meetings)

"Round Table 1" (Dec 1921) 315-320

"Round Table 2" (Jan 1922) 327-331, 334

"Ultimatum" 346-350

Nehru, Motilal 241, 253, 262, 273, 293, 312, 313, 353

Nehru, Jawarhalal 100, 273, 280, 293, 312, 313, 353

Nepstad, Sharon 375-376, 378

Noncooperation 193-203, 207-208, 210-21? 236-237, 285-287, 290-291, 359-362, 362-363 (*see also*, Boycott; Khilafat)

Evolution of the plan 205-208, 250

Progressive Nonviolent Noncooperation 17 23, 198, 201-202, 208-10, 222, 236-237, 249, 268, 285, 289-293, 319, 326, 334, 336-7, 342-343, 358, 360-361, 366, 383, 392, 396-397, 400

Opponents, Approach to,

British Raj 41-48, 79-81, 127-130, 227-234, 250-252, 283-285, 315-320, 327-331, 334, 343, 346-350

Indian critics 43, 81, 130-133, 239-240, 272-275, 281-283, 315-320, 321, 327-331, 347, 351-354, 358, 359-361

Indian opponents 73-75, 77-79

Organising 12-26, 97-100, 100-105, 238, 260, 296, 339n64, 364-368, 371, 378-379, 400-401, 403, 405-409, 410-411

Parallel government 211, 280, 399

Patel, Vallabbhai 87, 91, 97, 142, 149, 339n64

Patel, Vitalbhai 339n64, 344

Pledges (*see* Vows and Pledges)

Prasad, Rajendra 16, 30n3, 35-36, 38n6, 39, 41-43, 56, 92, 226

Princely States 7, 175, 421

"Punjab Satyagraha" 246-247

Rai, Lala Rajput 203, 224n35, 245, 312, 353

Recruiting for the Raj 51

Reforms 29, 34, 38, 43, 47, 58, 74, 85, 89-9

124, 127, 136, 151, 167, 177-178, 186, 200, 210 228, 233, 242, 245-246, 250, 262, 264-265, 271, 276, 279, 296-297, 315, 332, 344, 358, 363, 376

Rothermund, Indira 12, 19, 76, 152-153, 183, 388, 405, 409

Rowlatt Bills 90-92, 97, 100, 127, 133-135, 165-167, 365

Rowlatt Satyagraha 19, 22-23, 53, 84, 97-100, 105-108, 110-112, 112-118, 124-125, 133-135, 138, 145, 149, 163, 165, 168, 172, 176, 184-185, 195, 199-200, 214, 218, 226-227, 233, 238, 254, 298, 361, 392-393

"Himalayan" blunder 112-118, 133

Roy, Kalinath 125, 129, 241

Sacrifice (*see* Suffering)

Sarabhai, Ambalal 77-78

Sarabhai, Anusaya 64, 76-78

Sastri, Srinivasa 120, 202, 214, 262

Satyagraha 12-14, 16-19, 21-24, 26, 33, 35, 38n5,n6, 40-41, 48-50, 62-63, 66-70, 71, 73-75, 77-8, 84, 90, 95-101, 110-112, 113-118, 103-125, 127-138, 142-145, 147-149, 153, 162-163, 165, 168, 172, 176, 179, 182, 184-189, 191-193, 195-197, 199-200, 204, 207, 214, 217-218, 220-221, 223, 226-227, 230, 233-236, 238-243, 245-247, 249, 251-252, 254, 261-262, 264, 267-268, 280-282, 285, 292, 298, 312, 339, 348, 357-359, 361-362, 3643-74, 382, 385-407, 411, 416, 423, 426

Gandhi's method 12-14, 45-48, 82-83, 134-137, 235-238, 285-287, 359-363, 390, 392-401, 402-11

Gandhi's philosophy 12-13, 389-391, 402, 403

Satyagraha Sabha 24, 91-93, 97-99. 105, 115, 117-119, 122, 124, 127, 130-131, 133-136, 145, 149, 168, 172, 179, 235, 238, 240-241, 262, 264, 267

Schock, Kurt 375

Secretary of State for India (Montagu) 127, 130, 137, 233

Sharp, Gene 12, 20, 42, 164, 368-372, 375-380, 384, 387, 393, 402, 409-140

Shridharani , Khrishnalal 12, 73n13, 143, 192, 297, 368-370, 398-399, 402

Sikh campaigns 293, 297, 332

Shraddanand, Swami 119-122, 241

Strikes

Students 294

Workers 62, 64-66, 70, 72, 76-80, 82, 91, 105, 143, 150, 166, 298, 304, 387n76, 397-398

Suffering 65, 69, 69n12, 71, 188, 312, 335-336, 341, 390-391

Surveys, as part of Satyagraha 38, 38n6, 64-65, 338, 340-342, 344-345, 351-352

Swadeshi 17, 22, 24, 94, 107-108, 116, 119, 128, 136, 138, 154, 158-160, 163, 168-182, 192, 206, 235, 238, 263-265, 267, 271, 273, 286, 289, 293-294, 296-297, 301-305, 307, 322, 324n58, 336-337, 341, 344-345, 359, 371, 383, 404, 407 (*See also*, Constructive Programme: Khadi)

Swadeshi Sabha 17, 22, 24, 158, 163, 165, 168-180, 192, 206, 235, 238, 264-265, 267

Swaraj (Independence) 23-24, 47, 87, 104, 140, 144, 146, 155, 164, 176-178, 186, 198, 212-213, 232, 234, 244, 248, 251-252, 256, 259-262, 264-268, 273-275,

277-280, 283-284, 286-288, 290-292, 295-298, 302-305, 307-308, 310-311, 313, 316-318, 320-321, 326, 328-331, 335-337, 342, 345, 347-351, 357-363, 365-366, 386, 388, 404

"Swaraj in One Year" 146-147, 251-252, 279, 296-297, 307-308, 318, 359, 362-363

Parliamentary swaraj 259, 280, 317-318

Symbolic or individual action by the leader 126, 52-53, 303-304, 304n55, 307, 409

Tax refusal 73, 198-200, 279, 292, 335, 352, 357, 404, 409

Tilak, Bal Gangadhar 29, 52, 58, 68-69, 85-86, 89, 91, 103, 150-151, 165-166, 232, 240, 242, 247n40, 254, 263, 270n44, 273, 279, 288, 295-297, 302, 353, 355

Tilak Swaraj Fund 297

Universities 208, 290, 293, 407-408, 413

Vaikom cordon (1917) 142-143

Viceroy

Chelmsford 85, 127, 130, 137, 167, 177, 194, 204, 227-233, 242-243, 284

Reading 298-299, 315, 317-318, 327, 334, 348-349, 352, 360-361

Willingdon 86, 421

Viceroy's Secretary (Maffey) 127

Vinthagen, Stellan 379-381, 391

Violence 216, 224-227, 226n36, 321

Vows 28, 55, 66-70, 75-76, 78, 80, 82, 95, 133, 168-169, 171-175, 179, 192, 264, 307, 311, 332, 344, 366, 383, 386, 389-391, 407-408

Pledges 59, 92, 94-95, 99-108, 114-116, 120, 125, 128, 134-135, 142, 227, 243,

299, 322-324, 352, 357, 362-363, 395, 397, 399, 401

Women 16, 59, 69-70, 143, 168-169, 175-177, 180, 271, 294, 296, 312, 314, 317, 321, 329, 338

Yajnik, Indulal 55, 57, 59, 60, 64, 73n14, 81, 93, 96, 151, 166-167, 176, 181n26, 210-211, 217n34, 232, 243, 254, 259, 282, 307

About the Author:

Bob Overy is an independent researcher. A former anti-nuclear-weapons activist and peace journalist, also community worker and town planner, he did a PhD in Peace Studies at Bradford on Gandhi. He then worked as an emergency planning officer for a "nuclear free" local authority, later transferring to central government to advise on legislation that prepares for emergencies in peacetime. He is now retired.

CPSIA information can be obtained
at www.ICGtesting.com
Printed in the USA
FSHW021254171219
65191FS